Henry D. Jencken

A Compendium of the Modern Roman Law

Salzwasser

Henry D. Jencken

A Compendium of the Modern Roman Law

1. Auflage | ISBN: 978-3-84604-960-0

Erscheinungsort: Frankfurt, Deutschland

Erscheinungsjahr: 2020

Salzwasser Verlag GmbH

Reprint of the original, first published in 1870.

A COMPENDIUM OF THE MODERN ROMAN LAW,

FOUNDED UPON THE TREATISES OF

PUCHTA, VON VANGEROW, ARNDTS, FRANZ MOEHLER, AND THE CORPUS JURIS CIVILIS.

BY

FREDERICK J. TOMKINS, Esq., M.A., D.C.L.

AUTHOR OF THE "INSTITUTES OF THE ROMAN LAW," ONE OF THE TRANSLATORS OF THE "COMMENTARIES OF GAIUS ON THE ROMAN LAW," ETC.

AND

HENRY D. JENCKEN, Esq.

BARRISTERS-AT-LAW OF LINCOLN'S INN.

"Deum esse omnis juris naturalis auctorem, verissimum est, at non voluntate, sed ipsa essentia sua, qua ratione etiam auctor est veritatis."—LEIBNITZ.

LONDON:
BUTTERWORTHS, 7, FLEET STREET,
Law Publishers to the Queen's Most Excellent Majesty.
DUBLIN: HODGES, FOSTER & CO. EDINBURGH: T. & T. CLARK: BELL & BRADFUTE.
CALCUTTA: THACKER, SPINK & CO. BOMBAY, THACKER, VINING & CO.
MELBOURNE: GEORGE ROBERTSON. BOSTON, U.S.: LITTLE & BROWN.
1870.

GLASGOW:
PRINTED BY HAY NISBET,
TRONGATE.

TO THE

RIGHT HONOURABLE JOHN

BARON ROMILLY

Master of the Rolls

THIS WORK

IS

BY HIS KIND PERMISSION, DEDICATED

AS AN

Expression of Deep and Sincere Respect

FOR HIS

LORDSHIP'S LEARNING AS A JUDGE

And also IN ACKNOWLEDGMENT

OF THE

INTEREST TAKEN BY HIS LORDSHIP

IN THE

ADVANCEMENT OF THE STUDY OF JURISPRUDENCE

IN THIS COUNTRY.

CONTENTS.

BOOK THE THIRD.

Possession.

BOOK THE FOURTH.

Family Relations.

BOOK THE FIFTH.

Real Rights.

BOOK THE SIXTH.

The Law of Inheritance.

BOOK THE SEVENTH.

OBLIGATIONS.

PREFACE.

The following work has been undertaken not only to supply a want which has been felt in our legal literature, but with the hope of awakening an interest in this country in the study of the Modern Roman Law. The Introduction will, it is thought, demonstrate the importance of this department of Jurisprudence, not only, as is usually supposed, to the antiquarian and to the scientific jurist, but likewise, and especially, to the practical lawyer. Up to the present time we possess no complete systematic treatise in English on the Modern Civil Law. The work of Mackeldey, translated by Kaufmann in New York, is incomplete, the first volume only having been published, thus omitting the more valuable part of his work, namely, the portions which treat of the Law of Inheritance, of Family Relations, and, the most important section of all, that on Obligations. There is, however, another defect attaching to Mackeldey's work. It is not a treatise upon the Modern Roman Law proper at all, and on that account it has been superseded as a text-book in Germany. The first portion of his book contains a history of the sources of the Roman Law, and belongs, therefore, to an elementary or institutional treatise; whilst the work in every other part shows signs of its having been written before the modern mode of treatment had obtained its present system and perfection through the labours of Savigny and his successors. It is quite unnecessary at the present period to extol the principles and maxims of the Roman Jurisprudence. These have long since been received into the legal systems of all the great nations of modern times, and of them Leibnitz observed that, "Next to the writings of the Geometricians, there is nothing which, in force and subtlety, can compare with the Roman Law."* The labours of the great jurists of Germany, pursuing the historical method, by a constant and careful study at the very source and origin of law, have evolved a system of which even

* Leibnitz says in the Epist. XV., ad Kestnerum, in reference to the importance of the study of Roman Law—"Dixi saepius, post scripta Geometrarum nihil exstare, quod vi ac subtilitate cum Romanorum Jureconsultorum scriptis comparari possit: tantum nervi inest, tantum profunditatis. Et quemadmodum remotis titulis et cæteris operis integri indiciis, demonstrationem lemmatis alicujus geometrici ex Euclide, aut Archimede, aut Apollonio aegre discernas, et ad auctorem suum referas; adeo omnium idem stylus videtur, tanquam ipsa recta ratio per horum virorum ora loqueretur; ita Jurisconsulti etiam Romani sibi gemelli sunt, ut sublatis indiciis, quibus sententiæ aut argumenta distinguuntur, distinguere stylum aut loquentem vix possis. Nec uspiam juris naturalis præclare exculti uberiora vestigia deprehendas. Et ubi ab eo recessum est, sive ob formularum ductus, sive ex majorum traditis, sive ob leges novas, ipsæ consequentiæ, ex nova hypothesi æternis rectæ rationis dictaminibus addita, mirabili ingenio, nec minore firmitate deducuntur. Nec tam saepe a ratione abitur, quam vulgo videtur.

Gibbon had but a faint conception when he wrote the brief and eloquent 44th chapter of his "Decline and Fall of the Roman Empire." The feebleness of our knowledge of the Roman Law as a practical existing system, has long been a subject for frequent comment with continental jurists. Lest we should be charged by those who have too long neglected their duty in this matter, with traditional misrepresentation, we will adopt the words of a writer, who is unknown to us, in our principal legal periodical:—"It has been our lot at different times," says that writer, "to fall in with eminent foreign jurists, who have been commissioned by their respective Governments to inspect and report on the state of the law and its administration in this country, and we have uniformly found them struck with surprise at the total ignorance of the Roman Law, evinced by our most eminent (and justly eminent) lawyers. These learned foreigners observed to us that the Corpus Juris Civilis ought to attract the notice of every cultivated and reflecting mind, were it only as containing an unparalleled collection of the doctrines and opinions of the great lawyers, in many successive ages, all working out the same legal principles, in their application to an endless variety of cases,—that the revival of the study of this great work, after a long and gloomy interval of barbarism, was the first thing which communicated to the legal legislation of modern Europe consistency, method, and refinement,

—and that this cause continued to operate on the Continent not only down to the epoch of modern codes, but most powerfully and most beneficially in their composition."—*Law Rev.*, vol. iii., 1845.

In this country, we believe we are correct in stating that nothing hitherto has been done for the systematic *teaching* of the Roman Law. In laying stress upon the importance of this study, we do not wish to depreciate the Common Law of our native land, for that law has derived its best elements from the Roman Law. Savigny replied to those who charged him with a desire to supersede the Jurisprudence of Germany as follows: —"For us Germans," says he—(let us read, Englishmen)—"as for many other nations, this foreign element, centuries ago, became a part of our legal life, and thus mistaken, or half understood, it often had pernicious effects, where, if rightly apprehended, it would enrich our proper legal life."

We believe that the present work contains the first attempt made in England to explain, compendiously and systematically, the Modern Roman Law. The aim of the Editors has been to give to the practising jurist in a compendious form the leading principle of the Roman Law now incorporated in the Civil Codes of Continental nations. The Council of Legal Education, without doubt, intended to furnish the Law Student with courses of lectures on this subject as pre-eminently practical and necessary; but, up to the present moment, no such course has, we are informed, been delivered. The lectures read, however interesting, have been too fragmentary, and inadequate to meet the requirements of the subject. What is needed, is a thoroughly systematic exposition of the Modern Civil Law, as received by those European and Transatlantic nations who have embodied the Roman Law in their juridical systems. These principles are indeed the *vox vivida* of the Jurisprudence of the present age, which should be heard in the lecture-rooms and from the tribunals of the Old and the New World.

When we turn to our Universities to ascertain the state of legal studies there, we find a condition of things, but little changed from that which existed a a few years ago. An able article, which appeared in the "Law Review," in speaking of the extraordinary indifference of the Universities to this all-important study, says:—"The bar and the bench are still supplied by doctors of the civil law, who have graduated at Oxford or Cambridge; but those learned Universities take little pains to prepare the civilian for his peculiar faculty. If we are rightly informed, in one of them at least, no course of lectures on either the history or the theory of the Roman Law has been delivered for the last fifty years. Learned civilians have certainly been formed in those academic shades, by private study; but professors to stand by the side of a Hugo, or a Savigny (to whom we might now add a Puchta, a

Von Vangerow, and an Arndts), neither University will presume to boast."

Since these words were published it is to be hoped that some improvement has taken place, but for reasons it is impossible to understand, the want of interest, of method, and of manner in the treatment of this branch of science, has precluded all satisfactory progress.

The University of Cambridge, prompted by the views propounded by the Royal Commission appointed in 1852 to consider the state, discipline, studies, and revenues of the University and the Colleges, appointed a Board of Legal Studies, consisting of the Regius Professor of Laws, the Professors of Modern History, English Law, and Moral Philosophy, and the Three Examiners for the Degree of Bachelor of Laws, to consult on all matters relating to law studies and legal examinations in the University. With all due respect for these gentlemen, it may be affirmed with the utmost correctness that they made recommendations, which, whilst they were an improvement upon the old régime, still manifest a most complete want of knowledge as to the requirements of the times; as well as of the recognised mode of studying the Roman Law in every University in Europe out of England. Even at Oxford, the great national seat of learning, identified in the past with the study of the Jurisprudence of Rome, up to the present time no efficient system has been inaugurated.

What, it may be asked, do we demand? The introduction of systematic, well digested teaching of the Roman Law, such as is found on the Continent—that is to say, courses of lectures upon—1, Institutiones juris Romani; 2, Historia juris Romani; 3, Systema juris Romani hodie usitati; in addition to instruction in general Jurisprudence. The first two branches must be the subjects of close study, in order that the practical jurist may understand the Roman Law as now in use, and as applicable to the endless variety of cases that arise in the transactions of a great commercial people. It ought never to be forgotten that the jurisprudence which has regulated the affairs of mankind for nearly three thousand years, so rich in its principles and so prolific in its examples applicable to practical life; should not be treated by its professors with the coldness and the pedantry of antiquarian research, but that it should be illumined with the warmth and the enthusiasm which an adequate and deep acquaintance with its precepts alone can impart. A formal and diffuse lecture, or a mere literary essay, coldly read, must always fail to awaken the sympathy and to evoke the ardour of the student. Goethe himself, the prince of writers in modern times, has observed—"To write is to abuse speech; and the possession of a solitary perusal is but a sad substitute for the living energy of language." Von Vangerow observes in his preface to the first edition of his great work on "The Modern

Civil Law":—"I hold it to be an essential requirement of lectures on the Modern Roman Law that the verbal discussions of the lecturer should not only comprehend in a fragmentary manner the several distinct parts of the law, but should present for the contemplation of the auditors the entire system as an organic whole. Of course, I here presume a free and characteristic delivery, one in which the professor is, at the time of his lecture, really self-active. Lectures that are dictated or read ought in common justice not to be given, for they are only destructive to the intellect of the professor, tending to convert his avocation into actual misery; whilst they lack the penetrative vitality which gives to a spoken lecture its real value." When will our teachers come to understand the truth of these profound remarks? Whilst the utmost system and arrangement pervaded the lectures of Savigny, and characterise those of Van Vangerow, as professors they would have never obtained their world-wide reputation if they had confined themselves to the *ipsissima verba* of their MSS. The ready utterance, the keen eye, and the courteous demeanour and sympathy of these great men, all brought into play, powerfully ministered to the advancement of the students, and to their own well-merited European fame. To the professors of the Roman Law in this country, now that some attention is being paid to the subject, we will venture to suggest the imitation of these great teachers, not only in their manner, but also in their patience and thoroughness, and their fidelity to the original sources. The great revival that has taken place in Germany has been the result of the careful, and, we had almost said, the loyal study of the sources of the law contained in the "Corpus Juris Civilis." This fidelity and recurrence to the great jurists of antiquity can never be dispensed with by the practical jurist.

The most, however, that we can venture to hope for this Compendium is that it will serve to map out accurately the great divisions of the subject, and trace to some extent the subordinate lines of these boundaries, presenting, as far as practicable, some passing explanations of the several leading Institutes, as these main divisions are termed. At a future time it is our intention, after having completed other works already commenced, to do more than this. The materials are all prepared for a fuller treatment of the Modern Roman Law, and also for the History of Roman Private Law—a subject, we repeat, essential to the exact comprehension of the development and the perfection of the existing Roman Jurisprudence. We have endeavoured to condense within the limits of the present work the treatises of Puchta, Arndts, Von Vangerow, and more especially of Franz Moehler. But we have not always confined ourselves to the literal text of these authorities. We have enlarged and incorporated the carefully transcribed and valuable notes derived from these authors; and we have often, indeed, cited the names and the very words of the great jurists of antiquity. We have introduced the principal authorities from the Roman sources, and the writers upon whose works this Compendium is founded. This Treatise, we believe, will be found both interesting and valuable. It was commenced by Mr. Jencken at the suggestion of the other editor more than ten years ago, and has occupied much of his leisure time. It is enriched, so far as our space would allow, not only with the fruits of independent research, but with the explanations of Von Vangerow himself, his statements having been treasured up by means of copious notes of his lectures upon every department of the Roman Law, taken by Dr. Tomkins in the lecture-room of the old Ruprecht University of Heidelberg. Reference has been also carefully made to the work of Glück, since he is the greatest of the commentators on the Civil Law, so far as practical comment is concerned. This work, including the register, is contained in fifty volumes, and may be found in the library of Lincoln's Inn. It was commenced by the jurist whose name it bears, and has been continued by Mühlenbruch and Fein; and Arndts is now, after an interval of some years since the death of the distinguished Mühlenbruch and Fein, proceeding with the completion of the work. The Introduction will present further particulars in regard to this great work, which, so far as it goes, is consulted by every Continental jurist. It will also, we believe, demonstrate the fact that the principles here explained have penetrated the legal systems of almost the entire civilised world.

The Authors desire to acknowledge with thanks the valuable suggestions and kind assistance they have received from W. G. Lemon, Esq., LL.B., of Lincoln's Inn, Barrister-at-Law; and also the aid rendered to them by the careful reading of the proofs by Mr. Alfred W. Hall.

LINCOLN'S INN,
June 30, 1870.

INTRODUCTION.

Roman Law, why adopted.

The Roman Law has been adopted into the legal systems of European and other nations, not by means of external force, but because the principles of the Roman Jurisprudence have been found to be readily suitable in every age to the requirements of an advancing civilisation. As Chancellor Kent correctly observes—"The institutions of every part of Europe have felt its influence, and it has contributed largely, by the richness of its materials, to their character and improvement. With most of the European nations, and in the new States in Spanish America, in the province of Lower Canada, and in one of the United States (Louisiana), it constitutes the principal basis of their unwritten or common law. It exerts a very considerable influence upon our own municipal law, and particularly those branches of it which are of Equity and Admiralty Jurisdiction." And he further says that "It is now taught and obeyed not only in France, Spain, Germany, Holland, and Scotland, but in the Islands of the Indian Ocean, and on the banks of the Mississippi and the St. Lawrence." So true, it seems, are the words of D'Aguesseau, that "the grand destinies of Rome are not yet accomplished, she reigns throughout the world by her reason, after having ceased to reign by her authority."

Not received in its purity.

The Imperial Jurisprudence of ancient Rome has not been received in its purity, but in a somewhat altered form, in what is now designated as the "Modern Roman, or Civil Law." Puchta,* speaking upon this point, says—"That it has been received by the force of scientific conviction, and that the Roman Law, like the philosophy of the Greeks and the intellectual works of antiquity, has in this way found an entrance into modern life, and been restored in modern times."

A brief historical sketch.

To trace the history of the Civil Law as it has been adopted from the reign of Justinian to the present day, would require more space than these pages will allow;† but it may be instructive to the student to furnish a brief historical sketch showing the assimilation of the Civil Law into the juridical systems of European and other nations. A full inquiry would disclose the causes that have given such preponderance to the Roman Law in the formation of the legal systems of modern times; and it would further guide us in deciding upon the vast importance of the study of the Roman Law as a firm and sound basis for the legal rules still required for the advancing jurisprudence of the civilised world.

Code of Theodoric II.

Previous to the reign of Justinian, in the year 493, the great Captain of the Ostrogoths, Theodoric the Second, displaced Odoacer, the conqueror of Rome

* Puchta. Pandekt, sec. 2.

† For the fate of the Legislation of Justinian both in the East and in the West, *see* Tomkins' Institutes of the Roman Law, pp. 186-203.

founding a Germo-Roman empire under the nominal supremacy of the Byzantine emperors. At his command a Code of Laws was framed, entitled the "Code of Theodoric II.," which was authoritatively published about A.D. 500. This Code, though superseded by the far more complete juridical system of Justinian (A.D. 533-535), known as the "Corpus Juris Civilis,"* continued to exercise an important influence upon the juridical systems of Europe, in consequence of its adoption, though in a modified form, by the Visigoths, under Alaric II. The rule of the Byzantine emperors terminated with the invasion of the Longobards (A.D. 558) under their leader Alboin. From that period to the conquests by the Carlovingians (A.D. 774), the Roman Law intermingling with the customs and feudal laws of the Longobards, became the prevailing law in Italy.

Code of Lothar.

The only collections or codes of laws that have descended from that period are the Codex by Lothar, or Rothar, A.D. 643, and a collection of edicts by Aistulf, A.D. 748, published under the title of "Edicta regum Longobardorum." The constant wars, and the disorganised state of the country, prevented any progress in the amelioration of the laws; and at the time that the German Emperor, Otto the First, A.D. 961, took possession of Italy, the laws established by the Carlovingians still continued in force. In the eleventh century, however, the Edicts, which had been supplemented by the addition of forms of procedure and also glossed, were collected into three books, and were published under the title of "Liber Longobardæ, or

Liber Longobardæ.

* Tomkins' Instit., pp. 142-183.

Lombardæ." In this form, instruction was given in the law school at the University of Bologna. This Code exercised an important influence upon the development of the Feudal Laws of Europe; and until the end of the fourteenth century continued in use in the surrounding nations of Germany, France, and Spain. At this period, also, by the amalgamation of this Code into the Feudal Laws in force in those countries, the Liber Longobardæ was in its turn superseded, and gradually fell into disuse.

Lex Romana Visigothorum.

The Visigoths, in the course of the fifth century, completed their conquest of the south-west of Gaul and the north of Spain. Alaric II., the great captain of that conquering race, finding that the Code of Theodoric II. was beyond the comprehension of his barbarous subjects, published, under his own authority, a Code of Laws in the year 506. This Code was entitled the "Lex Romana Visigothorum." Imperfect as it was, it resulted in securing the continuation of the Roman Civil Law in the south-western portion of Europe. In the

Codex Utinensis.

tenth century, under the title of the "Codex Utinensis,"* the rules of the Roman Law, and the Consuetudinary Laws, as then extant, were collected and republished as the authoritative code, according to Savigny for the Lombards, according to Stalberg for Istria, according to the opinion of others for the Curiensis Rhætia. It is interesting and important to observe in regard to the

Breviarium Alaricianum.

"Breviarium Alaricianum" that it contains not only a selection from the Theodosian Code; but also a number of the Novellæ of Theodosius, Valentinianus, Martianus, Majorianus, and Severus. In addition to

* The last edition by Hænel, 1849. Puchta Instit., vol. i., p. 687, et seq.

these constituent parts, which represent the "Leges," as they are termed, it is also worthy of note that the Breviarium contained in the portion which embodied the "Jura" the following fragments:—A compilation from the Commentaries of Gaius, which, although very corrupt, proved of great service in the reading and deciphering of the recently discovered Veronese MS.; extracts from the Sententiæ receptæ of Paulus; from the Gregorian and the Hermogenian Codes; and a passage from the Responses of Papinian.

Contained a Compilation of Gaius.

In the Kingdom of Burgundy the Lex Romana Burgundorum was superseded by the Code of Alaric II.; and hence it followed that one system of laws, imperfect it is true, but still permeated by the principles of the Civil Law, prevailed throughout the length and breadth of the south-west of Europe, known as the Droit Ecrit; whilst, in the northern provinces of the empire of the Franks the customary law, that is the Germanic Law, known as the Droits Coutumiers, prevailed. On this account the southern half of Gaul has been designated as the "*pays du droit ecrit,*" whilst the provinces of the north have been termed "*pays du droit coutumier.*" These customary laws were in part embodied in the Codes entitled the Lex Salica, the Lex Francorum Chamavorum, the Lex Ripuaria, and other less important Codes. Rude as these Germanic legal institutions appear to have been when contrasted with the exactness and elegance of the classical Roman Law, they were, nevertheless, not unsuited to the peculiar character and circumstances of the times; and they mark the boundary between the older law of the Roman Empire and the institutions and Codes of

Code of Alaric II.

Droit Ecrit and Droit Coutumier

Lex Salica, &c., suited to the times.

modern times. Thus the law continued for centuries; for we find that not until the year 1283 was any effort made to codify the local and customary laws, when Beaumanoir collected and arranged them in a work entitled "Li livres des Coustumes et des Usages de Biauvoizins." This Code consisted of seventy chapters, and continued in use until it was superseded in the fourteenth century by the Grand Coutumier of Charles VI., and the Somme Rurale of Bouteiller. These, again, were subsequently modified by the ordinances of Louis XI. The latter, termed "Ordonnances Royales," further adopted the principles of the Roman Law, and from the days of Francis I., who invited the celebrated civilian, André Alciat, of Milan, to settle at Bourges, the Roman Law became the common study of the French jurist. It is worthy of observation that, at the very time that Cuyas, or, as he is more usually denominated, Cujacius (who was born at Toulouse in 1522, and died 1590) and Domat were lecturing on the Civil Law at Brouges; the University of Paris, which was under the influence of the advocates of the customary law, actually prohibited, by the Ordinance of Blois, 1579, the study of the Roman Jurisprudence.

Usages de Biauvoizins.

Ordonnances Royales.

Civil Law proscribed at Paris.

The time, however, for resisting the influence of the Imperial Law had now ceased. Charles Dumoulin, an Advocate of the Parliament of Paris, and one of the most accomplished jurists of his age, possessing an intimate acquaintance both with the old French and the Roman Laws, not only codified the Lois Coutumiers, but gave a new impulse to the study of the Civil Law; thus preparing the way for the well-known Pothier. This writer occupies a place among the

Dumoulin.

Pothier.

most distinguished jurists that France or any other country has produced. Pothier, by his labours and his genius, exercised an important influence upon the juridical studies and the legislation of his country; inspiring both the jurist and legislator of France, with an earnest desire to adjust and to digest the incongruous laws which prevailed at that time. The Ordinances of Louis XIV., Louis XV., and, finally, those of Louis XVI., were destined to lead the way to the ultimate codification of the French Laws under the Great Napoléon. The Code Napoléon, as the Cinq Codes are termed—though in reality there are eight Codes, including the Codes Forestier, *Rural*, *et Fluvial*—owes much of its intrinsic worth to the exact and learned treatment of legal subjects to which the labours of Pothier gave so great an impulse.

Code Napoléon.

The distinguishing feature of the Code Napoléon is, that it incorporates as regards inheritance, family relations, and marriage law, the customary laws (Lois Coutumiers) of France with the Jurisprudence of Rome; whilst the laws of Rome, in respect to Obligations, the Rights of Property, rules of Procedure and Servitudes, have been accepted as a model.

Its principal features.

In Spain the Roman Law prevailed at the time of the conquest of that country by the Visigoths. In the sixth century King Chindasvind ordered a Code to be formed for his Gothic and Roman-Spanish subjects. This collection of rules, called the Fuero Juzgo, or rules or prescripts of laws, embodied the following juridical elements:—1, The Roman Law; 2, The German Law; 3, The Canons of the Councils. The Fueros or Codes, however, varied according as the provinces were more

Roman Law in Spain.

The Fuero Juzgo.

or less Roman or Gothic. The wisdom of the Moors did not permit of arbitrary interference with the laws of the conquered races that submitted to their rule; hence, during the eight centuries of their supremacy, the Roman Law was permitted to continue in force in the southern part of the Peninsula. In the north, the Roman Law, though modified, continued to vitalise the laws of that country. In 1254 a University was founded at Salamanca, which, following the example of Bologna, fostered the study of the Roman Law.

Roman Law taught at Salamanca

The Partidas.

In the years 1263–65, Alfonso published the Codes arranged under his direction, entitled the Partidas. Unfortunately, they were composed so carelessly and with so little skill, that they contradicted without amending the Codes of the Fueros Juzgos which were in force at that time. The Fuero Juzgo, in its original form, was published in Latin, and the Latin original was the authorised Code until the year 1788, when a Spanish edition appeared for the first time. In consequence, however, of the conflict of the local laws in the ancient kingdoms of Castile, Arragon, and Navarre; and the wide gulf that severs the southern from the northern population of Spain, no systematic arrangement of the laws of Spain has been found practicable; and though the legal literature of Spain may boast of the Códigos Españoles Concordados y Anatodos (12 vol., pub. 1817), and the Coleccion de Cortes de Leon y Càstilla, 1836 and '43, which contain a valuable collection of the laws of Spain, it has been found impossible up to the present time to codify the laws of the Peninsula. In the beginning of the nineteenth century the Código de Comercio y Código

Reason why no complete Code in Spain.

Penal were projected, and these are at the present time the only Codes in Spain having a national application. Thus the Roman Law has, from necessity, been cultivated with much ardour, and its principles adopted in almost every sphere of jurisprudence. It follows from this universal reception of the legal rules of the Roman Law by the nations of the Peninsula that these principles were destined not to be confined to the narrow limits of European nations, but to follow the track of the discoverer across the Atlantic to the New World. Even there, their course has not been limited by the range of the vast territories occupied by the Spanish, Portuguese, and French settlers of those countries; but they have been further accepted by the Dutch as well as by the Portuguese in their possessions in the East and at the Cape of Good Hope, and finally incorporated into the juridical systems of these important settlements.

Roman Law in the New World, &c.

In the north of Europe, including the kingdoms of Scandinavia and in Germany, the introduction of the Roman Law was far more tardy. This was owing in part to the love of freedom inherent in the Northern races; whilst in addition to this national instinct there existed the dread of Papal encroachment. There were also among these nations deeply rooted, aristocratic and national laws. The wars of the Ottos, the Frederics, and the Henrys, introduced into the German Imperial Court an Italian element. The laws of the Longobards—their Liber Feudorum—had been studied and embodied in the feudal systems of Germany. The Authenticæ Fridericianæ, as taught at that great school of learning Bologna, became the adopted law of the

In the North of Europe.

German empire. Nevertheless, the Civil Law found but little favour. The crude Code of Laws known as the Sachsen Spiegel, supposed to have been compiled by Eike, a magistrate of Thüringia; the Schwabenspiegel, published at a later date—the latter including a chapter on feudal tenures—appeared to suffice for the rude necessities of the times. At the Universities of Prague, Vienna, Heidelberg, Cologne, Erfurt, during the fourteenth and part of the fifteenth century, the Canon Law only was taught; but upon the revival of letters, the Civil Law was accepted as part of the necessary studies of the jurists in these new Institutions, whose existence heralded the advent of modern civilisation. This innovation speedily resulted in the introduction of Doctors of the Civil Law into the magistratures of the land. One half of the magisterial benches was occupied by civilians, one half by laymen. From this period the adoption of the Civil Law into the German jurisprudence may be dated.

Sachsen Spiegel.

Canon Law at the Universities.

Law in Russia.

In Russia, the empire of the Sclavonic race, the customary laws of that people long prevailed; and it was not until the peace of Olegs and Igars, in the year 912 A.D. and 945 A.D., that we find any foreign element introduced into their juridical system. In the year 1020 A.D., Jaroslow published a Code of Laws entitled Prawda Ruskaja, which contained a crude collection of the customary laws then extant. At a later period, in the year 1497 A.D., Iwan III. projected a new Code, and in the year 1550 A.D., Iwan IV. revised and published an edition of these laws. Such was the jurisprudence of Russia until the time of Peter the Great. This remarkable man infused a new element into the

Peter the Great.

juridical systems of his empire, by ordaining that the Roman Law should be taught at the Universities of Moscow and Kiev. The University of Dorpat, by the conquest of the Swedish Baltic provinces at that time, became an institution of the Russian empire, and was destined to exercise an important influence on the study of jurisprudence in that country. Thus the law in force contains a strong element derived from Roman sources. The Code published by Alexander I. in 1825, and the subsequently authorised Codes published by Nicolas I., 1832, and again revised, 1833, and authoritatively published in fifteen volumes, under the title "Corpus Juris Rossiæ," contain the results of the labours of the civilians of the Russian law schools, who have devoted their energies to the amendment of the laws of that vast empire.

Code of Alex. I.

Corpus Juris Rossiæ.

In the sixteenth and seventeenth centuries, upon the revival of letters, there arose in Holland the classical school of Jurists, which at a later period was succeeded by the systematic and synthetic teaching of the Germans. The influence of the Dutch classical school upon the study of the Roman Law was most important. The method they adopted was to follow what the Germans term the "Legal Ordnung," or the order observed by the compilers of the Pandects.

Classical School of Jurists.

Of the three great jurists upon whose writings this work is founded, it is only necessary to say a few words. George Friedrich Puchta, the son of a distinguished lawyer, was born at Cadolzburg, in Franken, on the 31st August, 1798. After studying at Nürnburg, in 1816, he proceeded to the University of Erlangen, where he commenced his tutorial life by lecturing as a

George Friedrich Puchta.

Privatdocent on the Roman Law. Subsequently he lectured upon Legal Encyclopädie—a term employed to denote a scientifically arranged survey of the entire domain of Jurisprudence—and also on Ecclesiastical Law. His advancement was rapid in his profession, but his life, unfortunately, was of short duration. In 1828 he attained the dignity of an ordinary professor at Munich, and there made the friendship of his colleague Schelling. In 1835 he was called to Marburg, in 1837 to Leipzig, and in 1842 he became successor to Savigny in Berlin. In Germany, the student who intends not merely to practice the law, but to become a professor, after taking his degree of Doctor utriusque juris, and after the defence of his published theses before the professors of the faculty in which he intends to lecture, commences his professional life as a Privatdocent or tutor. At this stage he announces the delivery of a course of public lectures, without requiring the ordinary fee. His next step is made when he is appointed by the Government a Professor Extraordinarius in the University, and the higher rank is attained when he becomes an Ordinary Professor. Puchta passed through all these stages. In 1844 he was made Councillor of the Superior Tribunal, and in 1845 he was nominated as a member of the Council of State, and appointed one of the Legal Commission; but died on the 8th of January, 1846, at the early age of forty-seven. This able man understood the law in its most profound conception, and viewed it as a disciple of the school of Schelling. He, moreover, possessed a rare clearness and exactness of thought and of expression; whilst both his lectures and his later works are models

Savigny's successor.

in these respects. His writings on Ecclesiastical Law are said to have made him many enemies. Puchta's most important works are the following:—"Grundriss zu Vorlesungen über Juristiche Encyclopädie und Methodologie" (Erlang., 1822)—Elements for Lectures upon Juridical Encyclopædia; "Civilistische Abhandlungen" (Bd. 1, Berl., 1823)—Treatises on the Civil Law; "Encyclopädie als Einleitung zu Institutionen Vorlesungen" (Berl., 1825)—An Encyclopædia as an Introduction to Lectures on the Institutes; "Das Gewohneitsrecht" (2 Bde., Erlang., 1828-37)—Customary Law; "Lehrbuch für Institutionen-Vorlesungen" (Münch., 1832)—A Manual for Lectures upon the Institutes of the Roman Law; "Lehrbuch der Pandekten" (Lpz., 1838, 6 Aufl. von Rudorff, 1852)—Manual of the Modern Civil Law; "Einleitung in das Recht der Kirche" (Lpz., 1840)—Introduction to the Canon Law; "Cursus der Institutionen"—Text-Book for the Institutes (2 Bde., Lpz., 1841-42, and Aufl. besorgt von Rudorff, Bd. 1, 1853). His Lectures on the Modern Roman Law (in 2 vols., Lpz., 1847-48, 3rd edition, 1852), as well as his "Kleinen Civilistischen Schriften"—Minor Writings on the Civil Law—were published by Rudorff, the latter in Leipzic in 1851.

His writings.

Karl Adolf von Vangerow was born at Shiffelbach, a village in Kurhessen, not far from Marburg. From his sixteenth year he has devoted himself to the study of jurisprudence. On the 23rd of January, 1830, he was advanced to the degree of Doctor of the Civil and the Canon Law; and the following Easter he commenced his professional career as Privatdocent in the University of Marburg. In 1833 he became Professor

Von Vangerow.

Extraordinarius, and in 1837 he was appointed Ordinary Professor in the same University. In the autumn of 1840 he was invited to the University of Heidelberg as the successor of the distinguished Thibaut, where he has remained the most popular Professor of the Roman Law in Germany. In 1842 he was appointed a Court Councillor in the Grand Duchy of Baden; in 1846 he was made a Privy Court Councillor; and in 1849 he became Privy Councillor in the same State. He is also a Knight of both German and Russian Orders. In Germany it is usual to mark distinguished literary and scientific ability in this way.

His writings.

Von Vangerow's inaugural address, delivered at Marburg in 1830, consisted of a commentary on l. 22. 1 cod. "de jure deliberandi" (6.30). He has also published the following works:—"De Furto Concepto ex lege XII. Tabularum," Heidelberg, 1845. Also a treatise upon the "Latini Juniani," Marburg, 1833. His highly valued work, entitled "Leitfaden für Pandektenvorlesungen"—Elementary work for Lectures on the Modern Civil Law—was first published at Marburg in three volumes in 1837 and the following years. This work has passed through several editions; the seventh was published in 1869. Von Vangerow has also written in Richter's "Jahrbuch" several critical works, and in the "Archives for Civil Practice," of which he has been a co-editor since 1841, a great number of valuable articles have appeared from his pen.

Ludwig Arndts.

Ludwig Arndts, Professor of Law at Munich, was born 19th of August, 1805, at Arnsberg. He sprang from a Catholic family, the members of which for several generations had obtained high positions in the administration of justice. His father, who was a Privy Councillor and a Director of the Superior Tribunal, died in 1812, leaving his son only seven years of age. The boy studied in the Gymnasium of his native place, and subsequently, in accordance with the German practice of entering several of the great schools, he became a student at the Universities of Bonn, Heidelberg, and Berlin; at the latter of which he obtained the degree of Doctor of Laws in the year 1825. In the summer of 1826 he settled in Bonn, and became in 1832 a member of the "Spruch Collegium," or Collegium Juridicum, and in 1837 Professor Extraordinarius. In 1839 he was nominated to the Ordinary Professorship in the University of Breslau; but before he entered upon the duties of the office he received a similar invitation to Munich, which he was induced to accept. At Munich in 1844 he was appointed a member of the "Legal Commission," and was entrusted with the drawing up of a Civil Code; but in the early part of the year 1847 he retired from the duties of the Commission. During a journey to Italy, undertaken in the winter of 1834-1835, Arndts made a collation of the Farnese MSS. of Festus, which was subsequently used by Müller in his edition of that writer. Arndts, however, both as a teacher and a writer, has devoted his attention more especially to the Roman Law. He has written a valuable, though very brief, work on the "Encyclopädie of Jurisprudence," and also on the subject of "Civil Procedure." In addition to several other elementary works, and especially his "Lehrbuch der Pandekten"—dedicated to Von Savigny, 1st ed., 1852, 6th ed., 1868, and used in the present work—he has furnished many contributions to legal periodicals, and to Weiske's Law Lexicon. In the year 1848 he was chosen in Straubing as a deputation to the Frankfort National Assembly, and was regarded as strongly German in his proclivities. At present he is Professor of the Roman Law in Vienna. It is not a little remarkable that Savigny, Puchta, and Von Vangerow were at different times associated with the Hessian University of Marburg. Savigny commenced his student life there in 1795, and took his Doctor's degree in the same University on Oct. 31st, 1800. Puchta was a Professor at Marburg in 1837, and Von Vangerow was for ten years identified with this school of learning, as student, tutor, and Professor.

The University of Marburg.

The three works which should be consulted by the practical jurist, to whom Moehler was indebted for the production of his manual, it may be observed, are very different in their characteristics. The Pandekten of Puchta, the eighth edition of which, published in 1856, is now before us, was edited by Rudorff after the author's death. It was the third edition of the work edited by the Berlin Professor. Between the years 1838 and 1846 five editions had been published by the author himself, and between 1852 and 1856 the three editions referred to by Dr. Rudorff. No work on the Modern Civil Law has ever appeared at once so compact and so philosophical. If Puchta had lived at the time of the early Roman jurists, when the luminaries of legal science were grouped into two constellations of surpassing brightness, he would have been found marshalled with the Proculians, the sect or

Peculiar features of these three works.

Puchta a philosophical jurist.

school that treated the law with philosophical freedom, and which derived its arguments from the appropriateness and utility of the law itself. Not that there is anything visionary or obscure in his writings, for they are singularly sharp and clear, both in conception and expression. Puchta had a mind which enabled him to grasp the law, not as consisting of a number of fragmentary and broken ideas, or even of separate institutes, but as one vast and symmetrical system. No legal treatises produced by the jurisprudents of modern times—not even the writings of Savigny—show more thought and philosophical beauty than the writings of Puchta, especially his Pandekten. In addition to the work referred to, we are fortunately in possession of his lectures on the Modern Roman Law, published by Rudorff after the author's death. These volumes, consisting of upwards of 900 pages, contain the last gift the immortal Puchta, to use the words of Rudorff, bequeathed to the legal profession.

Von Vangerow a great controversialist.

The Pandekten of Von Vangerow is a work upon the Modern Civil Law altogether unique. To the general reader it would be regarded as lacking the completeness and finish of Puchta. But to the advanced student Von Vangerow presents, in the extracts from the authorities and his discussions on the controversies, a mine of wealth and treasure, of which most other treatises upon the Roman Law afford us no conception. In his three volumes, containing almost as many thousand pages, we possess the most acute discussions on the controversies of the Modern Roman Law found in either ancient or modern writers. The great value, however, of these volumes, is only known to those who have used them as a text-book for his spoken lectures. During the winter session of the University of Heidelberg, for five months hundreds of students assemble in his class. They come from all parts of Germany, from France, Holland, Belgium, Italy, Spain, Greece, Russia, and the United States of America. Full and systematic, microscopically correct and accurate in his authorities and his definitions, his students become enthusiastic in their devotedness to the Professor, and to the subject of which he is so great a master. In his lectures one seems to have revived the fluency and promptness of the Great Roman jurists with the impressive eloquence of Cicero.

Arndts didactic.

The Pandekten of Professor Arndts, is a treatise quite different from the two preceding works. In a volume of less than 900 pages he presents, in a manner well suited for the student who has mastered the Institutes of the Roman Law, the doctrines of the Modern Civil Law. The book possesses neither the charm of Puchta's perfectly philosophical treatment, nor the critical acuteness of Von Vangerow, but it is pre-eminently a plain, able, and practical book; and as such may be consulted before either of the others. As a teacher in the school of which Von Savigny was so eminent a master, Arndts has been careful not to combine extraneous subjects with the Roman Law as it now prevails. He teaches as a master, avoiding institutional treatment, or historical or classical digressions. Hence his work is valued by those who are laying the foundation of future acquisitions with a view to their employment for practical purposes in the courts of law or in the realm of statesmanship.

We have already called attention to the important work of Glück now in course of publication. Glück was a professor in Erlangen, and published the first volume of his Commentary in 1797. He lived to complete the thirty-fourth volume, which was published in the year 1830. In 1832, Mühlenbruch, a professor in Göttingen, who is still spoken of in Germany for his fine style of Latin composition, published the thirty-fifth volume. He dedicated it to Dr. Carl Friedrich Zapernick, "a veteran jurist, and the nearest friend of the immortal Glück." Mühlenbruch commenced the work where Glück had left off, at the 28th Book of the Digest, Tit. 1, "Qui testamenta facere possunt," etc. He, however, only lived to publish the forty-third volume, at Erlangen, in 1843, in which he advanced the work to the 29th Book of the Digest, Tit. 29, "Si quis aliquem," etc. The part done by Mühlenbruch, on the Law of Inheritance, is held in the highest estimation on the Continent. He was succeeded in 1851 by Dr. Edward Fein, professor first in Jena, and afterwards in Tübingen, who published the forty-fourth volume in 1851, on Book 29th, Tit. 7 of the Digest "De jure codicillorum," and the forty-fifth volume, on the same subject, in 1853. After his death the work lay long idle, until, in 1868-69, Dr. Karl Ludwig Arndts, the author of the Pandekten, published the forty-sixth volume on "De legatis et fidei commissis." A new issue of the entire work is announced by the publishers at a moderate price.

Glück's Commentary.

Continued by other jurists.

It is now necessary to explain what is at the present time comprehended by the expression Pandekten, and also to refer to the sources from which its constituent

The term Pandekten explained.

parts are derived.* By the term "Pandekten," or Modern Civil Law, is understood the systematic exhibition of the actually existing Roman Justinian Law in relation to *private rights*. Hence, in lectures on the Pandects, it is not the theory of pure Roman Law that is given, but the Roman Law as applied at the present time is presented for the consideration of the student. Roman Law is in force in nearly all the States of Europe, but in Germany it is confined to the Minor States. Those countries in which the Civil Law is adopted are designated "Common Law countries."

Modern Roman Law—its sources.

The sources of the Modern Roman Law are—1st, The Roman Law in the form given by the Emperor Justinian. This Emperor caused a collection to be made of all the laws extant at his time, which compilation is divisible into four parts:—*a*. The Institutes for elementary legal instruction (published A.D. 533); *b*. The Pandects, containing extracts from the greater and lesser works on Jurisprudence, namely, Gaius, Ulpianus, Paulus, the *Vaticana fragmenta*, etc. (published A.D. 533); *c*. The Code, a collection of all the Imperial Constitutions from the time of Hadrian (published A.D. 534); *d*. The Novels, which are the separate Constitutions of Justinian dating from the year A.D. 535. The collective title employed for these four component parts is that of "*Corpus Juris Civilis*." Its vitality extends only so far as it is glossed, *i.e.*, as far as the glossators have, by their remarks, declared it to be applicable in practice. On the other hand, it has a specific value by virtue of the additions made by the glossators themselves, and also in conse-

The legislation of Justinian, &c.

* The following authorities may be consulted:—Von Vangerow, Pandekten, ss. 1—10; Puchta, do., 1—9; Arndts, do., 1—20; Savigny, Syst. I. 1—3.

quence of the additional translations into Latin of Greek Extracts; Excerpts from the Novels *(Authenticæ);* Laws of the German Emperors, either incorporated as a whole, or given in abstract, in the Code *(Authenticæ Fridericianæ.)*

2nd, The Canon Law, composed of four constituent parts viewed in their combined character, is termed the *Corpus Juris Canonici (clausum):—a. Decretum Gratiani*—Extracts from the Bible and from the Fathers of the Church (middle of the 12th century); *b. Decretales* (Gregorii IX.), composed of papal decrees transmitted in the year A.D. 1234, to the Universities of Paris and Bologna; *c. Liber sextus decretalium* (Bonifacius VIII.)—a supplement to the former collection, and also transmitted to the same Universities, A.D. 1298; *d. Clementinæ*—a supplemental collection added to the former by Clement V., transmitted to the University of Orleans A.D. 1313, and subsequently to the previously named Universities A.D. 1317. The Canon Law.

In addition to these, and later in point of time, we have the Decrees of the Council of Trent (A.D. 1545-1563) relating to Marriage. The rules of the Canon Law bear both upon temporal and spiritual matters.

3rd, The native German Law, partly contained in the laws of the empire, in part originated by force of custom, or accepted for its scientific merit. Of special importance, also, are the Imperial Laws:—The Code of Procedure of the Supreme Court of Judicature, 1555; the Notarial Rules of Maximilian, made in the year 1512; the Criminal Code of Charles the Fifth, promulged in the year 1532; the Decisions of the Diet at Speier, 1529, relating to the succession of first Native German Law.

cousins; the Police Regulations of 1577; and the Final Decree of the States of the Empire, made in 1654.

Influence of the constituent parts upon each other.

The Canon Law has in part modified the pure Roman Law, though in practice Modern Law has in many points reverted to the original purity of the Civil Law. The modifications that remain, but only these, constitute one of the sources of the Modern Civil Law. The Roman Law occupies in regard to the indigenous law of Germany not only the position of an auxiliary supplemental Code, which becomes operative whenever the Common Law is silent; but it has moreover entirely supplanted many peculiar Germanic juridical doctrines and institutions.

German Private Law.

Several characteristic German legal institutions have, however, remained, which are comprised under the title "German Private Law" (*Deutsches Privatrecht*). This and the Roman Law possess respectively, each in its own sphere, equal authority. To designate this relation it is customary to say that the Civil Law has been received in Germany (*recipirt*). The Roman Law becomes operative wherever there is no contradiction to its rule, either by the Statute Law or by Customary Law, or by special local laws: or where the principles of the German Private Law do not come into operation. For the German Laws of the Empire and Customary Law have still further developed the Roman Law. Local Law abrogates the Common Law, and German Private Law maintains an equal rank with the Roman Law, and forms a judicial sphere of its own. The inapplicability of the Roman Law is, however, only exceptional; hence the rule, in all countries under the Common Law, is, that he who appeals to the Roman

Law proceeds upon a firm basis (*fundatam intentionem.*)

The relative value of these elements.

The relative authority of the various sources of the Modern Civil Law is the following:—Existing Customary Law modifies all other law; the laws of the Empire qualify the Canon and the Roman Law; the Canon Law modifies the Roman Law. The doctrine that has been promulged in regard to the relative authority of the various parts of the *Corpus Juris Civilis* may be thus stated:—The Novels precede all other sources; the Code takes the precedence of the Pandects; and the Institutes precede the Pandects, if they determine anything positive: this last point is, however, questioned by some jurists, because it is argued that Justinian intended his legislation to be considered not simply in its parts, but as a whole.

Various methods of interpretation.

The scientific exposition of the Modern Roman Law has varied at different periods of time. The following methods must, however, be distinguished:—*a.* The exegetical method which strictly adheres to the order and thought contained in the sources of the law. *b.* The method which avails itself of commentary, treating the original text systematically, but with greater freedom; adhering, however, closely to the several parts of the text. These two methods were adopted by the Italian and French schools of jurists which flourished from the 12th to the 17th century. *c.* The systematic treatment developed by the Dutch and German schools, at first by the explanation of the text in accordance with its normal and legal arrangement; afterwards by the methodical system pursued in the Institutes; and finally, in the 19th century, the free arrangement of the subject matter, controlling and systematically harmonising the whole. It is to this systematic exposition of the Modern Roman Law that attention is especially directed. Its inauguration dates only from the commencement of the present century, and it has been pursued not only in the schools of Germany, but also in those of France. It is scarcely too much to say that it marks not only an epoch in the study of the Roman Law, but one also in the history of the human intellect, and is destined to exert a powerful influence upon the condition and progress of mankind. This modern treatment and study of the Jurisprudence of Rome, scarcely understood in England, and wholly ignored at our national Universities, must sooner or later, on account of its vast practical importance in our commercial relations, and for our high courts of judicature, receive the attention as well of the jurist as of the legislature.

BOOK THE FIRST.

LAW IN THE OBJECTIVE SENSE; ITS SOURCES AND ITS APPLICATION.

Section I.—*The State, Law, Sources of Law, and Different kinds of Enactments.*

Von Vangerow, ss. 11—110.
Puchta, ss. 10—21.
Arndts, ss. 21—28.
Savigny, Syst. I., 2, 3, 12, 14, 18, 25, 26, 28—30.
Instit. I., 2, de jure naturali, gentium et civili.
Dig. de legibus, senatusque consultis et longa consuet. (1—3.)
Dig. de constitutionibus principum (1—4.)
S. 3, Instit. de jure natur. (1, 2.)
Cod., I., 15, de mandatis principum.
,, I., 19, de precibus imper. etc.
,, I., 21, Ut lita pendente vel post, etc.
,, I., 22, Si contra jus, vel utilitatem.
,, I., 23, de diversis rescriptis, etc.
,, VIII., 53, quae sit longa consuetudo.
Glück, I., p. 427, et seq.

It belongs rather to the philosophy of Law than to a work upon the Modern Roman Law, to discuss the important questions relating to the origin of the State. The writers upon this subject in the eighteenth century, based the existence of the State upon the will of the persons composing it, or, as it was expressed, upon

The State.

"social contract." More recent writers have favoured the view which has regarded the State as resulting from natural causes, and as wholly independent of the will of man. Puchta held that the State reposes upon Divine appointment, and upon the will of man viewed as a member of an assemblage or group of persons considered as a nation, using the latter term not in a political sense. Among the ancients, Aristotle, and among the moderns, Walter, have characterised man as distinguished from his congeners, by the fact that not only has nature endowed him with speech; but that he is not bound to the condition in which she has placed him in the early stages of his existence: that he is, in other words, capable of progressive improvement. "Nature," says Aristotle, "who makes nothing in vain, has bestowed upon man alone the gift of speech. Speech places him in a position to point out what is useful and what is injurious; hence, also, what is right and what is wrong. The faculty which distinguishes man from all other animals is, that he has a nature which enables him to distinguish between virtue and vice."* An able French writer, treating upon this subject, says—"L'homme n'a point d'instinct; il a une liberté et une volonté. L' absence d'instinct dans l'homme fait qu'il a besoin de tout apprendre. La société est, si l'on peut parler ainsi, un instrument nécessaire à l'homme; et les révélations dont la société est dépositaire sont le seul moyen par lequel l'homme ait pu parvenir à connaître et à aimer."†

Opinion of Aristotle.

* Polit., 1, 2.

† Ballanche, Institutions Sociales, cap. 9. Oeuvres ii., p. 244.

Gradual formation of the State.

The State, in its complete form, could not have been attained by a single bound, but must have been reached by successive steps involving a long historical period. In the course of time, the family, held together by patriarchal authority, became transformed into a family State, governed on family principles. Several families thus ruled becoming united, there arose the race, or class. This group, in its turn, became split up into several branches, races, and families. It was in this way that a State arose composed of several related races, the State being a complex of smaller and greater unities which were originally held together by family relationship as the primary principle. In the very nature of things, a State composed of races belonging to the same family was a much less coherent body than the smaller gatherings or circles of persons of which it was composed. It is in the family that the vital strength of the community proper lies. Families are States on a small scale, and their federation gives rise to the larger and to the political body.*

Definition of Grotius.

The political body, or body politic, of an independent nation is termed the State. Grotius, following Cicero, says—"Est autem civitas coetus perfectus liberorum hominum, juris fruendi et communis utilitatis causa sociatus."† In other words, the State is constituted by an aggregation of individuals into a political unit. This unit consists in Oneness of Will. The power which compulsorily forces the will of the many into the *one*, is termed Law. Thus Law is the expression of

* *See* Jhering's Gesit des Röm. Rechts., Pt. 1., 162, et seq.

† Grot. de Jur. Bel. ac Pac., lib. 1, c. 1, sec. 14. Cic. de Repub., lib. 1, sec. 25.

the common conviction of a people, and is the Matter of the recognised rules which govern the external relations or conditions of a people. Such is Law in the Objective sense.*

The origin of the common will, the origin of law, is either—

Customary Law, or *Jus non scriptum.*

1st, The immediate popular conviction. Law thus originated is designated Customary Law, or *Jus non scriptum.*† It is regarded as Law, because it is the common conviction, and it is termed "Law by Custom," inasmuch as its existence is known by its recognition and practice in actual life. Hence it does not require for its validity either the express or the tacit consent of the legislator. An essential and marked characteristic of Customary Law is its reasonableness; it must neither overrule any superior law, nor be opposed to morality (*contra bonos mores*). Upon these points the judge has power to decide in accordance with the more enlightened public opinion, and also in harmony with the spirit of the Law. Customary Law is recognised as follows:—*a.* As common custom *(Consuetudo)*, the exercise of such custom must be received by virtue of some legal doctrine *(opinione juris)*; it must, moreover, have been enjoyed by continuous or unbroken use *(tenaciter servata.)*‡ Custom and

* The Romans distinguished the *jus civile*, by which they understood their national law; the *jus gentium*, or the law observed by civilised nations; and the *jus naturale*—that is, *quod natura omnia animalia docuit.* The latter is neither precise nor clear, for animals cannot be regarded as capable of rights in the juridical sense of the term.

† This takes place in accordance with the maxim, "Consuetudo non immerito pro lege censetur."

‡ Judicial and extra-judicial. The Judicial is termed the practice of the Courts, "*rerum judicatarum auctoritas.*" The practice of the tribunal has

Customary Law are said to stand related to each other, as essence and phenomenon *(Wesen und Erscheinung)*. *b.* The testimony of Experts. *c.* Records, and Legal Maxims. Moreover, the judge is required to test and approve, scientifically, the applicability of these various methods of understanding a question, and to determine, *ex officio*, upon their force and conclusiveness. The judge is further bound, officially, to obtain information; but he is not allowed to impose upon the party asserting the affirmative, the duty of proving the customary law. Hence the maxim—"*Jura noscit curia.*" He may, however, call upon the party alleging the custom to state his reasons for it. An actually existing custom possesses the same legal effect as the written law itself; it may either modify or explain existing law,* or fill up its deficiencies, and it may be employed by way of analogy. There are both general and special customs.

2nd, The deliberate activity of the legislator. The rule the legislator propounds is termed Law *(Jus scriptum)*. Law, in this sense, is the rule or enactment of the legislative body, which rule must be constitutionally established and duly published.

Jus scriptum.

A legal Precept is either a rule of law adapted to a class of undetermined hypothetical cases and persons; or it is a rule to meet a special or concrete case *(Constitutio personalis)*.

Legal precepts.

---

authority only in the forum where it has originated. There is a distinction which must be noted between the formal and the essential practice of the tribunal, in respect to that which is merely formal and in relation to the subject-matter of its knowledge. It is impossible, theoretically, to say at what point the judge is to adhere to the practice and custom as being in use or not.

* In the way of *desuetudo*, as also *consuetudo contraria*.

The former only are laws in the proper sense of the term. They are classified as follows:—

a. According to the source from whence they emanate. The Roman Imperial Laws were either *Edicta*, or *Decreta*, or *Mandata*, or *Rescripta*. In the last, in respect to the form, the officially affixed date and signature of the Regent, or of his authorised officer, were always required—*(datum loci et temporis.)* In that which is essential, they cannot affect acquired or vested interests. The plea against the Rescripta is termed the *Prescriptio mendacii.** If the judge allows the plea, the plaintiff loses all right arising from the Rescript. Upon whom the burden of proof falls in the "Praescriptio mendacii," is a point in dispute. The Rescript must be regarded as non-existent, and the party with whom the *onus probandi* would rest in its absence, upon him the burden of proof is held to lie.

b. According to their Matter, laws are either compulsory—*Leges præceptivæ, cogentes, prohibitivæ;* or non-compulsory—*Leges permissivæ, dispositivæ.*

c. Laws are classified according to their comprehensiveness into *jus generale*, that is to say, general rules; and *jus speciale*, or rules adapted to special cases, and forming the exception to the general rule. The latter give rise to *privilegia*. The *jus commune* is the rule corresponding or answering to the general leading principles embodied in the act of legislation. *Jus singulare* is the exception from the legal rule; it suspends the general principle laid down in the law for a definite relation; it gives rise to *beneficia*. *Jus*

* It proceeds either on the ground that something has been wrongfully stated (subreptio), or that the truth has been suppressed (obreptio).

universale is the common law of the land. *Jus particulare* is valid law only in certain parts of the State.

d. Laws are designated according to their efficacy—*perfectæ*, that is, such as declare every act in opposition to the same to be null and void; or they are *minus quam perfectæ*, that is, such as do not set aside a thing done, but punish the transgressor; or they are *imperfectæ* whenever neither the one nor the other of the above cases occurs; or, as it is expressed, they are laws without a Sanction.

SECTION II.—*Use of Legal Precepts. Interpretation.*

Von Vangerow, ss. 22—26.
Arndts, ss. 5—15.
Puchta, ss. 14, 14a, 15.
"Scire leges non hoc est verba earum tenere sed vim ac potestatem," l. 17, Dig. de legib. (1, 3.)
"In ambigua voce legis ea potius accipienda est significatio, quæ vitio caret, præsertim quum etiam voluntas legis ex hoc colligi possit." l. 19, Dig. de legib. (1, 3.)

THE law must be enforced by the action of the magistrate or judge. But in order that he may grant his aid, it is necessary that he should himself understand the law. The means employed for this purpose are denominated "Interpretation." Interpretation.

In the first place, the authenticity of the text of a law must be ascertained. This investigation is designated criticism, and it is divisible into elective and conjectural criticism. The judge must further provide for the constitutional promulgation and publication of the Law. This function, again, is termed "Interpretation" in the more extensive signification of the term.

By Interpretation in its restricted sense, is understood the development of the Matter of a juridical prescript or rule. The law may be explained by some act on the part of the legislature itself. This is termed Authentic Interpretation, which has the force of law,* or it may be explained by Customary Law (Usual Interpretation).† Both these species are comprised under the term Legal Interpretation. Contrasted with this is Doctrinal or Scientific Interpretation, which derives its authority from its own intrinsic truth.‡ It is necessary also to determine the exact meaning of the words employed in a law; when this is done, it is termed Grammatical Interpretation. Regard must likewise be paid to the intention of the legislator, and to the purport and origin of the law (Logical Interpretation). The legislature, by the language employed in the enactment, simply gives an index by which to ascertain the determination of its will. Thus the jurist is bound to adhere to the express words of the Statute, wherever such words convey absolutely the exact expression of the will of the legislature. He has, however, power to comprehend, within the scope of the law, all such cases as do not come immediately within the literal terms of the Statute, that is to say, to include in it, those cases to which the same principles are applicable *(ratio juris)*. To this extension of the law, the expressions Comprehensive and Legal Analogy are applied. But he must not comprehend within the

Authentic.

Scientific.

Grammatical.

Comprehensive and Legal Analogy.

* It is retrospective in its effect even though something new may have been added to the law.

† This may or may not affect the true intent of the law.

‡ The rules of interpretation for expounding the Matter of the sources of law are termed Hermeneutics.

Statute, cases which although they might be brought within its literal meaning, do not harmonise with the "*ratio juris*," as understood by the legislator himself.* Nor must he include cases where the legislator has, by the language employed, expressed more than was really intended (Restrictive Interpretation).† All these different kinds of interpretation are also applicable to what are denominated "*Jura singularia*" and "*Privilegia*," for these likewise are regarded as laws, and possess their "*ratio*," that is, their essential presumptive characteristics, to which also must be added their legal intention. But all analogy in the case of Jura singularia and Privilegia is completely excluded. "*Quod contra rationem juris receptum est, non est producendum ad consequentias*." The "*ratio legis*" is *the ground of utility* which has moved the legislator to enact the law, or, as it is sometimes expressed, to establish the *norm*, or rule. In the first place, the judge is bound to restrict himself to the letter of the law, and he must in no wise trouble himself with the "ratio juris." Hence every extension and restriction of the law, according to the "ratio juris," is inadmissible, and the rule is false which says, "Cessante legis ratione, lex ipsa cessat."

Restrictive Interpretation.

The *ratio juris*.

---

* Ubi eadem legis ratio, ibi eadem legis dispositio. Ανά λογον which is secundum rationem, is included. Analogy always presupposes certain gaps or omissions. Analogy, however, may be excluded by the express words of the Statute, and it may be also extended to Customary law.

† For example, when the law prohibits marriage with more than one person, but designs only to prevent Polygamy, for such cases the penal sanction of the law is not applicable to successive marriages.

SECTION III.—*Of the Relation of Legal Precepts to one another.*

Von Vangerow, I., ss. 19—27.
Arndts, ss. 10—15.
Puchta, ss. 17—19.

Relation of a law to existing laws.

EACH separate law enters into some kind of relation to other existing laws. Either it agrees with enactments already existing, as when the legislator simply re-affirms that which has been forgotten; or when he furnishes an interpretation of the same; or, again, the new law may abrogate what has gone before. In the latter case, two distinctions must be noted—either the new statute may utterly invalidate, or it may simply vary that which already exists. The complete neutralization of existing law by the enactment of a new legal precept, presupposes that the law has originated from the same source, and that it occupies the same sphere as the statute which it has superseded. Special laws of a subsequent date cannot annul general laws, but they may limit them. Again, a general law of a subsequent date cannot, and does not, necessarily—that is, *eo ipso*,*—annul a special law. The alteration of pre-existing laws by a new enactment may be such, that it gives greater latitude or expansion to the law, so as to extend its scope; or it may restrict it so as to exclude cases which formerly fell within the established rule. Such a new law stands related to the

Effect of a new law.

* For this object it ought to be expressly or tacitly made. "Lex posterior (jus posterius) derogat priori; lex posterior generalis non derogat priori speciali."

old law as an exceptional law—*jus singulare.* The exceptional law is, within its own sphere, regarded as *jus commune.* It may create a right *(privilegium favorabile)*, or it may impose an obligation *(privilegium odiosum).* If the exceptional law has reference to a definite and special object, it is termed "*privilegium rei;*" if attached to a certain legal relation, it is denominated "*privilegium causæ;*" if attached to personal qualifications, "*privilegium personæ.*"

These privileges are designated *beneficia,* in contradistinction to privileges in the more restricted acceptation of the term, which create a right limited to a particular instance, and are of no force beyond the specified case. They invariably point to a concrete subject, and presuppose a special legislative enactment *(Constitutio personalis).* When the new law upon the same subject differs from the old law, and the judge is required, subsequently to the publication of the new law, to give his decision, the question may be asked—In accordance with which of the conflicting laws is it his duty to decide? If the case has been fully established prior to the promulgation of the new law, his decision must be given according to the older law; but any case that may occur subsequently to the promulgation of the recent statute, must be dealt with by the judge in conformity with the later law.* The presumption always is, that the legislator contemplated only the application of the new rule to legal relations that should arise subsequently to its publication. It is, however, different where the law contains

* A published law is in force from the day of its publication, unless its efficacy is intentionally delayed beyond that period.

a retrospective clause,* or furnishes an authoritative interpretation of the earlier law, or has for its object the revocation of the entire statute. These are the exceptions. The rule is, that fully acquired rights must be respected. A fully acquired right *(Jus quaesitum)* is, however, valid only if the given presumptions upon which the application of the law rests† have actually arisen.

Conflict of laws.

Laws may also come into conflict in other modes. It is, for instance, possible that upon the same facts the laws of different places, although situated in the same or in a different State or States, may be regarded from a different point of view (Conflict of *Statutes*). Here the question arises: From what point of view has the judge to decide? According to practice the judge determines the case before him by the following rules:

In personal questions.

1st, In all personal questions the law of the *forum* applies, before which the parties to the suit, as the rule, must be cited; thus generally the law of the Domicil prevails *(Statuta personalia)*. These decide where the relation is one of personal capacity; as, for example, Minority, or personal condition; as Guardianship, or where the property, in the eye of the law, is taken into consideration as a whole (Universal succession).

In real.

2nd, Where the question relates to a thing, the law

* This cannot affect cases finally decided, as, for instance, suits determined by judgment.

† For example, a recent law establishes new principles in respect to succession by intestacy—as, for instance, that the agnate relatives shall give precedence to the cognate relatives. In this case the question would arise, whether the right of the agnate relatives has not already been established by the death of the intestate prior to the publication of the new law. It would be of no avail that the possibility of inheritance existed in them merely *in abstracto*.

of the place where it is situated determines *(Statuta realia)*. But the question must be restricted to one thing in particular, as distinct and separate in itself, for in universal succession, as a general rule, the *Statuta personalia* determine.

3rd, Moreover in those cases where the formal expression of the will comes into question as a dominant feature, the *Statuta mixta* become operative—that is to say, the law of the place where the contract was made or the offence committed *(Locus regit actum)*. As to the required forms, the law of the place where the transaction will become operative must be observed; and as to that which is material, the place of fulfilment must be regarded; nor can any other place be selected *in fraudem legis*. As to the procedure to be observed, it must be in accordance with the law of the place where the suit is brought. *Statuta mixta.*

Section IV.—*The Relation of Legal Precepts to Morals, Natural Law, and Equity.*

Von Vangerow, s. 29.
Arndts, s. 21, et seq.
Puchta, ss. 20, 21.
l. 43, Dig. de relig. (11, 7).
l. 1 Cod. de legibus (1, 14).

1st, Morality is not a source of law. Before the tribunal, only those acts are regarded which result from the free exercise of the will, not such as arise from coercion. It is only obedience to law that can be legally enforced. Morals.

2nd, Natural Law is not a source of law in the Natural Law.

strict sense of the term. The judge must decide in accordance with positive law, and where this is defective, he must supplement it in accordance with the spirit of positive law.*

Equity.

3rd. Equity (Æquitas) is for the judge no source of law, unless the legislator has prescribed that the judge shall in his decision take into consideration individual differences,† and it is in this that Equity consists.

Equity is based upon the principle, that in order to meet the exigencies of a concrete case, the judge may exceed the strict limits of ordinary right. The duty of the judge also compels him to consider the special circumstances of each particular case, and to decide not by any mere arbitrary subjective standard derived from his own mind, but according to certain determined rules applicable to each particular case as it may arise.

"Justitia est constans et perpetua voluntas jus suum cuique tribuendi."‡ In this latter sense, however, the signification is too comprehensive for Modern Jurisprudence, for in our days Equity has become a science founded upon the reasonings and the experience of the past.

---

* The judge cannot refuse to adjudicate in an action on account of the obscurity or the insufficiency of the law. *See* Code Nap., Art. 4.

† As, for example, in respect to capacity to act.

‡ Dig. Lib., tit. 1, l. 10, 11.

SECTION V.—*Application of Legal Precepts in respect to Persons.*

Von Vangerow, s. 28.
Arndts, s. 24.
Puchta, s. 22.

THE laws of a State are applicable to all persons residing within its limits (Territorial principle). Hence aliens are held amenable to the law. The Regent or Sovereign is also, in his private capacity, subject to the law of the land. Application of law.

BOOK THE SECOND.

RIGHTS IN THE SUBJECTIVE SENSE.

SECTION VI.—*Notion of Rights in the Subjective Sense.*

Von Vangerow, ss. 111, 112, 113.
Arndts, ss. 21—23.
Puchta, ss. 10—17.

Rights.

IN relation to Rights, three questions may be suggested. What are Rights? How do they arise? What are the means by which they are to be ascertained and determined? The term Right, according to modern usage, has two principal significations. It may be either the power or dominion which a person is entitled to exercise over an object, in which exercise there is involved the freedom of the will, and of which we shall speak more directly; or it may be used to designate a rule or system of rules, established to govern the affairs of mankind in the relations which men sustain to each other. This latter meaning of the term has been already referred to in the first section, and was there denominated Right in the *objective* sense. The former is denominated Right in the *subjective* sense. There is a close connection between these two meanings of the term. Right in the one sense implies *Power*,

In the objective sense.

in the other it denotes *Precept*. All Rights exist in the interest of freedom. It is here that they are rooted and nurtured. Since man has a free will, Rights are called into existence to guard freedom, because they tend to limit our free will. Rights and Morals stand related to each other in this respect, that they both refer to the intercourse of mankind. But they differ from each other in the following respects:—In Jurisprudence man is taken into consideration as a Person—that is to say, as a being possessed of free will. In Morals the whole question relates to the determination of the will for good (quid oportet); Jurisprudence views man only in so far as he is living in society with others. Morals give to man rules for his guidance both in thought and conduct, to the dictates of which he is bound in duty to yield, even though he should live in the closest solitude. Jurisprudence is conversant about the business of mankind, in as far as human affairs are external. Morals concern essentially the inward disposition and direction of the Will—the Mind. Jurisprudence controls the will of the individual in such a manner, that when independent wills come into conflict, they may be checked and restrained by external and competent authority. At the tribunal of Morals the restraints of law have no value. The will must be free in the accomplishment of that which is good. "Juris præcepta sunt hæc, honeste vivere, alterum non lædere, suam cuique tribuere."

Relation of Rights and Morals.

As to the origin of Rights, it must in this place suffice to say that, viewed as to their ultimate source, they are of divine ordinance. The fountain of all

Origin of Rights.

Right is to be sought in the Divine Will. But the development and the formal expression of Rights are a product of the activity of the human mind, finding its expression in the history of mankind. Thus Demosthenes says—"Τοῦτό ἐστι νόμος, ᾧ πάντας ἀνθρώπους προσήκει πείθεσθαι διὰ πολλά, καὶ μάλιστα, ὅτι πᾶς ἐστὶ νόμος εὕρημα μὲν καὶ δῶρον Θεοῦ, L. 2, Dig. i. 3. Sed et omnes gentes et omni tempore una lex et sempiterna et immutabilis continebit, unusque erit communis quasi magister et imperator omnium Deus, ille hujus legis inventor disceptator, lator." (Cic. de republ. iii. 17.)

Rights connected with civilisation.

Without pursuing this subject, it may be observed that the establishment of the Rights of a people is closely connected with its growth and advancement in civilisation. When those natural outgrowths of the human race which we designate families, blend into each other, and when, subsequently to this union, a universal conviction becomes so powerful as to bind all, then it is that a Right or Ordinance is called into existence. When, however, the Matter of this acknowledged rule creates and limits the Rights of a people, the Right in such a case is said to be Positive.

The knowledge and determination of Rights have been already suggested in the remarks on Interpretation. These will be sufficient to indicate that the mere acquaintance with the letter of the law does not in every instance imply a knowledge of the legal Rights themselves. The elucidation of a law may be derived from the legislature or by means of some other organon of interpretation. In every case the aim of legal interpretation must be the development of the thought residing in the law itself, of which the words of the statute can be at best but an imperfect and feeble expression.

Rights in the subjective sense.

Right, then, it may be observed, *in the Subjective sense*, is the dominion over an external object, arising by virtue of a legal enactment (Right in an Objective sense). It consists of absolute dominion, of which use may be unconditionally made *(Qui jure suo utitur neminem lædit)*, and it may be laid down as a general rule that a Right may be renounced by some special act of disclaimer.* Rights and Obligations are correlative conceptions. The relations of men to one another, originating in Rights and Obligations, are designated Legal Relations. Those individuals in whom Rights and Obligations inhere, or persons having a capacity for legal relations, are designated Men. In such cases Men are regarded as Persons.

SECTION VII.—*Of Legal Subjects—Persons.*

Von Vangerow, ss. 31, 32, 33, 34, 35—60.
Arndts, ss. 24—47.
Puchta, ss. 22—28.
Gai. Comm., pp. 57, 163. et seq.
Savigny Syst. II., 4 et seq., 171, 231, 235, 290, 324.
Glück II., 64 xxx., 432 xxiii., ss. 1209 et seq., xl. 1.
Dig. de statu hominum (1, 5).
l. 1, ss. 7, Dig. de inspic. ventre (25, 4).
l. 3, Cod. de postum. hered. instit. (6, 29).
l. 12 pr., l. 14 Dig. de lib et post. (28, 2).
l. 18 pr., l. 9 pr., s. 4, Cod. de reb. dub. (34, 5).

* Not always. For example, where the right goes hand in hand with an obligation, and the latter is not of a purely accessory nature.

l. 11, de capite minutis (4, 5). Inst. I., 16 de cap. dem.
s. 5, Just. h. t.
l. 5, Dig. de in jus. voc. (2, 4), l. 8, l. 10, l. 12, l. 28, Dig. de statu homin. (1, 5).
l. 6, Dig. de his. qui sui vel al. jur. sunt. (1, 6).
l. 8, ss. 11, Dig. de suis et legit. hered. (38, 16).
Cod. de hæreticis et Manichæis et Samaritis (1, 5).
„ de apostacis (1, 7). Cod. de Judæis et cælicolis (1, 9).
„ de paganis (1, 11).
For further authorities and the literature, see Von Vangerow I., 74—117.

Ulpianus says: "Partus, antequam, edatur, mulieris est vel viscerum," l. 1, Dig. de inspic. ventre (25, 4). To which Papinianus adds:—"Partus nondum editus homo non recte fuisse dicitum," l. 9, s. 1, ad leg., Falcid. (35, 2).

Paulus says:—"Qui in utero est, perinde ac si in rebus humanis esset, custoditur, quoties de commodis ipsius partus quæritur, quamquam alii, antequam nascatur, nequaquam prosit," l. 7, Dig. de statu hominum.

Justinian in l. 3, Cod. de postum. hered. instit. says:—"Et sancimus, si vivus perfecte natus est, licet illico postquam in terram cecidit, vel in manibus obstetricis decessit, nihilominus testamentum rumpi, hoc tantummodo requirendo, si vivus ad orbem volus processet, ad nullum declinans monstrum vel prodigium." To which may be added the words of Ulpianus:— "Quod dicitur filium natum rumpere testamentum, natum accipe, *etsi exsecto* ventre editus sit, nam et hic rumpit testamentum, scilicet si nascatur in potestate," l. 12, pr. Dig. de lib. et post. (28, 2).

Personality.

THE subject to whom the law concedes the exercise of the will possesses legal capacity. The attribute of being such a subject constitutes Personality. To be a Person, is to possess the capacity to enjoy Rights—to be the subject of rights.

Modern Law recognises every human being as a Person.* Accordingly, at present, every one acquires the capacity for Rights from the very moment of birth—1. That is, from the instant the child is separated from the womb of its mother,† so soon as it has given signs of life, even though life may be impossible‡—2. From the moment of its birth, if it possesses a human form and shape, and is not a *monstrum*, nor a *portentum*. The capacity for the enjoyment of Rights commences for the physical person at birth, and terminates only at death. No other mode of extinction is recognised in modern jurisprudence. Again, the party who affirms the death of a person in order to establish a right, must prove the same. In the Roman Law this proof must be given in conformity with the general rules of evidence. According to the German practice presumption of death is permissible. An absentee, whose residence cannot be ascertained, who has attained seventy years of age, and who, upon due citation, fails to appear; is presumed to have died at the moment that the judicial decree was published, declaring that the citation had been made in vain.§

Proof of death.

* In the Roman State there existed three grades of legal capacity, in which the greater presupposed and involved the lesser; the lesser, however, might exist without the greater. On the lowest step stood the free man *(status libertatis)*; on the second or higher in the scale came the Roman citizen *(status civitatis)*; and on the highest step stood the *paterfamilias (status familiæ)*. These distinctions, which qualified the condition of persons possessed of legal capacity, have now become obsolete.

† The unborn child is pars viscerum. But the nasciturus is, nevertheless, protected.

‡ Vitality is not necessary.

§ Presumption is no fiction. Hence if at a later period the actual date of the death of a person becomes known, the legal effect dates from this date, and not from the period presumed.

Presumption in the case of ascendants and descendants.

Another presumption of death is the following:—In the event of the simultaneous death of ascendants and decendants by some unnatural cause; when from the facts presented an uncertainty arises as to who died first. Here the presumption is that the adult child survived the ascendant; the ascendant, however, is supposed to have survived the child who was the minor. He who asserts in opposition to this rule priority in the order of death, is bound to prove it. These legal presumptions, it must be observed, are strictly limited to the persons named. Where no proof of death can be advanced, and when the "presumptio juris" fails, it is assumed that both died at the same instant, and the legal consequences that would have followed upon the death of one before the other do not come into operation. In modern political society every Person is treated as in the possession of legal freedom, though it is not every one who enjoys it to its fullest extent.

Existimatio.

The combination of high moral character with legal capacity exerts a retro-active effect upon such capacity. This undiminished possession of legal capacity is denominated honour—public honour, or, as it is termed in Roman Law, Existimatio—"Existimatio est dignitatis illæsæ status legibus ac moribus comprobatus, qui ex delicto nostro auctoritata legum aut minuitur aut consumitur."* Thus, "Existimatio," or honour, may be diminished by certain causes. The diminution of "Existimatio" by special legal precept is termed Infamia. The "Infamia" of the Roman Classical Law is

* Arndts, s. 29. Puchta, s. 119.

at the present time no institution of Modern Civil Law. This proposition, however, is considered by some jurists as doubtful.*

Good Name.

The common honour which belongs to every man by the mere fact of his possessing legal personality is quite independent of the favourable opinion of others. A Good Name, however, is something totally different. It consists in the public opinion that a person has not by his own misconduct rendered himself unworthy of his reputation. The man who does an act by which he places himself in a position involving the loss of the respect of his fellow-citizens, at the same time manifesting the utmost indifference to his public reputation—as by the choice of a dishonourable occupation (*levis nota*, or in a higher degree, *turpitudo*)—entails upon himself by his misconduct a diminution of his

---

Infamy.

* Infamy consisted in the disqualification for certain public and private rights, and involved the loss of the Jus suffragii, and of the Jus honorum: also the abstraction of the right and capacity to intercede; or to act as a procurator; or attorney in an action-at-law. Infamy is at times divided into *infamia immediata*, and *mediata*. The latter is the tacit legal consequence attendant upon judicial decisions in certain completed acts, either in a criminal suit (*judicio publici damnati*, under which are now comprehended all those who have incurred penal disabilities, or the infringement of a law originally made in the comitium to which punishment had been attached) or in judgments resulting from a civil suit; (as in the action pro socio, the actio directa, arising out of mandates, or guardianship, or conviction, on account of theft, fraud, &c.). *Infamia immediata* is the resulting infamy which attaches to certain unlawful acts, such as bankruptcy; prostitution; breach of contract, coupled with perjury by an adult; the marriage of a ward by her guardian before rendering accounts, &c. Infamy might also follow upon sentence being pronounced, awarding a punishment for the above offences. Punishment alone did not involve the loss of Existimatio in Roman Law. Infamy might be set aside by an act of rehabilitation, *famæ restitutio* on the part of the Regent. Consequential infamy, infamia directa, was superseded by the magistrate granting upon the ordinary grounds the "restitutio in integrum" to remove the stain from the man's legal reputation.

legal rights. Thus admission to public service, and to public dignity is barred to him; his testimony is regarded with suspicion; he cannot institute an "*actio famosa*" against a person of good repute; and if he have been instituted heir under a Will in which his brothers and sisters have been passed over, they may institute against him the *Querela inofficiosa Testamenti*. The *famæ restitutio* may, however, be effected by an act of the Regent.

In modern States every one possesses "*in abstracto*" the capacity for legal rights; but in order to be the possessor of such rights "*in concreto*" for many legal relations, certain capacities and conditions are presumed. On the other hand, certain qualifications and conditions affect the character of legal relations. Such are the following:—

Effect of birth.

1. *Birth during Wedlock, or Birth out of Wedlock.*— A child conceived and born in wedlock is legitimate. The conception of a child in wedlock is presumed by its birth when 181 days have elapsed from marriage, or within 10 months from the date of the dissolution of marriage.* Children not born in wedlock are either *liberi naturales* (concubine children), or *liberi adultereni* (children begotten adulterously), or *liberi incestuosi* (children born in incest), or *spurii* (children born simply out of wedlock), or *vulgo quæsiti* (the children of prostitutes). An illegitimate child has no father, only a mother.† Nevertheless, the illegitimate child

* Pater est quem nuptiæ demonstrant. Evidence against parentage is only admissible when it is impossible that parentage can be presumed.

† The child does not take the putative father's rank, nor stand in any relationship to his family.

has a claim upon his parent for maintenance, and inheritance by intestacy. By legitimation the defect attaching to the child's birth is eliminated, and it is treated as though it had been born in wedlock. The child conceived in a *matrimonium putativum* is considered as legitimate.

2. *Of Sex.*—Mankind is divided, as regards sex, into two classes, male and female. Hermaphrodites are classified according as the one or the other sex predominates. Ordinarily the two sexes enjoy equal rights, though exceptionally women are either favoured or disfavoured. They take a secondary place in all matters relative to public rights, and also in the family. They lack the "Jura publica," hold a subordinate position as regards the husband, cannot exercise the "Patria potestas," and have no power to *perpetuate a family stock;* hence the maxim, "Mulier finis et caput familiæ est." The privileges they enjoy they owe to their helplessness and weakness (*levitas sexus*). They are not allowed to be prejudiced by errors of law, and cannot be bound as sureties (*Senatus Consultum Vellejanum*). Of Sex.

3. *Age.*—Human beings are either of full age (*majores*) or of nonage (*minores*), according as they have attained the age of twenty-five or not. Minors are either full aged (*puberes*) or under age (*impuberes*).* Of Age.

---

* *Distinctions.*—The impubes is under the *tutela*, the pubes is under the *cura*. The former cannot bind himself by an obligation, nor contract a valid marriage, nor make a testament. His father may nominate a pupillary substitute. The pubes is restricted in the sale of immoveables. Not so the major. The pubes enjoys the privilege of pleading error in law, and also the relief afforded by the *in integrum restitutio*. The infant (*infans*) possesses no capacity to perform a legal act.

Boys do not attain puberty till their fourteenth year, girls till their twelfth. The period of minority is termed *pupillaris aetas.* Minors are designated *infantes* till their seventh year; after that period *infantiæ majores*, and are either *infantiæ* or *pubertati proximi*, according as they are nearer or more remote from the period of puberty. Complete puberty (*pubertas plena*) is attained by males at their eighteenth year, a period sometimes of legal importance.* Females attain to full puberty at the fourteenth year. Majority may also be granted by the State (*Venia ætatis*),† provided the age attained is twenty years in the case of males, and eighteen in that of females. After majority is reached,‡ to the period of old age, years have no special effect upon the condition of legal relations. Extreme old age, however, the limit of which is not defined, exempts from the liability to guardianship, and from the responsibility of being made a witness.

Of Health. 4. *Health* may be either bodily or mental. A human being may suffer from some incurable physical defect (*vitium*), or he may be afflicted with some incurable ailment (*morbus*), rendering the doing of certain acts impossible (*morbus sonticus*), for example

---

* The *Pater adoptans*, or person adopting, must be older than the person adopted by *pubertas plena*. Where alimony has been bequeathed to a person till puberty, it will be enjoyed by males till eighteen, and by females until fourteen years of age respectively.

† The *venia ætatis* may be set aside by the *in integrum restitutio.*

‡ It is not so when majority is secured by grant. He who requires power by virtue of the concession of majority to make a valid conveyance of immoveable property, must always obtain a decree of the magistrate for that particular purpose. It must also be understood that any advantages arising from contract or testament dependent upon the concession of majority, mature only upon the full age of twenty-five being attained.

—deafness, dumbness, blindness. It is this that gives to bodily health a legal importance. Impotence also requires to be especially noticed. Impotence may be either that of the *spado*, which arises from some internal cause, or that of the *castratus*, where impotence is produced by mechanical means. The *castratus* can neither contract marriage, nor even adopt children. Imperfect mental capacity is divisible according to its nature into two kinds. First, that weakness of mind which characterises the simple, idiocy (*simplicitas*); or feebleness of intellect or imbecility (*debilitas*); or, on the other hand, madness (*furor dementia*). An insane person has no legal capacity for the transaction of business, is subjected to a curatorship, and his ascendant may make a will for him. During lucid intervals, however (*dilucida intervalla*), he is capable of transacting business.

5. *Domicile.*—The ground of the importance of domicile rests upon this; that it is, so to speak, the centre of the domestic and civil sphere of a person's activity. A Domicile is either voluntary (*domicilium voluntarium*), or one prescribed by law. A *domicilium voluntarium* is acquired *animo et corpore.* The union of both will and act constitutes Domicile. Neither the act of the will alone, nor the fact of mere residence can create it. *Domicilium necessarium*—Children take the domicile of their father; a wife takes that of her husband; officials have their headquarters, or place of office for a domicile; persons banished, the place of their banishment. A person may, indeed, have several domiciles. The *domicilium necessarium* does not exclude the election or continuance of a *domicilium volunta-* Domicile.

rium; but where there is a conflict of (§ 3) laws, the dominant domicile governs.

Relationship.

6. *Relationship.*—By relationship is to be understood the bond subsisting between two persons, founded upon consanguinity or oneness of blood. Opposed to this natural relationship is a fictitious civil relationship arising from Adoption or Arrogation. In natural relationship one person has either lineally sprung from the other as an ascendant or descendant (*linea recta*), or both, or several persons have sprung from the same third person. Such relationship is termed collateral (*linea transversa*). Proximity of relationship is determined by grades. Each conception constitutes a grade, and hence the maxim "*Tot gradus quot generationes.*" The Canon Law, in computing the relationship of collaterals, adopts the following rule:—*In that degree in which the member of a collateral branch (and in the case of different collateral branches, the remoter person of the different branches) is related to the common ancestor, in precisely the same degree, is such person related to the person of the other collateral branch.** Collateral relationship is either of the whole blood, that is, the relationship of persons springing from the same pair, who are termed *Germani*, or of the half blood, that is, only one half of the pair stands in common relationship, the one to the other. When this relationship is on the part of the father, it is termed *consanguinei;* if on the mother's side, *uterini.* When it happens to be founded upon pure male descent, and by

Agnation.

conception in wedlock, it is termed *Agnation.* Hence

* In computing the degrees of the ascending and descending lines, the rule of the Roman Law must be observed—"*Tot gradus quot generationes.*"

Ulpianus says:—"Agnati sunt a patre cognati viriles sexus per virilem sexum descendentes, ejusdem familiæ."* When relationship is established by males and females, or generally by persons descended from another, or from some common third person, it is designated "Cognation." The final division is that into simple and complex relationship. It is simple whenever persons related derive their descent from the same source, having the same blood. It is complex whenever the relationship is derived from different sources.†

7. *Affinity.*—By this is understood the relationship which arises from cohabitation between either of the persons cohabiting with the blood relations of the other. This view of affinity, however, is admissible only according to the Canon Law: the Roman Law limited the definition, and confined affinity to similar relationship arising from cohabitation in wedlock. Degrees of affinity do not, properly speaking, exist, as such relationship is not based upon conception. Still there is an analogy between affinity and that closer relationship which is computed by degrees. Thus it is held, by analogy, that in the same degree in which a person cohabiting is related to his relatives, in the same degree of affinity stands the other concumbent with them. Affinity.

All human beings, regarded as individuals, are legally the subject of rights; and any deviation from this

* *Agnati* are those persons who are subjected to the same *paterfamilias*, or who would be subject to him if he were still alive.

† There are several kinds of affinity. 1. When two persons who are related beget children. 2. When two persons related to a third person beget children. There arises likewise by the commingling of personal and civil relationship manifold relationship.

rule constitutes an exception to the law. By such exceptional law, a subject capable of enjoying a right but having no physical existence may be created. Such a subject is termed a fictitious, or juridical (or moral) Person; because such a Person is simply an abstract conception. A legal Person of this kind is

Universitates.

either an aggregate of natural persons *(universitas personarum)*, or a combination or union of property *(universitas bonorum)*. Where a group of natural persons becomes a legal subject, or Person, this subject of such rights and liabilities is the collective

Universitates personarum.

body of persons.* Of these *universitates personarum* there are several kinds: 1. The State, in as far as it possesses property *(fiscus)*; 2. A community, such as *civitates, reipublicæ, municipia*; 3. The Church and Ecclesiastical Corporations; 4. Other Associations. There are several kinds of *universitates bonorum*,† such, for instance, as—1. *Pia corpora*, trusts for charitable or religious purposes; 2. The *Hereditas jacens*, or the vacant inheritance. To constitute a juridical Person, two things are necessary: 1. Primarily, the existence of what may be termed a basis to which Personality may attach. This may be either an aggregate of persons, or a community of property. 2. There must also be a legal precept, that is, a general rule of law, which predetermines when a juridical Person shall be

* The varying separate members of a Corporate Body do not constitute a *Universitas*. Where one of these separate members possesses a different legal existence, there is no *Universitas*, but a *Societas*. The *Universitas* continues through all the changes of the individual members, even though but one member only should survive.

† They possess full Rights of Property, Possession, Servitudes, Obligations, Rights of Actions, Heirship by Intestacy, &c.

founded; or there must be a *Constitutio personalis.* A juridical Person is dissolved* by the removal or destruction of the object for which it has been created; or it may be abrogated by the authority of the State, extinguishing its juridical corporate existence. A legal or juridical Person in the sense just explained is merely an abstraction, and, consequently, by its very nature requires some one to represent it, and to act on its behalf. Its affairs may be determined by the resolution of the majority† of the members, or by officers appointed for that purpose.‡

SECTION VIII.—*Objects of Rights, Things.*

Von Vangerow, ss. 61—79.
Arndts, ss. 48—55.
Puchta, ss. 23—28.
Gai. Comm., pp. 203—214.
Glück II., 472 et seq.; XVI., 98 et seq.; XXI., 1 et seq.
Inst. de rebus corporalibus et incorporalibus (2, 2).
  ,, de rerum divisione (2, 1).
Dig. de divisione rerum et qualitate (1, 8).
  ,, de religiosis (11, 7). Cod. de religiosis (3, 44).
  ,, l. 2, ss. 21, 22, ne quid in locus publ., &c. (43, 8).

---

* Property is taken care of, in the case of State-institutions, for the future organisation of the *universitas.* Otherwise, where the legal person happens not to be a State-institution, dissolution will depend upon the incorporating statutes. If there be no statute, the property is accounted as *bona vacantia.*

† All *Cives* who are entitled to vote must have notice and be cited. Those who appear at the meeting vote. The absolute majority decides. Their resolutions bind all. A *universitas* cannot be charged with the commission of delicts.

‡ They have power to entitle those for whom they act, and also to bind them. They are responsible for transactions that have been disadvantageously concluded. Several magistrates are jointly and severally liable; but they possess the *exceptio excussionis.*

Dig. l. 1, ss. 1—3, de fluminibus (43, 12).
„ l. 30 pr., de usurpat. et usuc. (41, 3).
„ de actione emti venditi (19, 1).
„ de instructo vel instrumento legato (33, 7).
„ de impensis in res dotales factis (25, 1).
„ de usuris et fructibus rel. (22, 1).
Cod. de fructibus et litium expensis (7, 51).
Dig. de usuris l. etc. (22, 1).
Cod. de usuris (4, 32).

Things.

THINGS are destined to minister to the wants of man. A thing is an object that exists in space *(Res corporalis)*.* This conception of a thing may be extended, so as to comprehend several distinct objects. A totality of things may be conceived—*a*. As a corporal unity composed of objects that physically cohere the one to the other. Such a unity is termed a *universitas rerum cohaerentium*, as a herd or a library; *b*. It may be an incorporal unity of objects not cohering the one with the other, and to such unity the expression *universitas rerum distantium* is applied. "Tria autem genera sunt corporum; unum, quod continetur uno spiritu et Græce ἡνωμένον vocatur, ut homo, lignum, lapis et similia; alterum, quod ex contingentibus, hoc est pluribus inter se cohærentibus constat, quod συνημμένον vocatur, ut ædificum, navis, armarium; tertium, quod ex distantibus constat, ut corpora plura non soluta, sed uni nomini subjecta, veluti populus, legio, grex."† But it is not every object that may possibly minister to the wants of man that is capable of being subjected to his legal dominion.‡ To this class belong all spiritual

Tria genera.

* *Res incorporales* are rights which exist apart from the property itself.

† l. 30 pr., Dig. de usurpat. et usuc. (41, 3).

‡ *Res extra commercium* as contradistinguished from *Res in commercio*. This

things, that is to say, things consecrated and used for religious purposes. Such things are denominated, *Res divini juris.* Of this nature also are—*Res sacræ*, or things absolutely consecrated to the service of God; *Res religiosæ*, or consecrated spots; *Res sanctæ*, that is, things placed under the special protection of the State. Next to be mentioned are those things which are termed "*Res communes omnium*," or things which every one must of necessity enjoy. To this class belong air and running water. Finally, there are things denominated *Res publicæ*, State property, as roads and rivers.* Res divini juris sacræ etc.

Ulpianus says:—"Viarum quædam publicæ sunt, quædam privatæ, quædam vicinales. Publicas vias dicimus, quas Græci βασιλικάς, nostri praetorias, alii consulares vias appellant. Privatæ sunt, quas agrarias quidam dicunt. Vicinales sunt viæ, quæ in vicis sunt, vel quæ in vicos ducunt. Has quoque publicas esse quidam dicunt; quod ita verum est, si non ex collatione privatorum hoc iter constitutum est."—Cf. Ulp. l. 3, pr. de loc. et itinerib. public (43, 7). "Viæ vicinales quæ ex agris privatorum collatis factæ sunt, quarum memoria non extat, publicarum viarum numero sunt." l. 2, s. 22, Dig. ne quid in loco publ. vel itin. fiat (43, 8).

Certain differences subsisting among things carry with them special legal consequences. Such are—

---

classification is based upon a possibility. Another classification rests upon the reality of an existing thing; the division into *Res in patrimonio* and *extra patrimonium.* For example, a knife is legally a thing *in commercio*, but, if at any time it be under the dominion of no one person in particular, because it is lost, it is *extra patrimonium.*

* There is a distinction between *flumina perennia* and *torrentia.* The latter are private property. On this subject see further Gaius, Comm. note *a*, pp. 208 and 209. Tomkins' and Lemon's Edit.

Moveables and Immoveables. 1. Moveableness and Immoveableness.—Under the term immoveables are included the soil *(Solum)*, and the things of the soil *(Res soli)*, as plots of land, with the plants and the buildings thereon. Whatever does not belong to this class of things is a Moveable. Moveables are, again, divided into live stock, which move by virtue of their own living powers, as slaves and animals, and things which do not thus move. According as such possess the power of locomotion or not, they are termed *moventes* or *mobilia*.

Fungibiles et non fungibiles. 2. *Res fungibiles.*—Fungible things, as they are now termed, are those things in regard to which it is immaterial whether exactly the same or some other thing of a similar kind be given in return. Fungible things are money, grain, fluids, unwrought metal, etc. *Res non fungibiles* comprehend all those things not included under the term fungible.

Mutui datio consistit in his rebus, quæ pondere, numero, mensura consistunt; quoniam eorum datione possumus in creditum ire, quia [Hal. quæ] in genere suo functionem recipiunt per solutionem magis, quam specie; nam in ceteris rebus ideo in creditum ire non possumus, quia aliud pro alio invito creditori solvi non potest.

Consumtibiles. 3. *Res consumtibiles,* consumable things, are things the value of which consists in their use or consumption, such as provisions and money.

Res dividuæ. 4. *Divisibility.*—Things are physically divisible (*dividuæ*) whenever they may be separated into parts without destruction of their substance. When a thing is thus divided, the different parts are termed *partes certæ*, and the several participators are said to possess *pro diviso*. A thing is said to be juridically divisible in as far as several persons may possess abstractly a share or portion of it (*partes incertæ*),* which they possess *pro indiviso*. This mode of division is applicable to all kinds of things.

Principal and accessory things

In relation to each other, things are either principal objects or accessory ones. Principal objects are those to which other things belong as accessory parts. A thing that is accessory is determined either by its use or by its natural dependence upon the principal object. Accessory things are divisible into four classes.

Fructus.

1. *Fruits*.—Which comprise, first, the organic products of a thing; secondly, other uses which result from the thing;—advantages which accrue from it, as, for instance, *Interest*. These are designated *fructus civiles*, the former *fructus naturales*. These may be possibly purely natural products (*fructus naturales*) in the more limited sense; or they may have been created by the direct agency of man, in which case they are termed *fructus industriales*. In regard to *fructus*, the following distinctions are made:—Some are *fructus pendentes*, as still in connection with the parent stock; others, *fructus separati*, or fruits severed from it; other fruits are termed *percepti*, or those reduced to possession;† others *fructus percipiendi*, a term applied to those fruits which might have been, but which, in point of fact, have not been gathered. These have been called neglected fruits.‡ *Fructus extantes* are those fruits which the possessor

* The entire legal right is divisible according to the quota or share.

† The *perceptio* is of importance in the acquisition of the property, and in the *remissio mercedis*.

‡ See Gai. Comm. p. 221. Tomkins' and Lemon's Edit.

has still in hand; *fructus consumpti* those consumed or sold by the owner.* For further remarks on Interest see hereafter.

Appurtenances.

2. *Appurtenances.*—By which term are understood things which are dealt with as parts of a thing, without, however, being actually such. These follow the fate of the principal object. Immoveables, as also moveables, may possess appurtenances. No presumption is admissible in respect to their quality, for this must depend upon each separate case. It is necessary to consider—1. Whether a thing is destined for the absolute use of another; 2. As to the duration of the appointment; 3. As to the realization of the same.

Outlays or impensæ.

3. *Outlays:* that is, expenditures made in the improvement of a thing. When made for the preservation of property, they are termed necessary *(necessariæ);* but where the outlays increase the value of the property or improve the same, *utiles;* where incurred for the purpose of making the object more agreeable, *voluptuariæ.* For necessary outlays, *impensæ necessariæ,* every one, save the thief, has a right of detention. For *impensæ utiles* there is given a *jus tollendi* to the *mala fide,* a *jus retinendi* to the *bona fide* possessor. For *impensæ voluptuariæ* the possessor has only the *jus tollendi.* This right must not, however, be asserted in a manner that amounts to chicanery, which would be the case if the accessory thing did not benefit the owner; nor where compensation for outlays is tendered;

* The *bona fide* possessor is answerable for the *fructus extantes* from the period of the *litis contestatio,* and, subsequently, the *mala fide* possessor must account for all fruits. On the *Litis contestatio* see Tomkins' Instit. Rom. Law, § 27.

nor where injury has been done to the dominant property by the removal of that which has been added.

4. *Accessory Things: (res accessoriæ).*—If accessory things are once added to a thing they are afterwards regarded as part of it, as, for instance, alluvial deposits. On this subject see also hereafter. Accessories.

Section IX.—*Of the different kinds of Rights.*

Von Vangerow, s. 19.
Puchta, ss. 46—71.
Savigny Syst. IV., 540 et seq.

According to their object, Rights are divisible into Personal Rights, Rights of Things, and Obligations. Personal Rights are either Rights inherent in the person himself, or such as are acquired over another. Rights over a third person are Marital Rights, Parental Rights, Rights of Children, and Rights of Inheritance. Rights of Things are proprietary Rights, Rights over the property of another *(servitudes).* Things are either the immediate object of proprietary relations, as property, possession, severed Rights of ownership; or they are mediate to the same, as Obligations. Rights.

The relations of property are determined by the Rights of Property.

Right regarded in the objective sense, and classified accordingly, is divisible into *lex generalis*, and *specialis*, emanating from the *jus commune* or the *jus singulare*. A right which is not founded upon a legal enactment, but upon a *constitutio personalis*, is termed a *privilegium*. Its source is found in some act of the legislature. The proof of such grant is supplanted by immemorial Privilegium.

usage. A privilege becomes extinct by expiration of time *(dies ad quem)*; by renunciation; by the destruction of the object to which it is attached; by revocation; by non-user; or by the death of the grantor, where the privilege was limited to the term of his life.

SECTION X.—*Origin and Termination of Rights.*

Von Vangerow, ss. 80, 111, 118, 119, 126, 132.
Arndts, ss. 56—91. Puchta, ss. 47—77.
Glück IV., 52, 54, 86, 167 et seq., 86, 472 et seq., 460; V., 468 et seq.; XXII., 262; XXXVI., 357.
Savigny Syst. III., 120, 287, 204, 8 et seq., 99, 115, 258, 204, 226; IV., 1, 586.
Inst. (2, 7); Dig. (XXXIV. 5); Cod. (8, 54), de donationibus.
Cod. de revocandis donationibus (8, 56).
l. 5, Cod. de inoffic. donat. (3, 29).
Cod. de donationibus, quæ sub modo conficiuntur (8, 55).
Dig. quod metus causa gestum erit (4, 2).
Cod. de his quæ vi metusve causa gesta erit (2, 20).
Dig. (22, 6); Cod. (1, 18) de juris et facti ignorantia.
,, (4, 3); ,, (2, 21) de dolo malo.
Cod. plus valere; quod agitur, quam quod simulate concipitur. (4, 22).
Dig. de conditionibus institutionum (28, 7).
Cod. de instit. et substit. et restit. sub condit. factis (6, 25).
,, de conditionibus insertis tam legatis quam, etc. (6, 46).
,, de his quæ sub modo legata vel fideicom. relinq. (6, 45).

Origin of a Right.

A RIGHT implies the existence of a subject entitled to its possession. A Right originates and terminates according as a person becomes entitled, or ceases so to be. The origin of a Right is termed its acquisition. Its termination is its loss by the person in whom it has existed. Where a right is first originated with acquisition, it is denominated an absolute acquirement; if

Absolute and relative acquisition.

it have already existed in a third person, it is said to be relative acquisition. Agreeing with this classification in some measure, though not identical with it, is that of original acquisition, or acquisition independent of the right of a third party, and derivative acquisition, or acquisition by transmission. In derivative acquisition two cases must also be distinguished: First, The right as possessed by the owner in the first instance passes to the transferee, who steps into his place ("*succedit in locum ejus.*") Such an acquisition of the rights of another, if made in accordance with some legal relation, is termed Succession. Succession occurs either as to certain or special rights (*singular succession*), or it may be to the entire property (*universal succession*). Secondly, Of the right as possessed by the person originally entitled a portion only may pass to the party acquiring it, or to the transferee.

Succession

The matters of fact presumed in the acquisition of a Right are either acts done with a view to its acquisition, or involuntary acts resulting in the same consequences, as, for example, forfeiture; or the acquisition takes place *ipso jure*, in consequence of events arising apart from the will of the person acquiring.

Termination of Rights.

Rights also terminate either by some act on the part of the person entitled, or independently of the same.* The cause that gives rise to the termination of the right may be such that the right instantly ceases on its coming into operation (*ipso jure*). Other causes resulting in the invalidating of a right, do not possess

* Facts, with which are linked the origin and termination of a right, are designated modes of origin and termination. They are like the rights themselves, variable in their nature.

the effect of annulling it, but only render the same inoperative *(ope exceptionis)*.* A loss which has its origin in the intention of the person entitled, and has been incurred with a view of benefiting a third party, is termed Alienation *(alienatio)*. Alienation and acquisition, it is manifest, must always go hand in hand. According to the Roman Law, the smallest possible rights were alienable. Where no transfer of a right to a third party is contemplated, the intentional loss incurred is termed a Renunciation. In every Renunciation there is presumed, firstly, The capacity of the person to renounce, and declared *animus renunciandi;* in Obligations, and in Pawn, the acceptance of a substituted Debtor.† An executed renunciation is irrevocable. Renunciations, however, it is to be observed, are never presumed.

Alienation

Renunciation.

Donation.

A special mode of alienation is known as Donation or Gift *(donatio)*. Donation or Gift always implies the actual diminution of the property of one person in favour of another, incurred with the "*animus donandi,*" and received by the donee with the intention of *accepting* the same. A *Donatio* is either *perfecta* or *imperfecta*, according as it is conditional or unconditional. A Donation may be made in almost every form as by a *dare*, a *liberare*, or an *obligare*. A Donation is made either *inter vivos*, or *mortis causa;* in the lifetime of the donor, or upon his death taking place. No special form is needed to complete the act of

Inter vivos or mortis causa.

* An adverse right is established. The important distinction between a right void *ipso jure* and *ope exceptionis*, a voidable or inoperative right, is this: the former is absolutely void, the latter may be repaired. According to the older Roman Law this distinction was still more important.

† When property is concerned, the will, the intention, alone suffices.

Donation. Many persons, are, however, prohibited from making Donations. Thus, the stewards of another's property, such as Tutors and Procurators, cannot make Donations to each other. Neither can husband and wife. Gifts exceeding 500 *Solidi* must be judicially published, as also Donations of rent charges, if extending over a certain number of years, and when exceeding the above-named sum. Donations by and to the Regent need not be judicially published; nor gifts made to ransom prisoners; nor such as are made to restore dilapidated houses; nor dotal gifts—*dos*. Donations may also be made from subordinate considerations, such as rewards for past services *(donatio remuneratoria)*; in furtherance of some particular object *(donatio sub modo)*; where, however, only that which remains as a residue is to be the gift, after the performance of some act required; an action lies on the part of the donee for the delivery of the gift. The donor, however, may avail himself of the *beneficium competentiæ*. The donee is only subject to eviction when he has caused some damage to the donor, or when the donee has promised that he would submit to it. Interest for delay is not allowed. As the rule, a gift once made *inter vivos* is irrevocable. The exceptions, however, to this rule are the following:—

When gifts, inter vivos, are revocable.

1. In cases of gross ingratitude; (injury, the causing of pecuniary losses to the donor, acts endangering his life, non-performance of obligations resulting from promises.) The action that lies in such cases is that of the *vindictam spirans*.

2. In the case of the subsequent birth of children.

3. In the case of the violation of the legitimate portion (*reductio*).

Gifts in contemplation of death (*mortis causa donationes*) will be more fully considered under the chapter on the Law of Inheritance, as they have a strong resemblance to legacies. For the origin and termination of Rights two things are of importance—namely, certain Acts and Time.

Acts.

1. *Acts.*—Every operation of the will upon the external world is denominated an act. It is only such, only overt acts that are termed juridical. Acts are divisible into positive acts, or acts of commission; and negative ones, or acts of omission; allowable, and forbidden or delicts; possible, and impossible. Acts which have in view juridical results are termed* legal transactions (*Rechtsgeschäfte*). It is quite possible that, in addition to the object aimed at, other results may follow which were not contemplated—as, for example, in entering upon an inheritance. In illegal acts consequences result quite independently of any act of volition on the side of the wrongdoer. Every juridical act presupposes the capacity of volition, or the direction of the will to a given end (resolve), and the manifestation or declaration of the same.

Volition.

a. Capacity of Volition.—Incapability of volition involves also incapacity to act. Hence the insane, the child under seven years of age, the juridical person,

* Legal transactions are either unilateral or bilateral; the first where the declaration of the will proceeds simply from one person; for example, as in the case of occupancy; the second where several persons concur in establishing a legal relation (*pactum est duorum pluriumve in idem placitum consensus*). This division is not identical with that which is employed in defining unilateral and multilateral contracts.

cannot, strictly speaking, act; but, by a fiction of law, the capacity to act is presumed in the last instance.

b. Direction of the Will.—This presumes an insight into the object aimed at, and also into the means employed. Persons lacking such insight are restricted in their power of action. As infants* (*impuberes*); minors (as regards alienation); and judicially adjudged prodigals.† In point of law, as the rule, it is a matter of indifference what the motive may have been that has prompted the will in a certain given direction. Motives are, however, in some exceptional instances of importance both in legal transactions, as well as in delicts or wrongs; as in Coercion, Mistake, Fraud. Coercion may be twofold, that is, *vis compulsiva*, which is mental, and psychological in its character; and *vis absoluta*, or physical force. The employment of force does not nullify an act done, but it may exempt from its more serious consequences.‡ In such a case the presumptions are, that there are what is termed *metus injustus ex parte inferentis*, a *metus non vani hominis*, a *metus majoris malitatis*, and a *metus* directed against the person himself under coercion. Coercion.

The effect of error or mistake upon acts involving the exercise of the will is cognisable— α. Where the mistake excludes the exercise of the will, in which case Error.

---

* By the aid of a tutor (*tutore auctore*) they are rendered capable of acting. *Sine tutore*, minors, that is *impuberes*, can only acquire rights. Not, as the rule, commit crimes; but *Malitia aetatem supplet.*, Tom. & Lem. Gaius., p. 563.

† They are treated, so to speak, as if they had no property (*interdicitur bonorum administratio*). They may be guilty of criminal offences.

‡ For *bona fide* contracts there is given the action *ex contractu*. For contracts *stricti juris*, the *actio quod metus causa*, and the *in integrum restitutio*; where no performance has taken place, the *exceptio metus*. The legal remedies *propter metum* operate *in rem*.

the maxim applies *errantis nulla est voluntas; β*. Error excludes *dolus* and *mala fides*, and consequently all legal disadvantages that may result from them; *γ*. Where there is *bona fides*, and advantages accrue, although a person act under an erroneous impression of being in the right, and though he be really in error, still the bargain cannot be set aside*; δ. Mistake protects against loss, in many cases when there is delay; † ε. *Mistake* entitles to restitution; ζ. *Mistake* on the part of a creditor excludes the application of the rules of law arising out of the *Senatus Consultum Macedonianum* and *Vellejanum; η*. The actions given by the Aediles presume mistake; ‡ θ. *Condictio indebiti* is founded on a presumption of error. As a rule, regard is paid only to an excusable mistake, or *Error justus*, as it is termed; and it is contrary to rule to say that a mistake in fact *(Error facti)* only, not a mistake in law *(Error juris)*, is to be regarded. Mistake in law is excusable where the party in error has had no opportunity of ascertaining the law; but here the burden of proof lies on him who makes the assertion.§ On the other hand, any mistake in fact is prejudicial where it arises from gross neglect. In cases of mistake *in fact* the remedy is *in damnis* and *in compendiis*; in the case of mistake in law the remedy lies *in damnis* only.||

Error justus.

---

* *Usucapion. Actio Publiciana.*

† *In tempus utile* the periods of time which have been allowed to lapse under some mistake are not reckoned.

‡ The purchaser is under a misconception, is not aware of the statutable illegality inherent in the thing sold.

§ Si quis copiam jurisconsultorum non habet. There are privileged persons, namely, soldiers, women, minors, the ignorant *(rustici.)*

|| By *Damnum* is to be understood the positive and negative injury, and is

The third motive which must be considered is that of fraud (*dolus*), which is, the intentional use or presentation of an error, from a greed of gain. Where the mistake is such as to exclude the action of the will of the person in error, the act becomes absolutely null and void. In all other cases the remedy is the same as in the case of *Metus*. The *actio doli* is an action *in personam*, not an action *in rem*. Fraud.

c. Expression of the Will.—The will must be manifested by some external act: it must be declared. This is required in order that by the realisation or declaration of the intention it may be shown that the party wills. The declaration by which a person is regarded as giving expression to his will is termed *consensus*. It may be either *express* (*consensus expressus*), or *tacit* (*consensus tacitus*.)* Such *consensus* is evidenced by acts from which the will is presumed. These acts are termed conclusive acts. The mode in which the will is expressed determines the form of the legal transaction. There are certain definite forms prescribed by law for certain legal acts. These are termed formal or solemn acts.† The declaration and also the will must co-ordinate or agree with each other. A legal transaction where the will and its declaration are purposely made to differ, so that something else is intended, and not that which is actually done, is termed a simulated transaction. Only that which Manifestation of the Will.

termed either *damnum emergens* or *lucrum cessans*. By *compendium* is understood the gain which would not have accrued to a person but for some mistake. Mistake in law is not allowed in Usucapion of *fructus naturales*.

* Silence suffices under certain circumstances, as where a person has remained silent, when he might or ought to have spoken.

† Hence deaf and dumb persons are excluded from many legal transactions.

was intended has validity, not that which is simulated. (*Plus valet quod agitur quam quod simulate concipitur.*) He who maintains that he has been simulating must prove it. Frequently the disagreement between the will and its declaration is not intended, but is unpremeditated and consequent upon some mistake; or it results from some imperfect mode of expression. As applicable to such a case, the rule "*errantis nulla est voluntas*" has already been mentioned. The imperfection of the expression used renders the declaration either ambiguous, where the meaning said to be in accordance with the will has to be ascertained by interpretation;* or the utterance of the will is of no effect as expressive of the intention of the parties; in which case no legal transaction is perfected.

Protest.

To guard against a prejudicial interpretation of acts as representing the intention of the parties, *Protest* is sometimes employed. This is available not only in the case of our own acts, but also in those of others. Related to Protest is what is denominated *Reservation.* This takes place in transactions when in the transfer of a right or rights, some right is

Reservation.

* In interpreting the law it is necessary to bear in mind that intention and its declaration are equally essential. Where the intention is conveyed by the employment of words, the person interpreting must render the meaning conformably to the ordinary acceptation of the words used. It is only when the meaning is utterly obscured that regard must be paid to the peculiarity of the speaker's diction, or to the usage of words in his native place. Finally, the meaning must be taken in such a sense as shall not invalidate or set aside the transaction (*rei gerendæ aptior*). It may also be observed that, where a doubt exists, the interpretation is in favour of the person liable; and further, that certain "*Causæ favorabiles*" exist in which an interpretation favourable to certain parties is allowed, such as *dos* in favour of the wife, in the case of liberty, and also in testamentary dispositions.

reserved from the complex of rights which has been transferred. The following questions may be suggested:—May not the intention be carried out by the intervention of a third person? Or may not a third person act on behalf of another? Or may not acts be done on behalf of another which shall be deemed as legally valid, and as binding as though the principal himself had performed them? In answer to such questions it may be stated that illegal acts allow of no representation. Again, in legal transactions, as the rule, representation is excluded. Further, in certain cases, the agent must possess a special qualification, which renders the performance of all acts except by a properly qualified person void. Exceptionally, however, rights may be acquired—1. By persons who are under our *potestas*, or representatives by necessity; 2. By free representatives. But according to the Modern Law the representative acquires in the first instance both the rights and liabilities for himself, and those under him take these only mediately through him. There are, however, acts which cannot be effected through the person of a representative. For example, the making of a will. Representation may have its origin—1st, By virtue of certain relations conferring authority, as by the *potestas*; 2nd, By the constitution of a juridical Person; 3rd, By virtue of some office, or by commission. An authorised representative is termed a *Procurator;* the one by whom he is empowered is called the *Dominus*. The representative of a juridical Person is the representative of its will, not so the *Procurator*. His acts only affect the principal in so far as they are consonant with the intention of

Representation.

By whom Rights may be acquired.

Origin of Representation.

The Procurator.

the *Dominus*. The Procurator is bound to act in pursuance of the power delegated to him *(Procura)*. A power of attorney *(Procura)* may be special or general, according as it defines the business to be done or not. A *Procurator omnium bonorum* may either only have the *Custodia*, that is, the charge or care of maintenance; or he may be entrusted with the *Administratio*, that is to say, the entire management of the property. Only in the latter case is he allowed to alienate; but he is not permitted to do anything from motives of mere liberality. When the Procurator has received no special instructions to guide him in the administration entrusted to his charge, he is said to have a *Libera Administratio;* but, even in the *Libera Administratio*, he must be guided by the probable will of the *Dominus*, for it is his duty not to alienate, except in cases of necessity. The acquiescence in the transaction of another, of which mention has just been made, must precede the transaction to which it has reference. But it may take place subsequently; and in this case the consent given to that which has been done, is termed *Ratification.* This especially occurs where a third party has disposed of an object for the alienation of which he possessed no legal authority. Acquiescence may occur, however, by virtue of the Ratification of one's own prior acts in some business in which one has the option either of rescinding or of revoking the same. In the latter instance Retrotraction takes place; in the former it does not necessarily, and certainly not where the duly acquired rights of a third party may be prejudiced, or where the legal transaction intended to be confirmed

Procurator omnium bonorum.

Ratification.

could not be amended by any Ratification. In the latter instance it takes effect from the moment of the remedying of the defect. There is a *Ratihabitio expressa, et tacita*, by the conclusive acts of a party. Formal matters admit of no Ratihabition, for they must be made in accordance with the prescribed forms.

The matter or substance of a legal transaction is determined on the one hand by the will of the party; on the other hand it is regulated by the lawful nature of the legal transaction. The essential elements of a transaction, without which the transaction itself could have no existence, and upon which even the will of the party can have no influence, are termed *Essentialia negotii*. Constituent parts which, under the presupposition of the existence of an act, are its legal and natural consequences, which also may be subject to the control or change of the will, are termed *Naturalia negotii*. Incidental collateral appointments which are entirely dependent upon certain stipulations are designated *Accidentalia negotii*.* **Essentials of a transaction.**

Collateral appointments modify the principal ones, which they have power to extend, to confirm, or to limit. Such are Conditions, Days, and Modes. Under the term CONDITION *(Conditio)*, we understand that undetermined matter of fact upon the taking place or not taking place of which legal consequences are made to depend.† A Condition is termed *Suspensiva* where the commencement, *Resolutiva* where the termination, **Conditio.** **Suspensiva, Resolutiva, etc.**

---

* He who maintains the *essentiale* must prove it. The *naturale* is presumed, except where it is something very unusual. The *accidentale* must be proved.

† For example, a legal transaction, wholly so or in part.

of a legal transaction is dependent on it. The Condition is termed *Negativa* or *Affirmativa*, according as the validity of a transaction is made to depend upon some event happening or not happening, as the case may be. It is designated *Potestativa* if the uncertain event is a perfectly free positive act of the party who must create it. Where the circumstance is an accidental event, it is designated *Casualis*. Where it consists of an admixture of freedom and chance, it is termed *Mixta*. Where an uncertainty exists as to the occurrence of a Condition, the phrase *Conditio pendet* is used; where, however, it has taken place, *Conditio existet;* where the same has failed altogether, *Conditio deficit*. A transaction entered upon subject to a *Conditio Suspensiva* does not exist pending the continuance of the Condition *(pendente conditione)*, though when a transaction has been made under a *Conditio Resolutiva*, it is regarded as existing, notwithstanding the *deficiente Conditione*. The existence of a Suspensive Condition gives rise to the actual relations dependent upon its taking place. With the existence of the *Conditio Resolutiva* the relation ceases.* The change thus effected dates from the day of the inception of the transaction. It originates and terminates retrospectively; hence the maxim, "*Conditio existens retrotrahitur ad initium negotii.*" The Affirmative Condition is perfected the very instant the conditional event occurs in the manner in which the stipulator intended. The Negative Condition is regarded as fulfilled whenever a "*factum contrarium*" has become utterly

* Property reverts *ipso jure*, there arises not merely an obligation *ad rem restituendam*.

impossible. The non-fulfilled Condition is, by a fiction of law, supposed to have taken place whenever he who would become liable upon the Condition being accomplished, renders by his own acts the performance impossible: so also, if the party to be benefited renders the happening of the conditional event impossible by an act of his own; for in this instance he is presumed to have waived his right.* There are numerous *Pseudo* Conditions—*Conditiones in præsens vel præteritum relatæ; Conditiones necessariæ*—that is, those of which it is certain that they must arise, or that they cannot possibly take place; *Conditiones impossibiles*—that is, impossible according to the nature of the legal enactments; *Conditiones turpes*, immoral conditions; *Conditiones tacitæ*, or *juris*—namely, Conditions that uphold a state of things which, by the nature of the legal transaction, might have been already suspended. Pseudo Conditions

Certain Conditions are inadmissible: Impossible Conditions† are regarded as if they had never been inserted by the testator in his will; also *Conditiones turpes*, and Conditions incompatible with the nature of the transaction, for instance, in the case of marriage. In every transaction the *Conditio perplexa*—that is to say, a Condition opposed to the very nature of the transaction itself, is inadmissible. In all such cases the transaction becomes null and void.

---

* This consequence does not ensue whenever the existence of the Condition is dependent upon the will of the party conditionally entitled or conditionally bound; and for this reason, that it remains with them to permit the existence of the Condition.

† Equally so those which are of so perplexing a character that their difficulty amounts to an impossibility. It is immaterial whether the person imposing the condition knew of this or not.

Time.

Time *(Dies)*, by which is to be understood that moment or period, upon the arrival of which certain legal consequences depend. This point of time, however, must not be uncertain.* It is this, indeed, which marks the difference between the period of fulfilment or *Dies*, and the Condition *(Conditio)*. The Condition affects the existence of the relation, not so the *Dies*. The latter concerns the enforcement of the validity of the relation affecting the exercise of the right; it suspends the *Dies veniens*, not the *Dies cedens;* the *Conditio* suspends the *Dies cedens* and *veniens*. The *Dies* is either *a quo* or *ad quem*. The termination *ad quem* does not annul the relation *ipso jure*, but only supersedes it by the aid of a plea or *exceptio*. Retrotraction cannot take place. The appointment of a fixed time *(Dies)* is not admissible in all transactions; for example, in the institution of an heir.

Mode.

MODUS.—Mode is the charge which any one who gives a thing imposes upon it, as the purpose and intention of the Gift. Hence it points to the determination of the object. The charge must neither be reciprocal in its nature, nor suspend *(sub modo)* the rights that have been granted. The *Modus* has in its very nature something of a compulsory character. The donor and his heirs are entitled to an action for performance in the case of lucrative transactions, also for restitution *(condictio causa data causa non secuta)*. In certain cases, as an exception, the *Modus* is not enforcible when it ordains an impossibility, or creates the charge in the sole interest of the party burdened,

* The *When* may be uncertain. The *Dies incertus*, if it be uncertain whether it happen, is a Condition.

or where the party benefited is unable to perform that which is required of him without fault on his part, or where the charge imposed was not made on account of the *Modus*.

It has been already stated that the requisite for a legal transaction—indeed, for any business transaction—implies the capacity to act. But a further requisite of a legal transaction is, that the business itself should be both possible and lawful, otherwise it is null and void. And lastly, the actual completion of the transaction is necessary, and that too, possibly, in the form prescribed by law.

When in a legal transaction some lawful requisite is wanting, the transaction becomes void *(nihil agit)*. This defect in a lawful requisite may have been present from the very commencement of the transaction, or it may have arisen subsequently.* In either case, the invalidity manifests itself either as an absolute nullification of the transaction *(negotium nullum, inutile)*—that is, it becomes *ipso jure* void at law; or the transaction becomes voidable, or to use the expression of Judge Story, it is "rescindable:" the transaction, however, remains valid until set aside at the request of one of the parties interested,† or till its effect is contested by means of a plea *(ope exceptionis)*. That which is invalid does not, however, destroy that which is valid. Where the parts unaffected still continue in force, thus constituting a new transaction, such a continuance is Conversion.

* But a testament that becomes void after it is made, has the effect of rendering a former one likewise void.

† There is, however, no *querela nullitatis*. The actions brought must be the same actions as would be employed if no legal transaction had existed at all.

termed a Conversion.* The validity of a transaction dates from the time of its inception. If void from its very commencement, the invalidity becomes irremediable, and the removal of the cause will not remedy the flaw. Hence the rule of Cato—"Quod ab initio vitiosum est, non potest tractu temporis convalescere." A voidable or rescindable transaction may, however, convalesce.

Influence of time.

Time is the second principal cause of the origin and termination of rights. Time exercises a threefold influence:—*a*. At certain periods certain judicial matters cannot be performed *(feriæ)*; *b*. At certain periods certain juridical acts must be undertaken, such periods are denominated Terms, fixed periods of time; *c*. Upon the expiration of those periods of time in which a certain condition of things has existed, Rights, or certain relations in fact, upon which juridical effects depend, are entirely changed. Thus, there may be an entire change of ownership effected by the length of the time of possession, when there has been an "animus rem sibi habendi."† To this category belong those rules of law which are known under the generic term of Prescriptions—change of rights by the expiration of a given time, in which they are, or are not, exercised. The phrase "Acquisitive Prescription" is employed when a right is acquired, and "Extinguishing Prescription" when such is forfeited. It is not unusual for these to concur.

Prescriptions.

* A Conversion requires that those who have the control of the transaction, the "Disponents," as they are termed by civilians, or the contracting parties eventually give their consent.

† See also on the doctrine of the "Cretio."—Comm. Gaius II., 164—173, and note *k*, pp. 347, 348. Tomkins' and Lemon's Edit.

Triple division of time.

There are three divisions of time necessary to be noticed; namely, days, months, and years. A day is understood to consist of twenty-four equinoctial hours. Months are of various lengths. A calendar month has thirty days. The year comprises three hundred and sixty-five days; every fourth year a day is intercalated, a day being added between the twenty-third and twenty-fourth day of February in Modern Roman Law, in the place of the *mensis mercedonius* of former times.* Ordinarily a year means three hundred and sixty-five days.

A period of time is computed either by including all the moments of time *(tempus continuum)*, or without reckoning the passing moments, pending which a certain given transaction could not take place *(tempus utile)*. The impediment in the party to the transaction may arise from sickness, absence, imprisonment, or excusable error; or it may be in consequence of the impossibility of finding the person of the other party to the transaction; or it may be attributable to some other circumstance, as the impossibility of doing something before a certain given day. The *tempus utile* never occurs during periods by the lapse of which something is to be gained. It occurs only in the delay of judicial proceedings. The "*tempus continuum,*" however, may be regarded as the rule. The time in question must be prescribed by a rule of law, and can never exceed one year.

---

* The intercalated day is not computed in periods of time fixed by law as a distinct day, but the twenty-fourth and twenty-fifth of February in leap-year constitute but one day. The twenty-fourth of February, however, in contracts, is regarded as a separate and distinct day, and will be reckoned as such.

Computation of time.

The Roman Law distinguishes two methods of computing time: civil time, and natural time. The latter consists in this, that the time is computed *a momento ad momentum;* the former is reckoned by entire days.* Thus, the hour of the day at which an occurrence took place is not asked. The computation of time by civil reckoning is the rule,† and it comes into application where the acquisition of a right depends upon the lapse of a certain time, in which case any hour or moment of the day suffices; but where the loss of a right depends upon lapse of time, the last day must have wholly expired.

Immemorial Prescription.

There is still another and quite peculiar kind of Prescription; namely, where a certain condition of things is continuous throughout an undetermined period of time. This state of things gives rise to legal consequences *(Prescriptio Immemorialis).* The commencement of a Right in this case is said to be beyond the memory of man; hence it is assumed to have been lawfully acquired. Time immemorial *(vetustas)* furnishes the foundation of the proof of a lawful acquisition of a Right.‡ It is presumed—1. That no one is alive who, from his own personal knowledge, or by hearsay, has any acquaintance with the matter.

---

* This must include both the day of the commencement of anything and the last day. Consequently the period of a year commencing to run from the 1st of January, terminates on the 31st December, and not as Savigny thinks, on the 1st January of the following year.

† Natural computation of time occurs only in the *minor ætas,* and in the case of the period allowed for appeal.

‡ Time immemorial is only subsidiary in its nature, and only becomes operative, as the rule, where no other proof can be adduced, namely, where the lawful origin of a certain condition presumes a magisterial concession *(vetustas pro lege habetur).*

2. That no one is living who has any information respecting the matter from any deceased person, or who has either seen or heard the persons who have, or who had such information. Time immemorial is presumed where, either by witnesses, or by documentary proof, the continued existence of a certain state of things is shown to have remained during two generations. This presumption is set aside by the proof on the other side, that at a certain time the circumstances upon which the Right is founded had then commenced, or that it never existed as an Obligation.

Section XI.—*Exercise and Collision of Rights.*

Von Vangerow, s. 131.

Exercise of a Right.

The exercise of a Right consists in the doing of those acts for which the Right imparts the qualification. But it may happen that Rights collide in such a manner that although they may co-exist they cannot be simultaneously enjoyed. When a limiting Right is in collision with a limited Right, as, for example, Servitudes or Easements with Property, the limited Right takes the preference; it merges into the unlimited Right in the Person entitled, that is to say, the collision gives rise to what is technically termed "Confusion." When several Persons have an exclusive Right to one and the same object, the Person whose Right is founded upon general precept must yield to the Person whose Right is based upon a *privilegium* or upon a *jus singulare.* But if all equally rest upon general precept, but one is specially favoured, this one has the preference. Where, however, Rights are equal, that Person is preferred who seeks by means of his Right to avert some danger. When Rights collide in a third Person, possession in the first instance determines; where neither is in possession, division takes place; should this be impossible, recourse must be had to the lot.

Section XII.—*Of the Securing of Rights.*

Von Vangerow, ss. 182 et seq., 189 et seq., and for the authorities for the actions compare Von Vangerow, Abschnitt II., vol. I., p. 213 et seq.
Glück II., 8, 43, 81 et seq., XI., 745, 789 et seq.
Savigny Syst. II., 83; V., 1 et seq., 37, 119 et seq., 160, 198 et seq., 265 et seq.; VI., 1; VII., 20, 47, 90, 161, 191, 211, 312, 322, 326.
Dig. qui satisdare cogantur vel etc. (2, 8).
„ de stipulationibus prætoriis (46, 5).
Instit. de divisione stipulationum (3, 18).
„ de satisdationibus (4, 11).
Cod. de satisdando (2, 57).
Dig. quibus ex causis in possessionem eatur. (42, 4).
„ de rebus auctoritate judicis possid., etc. (42. 5).
Cod. de bonis auctoritate judicis, etc. (7, 72).

Cautiones. To secure the future acknowledgment of legal claims, and to insure the performance of assumed obligations, Guarantees, or Sureties *(Cautiones)* are employed. These are certain acts done for the purpose of guarding against the violation of a future Right, or for the reparation of injury already inflicted, according to the grounds that impose a liability to provide security. Guarantees are divisible into Voluntary, namely, those originated by agreement, or by testamentary disposition, and Necessary (legal, judicial) Guarantees. They are further classified, according to the remedies they furnish, into Verbal Guarantees (promises, oaths) and Real Guarantees (pledges, suretyships). The *Cautiones necessariæ*, and Guarantees by agreement, are, for the most part, Real Guarantees; namely, where the intention is to avert some impending danger. The Fiscus and Municipal bodies are only liable to furnish a verbal promise of surety. Promises upon oath are required—1. In cases where a Real Guarantee cannot be provided; 2. Where a person owns large immoveable properties. The party whose duty it is to give bail, is bound to make good any deficiencies that may arise, and to supplement that which is inadequate. When, however, the secured right itself becomes extinct, the suretyship terminates. The act by which a guarantee may be created is either by judicial disposition, or by sequestration, or by a *Missio in possessionem*, or by arrest. The *Missio in possessionem* is the putting a person into the possession of the property of another, or into possession of some particular thing *(in rem)* by decree of a Court. The party installed in the first instance obtains the right of detention only. He only obtains possession and right of property *ex secundo decreto*. The party installed acquires the right of a pawnee from the moment of his obtaining the legal possession. **Missio in possessionem.**

Another remedy whereby to ward off attack is denominated Self-help. As a rule, the exercise of Self-help is forbidden.* It is, however, permissible to repel illegal attacks upon lawful conditions where no more than necessary force is employed. Detention **Self-help.**

* For example, by the Decretum Divi Marci, which forbids the debtor from seizing anything, and then by its precept forbids any one under pain of forfeiture from seizing the property he claims by his own unauthorised act.

also is a species of Self-help, that is, the withholding in the first instance of a thing until the claim put forward has become satisfied. It is always presumed that the possession is not *vitiosus*, that is to say, it must be *nec vi, nec clam, nec precario*, and that a *vinculum* exists between the claim and the property detained. To this rule there are only two exceptions, namely, in the case of what are denominated chirographic and pawn creditors.*

Civil Process.

The positive recognition, the actual protection of a violated right is attained only by appeal to a judge. For the judicial settlement of contentious differences between private Rights, a legal order of proceeding is prescribed, denominated Civil Process. This Process is connected with Private Right; for the violation as well as the legal remedy induce a certain natural reaction upon the subject-matter of the injured and violated Rights themselves.

The Action

Proceedings are commenced by Action. The *Actio* is the legal remedy by which a private person, called the actor or plaintiff, enforces a private lawful claim. By the term *Actio*, however, is likewise meant the right of instituting legal proceedings. The possibility of exercising this right is co-existent with the right itself. Actions are, according to their legal origin, either *civiles (ex lege)* or *honorariæ;* the latter are those given by the prætors, or the ædiles *(prætoriæ, aediliciæ)*. They are also designated *directæ* and *utiles*† according

* That is to say, they must stand in a juridical relationship (*nexu*) to the object retained. For example, when expenses have been incurred upon the thing.

† Where greater latitude is given by means of a fiction of law; the action is termed an *Actio ficticia*.

as they are restricted within their original sphere of action, or are extended beyond it. Again, Actions are, according to their origin, either real or personal.* According to their object, actions are divisible into— 1. Those instituted for the purpose of obtaining a judgment against the defendant, who is called the *reus;* 2. Those which proceed for the preliminary recognition of a certain relation *(actiones præjudiciales).* 3. Those which are available for some certain specific object *(certum),* all *in rem actiones,* or some uncertain object *(incertum).* The latter are all *bonæ fidei actiones.* 4. For the purpose of simply reinstating in a former position *(rei persecutoriæ),* or penal *(pœnæ persecutoriæ),* or including both objects *(mixtæ).* Again, according to the mode of procedure adopted, actions are divisible into *ordinariæ* and *extraordinariæ.* This is an ancient distinction of procedure. The Extraordinary was marked by this peculiarity, that the entire process was conducted before the same tribunal. To use the technical expression, the same magistrate had cognisance both *in jure* and *in judicium.* In the Ordinary Action the suit was commenced before the magistrate who controlled the proceedings, and the proof was given before the Judices, or Recuperatores, or the Arbitri, or other similar judges.†

How divided.

The classification of Actions into *in jus conceptæ* and *in factum conceptæ,* according as the plaintiff framed his demand upon the *jus civile,* or upon the formula of

* *Actiones in rem scriptæ* must also be mentioned. These are Actions arising out of obligations which may be brought against any third person; for instance, the *Actio quod metus causa.*

† See Gaius, pp. 583 et seq. Tomkins' and Lemon's Edit.

the Prætor, is likewise an ancient division. Another early distinction was made between *Actiones in factum* and *Actiones vulgares*, according as the Action had been determined beforehand by the Edict with a prescribed formula, or first established for a particular or concrete case. The ancient division into *Actiones stricti juris*, and *bonæ fidei*, has become obsolete. At the present day all Actions are *bonæ fidei*. The classification into *Actiones arbitrariæ*, and *non arbitrariæ*, has likewise been superseded, because the principle of condemnation in pecuniary damages *(condemnatio pecuniaria)* has been abolished.* The process by Interdict has also been abolished; but a summary proceeding has been instituted in its place. Hence it is still of importance to ascertain whether formerly an Interdict would have been instituted or not. Originally the Interdicts were commands of the Prætor, in which he ordered something to be done, or not to be done. The injunction of feasance, or of non-feasance, gave rise to the division of Interdicts into *prohibitoria*, *restitutoria*, *exhibitoria*. At a later period, under the term Interdict was comprised the petition for such injunctions. Such petitions were especially employed in cases of disputed possession. Interdicts were also divisible into *Interdicta retinendæ*, *recuperandæ*, and *adispiscendæ possessionis*. Another, and further classification of Interdicts; was that into *simplicia* and *duplicia*, according as the part of the litigants was distinctive or not. As for example, according as the one party was plaintiff, and only such, and the other defendant, and only defendant; or both

All Actions are at present *bonæ fidei*.

Interdicts

How divided.

* Where formerly the *Actio arbitraria* was available, there now exists in its place what is termed *juramentum in litem*.

haracters were combined in each of the parties to the uit. For example, in the *Interdicta uti possedetis* and *trubi*.

Actio nata.

To commence an Action it must be what is denomi-ated *nata*. In order to give rise to it, there must be ome ground or cause, some infringement of a Right. ny person may avail himself of an Action, and that t such time as he may think best, this right continues ntil the legal period prescribed has elapsed. There re exceptions to this rule: the citation by Edict, *cum ræjudicio præclusi*, and the *provocationes ex lege diffa-ari*, and *ex lege si contendat*.

How Right of Action terminates

A Right of Action terminates with the extinction f a Right to which it is annexed. But, apart from is, a Right of Action becomes absolutely destroyed -1. By the death of the Party; 2. By Prescription; nd 3. By Confusion or Merger. It is also, of course, xtinguished by the actual employment of the Action.

1. *By the death of the party*. As a rule, Actions are oth active and passive—that is to say, they are avail-ble, as it is expressed, both for and against the Person. hey are *in* and *ad* the heirs. But *Actiones populares*, d *Actiones ex delictis*, are, however, personal, and do ot avail as against the heirs. Nor do the *Actiones enales*. In the case of the *Rei persecutoriæ ex delicto* e Action lies against the heirs, but only in as far as ey have been enriched; so likewise in the *Actiones* ising out of contract, heirs are liable for the *Dolus* the testator. Excluded from active Actions which e transferable are—

Popular Actions.

The *Actiones populares* (which every citizen may ing), and the *Actiones meram vindicatam spirantes*

(*Actiones injuriæ; Querela inofficiosi testamenti;* Revocation of a gift; *Actiones sepulcri violati; Actiones de effusis; Actiones de mortuo inferendo*). These Actions pass *in* and *ad heredes* from the instant of the *Litis contestatio*.

Actiones temporales et perpetuae.

2. *By Prescription.* According to the more ancient Roman Law, actions were perpetual, only a few being limited as to the time in which they might be brought. These were termed *temporales*, whilst the others were designated *perpetuæ*. Theodosius the Second limited the time of bringing Actions, with but few exceptions, to a period of thirty years. Four conditions are now necessary to bar an Action by Prescription:—*a*. The Action must be *nata*, that is, according to Puchta, a fact must have occurred manifesting some breach on the part of the party bound, in respect of the duty undertaken;* or in the case of real rights a state of things must have intervened, or a fact must have taken place hindering the enjoyment of the Right; *b*. The thirty years, reckoning from the moment of the *actio nata*, including also the very last day, must have completely elapsed;† *c*. *Bona fides; d*. There must be no interruption, which may be brought about by the commencement of a suit,‡ by Protest, by acknowledgment on the part of

Conditions necessary to bar an Action.

* Von Vangerow is opposed to this view. He maintains that no violation of a Right is requisite in order that an Action may be *nata;* and affirms that the Action is *nata* the very instant that the Obligation which binds the debtor attains its complete and mature existence.

† Minors, infants, and children possess privileges beyond this. There are also Actions limited to a shorter period. For example, penal Actions by the Prætor, etc.

‡ If an action remains dormant for forty years, the right becomes barred by prescription of the *lis pendens*.

he debtor, by *mala fides superveniens*. Prescription ·perates as a Plea. Hence, although the Right of ·ction is extinguished, the right itself of the party ·ntitled is not lost. Puchta and Arndts think ·hat it may, on the contrary, survive as a *naturalis* ·*bligatio*, and that it may be protected in some ·ther form.* For example, By *soluti retentio*, mort- ;age, suretyship.

3. *By Concurrence*—Which exists where several ·omplete legal actions come into contact, or converge ·t one point. This point of contact may be—1. The ·ediate ground or cause of their origin (Fact); 2. The ·mmediate origin or cause (Right); 3. The Person ·ho may be entitled to several Actions, or against ·hom several Actions may be brought; 4. The object ·nd purport towards which the several Actions are ·irected. The community of the mediate cause, and ·he mere merging in the same person operate as a ·umulative Concurrence; that is to say, the several ·ctions are independent of each other, or they exist ·y the side of each other. But the unity of the object, ·nd the point of contact in the immediate origin or ·ause† (coupled with an object in common) produce ·lective Concurrence; so that one Action abrogates ·ne other. But this effect becomes operative only ·fter the bringing of an Action where several demands ·re incompatible with each other, either intrinsically ·, or by virtue of some legal precept;‡ or where the ·ction has been satisfied (as far as there is identity

Concurrence of Actions.

---

* Von Vangerow is opposed to this view.

† Injury to property belonging to several persons.

‡ Actio redhibitoria and Quanti minoris.

of object),* when the second Action falls to the ground.

Exceptio or Plea.

When the Defendant intends to resist the Action brought against him,† he either traverses the statement of facts made by the Plaintiff; or he admits the cause of Action, but brings forward new facts which, provided they be true, totally or partially answer the allegations put forward on the other side. This is the essence of a Plea *(Exceptio)*. It consists in the adducing of facts either barring or destroying the Right.‡ Where the facts utterly defeat the Right of Action, the Plea is termed a Peremptory Plea *(peremptoria)*. Where the Plea suspends the Action for a time, it is termed a Dilatory Plea *(dilatoria)*.§ As the rule, a Plea is what is denominated "Res cohærens"—that is to say, every one who enters into a definite relation has a right to use it. Commonly this Plea is *in rem*—that is to say, adverse to the party making the claim repelled. By the *Exceptio doli (generalis)* is to be understood a plea set up by the Defendant—that the Plaintiff, although better informed, nevertheless brings his action. This Exception comprises several Pleas. The Plea becomes extinguished by the extinction of the cause; or by the expiration of the time allowed for pleading; or where the subject-matter in dispute partakes of a penal character.||

Peremptoria. Dilatoria.

Exceptio doli.

* Condictio furtiva and the Rei vindicatio.

† Apart from and in addition to the probable carrying into effect of the rule of law on which the Plaintiff relies.

‡ The answer made by the Plaintiff is denominated *Replicatio;* the Defendant's further answer is called *Duplicatio;* the reply again to this is the *Triplicatio;* after this comes the *Quadruplicatio.*

§ For example, the premature bringing of an Action.

|| A Surety who denies his liability as such, forfeits as a penalty the *Exceptio divisionis.*

Litis contestatio, and its effects.

A specially important period of time in Civil Actions is that known as the *Litis contestatio*. The meaning of this term has greatly varied from time to time. In modern practice it is understood to be that stage of the process at which the Defendant enters upon the special statement of the facts of the case. Its effects are the following:—1, A new obligation is created* transmissible *in* and *ad heredes;* 2, The Litigants agree to abide by the future decision of the Court; 3, Also to await the judicial decision—that is, not to employ any other mode of enforcing their Rights; 4, Inalienability of the matter in litigation or non-cessibility of the Right of Action; 5, The *Litis contestatio* forms the basis upon which the judicial decision rests, as far as regards the existence of the Right † and the extent of the liability or of the demand; ‡ 6, Where variable circumstances determine who is to be the Defendant (ownership—possession—as, for example, in the case of Noxal Actions), the time of the *Litis contestatio* decides. The party not in possession, who *liti sese obtulit*, is answerable after the *Litis contestatio*, or the issue joined, just the same as

* The new obligation thus created includes the entire force and scope of the Action. The legal condition of the Plaintiff remains unchanged. Thus rights of mortgage or other rights remain unaffected.

† In Real Actions the Plaintiff, if he should happen to be owner at the time when the judgment is delivered, is not for that reason to be non-suited. But how is it, it may be asked, if the action lies at the time of the determination of the *Litis contestatio* or issue, but subsequently the Right becomes void? In the case of *actiones in personam* the plaintiff is non-suited, so also in the *actiones in rem*, should reasons occur affecting the established obligation through the *Litis contestatio*. For example, the accidental destruction of the object by a *bona fide* possessor.

‡ Here the question arises, At what period of time shall the valuation be made? According to the time of the judgment.

the real owner; 7, The Defendant is from the period of the *Litis contestatio* regarded as a malæ fidei possessor, both in respect to the thing itself and its fruits.

Proof of facts must be adduced

In order that the judge may decide upon a question in litigation, it is necessary that the parties to the Action should satisfy him of the truth of the facts submitted for his decision. But they must not only satisfy the judge; they must also prove the facts adduced. Facts that must be proved, and such as affect and are relevant to the decision to be given, are uncertain facts—that is, such as are disputed by the other party.* The burden of proof (*onus probandi*) is thrown upon him who asserts a fact in support of his claim, or in support of his exemption from a claim. The Plaintiff commences in the first instance. If his proof fail, or if it be set aside by rebutting evidence, he is non-suited. The Defendant follows the Plaintiff with his proofs. The general rule of evidence is "*affirmanti non neganti incumbit probatio.*" This rule, however, has no other meaning than the following:—Whenever a Person, whether Plaintiff or Defendant, adduces a fact with a view to establish an intention, he must prove in every case whatever he alleges. The means of proof are:—

On whom *onus probandi* lies.

Rule of evidence.

Means of Proof—Persons.

1. *Persons.*—As the judge who resorts to ocular inspection, drawing his conclusions from the evidence

* Notorious matters of facts are incontestable; so also are *præsumptiones juris et de jure.* With the latter, counter proof is not admissible. The *præsumptiones juris* are somewhat different. Facts based upon conjecture may be repelled by counter evidence adduced on the other side; for instance, the unconditional nature of a transaction, the *naturalia negotii.* The *præsumptiones hominis* (*facti*) are such probabilities as only support the evidence.

of his senses, Witnesses, Experts,* and the Suitors themselves by their admissions † on oath. ‡

2. *Things* (*Records*).§—By the *Litis contestatio* the Things.

---

* Witnesses are third persons who give evidence simply upon what they have observed by their senses. Experts are those who draw inferences from what has been observed. Witnesses. Experts.

† Confession is either Judicial or Extra-judicial. Judicial Confession is such as is made in the particular litigation after Action brought, before a competent judge, and in the presence of the parties themselves. Further, in Confessions of this nature, evidence to the contrary is not admissible (*pro veritate habetur*). Extra-judicial Confessions may be understood by duly considering the nature of a Judicial one. Whoever appeals to Extra-judicial law must prove the same; proof, however, to the contrary is admissible. Confession

‡ The oath—the affirmation of truth by appeal to the Deity—is intended either to confirm a promise made (*juramentum promissorium*), or it is made in confirmation of the truth of a statement of a fact (*juramentum assertorium*). An oath also is either Judicial or Extra-judicial. The latter occurs principally in confirmation of an obligation. The former is *delatum*, when the party burdened with the proof in lieu of proof imposes upon the opposite side an oath in substantiation of the statements made; it is *relatum* where the opponent refers it back; it is *necessarium* where evidence that is incomplete has to be perfected (*suppletorium*), or an improbable, imperfect proof (*purgatorium*) of the opposing party, on whom the *onus probandi* rests, has to be rebutted. The presumptions of an oath are:—1. *Judicium in jurante:* 2. As to the object in promissory oaths; this must be *justitia in jure jurando;* and in assertory oaths, the subject-matter must be of a character suitable for a legal transaction: 3. In respect of the determination of the will, Coercion, Fraud, and Error affect the transaction; in promissory oaths *Relaxatio* or Waiver; in assertory false oaths, the party affirming the same must make restitution of that which he has obtained by the perjury. False evidence disclosed before verdict is utterly void; if after judgment, compensation must be made for the injury sustained, and likewise restitution. The rule in regard to the administration of oaths is, that they must be taken orally, not in writing. An oath once taken, makes all averments so made judicially true; and what has been promised must be carried out, unless such promises are immoral, or *contra bonos mores.* The *juramentum in litem* constitutes a further form of judicial affirmation on oath. It is that form of oath in which the plaintiff in *actiones arbitrariæ* and *bonæ fidei,* which are employed to obtain a *restituere* or an *exhibere,* appraises the extent of his own damage, when the defendant fails to render the demanded restitution, either from disobedience, or from *dolus,* or *culpa lata,* or from inability. There is no *jusjurandum in litem affectionis.* Oath.

§ Records are either public or private. The former furnish complete proof Records.

parties submit themselves to the final issue of the legal controversy; by the proofs adduced they enable the judge to gain an insight into the subject matter in dispute; the judgment determines the existence, or the non-existence of the legal claim. Hence the maxim "*Res judicata pro veritate habetur inter partes,*" that is to say, by virtue of a legally valid sentence* a right is formally created. But the effect which results from the sentence does not reach beyond the parties to the suit and their successors *(inter partes).* It extends, however, to third parties exceptionally, as, for instance, in the case of the invalidity of a testament; in an indictment; in a judgment upon the *status* of a person; in judgments in cases of real servitudes; in joint-ownerships; and in other similar instances.

The maxim "Res judicata pro veritate," etc.

The *Actio judicati,* and the *Exceptio rei judicatæ.*

The benefits of a judgment are secured to the victorious party by means of the *Actio judicati*, or by the *Exceptio rei judicatæ*, which may be pleaded either by the plaintiff or the defendant. The newly created obligation is enforceable by the *Actio judicati.*† The *Exceptio rei judicatæ* bars every claim which may be adverse to the Matter of the judgment *quotiens inter easdem personas eadem questio revocatur.* In respect to the requisites for the identity of a legal contention, two things are needed—1, The *Exceptio* falls to the

for and against all the world. Private records containing matter which is prejudicial to the party publishing them, are evidence against such person, and if the record contains a disposition of the party making it, such disposition is valid against third parties.

* A Sentence is legally valid if it cannot be further disputed by ordinary judicial means; as by Appeal, or by Restitution.

† In Personal Actions the debtor has a period of four months; in the case of Real Actions, nine months.

ground when no identity exists; even though the subsequent action may resemble the former one; 2, The *Exceptio* is maintainable where the identity is actually present, though the previous point in litigation and the new one may be somewhat dissimilar.* In Personal Actions, identity of Right results from similarity of origin; but in Real Rights, and in Real Actions, the mode of origin is immaterial.†

The In integrum restitutio.

A perfectly rightful application of a legal principle may be violated by any one on the ground of the circumstances in which he is placed, since the application of strict legal Right may prove detrimental to the party entitled. On the other hand, against the Right itself protection may sometimes be obtained by the *In integrum restitutio*, by means of which a person is restored to the same position in which he was placed before the occurrence of the injurious event. The *In integrum restitutio* is a mode of adjustment between law and equity, and it had its origin in a Prætorian source. It is presumed that there exists an injury caused by the operation of the law itself *(laesio)*, which must neither be altogether unimportant, nor have been caused by the neglect of the party aggrieved. Moreover, it may have arisen from some loss, or from the deprivation of some possible gain,

* For example, a suitor has instituted the *Hereditatis petitio*, and has been non-suited upon which he proceeds by the *Rei vindicatio* for certain definite things. In this case the *Exceptio rei judicatæ* comes into operation. Thus the distinction between the whole and part is irrelevant.

† Real Rights are not converted into any other Rights when the nature or mode of their origin has been changed. But the plaintiff, who claims upon a different ground, sues under a new obligation. Thus a Personal Action, but not a Real Action, may be reinstituted by virtue of a declaration assigning a different ground for the origin of the Right.

against which the ordinary procedure affords no remedy. Further, there must be a lawful reason or ground for claiming Restitution, or, as it is expressed in other words, a *justa causa restitutionis*. Such reasons are the following:—

Justa causa restitutionis:—Minority.

1. *Minority*,* even when the minor himself has been the cause of the injury. But Restitution is barred in all cases where the transaction has been confirmed by the oath of the minor; when he has acted deceitfully; when the Restitution is based upon an immoral or improper consideration.† A surety, however, cannot avail himself of the Plea of minority *(minor ætas)* with a view to the obtaining of Restitution in the case where he has become surety for the very purpose of guaranteeing a credit. All *universitates personarum* are entitled to such Rights of Restitution as are available for minors.

Absentia and *Generalis clausula.*

2. *Absentia* and *Generalis clausula.*—Restitution in this case is termed the *Restitutio majorum.* The following cases must be distinguished—*a.* When a person has suffered damage to his property, or has lost a suit on account of absence, which has resulted from just fear, or from absence on public business *(rei publicæ causa)*, or in consequence of imprisonment, or from being reduced to slavery; *b.* When a person has

---

* Provided that the business was not without the peculiar circumstance void; for instance, when a contract has been made without the consent of a guardian.

† If a minor, eighteen years of age, has borrowed money to redeem from imprisonment a person to whom he is heir. When two relatives have agreed as between themselves to the respective Rights resulting from the death of either the one or the other of them. When a minor demands Restitution from another minor.

suffered such loss, because his opponent was personally absent, or in bondage, or in slavery, or has failed to appear in defence, or has withdrawn from the Action, or could not be cited *in jus; c*. When any one has sustained such loss by denial or delay of justice. In addition to these distinct cases, there is also added the clause: "*item si qua alia justa causa esse videbitur, in integrum restituam.*" The meaning of which clause is, that Restitution shall take place whenever the due perception or realization of a Right has been prevented by any external effective impediments.

3. *Error.*—Restitution is granted *ex generale clausula* on account of error; or on the ground of delay *(mora)*. But another kind of Restitution exists on the ground of error, on account of delay, and against positive acts. This principally occurs in the case of disadvantages in the procedure. Restitution on account of *dolus* and *metus* has become obsolete in the later law. Von Vangerow, however, opposes Puchta's view on this point. Error.

As Restitution is but a subsidiary legal remedy, it is only employed in cases of necessity. It may be claimed by the party injured, his assignees, and his universal successors. As the rule, it is *in personam*, not *in rem*.* Restitution must be pursued *intra quadriennium continuum*, that is, within four years. With minors this period commences to run from the moment of their attaining their majority; with absentees, from the instant of their return. Other cases of Restitution

Restitution a subsidiary remedy.

Must be pursued within four years

* It is, however, *in rem* when it would otherwise be inoperative, or where the third party in possession is *conscius;* when it is urgently necessary that the party claiming should be reinstated in the possession of the thing claimed.

date from the period of the wrong done. In order to obtain Restitution, it is necessary that an application should be made. After completed investigation the judge reinstates the applicant for Restitution in the possession of the alleged Right *(judicium rescindens)*, and leaves it to him to make use of his Right *(judicium recissorium)*. But the two decrees may be combined. Pending the course of proceeding for Restitution, the *status quo* remains unaffected. Upon Restitution being decreed, everything must be reinstated as far as possible in its former position. Each party must return what he has received from the other, with all accessions and parts.* As to third parties, Restitution has only a beneficial effect so far as their interests are inseparably connected with that of the person obtaining it.†

* This does not occur: 1, Where the minor sues; 2, Where the defendant is guilty of *dolus*.

† For example, Sureties may claim on the ground of the enforced Restitution obtained by the principal debtor. For instance, the father guaranteeing as a Mandans is liable for the delict of another.

BOOK THE THIRD.

POSSESSION.

Section XIII.—*Theories, Notion, Legal Character, and Mode of Possession.*

Von Vangerow, ss. 198—210.
Savigny, "Das Recht des Besitzes."
Dig. de acquirenda vel amit. possessione (41, 2).
Cod. de acquirenda et retinenda possessione (7, 32).
Dig. l. 3 pr. hoc tit. de possessione.
,, l. 30, s. 1 hoc tit. eod.

Savigny, Bruns, and Pfeiffer on Possession.

The treatise of Savigny on Possession is so well known, that a mere reference to it is all that is needed in this Compendium. It was his first work, and was written in a very short space of time, while he was a young man. At a later period a writer named Bruns, working upon the plan laid down by Savigny, enlarged the scope of the subject so as to explain the notion entertained in relation to Possession in the Middle Ages and also at the present time.* Pfeiffer has examined and criticised with great acerbity the treatise of Savigny, in a work showing ability, but in language unsuitable for juridical discussion.†

* Bruns. "Das Recht des Besitzes im Mittelalter und in der Gegenwart." Tüb. 1848.

† Pfeiffer. "Was ist und gilt im Röm. Rechte der Besitz?" Tüb. 1840.

Controversy on the nature of Possession.

It may be useful to remind the reader that there has been much controversy among jurists as to the precise nature of Possession itself. Savigny's title of his great work on this subject has been strongly objected to; and it has been asked, "Is Possession a Right? and, if it be, to which class of Rights does it belong?" Without discussing this question fully, it is not disputed that a person may stand in such a relation to a thing, that *in point of fact* it is thrown under his dominion. In such a case the person becomes Dominus *in fact*, at least as far as relates to the particular thing. Thibaut, the predecessor of Von Vangerow at Heidelberg, who took part in the discussion provoked by the work of Savigny, affirmed that Possession consists in the exercise, in point of fact, of a Right. This may be philosophically correct when the idea of Possession is regarded in the most extensive signification of the term; but such is not the idea of the Roman Law. One may, indeed, speak of the Possession of a Right of Claim, or Obligation; or of the Possession of Family Rights; or the Possession of Rights of Inheritance; but it does not admit of a doubt that such an extended idea of Possession was quite foreign to the classical Roman jurists. There is only one apparent exception to this view, and that is in the case of Servitudes. It is said that the *jus servitutis* gives rise to *quasi* Possession. But even in this case the Romans did not speak of a true or actual Possession, but merely intimated that in the case of Servitudes there is a similar exercise of Right, if it may be so expressed, to that which exists in the case of actual Possession. Hence the maxim,

Thibaut's view.

"*Usus pro possessione est.*" Strictly speaking, Possession is a pure matter of fact, and not a legal idea. Possession also, it should be observed, may arise as the consequence of a Right; or, on the other hand, Possession may be the *causa efficiens* giving rise to a Right. When it is the consequence of a Right, we speak of the *jus possidendi.** This idea of Possession, however, is the least important one. It is only when Possession is the source and origin of a Right that we can speak of a *jus possessionis*. Hence it will be seen that it is not out of every Possession that a *jus possessionis* can arise. When, for instance, a person holds a thing in the name of another, and for a third Person, a *jus possessionis* is inadmissible. *Jus possessionis* always implies the Possession of the thing for oneself. When we hold a thing in the name of another, it is simply regarded as Detention, and it is denominated "*Naturalis possessio.*" Here there is no "*animus rem sibi habendi,*" and it is only when such *animus* exists that we can correctly speak of Possession. In answer to the question, "What is Possession?" Savigny says that it is a *factum* and a *jus*—a fact and a Right. This, however, is held to be a mistake, and Possession is at present regarded as simply a *fact* and not a Right. But it may, without doubt, be the *causa efficiens* giving rise to a Right. Possession in this case is, to speak exactly, *a Fact engendering a Right*.

True notion of Possession.

Distinction between *Jus possidendi* and *Jus possessionis.*

Mistake of Savigny.

An important distinction already hinted at in regard to Possession is, that it is either natural (*naturalis*) or civil (*civilis*). There has been in the past much

Possession may be *naturalis* or *civilis.*

* For a fuller discussion of this subject, see Gaius, Tomkins & Lemon's Edit., note *y*, p. 257, et seq.

Three theories—Savigny's. discussion upon this division, and at present there are three different theories which require to be noticed. The prevailing theory is that of Savigny, who regarded *possessio civilis* as that Possession which leads to Usucapion; *possessio naturalis* being every other kind of Possession. Savigny has presented a tabulated form in which he denotes very clearly his ideas upon this point.* Thibaut's. Thibaut's theory, which has found numerous defenders, is, that by *possessio civilis* is to be understood that Possession which entitles the possessor to avail himself of the Interdicts; whilst *possessio naturalis* is the holding of a thing in the name of a third party. Thibaut did not think with Savigny, that *possessio naturalis* could be taken in a double sense. The third view is that in which the division of Possession is derived not from its operation, but from the fundamental notion of Possession itself. In the views of both Savigny and Thibaut, the effect and operation of the Possession is regarded. Von Vangerow's theory. Von Vangerow is of opinion that both Savigny's and Thibaut's views are fanciful, and that the real test which decides the nature of Possession is the existence of the "*animus rem sibi habendi.*" Where there is "*animus domini*" the Possession is *civil;* where this does not exist, the Possession is *natural.* When, however, the *animus domini* is not legally possible, the Possession is only *natural.* Impediments to Possession. Hence, for example, when a slave holds anything with *animus domini*, because this is legally impossible, it is not a *civil* Possession. Again, and for a similar reason, if a man holds anything *extra*

* Recht des Besitzes, p. 131.

commercium, animus domini, it is merely *natural* and not *civil* Possession. Thus, the man who holds a *pignus*, and the *emphyteuta* have merely *natural* Possession, as from the nature of this tenure all idea of *animus domini* must be excluded. Or again, when a man has *animus domini* in regard to a thing which it is absolutely impossible for him to own, in this case there can be no *civil* Possession. Again, when a thing is stolen, it is a delict or wrong, and constitutes a legal impediment; it is not a case of what is merely forbidden, but it renders *civil* Possession impossible. Without pursuing this subject farther in this place, it must suffice to refer the jurist to the works to which reference has already been made.* The definition of Possession now accepted is the following:

Definition of Possession.

Possession is the exclusive holding of a corporal thing. This holding, however, as we have already seen, may be either consequent on a Right, or it may be merely a *fact* independent of any recognised corresponding Right. The exercise of Dominion continues in force *as a fact*, until by legal means an adverse Right has been proved and judicially rendered valid. This actual relationship takes the character of a lawful Right, because in it the will, that is to say, the Personality, is shown to be operative.

Detention and Juridical Possession.

The holder of a thing stands either in such a relation to the thing held, that he combines with the physical holding the intention (*animus*) of acquiring a proprietary Right, which is termed "*animus rem sibi*

---

* *See* Gaius II., 89, 90, 94, 95; IV., 138—170. Tomkins and Lemon's Edit. Also Bruns' work, where the view of Von Vangerow, adopted by the present writers, is defended and established.

habendi;" or the possessor sustains such a relation, that he recognises the intention of another Person to obtain the Ownership. In the latter case, the holding* is termed "Detention;" in the former, "Juridical possession." The person who takes Possession of a thing for another as the *detentor*, is not regarded as being in the Juridical Possession of the thing. But necessity has compelled the recognition of the Possession of the Sequestrator as a Juridical Possession, and likewise that of the Mortgagee, and of the Person who was said to hold a *precario*. This transmitted Possession is termed "Derivative Possession."

Derivative Possession.

Possession *justa* and *injusta*.

Possessio is either *justa* or *injusta*, according as the ground or *causa* upon which it is founded, or the mode of its origin, is legally permissible or non-permissible. The three vices of Possession are denominated *vi, clam, precario*.† As to Juridical Possession, the mode of inception is immaterial; hence the thief who takes a thing *animus possidendi* is juridically in Possession. But Possession ripening into Usacapion must rest upon a *justa causa*. Such Possession maturing into Usucapion, we have seen, is designated *civilis possessio;* but mere Juridical Possession only, it should be remembered, is denominated *naturalis possessio*.

---

* The Romans designated this by *Habere, Tenere, In possessionem esse*. The Juridical Possession they denoted by the word *Possessio*.

† "Nemo sibi ipse causam possessionis mutare potest." This rule was formerly of more importance than at present. Its meaning is, that when Possession, for instance Detention, has once taken place, it cannot by the mere change of the *animus* be transmuted into another mode of Possession. Detention cannot by the mere will of the *detentor* be changed into Juridical Possession.

Section XIV.—*Acquisition and Loss of Possession.*

Von Vangerow, ss. 202—210.
Savigny, "Besitz.," s. 21, 284 et seq., 77, 119, 128, 185, 237, 274, 328, 372, 388, 406, 420, 475.
" Syst. III., 49.

He who has capacity to own Property, is also capable of acquiring Possession. Hence Juridical Persons, the insane, children, and all who are by nature incapable of exercising free will, have still the capacity to possess. Several Owners cannot possess the same entire thing. This follows from the exclusive nature and character of Possession. The same thing may, however, be owned by several Persons according to ideal parts, provided that the several parts are determined by a juridical fact,* and such parts are known to the Possessor. The severance need not be a physical act, it is not made in the *corpus* itself, but the severance is made entirely in the mind (*animus*). What Persons may acquire.

There are, however, some things which cannot be possessed:— Things which cannot be possessed.

1. Those which cannot be the subject of Property.†
2. All incorporal things.
3. Integral parts, namely, such as essentially belong to one another.
4. Corporal‡ independent parts, the relations of which to the whole is so constituted that their actual control

* For example, joint purchase.

† *Res extra commercium*, etc.

‡ For example, the limbs of an animal cannot be possessed apart from the body of the animal, because they have no separate existence; since only that can be possessed which has a separate independent existence.

apart from the thing itself cannot be conceived of. For example, a person acquires the Possession of a carriage, that is, of a thing consisting of component parts; in which case the acquisition of the Possession of a wheel, *quoad corpus*, is quite permissible. The *animus* might also have been directed to the wheel; but this intention could not be ascertained, because the *corpus* invariably extends to all the parts. Hence the Possessor of the whole is not Possessor of the separate parts, as long as they continue in connection with one another, so as to form constituent elements.* It is different when any one who is already in Possession of a separate thing chooses to combine it with a thing already possessed by him. In this case he possesses the part in the whole, for he has not lost the Possession of the part, either *corpore*, or by giving expression to any *animus non possidendi*.

Conditions of Acquisition of Possession.

The Acquisition of Possession is based upon two conditions:—

1. Upon the Apprehension of the thing, that is, some bodily physical act by which a Person places himself in such relation to the thing, that a consciousness arises in the mind of the Person of physical dominion over the Acquisition.

2. By the intention *(animus)* of having the thing for oneself. Instead of acquiring Possession in one's own person, it may also be obtained through a Representative.† This, it is to be noted, presupposes:

---

* This is a rule of much importance in Usucapion.

† Representatives are Persons who, on account of a definite juridical relation, take the place of another Person. Such, for example, are Guardians, Mandatories, etc., etc.

1. That the Representative acquires the holding of the Property, not with the intention of possessing it himself,* but for the Person whom he may represent.

2. That the party represented in such a case, has the *animus possidendi*. A Substitution, however, only takes place exceptionally in the case of the Acquisition of a Peculium by juridical Persons, and by Persons under the *tutela*. A peculiar mode of Acquisition of Possession by Substitution is that known as the *constitutum possessorium*, which is the declaration of a Juridical Possessor, that for the future he will hold in the name of a third Person, that which he has hitherto held in his own name.

Constitutum possessorium.

Possession is lost *corpore vel animo*, which need not here be cumulative *(possessio amittitur vel corpore vel animo)*. It suffices in reference to one or the other point, *contrarium actum est*. Thus, in respect to the *corpus*, if the Possessor, by any state of things whatever, is effectually barred from exercising physical control over the thing. Still, the Ownership of a piece of ground cannot be forfeited by a third Person taking Possession of it during the absence, nor without the knowledge of the Owner. Possession, however, is first lost when a third party endeavours to prevent the exercise and enjoyment of the Possession ("Dejection"). Possession held for us by a Representative is not lost in the Person of the Representative *corpore*, but it is lost *animo*. † Possession

How Possession is lost.

* There is an exception to this rule. When the Representative has the intention of acquiring for himself or a third Person, but the transferor (*Tradens*) intends to convey to the Representative, in this case the Representative acquires.

† In the case of the Ouster of the owner, the Possession still remains if the Representative continue to maintain himself in it.

exercised by a Representative is lost *corpore* only upon an event happening affecting the Person of the Representative, and causing the loss of the Possession through him, hence not by mere change of mind on the part of the Representative, for example, by an intention on his part to possess (*animus domini*), where he intends to hold for some third party, or by his becoming unfitted for the exercise of the will.

SECTION XV.—*Operation and Protection of Possession.*

Von Vangerow, ss. 335, 336, 295.

Effects of Juridical Possession.

THE following are the effects of Juridical Possession:—

1. The Acquisition of Possession is a mode of acquiring Property.

2. Possession continued for a certain period of time creates Ownership (Usucapion).

3. Possession leading to Usucapion is converted by a fiction of law into Ownership, and is protected by the *Publiciana Actio*.

4. Simple Juridical Possession is protected by the Possessory Interdicts* (*Interdicta Retinendæ* and *Recuperandæ Possessionis*).

Possessory Interdicts.

Disputed Juridical Possession is protected by the *Interdictum Retinendæ Possessionis;* where land is in question, by the *Interdictum Uti Possidetis;* where moveables have to be protected, by the *Interdictum Utrubi*. The object of these Interdicts is to determine which of the

* It has been already stated that the *causa possessionis* was immaterial as regards the existence of a Juridical Possession. From this it follows that the *injustus possessor* has also the possessory remedies allowed him. These are, however, not allowable against the Person from whom the party in possession holds either *vi*, *clam*, or *precario*.

two parties, where both claim the Right of Possession, is entitled to it. The aim of these legal proceedings is preparatory to the suit respecting the Ownership, and they are employed in order to determine which of the parties to the record shall be regarded as the possessor (*petitor*). It must be observed that, from the very nature of the Interdicts already mentioned, results their twofold character (*duplicia*). The same proof is required from both parties when one has obtained the possession *vi*, *clam*, or *precario*, or the other has lost it through one or other of these three vices. The suitor who furnishes the conclusive evidence is successful in the cause. If neither side is able to do this, the strife remains undecided (*nihil agit*); and the party to the suit who is not satisfied with this must have recourse to the *petitorium*. In the case of the *Interdictum Retinendæ Possessionis*, there exists a *Præscriptio Annalis*. If the Person is still in Possession through whom the rightful Possessor has lost his Possession, either *vi*, *clam*, or *precario*, there may be instituted against him, as already stated, the *Interdictum Retinendæ Possessionis*. But if he is no longer in Possession, the *Interdictum Recuperandæ Possessionis* must be employed; and in questions relating to land, the *Interdictum de Vi*.* Against the receiver of a *Precarium*, who is no longer in possession, the *Interdictum de Precario* lies, which is not limited to one year like the *Interdictum Retinendæ Possessionis*. The Donor has it from the time of making the Gift. The *Interdictum*

Præscriptio Annalis.

* This Interdict can only be had recourse to in the case of land, where Juridical Possession existed at the time of its loss, by violence (*Vis atrox, Dejectio*).

proceeds for Restitution and compensation for damages sustained by *dolus* or *culpa lata*. It passes to the heirs *(ad heredes)* of the Donor, and against the *heredes* of the donee; only, however, to the extent that the latter have been benefited.

SECTION XVI.—*Quasi Possession of a Right.*

Von Vangerow, s. 210.
Savigny, s. 44 et seq., p. 574 et seq.
l. 20, Dig. de servit. (8, 1).
l. 7, Dig. de itin. actuque priv. (43, 19).

Effects of Juridical Possession

JURIDICAL Possession consisted in the independent enjoyment of the Property held. The effect of such Possession was to entitle the party to the protection of the Interdicts and to Usucapion. These consequences, however, it must be observed, attached to the exercise of other Rights, namely, Incorporal Rights. A legal relation was created analogous to Possession. This is now designated *juris quasi possessio*. This so-called *quasi possessio* is only possible where permanent Rights exist. Quasi Possession, according to the Roman Law, consists, as we have already stated, in the user of Servitudes or Easements, and in Superficies, or things above the ground. According to the Canon Law, and the German Law, and Custom, other Rights also come under this category.

Quasi Possession.

How acquired.

Quasi Possession is acquired, *corpore et animo*. The actual enjoyment corresponds to the corporal relations.* The *animus* consists in this: That the user is exercised

* In positive Easements, the doing of an act; in negative Easements, the prohibiting of an act.

with a view of acquiring the Right. Quasi Possession is annulled by some adverse proceeding (*contrarium actum*).

Remedies in Quasi Possession.

Quasi Possession is in part protected by the Interdicts of the *corporis possessio;* partly by some peculiar remedies. The Interdicts of the *corporis possessio* are employed in those cases in which the Detention of the thing which constitutes the object of the Right in question, is presumed. Hence in Personal Servitudes they are also applicable to those Rights, the exercise of which is united with the thing for which the Right is appointed.* For a like reason, also in the case of the Positive Servitudes of the *prædia urbana.* For the protection of the Servitudes *prædiorum urbanorum* the Prætor introduced special Interdicts, that is to say, the *Interdictum itinere*, the *Interdictum de aqua*, and the *Interdictum de fonte.* In these Easements, it is true, the Right of enjoyment is coupled with the dominant land; but a hindrance to the exercise of the enjoyment by no means constitutes a disturbance of the Possession of the thing.

Interdicts for the protection of servitudes.

* A disturbance of the enjoyment of a holding is a disturbance of the Possession. The party who disturbs me for the sake of placing a beam in the wall of his neighbour, disturbs my Possession.

BOOK THE FOURTH.

FAMILY RELATIONS.

SECTION XVII.—*Of Marriage.*

Von Vangerow, ss. 211—228.
Arndts, ss. 393—418.
Puchta, ss. 411—429.
Gai. Comm. I., 58—65.
Savigny Syst. II., 13 et seq.; IV., 165 et seq.
Glück, XXII., 375; XXII., 376 et seq.; XXIV. 98, 395, 425 et seq.; XXV., 78 et seq., s. 1242; XXVI. 1253 et seq.; XXVII., s. 1274; XXVIII., 14, 49, et seq.
Instit. de nuptiis (1, 10).
Cod. ,, ,, (5, 4).
Dig. de ritu nuptiarum (23, 2).
Cod. de incestis et inutilibus nuptiis (5, 5).
,, de interdicto matrimonia inter, etc. (5, 6).
,, si quacumque præditus potestate vel, etc. (5, 7).
,, si nuptiæ ex rescripto petantum (5, 8).
Dig. de divortiis et repudiis (24, 2).
Cod. de repudiis et judicio de moribus sublato (5, 17).
Instit. de patria potestate, s. 1, (1, 9).
l. 30, Dig. de R. J.
Dig. de sponsalibus (23, 1).
Cod. ,, ,, et arrhis sponsalitiis (5, 1).
,, si rector provinciæ, etc. (5, 2).
,, de sponsalitiis, etc. (5, 3).
l. 51, Dig. de donationibus inter vir. (24, 1).

Dig. de jure dotium (23, 3).
Cod. de jure dotium (5, 12).
,, de dotis promissione et nuda pollicitatione(5, 11).
Vaticana Frag., s. 115.
l. 77, Dig. de evict. (21, 2).
l. 22, ,, de pactis dotalibus (23, 4).
Dig. soluto matrimonio dos quemadmodum petatur (24, 3).
,, de impensis in res dotal. fact. (25, 1).
Cod. de rei uxoriæ actione etc. (5, 13).
,, soluto matrimonio dos quemadm., etc. (5, 18).
,, ne pro dote mulieris bona, etc. (5, 22).
l. 5, Dig. de divortiis (24, 2).
l. 6, ,, de collatione (37, 6).
Cod. de donationibus ante nuptias vel propter nuptias et sponsalitiis (5, 3).
Dig. de pactis dotalibus (23, 4).
Cod. ,, ,, conventis tam super donatione ante nuptias, etc. (5, 14).
Cod. de donationibus inter virum et uxorem (5, 16).
Dig. de actione rerum amotarum (25, 2).
Cod. de secundis nuptiis (5, 9).
,, si secundo nupserit mulier, cui maritus usumfructum (5, 10).
Nov. 22, c. 22—48.
,, 39, c. 2,

It is sometimes said that Marriage is the foundation of family relationships and family Rights; but Von Vangerow and other jurists are of opinion that this is not correct. The "Patria Potestas" seems to be the root of family relationship. The whole theory of Marriage cannot be developed in a treatise on Modern Roman Law, but chiefly the influence exerted by the marital condition on Property. The forms now observed at the entrance into the marriage state, and the mode by which the marriage bond may be dissolved, Source of Family Relationship belong properly to the Ecclesiastical Law of the Protestant and Roman Catholic Churches, modified, however, by the principles laid down upon this subject in the Canon Law.

Definition of Marriage.

Marriage may be defined as the union of the sexes, voluntarily entered into for the whole period of the lives of the parties, by means of certain prescribed legal forms. Modestinus says, "Nuptiæ sunt conjunctio maris et feminæ, et consortium omnis vitæ, divini et humani juris communicatio." Again, in another passage, he says, "Nuptiæ autem sive matrimonium est viri et mulieris conjunctio, individuam vitæ consuetudinam continens."

Not strictly a legal relation.

Marriage itself, although not strictly a juridical relation, has acquired this characteristic by reason of its great importance, and the wide-spread influence it exercises on all the conditions of social life. Viewed, however, as a legal relation, it is the Right which, by mutual consent and reciprocally, man and wife possess in each other, resulting from their union for life. Hence the maxim of Ulpianus, "Nuptias, non concubitus, sed consensus facit." In reality, the union of the sexes must be regarded as a purely natural relationship, which first becomes of legal importance when it has been entered upon in the form prescribed by law. The resultant effects proceeding from Marriage are the following:—

Resultant effects of Marriage.

1. Those which affect the personal relations of husband and wife to each other.

2. Those which relate to their Property.

3. Those which have reference to their children begotten in wedlock.

From the very earliest times of Rome the monogamic principle which still prevails in the Modern Law has been fully recognised: namely, that one man should be joined only to one woman. In ancient Rome, until the time of the Emperor Justinian, concubinage was permitted, regulated however by the same principle. Concubinage was expressly recognised by the Lex Papia Poppaea. But, even in the case of legal concubinage the monogamic principle always prevailed. The concubine was never an *uxor*, nor a *materfamilias*, and she remained in the same rank, and sustained the same family relations after she became a concubine as before. The wife, however, entered into the rank and dignity of her lawful husband. The children of a concubine were *spurii*, using that term not in its limited, but in its more extensive, signification. They were *liberi naturales*, and were held legally to have no father, but only a mother (*sine patre sunt*). Still, the man who had begotten them was bound to provide alimony for them, and this marked the distinction between the *spurii*, in the strict sense of the term, and the *liberi naturales*. Concubinage was a *licita consuetudo* even long after Rome became Christian, and hence we find Titles in the Digest referring to this relation of the sexes. Further, concubinage was forbidden in the East by Justinian in his Novella 91, and in Germany by the Reichs Polizei-Ordnung passed in 1567 (title 26).

Roman Monogamic principle.

Concubinage.

Concubine Children.

By the ancient Roman Law no special forms were required to constitute Marriage; but simply the consent of the contracting parties. There were, however, forms for Marriage as in the case of *conventio in manum;*

The Ancient Law required no special forms.

but these were marriage *rites*, and not necessary to its validity. Marriage was always *solo consensu*. Hence Paulus says, "Nuptiæ consistere non possunt, nisi consentiant omnes, id est, qui coeunt, quorumque in potestate sunt."

Right of Husband and Wife to Fidelity.

A common Right of both man and wife is their mutual claim to Fidelity. The husband has also a special claim to *reverentia* from his wife; she, on the other hand, claims from him support and protection. She also acquires, as already stated, the name, status, and position of her husband, and becomes subject to his judicial status. Husband and wife cannot institute any *actio famosa* or *pœnalis* against each other, they cannot be compelled to bear witness against each other, nor make a donation to each other during Marriage, and they may both avail themselves of the Plea of competency. The principles of the Roman Law respecting the contracting and dissolution of Marriage are now no longer applicable, we may therefore omit further mention of them. The Roman Law proceeded upon the principle that Marriage did not alter the

Property Relations.

Property relations of man and wife, but it did not carry the doctrine of separation of goods, nor the dotal system, to the utmost limits; for it only extended the privilege subject to certain limitations as regards the Rights of Property after Marriage.

Opposed to this principle is the doctrine of the community of goods, which has been embodied into the judicial systems of France, Holland, the greater portion of the German Empire, and some other countries—a principle, no doubt, originating in the customs of the ancient Teutonic races that overran and conquered Europe.* The *Code Napoléon* gives the amplest expression to this law in the six sections contained under the chapter on the Laws of Marriage.†

Six Sections of the *Code Napoléon.*

These celebrated Six Sections express the Common Law of the land in France, the *Lois Coutumiers* of the Franks.‡ In juxtaposition to this law is that of the *Régime Dotal*, which has all but literally adopted the rules of the Roman Law.§ In dealing with this question as part of the Modern Roman Law, it must not be forgotten that the Codes of those countries, that have incorporated the Civil Law with their juridical systems, have modified the rules that have now to be considered; but they have only modified them, and not materially affected their principles. The Precepts of the Roman Law as regards Family Relations and Marriage may be studied as a sure guide to the right appreciation of the juridical doctrines upon which the Modern Law has been established.

The Dotal System.

According to the Roman Law, as already stated, Marriage does not effect a complete change in the relations of the Property of husband and wife. The Property relationship arising out of Marriage is designated the system of Separate Property, or the Dotal System. By this system the wife retains the Ownership of all that she has acquired during her Marriage. Should she, however, not be able at any time to disclose the source of her acquisitions, a

* Arntzenius Instit. Jur. Bel. Civ., pt. 2, tit. 4, s. 4.

† Code Napoléon—Div. Contrat de Mariage, etc., sects. i. to v., Arts. 1401, 1496.

‡ For an account of the origin of this Law the previous works may be consulted.

§ Code Napoléon, Cap. iii., ss. 1540, 1581. Du Régime Dotal.

Gift by the husband is presumed. This presumption is termed the *Præsumtio Muciana*, and the effect of it is that he may claim these acquisitions. It would, however, be quite erroneous to suppose that Marriage exerts no effect upon Property. On the contrary, property relations exist, which, although they presuppose a constituting act, yet acquire their peculiar legal character by virtue of Marriage. Again, Marriage produces *ipso jure* an effect upon Property. One of the most important of these effects calls for particular notice in this place.

Præsumtio Muciana.

Dos.

1. The *Dos.*—The Marriage Portion, or *Dos*, comprises everything which the wife has contributed, or which has been contributed on her behalf to the husband in aid of the burdens imposed by Marriage. Even an *extraneus* may constitute a *dos*. The *dos* must be an addition to the husband's Property.* It may consist in the creation of a Real Right, or in the remission of one, or in the renunciation of a claim; it matters not in what form it is made, provided the Estate of the husband has become enriched. It follows from the very nature of the *dos* that the use of the things constituting it must be permitted to the husband, and further, that, *sine matrimonio nulla dos*. The *dos* is created from the moment that the Estate of the husband has been increased *dotis nomine*. There exist two modes of constituting a Dowry—*a*. The *Donatio dotis*, as, for instance, when a thing is made over in Ownership, or a Right is assigned, etc.; *b*. The *Promissio dotis* to the husband.

* The marriage outfit, that is to say, the things necessary for the household, may constitute either the entire *dos*, or only a part of it.

Since the *Promissio* founds a Right of Action, and an Action in itself benefits the Estate of the husband, the *Promissio* is regarded as constituting a Dotal Gift. Thus the subsequent *numeratio*, as it is termed, is only the fulfilment or carrying out of the Gift. No Action, however, can be brought before the celebration of the Marriage; and the claim for the Fruits, and for Interest, arises only after the expiration of the second year. Where the father or grandfather on the paternal side has promised a dower, it is not necessary, in order to give to this paternal promise a legal validity, that a particular or detailed specification of the dotal goods should have been rendered. In the case of an *extraneus*, such a promise would not be binding.

Different kinds of Dower.

Generally, the constituting of a *dos* is a voluntary act, when it is termed *dos voluntaria*. Exceptionally, however, certain Persons are obliged to furnish a Dower, in which case it is termed *dos necessaria:* the father, the grandfather, and sometimes the mother, and the *stuprator* of a woman. The *dos* which has been furnished out of the Estate of the father, or by the paternal ascendants, is termed the *profecticia;* the *dos* which an *extraneus* furnishes, under the condition of its being repaid by the husband, is designated *recepticia.* A further classification of the *dos* is that into the *dos venditionis causa æstimata*, and *dos taxationis causa æstimata.* The first arises where the *dos* has been given in such a manner that the husband is required to restore only the estimated value, and not the goods. The husband is said to possess in this case, *pro emptore;* he must bear the risk, and he may claim what is termed "Eviction." It is only when he becomes insolvent that the things themselves, not their value, are to be regarded as the Dotal Property. The *dos taxationis causa* arises where the husband is required to return the property itself given, as a *dos in natura*.

Husband's Right to the *Dos*.

During the continuance of the Marriage the husband is regarded as the Owner of the Dotal Property so fully and completely, that he is legally entitled to its free control and use; and further, he is neither bound to render accounts, nor to find Security. He is, moreover, entitled to employ the *Vindicatio* against every Possessor of the Dotal Property, even against his own wife. He likewise possesses the amplest Right of Alienation, with the exception, however, of the *fundus dotalis*. This he cannot alienate or mortgage, not even with the consent of his wife. Again, he must not effect any alteration in the legal relations of her Real Rights. Such an alteration would be held to take place by the prosecution of any one of the divisory Actions, if Property held in joint Ownership should happen to be given as a *dos*. Thus the husband is precluded from instituting this Action, although a third party might do so. Any Alienation made is void, and the wife may declare it to be void, from and after the time that she becomes entitled to demand the Restitution.

Von Vangerow is of opinion that the husband may even vindicate the alienated *fundus* upon giving indemnity to the defendant. Puchta and others differ from him on this point. There are, however, exceptions to the general rule just given, which must be noted. These are the following:—

1. In the case of a *fundus æstimatus*.

2. When it is certain that the *dos* does not revert to the wife or her heirs.

3. When by a valid *permutatio dotis* something else is given in lieu of the *fundus*.

To these cases the prohibition does not apply.

Collateral with the Rights of the husband already mentioned, and with a view to the future operative Rights of the wife, there is imposed upon him the constant attendant duty of *diligentia*. Moreover, the wife is not altogether without a remedy as regards her *dos*, even during the period of her Marriage. She may claim that the *dos* shall be applied according to its object. She is exempt from providing Real Security, when she expects to receive a piece of ground as a Dotal Gift. She may adopt precautionary measures for the preservation of her *dos;* she may, in case of Eviction, and even during Marriage, look to the Auctor of the *dos*, and she may claim half the Treasure-Trove found on the *fundus dotalis*. If her husband becomes poor, or a bankrupt, the wife is entitled to reclaim her Dower. The Right of the husband to the *dos* is extinguished by the termination of the Marriage, and when this takes place he must return the Dower. He can only retain it when it has been secured to him by agreement. When the death of the husband dissolves the Marriage, the *dos* is claimed by the wife and her heirs, unless, indeed, it has been constituted by a third party, and its return has been stipulated for under this condition. If the Marriage is dissolved by the death of the wife, the heirs are entitled to claim the *dos adventicia*, except when the *extraneus* who has constituted the *dos* has reserved this Right to himself *(dos recepticia)*. But in

Rights of the Wife.

Rights of her Heirs.

the case of the *dos profecticia*, the person who has constituted it takes precedence of the heirs. The father, the heirs, and the wife have also a claim for Restitution, though it may not have been promised to them. As far as relates to land, Restitution must take place immediately upon the dissolution of the marriage, and in the case of Moveable Property within a year. The subject matter for Restitution is what the husband has received *dotis nomine*. To this, however, must be added all Fruits and Accessions before and after the marriage. Fruits acquired during Marriage accrue to the husband. But the question has been asked, who is entitled to take the Fruits of the last dotal year? In this case the Fruits are divided according to the time and duration of the Marriage. Some are of opinion that it is not the Fruits of the dotal year, but the Fruits gathered during the year of harvest that are to be apportioned. The husband, on his part, is, however, entitled to claim compensation for his outlays on the Dotal Property.

Dotal Fruits.

Husband's claim for *Impensæ*.

Impensæ necessariæ, as they are termed, diminish the *dos*, *ipso jure*. Still, the husband has no Right of Retention for *impensæ utiles* and *voluptuariæ*, but he is permitted to avail himself of the *Actio mandati*, the *Actio negotiorum gestorum*, and has also a *jus tollendi*. The Action which lies for the Restitution of the *dos* is *Actio ex stipulatu*. This Action was given by the ancient Law only when Restitution was stipulated for, otherwise the Action given was that of the *Actio rei Uxoriæ*, which never passed to the heirs. The Plaintiff is the party entitled to obtain the Restitution; the Defendant, the husband and his heirs. In addition to the above, the wife has the *Actio hypothecaria* by virtue of her legal mortgage, and also the *Actio in rem* against every Possessor of her Dotal Property. The Property which the wife has brought to her husband upon her Marriage, but not by way of Dower, is termed her *Paraphernalia.* As to this Estate, her Ownership and her control remain undiminished.

2. The *Donatio Propter Nuptias* (or, to employ the Byzantine name, the *Antipherna*).—This, in its nature, is analogous to the *dos*, and it consists of that complex of Property which is brought in by the husband for the relief of the burdens imposed by Marriage. The wife, on her part, has a legal Right of Mortgage to the same; and if the Marriage be dissolved by the fault of the husband, the *donatio* reverts to her. This custom, however, has now become obsolete. *Donatio Propter Nuptias (or Antipherna).*

3. The relations of Property subsisting between the husband and the wife, however, may be otherwise regulated. The Agreements by which this is effected are termed "*pacta dotalia.*" By these, for instance, it may be determined that the husband shall have during the Marriage the Ownership, the Usufruct, and the control of the *Paraphernalia.* Such *pacta dotalia* do not require any particular form, and they may be concluded upon, before, at the time, or after the celebration of the Marriage itself. They must not, however, contain anything repugnant to the aim and object of the Marriage contract itself, nor must they be opposed to good morals, nor be contrary to the purport of the *dos*, so as to diminish or endanger the Rights of either the husband or the wife in regard to it. For example, the *pacta* must not exclude the *Pacta Dotalia.*

Right to competency, nor the claim for compensation, nor the Right to the enjoyment of the Fruits, nor liability incurred for *culpa*, nor the deferring the legal period for Restitution, etc.

Effects of Marriage on Property.

After the above explanation of the various legal rules exerting an influence upon the Property relations of the husband and the wife, it becomes necessary to consider the effects which Marriage has *ipso jure* upon these relations themselves.

Donations Void.

1. All Donations between husband and wife are void, and that not only between the husband and the wife, but if made to any person who is connected with the husband by the bond of the *patria potestas*. The Donor can not only vindicate the things given, but he or she may even vindicate those things that have been purchased with any money given. Where the things donated are no longer in existence, their value may be recovered by means of the *Condictio* to the extent that the Donee has been benefitted. But according to an *Oratio Severi*, the Gift convalesces, or becomes valid, if not revoked prior to the death of the Donor. Puchta maintains that the same holds good in regard to promises of Donations, but Von Vangerow denies this. It is, however, Gifts only that are void, not other acts of liberality. Again, Donations are allowed that do not impoverish the Donor, nor enrich the Donee; also, reciprocal Gifts, and Donations made for the purpose of the reconstruction of buildings in a state of ruin.

No *Actio Furti* between Husband and Wife.

2. Neither husband nor wife can institute against each other the *Actio furti*. Both husband and wife must strike out the element of theft, and choose an Action proper and suitable to the circumstances of

the case. To this important rule there are only two exceptions:—*a*. Where the purloinment takes place at the very moment of a contemplated separation; in this case the *Actio rerum amotarum* is given. *b*. Where it occurred before marriage, and divorce subsequently takes place, in which case the *Condictio furtiva* lies.

3. When husband or wife gives to the other a just cause of separation, the guilty party suffers a pecuniary penalty. The guilty wife loses her *dos*, so far as she might have reclaimed it after the dissolution of the Marriage; where no *dos* has been constituted, she loses one fourth of her Property, the Ownership of which goes to the children, the Usufruct to the father. In the case of the wife's adultery the penalty is increased to a third. The guilty husband loses the *Donatio propter nuptias*, and when none has been constituted he forfeits one fourth of his Property in favour of his children, the mother having the enjoyment of the Usufruct. When there are no children, the Property goes in both cases to the innocent husband or the innocent wife, as the case may be. **Penalties imposed on Husband and Wife.**

4. *Prejudice to Property* arising from a second Marriage, or, as it is termed, "*Pœnae secundarum nuptiarum.*" *a*. The husband or wife entering upon a second Marriage sacrifices whatever he or she has received by virtue of the first Marriage, whether by inheritance or from some other beneficial source. *b*. The husband or wife who proceeds to a second Marriage, loses also all Property in that which he or she has inherited, or which he may inherit from a child, *ab intestato*, so far as it has been derived from the Property of the deceased husband or wife. The **Penalty upon Second Marriage.**

Property goes in these cases to the children of the first marriage, according to the principle regulating Succession by Intestacy. The party marrying a second time retains, however, the Usufruct. *c.* The husband or wife entering upon a second Marriage, cannot give to the second spouse more than the minimum amount (*inter vivos* or *mortis causa*) reserved to a child of the first Marriage. Whatever has been given in excess of this, is divisible amongst the children of the first Marriage. *d.* The *Binubus* or *Binuba* cannot revoke any Gift made to the children of the first Marriage for any given reason, excepting only where the child has made an attempt upon the life of the parent, or has actually outraged the parent, or has caused the parent loss of Property. *e.* The *Binuba* loses the Guardianship and Right of the bringing up of the child. *f.* When the *Parens binubus* has been instituted as the heir, and the children as legatees, the *Parens* is no longer exempt from the liability to find Security.

5. Prejudices by a violation of the year of mourning. A woman who re-marries within a year of the dissolution of her previous marriage, either by the death of her husband or by divorce, is subject to the following disadvantages:—She suffers *infamia*. This, however, has been abolished by the Canon Law. She sacrifices in favour of the nearest relatives of her husband all she may have received from him; she cannot possibly give more than one-third of her fortune to her second husband; she cannot acquire Property either by Gift or Legacy, and can only inherit from relatives *ab intestato* as far as the third degree. Should there be children of the first Marriage, in addition to

these penalties, the general consequences of a second marriage take place.

SECTION XVIII.—*Rights of Parents and Child.*

Von Vangerow, s. 228.
Arndts, s. 419.
Puchta, ss. 430—431.
Dig. de agnoscendis et alendis liberis (25, 3).
,, de inspiciendo ventre custodiendoque partu (25, 4).

Right of Mother and Child.

A CHILD may employ the *Actio de partu agnoscendo* against his parents for the acknowledgment of his relationship. The mother may avail herself of this Action, but she sacrifices this Right if she fail to give notice of her pregnancy to her husband, or to the person in whose *potestas* he is, within thirty days after the dissolution of Marriage, for it is only in this case that the rule of the *Senatus consultum Plancianum* applies. Actions for Infamy, or Actions based upon *dolus*, cannot be instituted by children against their parents; nor can the *Jusjurandum calumniæ* be demanded from a parent. Parents also have the *Beneficium competentiæ* against their children.

SECTION XIX.—*The Patria Potestas, or Paternal Power.*

Von Vangerow, ss. 229—260.
Arndts, ss. 420—438.
Puchta, ss. 432—445.
Gai. Comm. I., 55.
Glück XIV., 423 et seq., 267, 400, 302, 317; XXVIII., 183; XXXV., 190 et seq.
Instit., de patria potestate (1, 9).
Cod. ,, ,, ,, (8, 47).

Dig. de his. qui sui vel alieni juris sunt (1, 6).
Cod. de donationibus, etc., a parentibus in liberos factis (5, 16).
s. 6, Instit. de inutil. stipul. (3, 19).
l. 2 pr., Dig. de contr. emt. (18, 1).
l. 4, „ de judic. (5, 1).
l. 16, „ de furt. (47, 2).
l. 56, s. 1, de fidejussorib. et mandat. (46, 1).
l. 38, s. 1, 2 de condict. indeb. (12, 6).
Dig. de peculio (15, 1).
l. 31, s. 2, Dig. de donatib. (39, 5).
l. 1, s. 5, Dig. de adqu. v. am. poss. (41, 2).
l. 3, s. 4, Dig. de minor. (4, 4).
Dig. de castrensi peculio (49, 17).
Cod. de castrensi peculio militum et præfectianorum (12, 37).
„ de castrensi omnium palitinorum peculio (12, 31).
„ de bonis maternis et materni generis (6, 60).
„ de bonis, quæ liberis in potestate constitutis, etc. (6, 61).
s. 4, Instit. de inutil. stipulat. (3, 19).
l. 130, Dig. de V.O. (45, 1).
l. 141, Dig., s. 2, de V.O.
l. 57 pr., Dig. de judic. (5, 1).
l. 39, „ de O. et A. (44, 7).
l. 44, 45, „ de peculio (15, 1).
l. 1, s. 9, „ de separat. (42, 6).
Instit. quod cum eo, qui in aliena potestate est. (4, 7).
Dig. quod cum eo, qui in aliena, etc. (14, 5).
Cod. „ „ „ (4, 26).
Dig. quod jussu. (15, 4).
„ de peculio (15, 1).
„ quando de peculio actio annalis est. (15, 2).
„ de tributaria actione (14, 4).
„ de in rem verso (15, 3).
„ de S.C. Macedoniano (14, 6).
Cod. ad S.C. Macedonianum (4, 28).
Dig. de liberis exhibendis item ducendis (43, 30).
Cod. de liberis exhibendis seu de ducendis, et de homine libero exhibendo (8. 8).

l. 1, s. 2, de R. V. (6, 1).
Instit. de adoptionibus (1, 11).
,, de adquisitione per arrogationem (3, 10).
Dig. de adoptionibus et eman. (1, 7).
Cod. ,, ,, (8, 48).
l. 7, Cod. de hered. instit. (6, 24).
Instit., de acquisitione per arrog. (3, 10).
Gai. Comm. I., 101, 102.
Cod. de naturalibus liberis et matribus eorum, etc. (5, 27).
Nov. 74, 89.
Instit. quibus modis jus potestatis solvitur (1, 12).
Dig. de, etc. emancipationibus et aliis modis, etc. (1, 12).
Cod. de emancip. liberorum (8, 49).
Dig. de obsequiis parentibus et patronis præstandis. (37, 15).
Dig. de agnoscendis et alendis liberis vel parentibus, etc. (25, 3).
Cod. de alendis liberis ac parentibus (5, 25).

Rights of the Father

THE special Rights which belong to the father by virtue of the *patria potestas* relate in part to the Person and in part to the Property of the children. As far as relates to the Person, he has the Right of administering correction; the Right of appointing Guardians by a Testament; the Right of what is denominated Pupillary Substitution, and of sanctioning Marriage; the Right to demand an acknowledgment of the paternal authority, for which purpose there is given him the *Actio de patria potestas;* and, finally, the Right to prohibit the detention of the child subject to his power. To secure this last Right there is given to him the *Interdictum de liberis ducendis*. In regard to the child's Property, this Right extends to the *Peculium* of his children. By *Peculium* is to be understood that complex of Property which the father permits his child to have for his own free administration. According to the most ancient Law, all the acquisitions

Peculium, and the Rights of Father and Child to its enjoyment.

of the child went *ipso jure* to the father; by the modern Law the child retains his acquisitions for himself. From this, however, is to be excepted what the child acquires *ex substantia patris*, which belongs entirely to the father, either in absolute Ownership or in Usufruct. This is the so-termed *Peculium profecticium*. All other acquisitions fall into the Ownership of the child; but the father is entitled to enjoy their Usufruct. Upon this point we must distinguish between *bona adventicia* on the one side, and *bona castrensia*, the *bona quasi castrensia*, and *adventicia irregularia*, on the other. On *bona castrensia vel quasi*, that is to say, on the Property acquired by a *filius familias*, either as a soldier, a public officer, an advocate, a clergyman, or by gift from the Prince or Princess, the father has the Exclusive Usufruct. On the *bona adventicia*, that is, Property otherwise acquired, the father has also the Usufruct. To this category, moreover, especially belong the *bona materna* and *materni generis* of the children; their *lucra nuptialia*, and all that may possibly revert to them, upon either the father or mother entering into a second marriage.

Right of Son to the Usufruct of it.

As to the *bona adventicia* there are several exceptions, where the son is entitled to the Usufruct:—

1. Where a Gift has been made to a child subject to this condition.

2. In the case where the child makes some acquisition against the will of the father.

3. Where the child of a *furiosus* takes an Inheritance.

4. Where the father is required to make an immediate Restitution of a Testamentary Trust, on the termination of the *patria potestas*, in consequence of his bad management.

That which a child acquires in these four instances is termed *bonum adventicium irregulare*. The difference between *adventicium irregulare* and *castrensia vel quasi castrensia* is as follows: That the son is only regarded in reference to the latter as a *pater familias*. It is only as regards this that he has the right of testamentary Disposition and Power to enter into a legal transaction with his father. During the continuance of the *patria potestas*, any existing obligatory relations entered into between the father and the son can exert no influence whatever either upon the one or the other. After the termination of the *patria potestas*, such relations operate only as *naturales obligationes*, and that with respect to the fate of the *peculium*. But as regards the *bona castrensi*, or *vel quasi*, the son, viewed in his relation to the father, is regarded as if he were a stranger. *Bonum adventicium irregulare.*

The *Patria Potestas* may be acquired— How *Patria Potestas* may be acquired.

1. By Conception in lawful and valid wedlock.

2. By Legitimisation; the father of an illegitimate child may bring the child under his *potestas* by subsequently marrying the mother. In such a case there arises what is denominated a *Legitimatio per subsequens matrimonium*, or by the Rescript of the Sovereign, which is termed *Legitimatio per rescriptum Principis*.

3. By Adoption and Arrogation. By the former is to be understood that legal transaction by virtue of which a Person who has been already subjected to the *patria potestas* is brought under the *potestas* of another. By the second is to be understood that legal transaction by which a Person who is *sui juris*, or in his own *potestas*, is brought under the *patria potestas* of another. In both these cases it is always and absolutely necessary Adoption and Arrogation.

that the Person desiring to adopt should be capable of doing so. Those Persons are incapable who are absolutely impotent; and also, those who are not at least eighteen years older than the party adopted. That is to say, there must be the *pubertas plena* on the part of the *pater adoptans;* and, finally, what is termed an Adoption *ad diem* is not allowable. These propositions are founded upon the rule *Adoptio imitatur naturam.* The doctrine just explained rests upon the special grounds that no one can adopt who has children of his own, unless, indeed, the Adoption does not operate as an injury to his own children; that a Guardian shall not, before rendering his accounts, arrogate his Ward; that the poor shall not adopt the rich; that the father shall not adopt his illegitimate child.

Who cannot Adopt.

Requisites for Arrogation.

For Arrogation, it is especially necessary that he who arrogates should have acquired an advanced age; that the Person to be arrogated should acquiesce, and if he be a minor, that a prior investigation should determine the desirability of the Arrogation. Further, in the case where the party arrogated is a minor, security shall be given by the Arrogator that in the event of the death of the minor before attaining his majority, the Property belonging to him shall be handed over to those to whom it would have come if the Arrogation had not taken place.

Effects of Arrogation.

The effects of Arrogation are—

1. The Arrogator acquires the *patria potestas.*

2. The party arrogated steps into all the Rights of a *filius familias*, but suffers a *capitis deminutio*, because he ceases to be a *pater familias.* These results were, by the ancient Roman Law, connected with the act

of Adoption. But by the Emperor Justinian it was ordained that where the natural father gave up his son or his daughter to another person in Adoption, the ancient effects should only take place when the *pater adoptans* was the natural ascendant of the child. Otherwise the child continued under the *potestas*, and in the family of its natural father; and only in the case where the *pater adoptans* died during the period of the Adoption did the child have an intestate Right in the Estate of the adoptive parent.* This principle is, however, limited to the case of Adoption, and is not applicable to that of Arrogation, and the adopted child of a woman holds a similar relation, for women cannot possibly possess the *patria potestas*. This relationship is termed *Adoptio minus plena*. In German Law, when the natural parents receive back the adopted child *as a child* into the family, the *Adoptio minus plena* is dissolved. Finally, it is to be observed in respect to the formal part of Adoption, that it must be made in the presence of the competent authorities. Arrogation by the Rescript of the Prince must be so effected that the Adoption shall not take place in opposition to the wish of the person adopted; and as regards Arrogation, the consent of the person to be arrogated, or that of his Tutor, is necessary. In the mode employed to express dissent it is implied that it is not necessary that *formal* assent should be given.

How the *Patria Potestas* is dissolved.

The *Patria Potestas* is dissolved :—

1. When the *pater familias* to whom it appertains dies, or suffers a *capitis deminutio*, either *maxima* or

* The proceedings in Court are commenced by protocol.

media; when the grandchildren fall under the *potestas* of their father, he having been, till the death of the grandfather, under his father's *potestas.*

2. When the child who was subject to the *patria potestas* dies, or suffers the *capitis deminutio maxima* or *media.*

3. When the son attains some high official position.

4. When the father forfeits his Right by exposing his son, or by pandering for his daughter.

5. When the father allows himself to be arrogated, in which case, the Arrogator himself acquires the *potestas.*

6. When, by Adoption, the *potestas* passes to the adoptive father.

7. By the Emancipation of the child.

Definition of Emancipation.

Emancipation is that act by which the father, under public authority, releases his child from his *potestas,* with a view to his child becoming *sui juris.* The form of this transaction is either a declaration on the part of the father, in the presence of a competent judge, and in the presence of the child, which is termed the *Emancipatio Justinianea;* or the declaration made by the Regent, upon the petition of the father, which is denominated *Emancipatio Anastasiana.* The requisites for Emancipation are :—

Requisites for Emancipation.

1. The consent of the father, save where he ill-treats the child, or has accepted a legacy which has been bequeathed to him, subject to the condition of his emancipating his child; or where the *impubes* who has been adopted or arrogated, upon subsequently attaining his majority, proves that he has been damnified by the Adoption or the Arrogation.

2. The consent of the child, except where it is an adopted child, or an *infans*.

According to German Law, the Paternal Power is also terminated when the son supports his own home, and when the daughter marries. This is termed the *Emancipatio Germanica*.

SECTION XX.—*Guardianship*.

Von Vangerow, ss. 261—294.
Arndts, ss. 439—462.
Puchta, ss. 321—358.
Gai. Comm. I., 142—200, pp. 142—202 (Tomkins and Lemon's edit.)
Glück XXVIII., 435; XXVIII., 468 et seq.; XXIX., 1 et seq., 50, 199 et seq., 253, 315, 400; XXIX., 173, 184; XXX., 1, 253 et seq.; XXXI., 41, 55, 161; XXXII., 3 et seq., 107, 293, 444; XXXIII., 73 et seq., 199, 259 et seq.
Instit. I., 13—26. Dig. XXVI., XXVII.
Cod. V., 28—75.
l. 2 pr., s. 1, Dig. de tutelis (26, 1).
Instit. de tutelis (1, 13).
" qui testamento tutores dari possunt. (1, 14).
Dig. de testamentaria tutela (26, 2).
Cod. " " (5, 28).
s. 2, Instit. qui test. tut. dari poss.
s. 27, Instit. de legat. (2, 20).
Dig. de confirmando tutore (26, 3).
Cod. " " (5, 29).
Dig. de legitimis tutoribus (26, 4).
Cod. de legitima tutela (5, 30).
Instit. de legitima agnatorum tutela (1, 15).
Cod. quando mulier tutelæ officio fungi potest. (5, 35).
Cod. si mater indemnitatem prom. (5, 46).
Nov. 118, c. 5.
l. 11 pr., de testam. tut. (26, 2).
Instit. de legitima parentum tutela (1, 18).

Instit. de fiduciaria tutela (1, 19).
Gai. Comm. I., 188, 175, 185.
Instit. de Atiliano tutore et eo qui etc. (1, 20).
Dig. de tutoribus et curatoribus datis ab his, qui jus dandi habent (26, 5).
Dig. qui petant tutores vel curatores et ubi petantur (26, 6).
Cod. qui petant tutores, etc. (5, 31).
Cod. qui dare tutores vel cur., etc. (5, 34).
Instit. de excusationibus tutorum vel curatorum (1, 25.)
Dig. de excusationibus (27, 1).
Cod. „ „ etc. (5, 62).
„ si tutor vel curator falsis alleg., etc. (5, 63).
„ „ „ rei publicæ, etc. (5, 64).
„ de excusationibus veteranorum, (5, 65).
„ qui numero liberorum se excusant (5, 66).
„ qui morbo se excusant (5, 67).
„ qui ætate se excusant (5, 68).
„ qui numero tutelarum (5, 69).
Vaticana fragmenta tit. IV. de excusatione, ss. 123—248.
l. 1, s. 5, Dig. quando appelland. sit. (49, 4).
Instit. de satisdatione tutorum vel curatorum (1, 24).
Dig. rem pupilli vel adolescentis salvam fore. (46, 6).
Cod. de tutore vel curatore, qui satis non dedit (5, 42).
l. 7, s. 1, Dig. de curat. fur. (27, 10).
Dig. de administratione et periculo tutorum (26, 7).
Cod. de administratione tutorum vel curatorum (5, 37).
Dig. ubi pupillus educari morari debeat (27, 2).
Cod. ubi pupilli educari debeant (5, 49).
Cod. de alimentis pupillo praestandis (5, 50).
Dig. de rebus eorum, qui sub tutela vel cura sunt (27, 9).
Cod. de prediis et aliis rebus minorum sine decreto, etc. (5, 71).
„ quando decreto opus non est. (5, 72).
„ si quis ignorans rem minoris esse (5, 73).
„ si major factus alienationem factam, etc. (5, 74).
Nov. 72, c. 5, 6, 7.
Instit. de auctoritate tutorum (1, 21).
Dig. de auctoritate et consensu tutorum et curat. (26, 8).
Cod. de auctoritate praestanda (5, 59).

Dig. quando ex facto tutoris vel curatoris (26, 9).
Cod. ,, ,, ,, (5, 39).
l. 17, s. 1, Dig. de solut. (46, 3).
l. 3, s. 1, Dig. ad adm. et peric. (26, 7).
s. 1, Instit. de satisdatione tutor. et curat. (1, 24).
Cod. de dividenda tutela (5, 52).
Dig. de tutelæ actione (27, 3).
,, de contraria tutelæ et utili actione (27, 4).
,, de heredibus tutorum et curatorum, etc. (27, 7).
Cod. arbitrium tutelæ (5, 51).
,, de heredibus tutorum et curatorum (5, 54).
,, de contrario judicio tutelæ (5, 58).
Dig. de tutelæ et rationibus distrahendis (27, 3).
,, de fidejussoribus et nominatoribus (27, 7).
Cod. si mater indemnitatem promisit (5, 46).
Dig. de magistratibus conveniendis (27, 8).
Cod. ,, ,, (5, 75).
Instit. quibus modis tutela finitur (1, 22).
Cod. quando tutores vel curatores esse desinant (5, 60).
Instit. de suspectis tutoribus vel curatoribus (1, 26).
Dig. eod. tit. (26, 10).
Cod. eod. tit. (5, 43).
Dig. de eo, qui pro tutore prove curatore negotia gessit (27, 5).
Cod. eod. tit. (5, 45).
Dig. quod falso tutore auctore gestum esse dicatur (27, 6).
,, de curatoribus furioso et aliis extra etc. (27, 10).
Cod. de curatore furiosi vel prodigi. (5, 70).
l. 3, s. 1, Dig. de tutelis (26, 1).
l. 12, pr. 1, Dig. de tutor. et curator. dat. (26, 5).
Dig. de curatore bonis dando (42, 7).
,, de ventre in poss. mittendo etc. (37, 9).

THE Romans had no express term to designate what we denominate Guardianship, but they employed the words *Tutela* and *Cura*, as denoting *species* of an undefined genus. What the modern Germans name *Vormundschaft*, and we call Guardianship, originated in the necessity, which must have been early felt, that

Introductory.

Nature of Guardianship.

persons needing protection on account of their inexperience or weakness should be aided or protected by the laws of the State. Guardianship exists for the benefit of those persons who are indeed *sui juris*, but who, nevertheless, on account of youth, or for some other reason, are incapable of taking care of themselves, or controlling properly their own affairs. Puchta was of opinion that its proper position in the systematic treatment of the Law is under the head of Obligations. Guardianship has lost the character which it originally possessed in ancient Rome, of being a strictly family Right, but it continues to retain its original characteristics of being a family duty. Even the person who has been nominated as a Guardian assumes somewhat the character of the parent of the Ward. The peculiar nature of Guardianship can only be explained when viewed from the stand-point of family connection. It is for this reason that it becomes necessary to treat of the theory and doctrine of Guardianship, under the category of Family Law.

Two kinds, *Cura* and *Tutela*.

As already intimated, two kinds of Guardianship exist, namely, *Tutela* and *Cura*. Both kinds possess this feature, that they are strictly public appointments, by virtue of which the holder of the office is called upon to administer and conduct the affairs connected with the Property of a third party, who is himself incapable of doing so on account of certain personal disqualifications. This definition gives the notion contained in the species of Guardianship designated *Cura*. In order that Guardianship may exist in the form known as the *Tutela*, it is essential that an *impubes* should be the Ward, whose personal incapacity to act for himself the Guardian removes by supplying the defect in his Ward's personality. The *Auctoritatis interpositio*, as it is called, which is the characteristic function of the *Tutor*, distinguishes it from that of the *Curator*. A Tutor is appointed to take charge of an *impubes* who has become free from the *patria potestas*. A Curator is appointed for an *impubes* under certain circumstances, as also for *puberes minores*, *furiosi*, *prodigi*, and incapacitated persons; for the last, however, only at their own request. Where, however, *puberes minores* already possess a Tutor, no other person is appointed as the Curator, but the Tutor becomes the Curator. The person is not changed, but the office; the sphere of action is altered when the *Auctoritatis interpositio* is abrogated.

Function of the *Tutor*.

Creation of Tutelage; and kinds of *Tutela*.

A Tutelage is created either by testamentary disposition, or by law, or by magisterial appointment. The testamentary Tutela (*Tutela testamentaria*) requires that the Minor should be in the power of the testator; that the Tutor should possess the *testamenti factio*, and that he should be nominated in a testament, or in a confirmed codicil. When such is the case, it is a *Tutela testamentaria perfecta*. When, however, the testator has no power over the Minor, the Authorities in many instances will confirm the appointment; as for instance, when the father has appointed a Tutor for an emancipated Minor, or a Tutor has been appointed by the mother, or where a Tutor has been appointed by any one for the person whom he has instituted as his heir. But such Tutela, which is termed the *Tutela testamentaria imperfecta*, first becomes operative upon the obtaining of a confirmatory decree. The *Tutela legitima* proceeds upon the principle that the nearest intestate heir of the Minor, who is capable of accepting the responsibility, is bound to accept the office. The *Tutela* by magisterial decree, or as it is termed, *Tutela dativa,* occurs where a Tutor is needed for some special business, or where no testamentary or legally nominated Guardian exists. Of these three kinds of *Tutela* the testamentary takes the precedence of the other two. The *Tutela* by operation of law *(Tutela legitima)* does not come into existence until it has been decided that no testamentary *Tutela* exists. Until this is determined, and for the intermediate time, a *Tutor dativus* is appointed; so also if the legal Tutor should be for a time prevented from accepting the office. In the event of no Tutor being appointed by testament, and also where no legal Tutor accepts the office, one is immediately appointed by the lawful Authorities.

Appointment of *Curator.*

The foundation upon which the appointment of a Curator rests, is in every case the decree of the proper Authorities. But the nomination of a Curator in a testament by a father or a mother will be confirmed by the Court, provided no grounds for objection exist.

Petitio tutoris sive curatoris.

For the appointment of a Guardian all Persons are entitled to petition who have a legal interest in the nomination, and such an application is termed *Petitio tutoris,* or *curatoris.* The persons liable for the office, where the above decline to accept the *Tutela* or *Cura,* are the heirs by intestacy. Should they fail to undertake the duty within the space of a year, they forfeit their Right of Inheritance. Persons incapable of Guardianship are the following:—

1. Women, except a mother and a grandmother.
2. Bishops and monks.
3. Soldiers.
4. Minors.

Persons incapable of Guardianship.

Not absolutely incapable, but, nevertheless, persons not deemed admissible to the office of Guardianship are: *Furiosi, Muti, Surdi, Prodigi.* The appointment of such persons to the duties of Guardianship is indeed valid, and can only be set aside by the decree of the Court. Such persons are also superseded when these disqualifications arise after their entering upon Guardianship. Moreover, certain persons are excluded from certain kinds of Guardianship. That party is excluded who obtrudes himself into the office. Again, those persons are excluded who, at the time of the making of the appointment, were either creditors or debtors of the Ward. If the father or mother has forbidden a person from being appointed, such person cannot be installed. The bridegroom cannot be the Guardian of his bride, nor the husband that of his wife.

Duty to accept the office.

As Guardianship is a *munus publicum*, every one qualified to become a Guardian is bound to accept the office, with the exception of the mother and the grandmother. There are, however, several legal grounds of Excuse, or *excusationes*, as they are termed, by which a person may relieve himself from the duties of Guardianship. Other grounds of Excuse give an absolute Right to decline a proffered Guardianship. These must be carefully noted—

Grounds of Excuse.

1. The holding of some public or clerical office.
2. The administration of the affairs of the Prince or the Fiscus.

3. Admission into the Privy Council of the Prince.

4. Absence on business on behalf of the State.

5. The holding of a public post of instruction, or one connected with science or art, or that of a practising physician.

6. Also, if a man has three, four, or five children born in wedlock, and still living in Rome or in Italy, or in the Provinces.

7. The administration of three *Tutelae* in the same family, so far as the *paterfamilias* is liable.

8. Poverty or sickness, or having attained seventy years of age.

9. Inability to read and write, and the want of business knowledge where this is required.

10. The removal of the residence of the Guardian from the place where he has been called to discharge the duties of the Guardianship.

11. Where the Property to be administered lies at too great a distance for its administration.

12. When the nomination of the Guardian has been made from a feeling of hatred.

13. When a dispute exists in regard to the Inheritance between the person nominated and the Ward.

Grounds of Resignation.

There are also grounds of Excuse which give the Right to a Guardian of resigning a Guardianship already undertaken. These are—

1. Removal to a distance beyond the seas upon business on behalf of the State.

2. Admission to the Privy Council of the Prince.

3. Poverty and sickness.

4. Change of Domicile with the consent of the Prince, provided the Regent is aware of the

Guardianship. All these excuses must be pleaded before the Court of Wardship within fifty days, reckoning from the day that the event becomes known. Within four months they must be proved. During the procedure, grounded upon the alleged Excuse, an *ad interim* Guardian is appointed. The Rights and duties of the Guardian date from the very moment that he has notice of his appointment. His chief duties are— Duties of a Guardian.

1. To obtain a decree of the Court, by which his appointment as Tutor or Curator becomes legalised; by virtue of which the administration is made over to him, whether it be a *tutorium* or a *curatorium*.

2. To take the oath of office of Guardian.

3. To furnish adequate and proper Security.

4. To draw up an Inventory.

After this his care for the *Person* and the *Property* of the Ward commences. The duties as to the Person of the Ward are to defend, to nurture, and to train him, which duties he fulfils under the inspection and with the co-operation of the Court. Whilst, however, this is the rule the paternal direction must always be regarded. The most important function of the Guardian is that of the administration of his Ward's Property. He is answerable only for *diligentia in concreto*, but he becomes liable for *omnis culpa* when he has obtruded himself into the office of Guardianship. He must, according to the German Law, render his accounts every year. The ruling and chief principle of his administration must be that he must take care both to preserve and to increase the Property of his Ward. Hence he must not allow anything to perish, a rule Care of the *Person* and *Property* of the Ward.

which renders it imperative upon him to dispose of all perishable articles; he must collect outlying capital in due time; and invest incoming moneys in good securities. Money in hand he is obliged to invest within six months; newly acquired income within two months. He must further cultivate, or let immoveable Property, and he must, as much as possible, limit the expenses of his administration. Acts of liberality are forbidden, except where the withholding of the liberality might subject the Ward to disgrace. He must likewise pay his Ward's debts without waiting to be sued by process of law. The Right of Alienation which also appertains to the Administration of the Guardian, and which was unrestricted by Ancient Law, has been so curtailed by the Modern Law that the Guardian is not at present allowed to alienate anything without a decree of the Court. Moreover, Alienation must be taken in its widest signification, as including every alteration in the real legal relations of the Ward. As for instance, an acquisition with a *reservatio hypothecæ*.

Restricted Right of Alienation.

Right of Pupil to the *Vindicatio*.

Any Alienation in violation of a prohibition is void, and the Pupil may vindicate the things alienated upon the payment of their price, so far as the Alienation has benefitted his Estate.

The following is the evidence required to be given: The Minor must prove that the property belonged to him. The Defendant must prove that the Alienation was made by the permission of the authorities. The Ward must further prove the defect in such alleged authority where he intends to protect himself by this Plea.

Excepted from this restriction upon Alienation are—

1. Fruits and surplus and perishable things. What the Guardian may Alienate.

2. When the Alienation is allowed by the Testator.

3. Things whose sale the Regent authorises.

4. When the Plaintiff affirms the Alienation on oath.

5. When the sale has been compulsory; as, for example, where one *socius* demands the *dissolutio* of a *communio*.

6. Property which has been mortgaged to the Ward, when he could not otherwise obtain money.

A sale originally void may convalesce— How a Sale may Convalesce

1. By the ratification of the Minor upon his obtaining his majority.

2. Where the Ward succeeds to the Inheritance of the Guardian, or the latter to that of the Ward.

3. By Prescription, after the expiration of five years.

Transactions appertaining to the administration of the Guardianship are undertaken either by the Guardian in the place of the Ward, or by the Ward himself, in those cases where such a representation is allowable. In the latter instance, however, a distinction has to be made between the *Impubes* and the person under a *Curator*. Where a person acts under the *cura* he does not need co-operation on the part of the Curator, but simply his assent, which, in the case of the Curator's absence, may be given either before or after the the transaction. But where an *Impubes* is required to transact any business, the co-operation of the Tutor is required, and his *auctoritatis interpositio*, by means of which a natural act or transaction is converted into a juridical one. *Auctoritatis Interpositio.*

In the case of utter incapacity to transact business,

as where the Ward is an *infans* or a *furiosus*, there can be no completion of the legal person by the *Auctoritatis interpositio*. The Tutor, who interposes his authority, must be present at the time of the transaction of the business, and must give his assent forthwith, clearly, in express and verbal utterance. Hence it follows that the Tutor cannot interpose his authority in a transaction by which he himself is to derive an advantage *(Ipse tutor in rem suam fieri non potest)*.

Tutor *gerens* or *honorarii.*

Where there are several Tutors, the interposition of the authority of one suffices. Where there are several Guardians, the administration may be preferentially entrusted to one. This person is called the *tutor gerens*, the others are termed *honorarii*. These have to find Security just like the *tutor gerens*, and are liable as he is. The *Tutela* may also be subdivided into divisions and subdivisions, or as the Germans denominate it, into *Regionen und Branchen*, in which case each Tutor, as far as regards the sphere of action of the others, holds the place of the *Tutela honoraria*. By the administration of the *Tutela* the Guardian may become civilly liable.

Obligations and Actions arising out of Guardianship.

These Obligations become enforceable after the termination of the Guardianship by the *Tutelæ actio directa* and *contraria;* and in the case of the *Cura*, by the *Actio utilis directa* and *utilis contraria*. The direct Action proceeds for the rendering of the Accounts, surrendering of the Property, and compensation for all injuries. The Plaintiff is the Ward, or his Heirs; the Defendant is the Guardian, or his Heirs. The Action may be brought against the Heirs, as well as against the Guardian, if the suit has advanced as far as the *litis contestatio* during the lifetime of the Guardian.

Should the Action be brought against the Heirs, for acts done by the Guardian, they are only answerable for *Dolus* and *Culpa lata*. Where there are more Guardians than one, they are all liable *in solidum;* the party attacked may, however, defend himself by the *Beneficium excussionis*, the *Beneficium divisionis*, and the *Beneficium cedendarum actionum*.

If the Guardian has embezzled any of his Ward's Property during the period of the Guardianship, he is liable not only to the *Actio tutelæ*, but also to the *Actio rationibus distrahendis*, which is brought for twice the amount abstracted. This Action, however, can only be instituted after the termination of the Guardianship. Besides the Guardian and his Heirs, the Sureties are also answerable; and further, *in subsidium*, the *Affirmatores*, as they are termed (that is, those persons who have guaranteed the fitness and suitability of the Guardian), and likewise the *Postulatores* (or those persons who have proposed a party as a fit and proper person as a Guardian). Where the Ward has not been able to recover his Property, either from his Guardian or the last-named persons, he may institute the *Actio tutelæ subsidiaria* against the Superior Court of Wards, or, as it is termed by the Germans, the "*Obervormundsschaftsbehörde*." The Court must, under these circumstances, prove that it has fulfilled all the duties legally imposed upon it. When any one acts as Guardian who had no right, either as a *protutor* or a *falsus tutor*, he is placed, as regards the Ward, under the same Obligation as a proper Guardian, and the *Actio protutelæ* lies against him. This Action may be instituted at any moment. The *protutor* has neither

Liability of Sureties.

the title to administer, nor the capacity to interpose, a valid authority. Things that have been alienated the Ward may sue for by the *Vindicatio*.

Superior Guardian.

Reference has already several times been made to Superior Guardianship. With what office, it may be asked, is the Superior Guardian combined? Who is this Officer in any given concrete case? The Superior Guardian is the ordinary judicial tribunal, and the office is held in any given case by the judicial tribunal of the place where the Ward is domiciled. The functions of the Superior Guardian refer, as already observed, to the appointment and installation of the Guardian, and also to the conduct of the Guardianship and its termination.

How Guardianship is terminated

Guardianship is terminated:

1. As soon as the Pupil becomes of age, or when he dies previously to that event.

2. When he comes under the *patria potestas*, in which case he suffers a *capitis deminutio*.

3. When the Guardian dies, upon which event the next Guardian takes his place.

4. When the Guardian becomes incapacitated.

5. When he, upon proof of any other valid excuse, surrenders his office.

6. When the Mother or the Grandmother have been the Guardians, and they enter upon a second marriage.

7. When the time expires, or a *Conditio resolutiva* takes effect.

8. When the business for which it had been created is completed.

9. When the Guardian is removed.

Not only may others besides the Ward apply to the Court for the removal of a suspected Tutor, or make what is termed a *suspecti postulatio*, but proceedings for his removal may be even instituted *ex officio*. Thus in some cases the co-Guardians are bound to take legal proceedings. The *accusatio tutoris suspecti* can only be instituted against the Guardian so long as he is in office, and the ground for this proceeding must always be some violation of duty on his part. Should this presumption be proved to be well founded, he is removed, and the reason for his removal stated; for if *culpa lata* or *dolus* has been the cause of his removal, the consequence to him is Infamy.

BOOK THE FIFTH.

REAL RIGHTS.

SECTION XXI.—*General and Introductory.*

Von Vangerow, ss. 295—337.
Arndts., ss. 22, 126—129.
Puchta, ss. 140—143.
Gai. Comm. (Tomkins and Lemon's edit.), p. 581, note *a*.
Instit. de rerum divisione (2, 1).
Dig. de acquirendo rerum dominio (41, 1).

A REAL RIGHT is such, that its Matter, or Substance, determines the legal subjection of an external Object. Ownership This subjection or dominion, is either partial or total. Complete power over a Thing constitutes Ownership, or Property. Every *jus in re* is formed out of the elements which constitute Property; that is, from the several constituent separate Rights which may be severed and transferred to a Person who is not the Owner. The *Emphyteuta* and *Superficiarius* possess the greatest number of Rights, or Claims, short of absolute Ownership; next to them the Mortgagee, and finally the Person entitled to a Servitude. These *jura in re aliena*, as they are termed, continue where they have once originated, even though the Property itself may subsequently change Owners. There is, however, an exception to this rule, in the case of what are designated Revocable Rights.

No special rule can be laid down for determining the origin of Real Rights. Sometimes they originate like other Rights; but, on the other hand, *all* Rights of Things do not spring from similar principles, or sources. Rights of Things are terminated, either by the destruction of the subject matter, or by the withdrawal of the Thing from Commerce. Property in wild animals ceases the moment they regain their condition of natural freedom. Alienation by the *Fiscus*, by the Prince or the Princess, and by the Regent, extinguishes all Real Right in the Thing alienated.*

No special rule for the determination of Real Rights.

SECTION XXII.—*Of Property or Ownership.*

Von Vangerow, ss. 295 et seq.
Arndts, ss. 130—174.
Puchta, ss. 144—178.
Gai. Comm. II., 1—97; IV., 36.
Savigny, Syst. III., 369; Recht des Besitzes, ss. 37—39.
Glück VIII., 26, 311; XVI., 41 et seq.
l. 25, pr., Dig. de verb. sig. (50, 16).
Dig. de aqua et aquæ pluviæ arcendæ (39, 3).
Instit. quibus alienare licet vel non (2, 8).
Cod. de rebus alienandis et de prohib., etc. (4, 51).
Dig. de tigno juncto (47, 3).
Instit. s. 29, de rerum divisione (2, 1).
Dig. XLI.
Dig. de adquirendo rerum dominio (41, 1).
Cod. de thesauris (10, 15).
Cod. Theod. de thesauris (10, 18).
Instit. de usucapionibus et long. etc. (2, 6).

* The party injured, however, may claim Compensation at any time within four years.

Dig. de usurpationibus et usucap. (41, 3).
Cod. communia de usucapionibus (7, 30).
l. un. Cod. de usuc. transformanda (7, 31).
Dig. VI., 1, Cod. III., 32, de rei Vindicatione.
Dig. de Publiciana in rem actione (6, 2).
Dig. (43, 17), Cod. (8, 6), uti possidetis.
The above contain the principal authorities; but for additional see Von Vangerow, in ss. 295 et seq.

Definition of Property.

WHAT, it may be asked, is the notion of Property? To this question it may be replied that Property is the *legal* total dominion over a corporal object. When a Thing belongs to a Person, he may do with it whatever he pleases. What the *Possessor* of a Thing is in point of *fact*, that the *Owner* of Property is in regard to the object he owns in point of *law*. The Right of Property was always regarded by the Romans as *corporal;* other Rights they looked upon as *incorporal*. In modern times we often hear persons speaking of their Property as consisting in some Right, or Claim, or Obligation. This is to be regretted as it leads to confusion, for there is no Property, strictly speaking, in Rights.

Extended to a *Universitas Rerum Distantium.*

The Romans always limited Property to corporal Things, with but one important exception, that of a *Universitas Rerum Distantium*. As the rule, no mere abstract idea or notion can be the object of Property. We speak of the Ownership of a book, or of a certain animal; but the Romans also included the notion of a library and of a flock; and the *universitas* might be sued for by means of the *Vindicatio*. This abstract idea implied in a *universitas*, regarded as Property, constituted the only exception to the general rule. Further, although Property is defined as the legal total *dominion* over a corporal object, it does not, by any means, follow that an Owner sustains such a relation to his Property that he has in point of fact the actual dominion over the Thing he owns. For example, when an Owner permits a person to enter his house as a Superficiarius, or his land as an Emphyteuta, or a Usufructuary, the ground landlord is still the Owner, although the Usufructuary has a *jus utendi fruendi*. These are mere restrictions of his Ownership for the time being, and when they fall away, the Property reverts immediately into the full, entire, and unlimited power and dominion of the Owner without any new Acquisition whatever. Paulus says: "Recte dicimus, eum fundum totum nostrum esse, etiam quum ususfructus alienus est, quia ususfructus non dominii pars, sed servirtutis est, ut via et iter; nec falso dici, totum meum esse, cujus non potest ulla pars dici alterius esse; hoc et Julianus, et est verius." *

Again, an Owner has the entire control over the *substance* of his Property, and the fullest *jus utendi fruendi*. In addition to this he also acquires a new Right of Property in all the Fruits as soon as they are separated from the fruit-bearing Thing. He has, further, a *jus alienandi*, or power to dispose of his Ownership whenever he pleases; or he may even limit his Ownership by carving out of it *jura in re aliena*. Again, he has a *jus possidendi*, and may exercise his dominion in point of *fact* in the most extensive manner he pleases; and lastly, he has the power to avail himself of the *jus vindicandi* without any one challenging his Right. Hence the maxim, "*Ubi meam rem invenio, ibi vindico*." Rights of an Owner.

* l. 25, pr., Dig. de V. S. (L. 16.)

Sole and Joint Ownership

When this lawful dominion over a corporal Object, denominated Ownership, resides in one person, it is termed Sole Ownership; it is Joint Ownership where several persons share the Property in common, each Owner being entitled to a portion according to an *ideal* division. Each person may dispose of his share, but the Thing itself can be alienated only by the consent of all the Joint Owners.

Limitations of Ownership

Ownership obviously, by its very nature, confers the largest Right to the enjoyment of the Thing owned, but it may be subjected to certain limitations. These restrictions are reducible to two kinds; either the Owner is prohibited from doing certain acts, or he must on his part permit certain acts to be done. The limitations denominated *jura in re*, and the so-called Servitudes or Easements fall under both heads.*

When Alienation is void.

Prohibited Alienations come under the first class. Such are either restricted by some law or judicial decree, or by testamentary disposition, or by contract. Alienations which have been made in disobedience to a lawful prohibition, or to the decree of a Court, are absolutely void. Alienations, in violation of some private prohibition (Agreement, Testamentary Disposition), only become void, when the Alienation has been prohibited under the penalty of rescinding the Tradition, or if the Thing, in the event of Alienation, has been made over to a third person.

* No one may build in such a manner as to exclude the air from a neighbour's *area* or plot of ground. A neighbour likewise is permitted to gather the fruits which have fallen from his trees upon another one's ground; the branches of trees may project fifteen feet over a neighbour's ground; and Right of Way, when absolutely necessary, must also be allowed. The bulging out of a neighbour's wall, if it does not exceed six inches, must be submitted to; so also the digging and searching for ores.

Mere Prohibition by agreement does not make Alienation void, unless a *conditio resolutiva* attaches. Only a Personal Action lies against those who alienate in violation of a Prohibition. There is a peculiar limitation of Property in connection with the *Vindicatio*. Where the *tigna*, or beams, of another person have been built into an adjoining house, neither the *Actio ad exhibendum* nor the *Vindicatio* lie, at least, not as long as the *tigna* remain in contact with the house (Vineyards, etc.)* Finally, Ownership may be limited in point of duration. This may depend upon a *Condition*, or upon a *limitation in time*. It is to such restrictions that the phrase "*dominium revocabile*" is applied. In the first instance, we speak of *dominium revocabile ex tunc*, in the latter the *dominium revocabile ex nunc*. The former operates retrospectively, annulling the Ownership; the latter operates *in futuro*. The latter is not a restriction of the Property, but it limits the Owner in its use; the former only is a restriction affecting the Property itself. The Property passes with the existence of the Condition *ipso jure*, to the person to whom the Condition in the given case applies.

Tigna.

Dominium revocabile ex tunc and *ex nunc.*

All the Rights hitherto conferred by the Person entitled become void (*resoluto jure concedentis resolvitur jus concessum*). Property apart from a *conditio resolutiva* is, upon transfer, *revocabile ex tunc* in certain legal cases, namely, in regard to the *lucra nuptialia*, in *pœnae secundarum nuptiarum*, and in cases of Right of Redemption.

---

* By way of Compensation the *Actio de tigno juncto* is given for twice the amount of the Property claimed. *Tigna* comprise all building materials, and poles, and palings, used in Vineyards for the support of vines.

Requisites for the Acquisition of Property.

The Acquisition of Property presupposes:

1. A Subject capable of acquiring, which capacity in the present day every one enjoys who is possessed of the power of volition.

2. An Object that may be acquired *(res in commercium)*.

3. A certain Transaction, or legal act of Acquisition.

Two modes to be distinguished

Two modes of acquiring Property must be distinguished, the one arising from Possession, the other arising without Possession:

By Possession.

I. *Acquisition of Property by Possession.*

Occupancy

A. The first mode of Acquisition to be mentioned is Occupancy, which consists in the taking Possession of a *Res nullius*. There are several kinds of Acquisition by Occupancy: *a*. That of wild animals enjoying their natural freedom (Bees are treated as wild animals). *b*. Acquisition by the Occupancy of a treasure *(thesaurus)*, that is, of valuable moveable Things hidden for so great a length of time that the original Proprietor cannot be found. A Treasure-Trove discovered upon one's own ground, or upon a *locus sacer*, belongs wholly to the finder; if found upon the land of another, or in a *locus religiosus*, the half only can be retained by the finder. *c*. The *Occupatio bellica*. *d*. The Occupation of special Things (Specification). The Person who, by manufacture, changes the raw materials owned by another, in such a manner that it is rendered impossible to reduce them to their former condition, becomes the Owner of the new fabric. The Specificator, as he is termed, may have acted *bona* or *mala fide*, but it is quite immaterial.* He holds a new Thing by Occupancy, and hence he becomes the Owner of it. These rules also hold good where any raw material of one's own has been mixed with that belonging to another Person. *e.* The Occupation and cultivation during two years of arable land which has been left uncultivated for a long period, conveys Ownership to the Occupier.

B. *Tradition.* A mere Agreement does not suffice to transfer Property. Hence the important maxim, "*Traditionibus et usucapionibus dominia rerum non nudis pactis transferuntur.*" According to the Roman Law the only exception to this rule was in the case of a *Societas omnium bonorum.* The intention to transfer must receive a physical embodiment in some tangible form. Such transfer of Possession is what is designated Tradition. In order to acquire Property by Tradition it is necessary: Tradition.

1. That the traditor or transferor, as Owner, or his Representative, should be capable of transferring the Property. Requisites for Tradition.

2. That the transferee should be capable of acquiring the Property.

3. That there should be a *justa causa traditionis,* that is to say, an external fact or transaction embodying the intention of both parties; of the one party to transfer the Property, and of the other to acquire it. Such a transaction, for instance, is presented in the case of a Sale or a Donation.

4. Possession must be given in accordance with such *justa causa,* or if the other side is already in

* It is immaterial for the Acquisition of the Property. He cannot, however, escape a claim for Compensation.

Possession, undisturbed enjoyment must be conceded. By imposing a Condition upon the *justa causa*, the Property only becomes acquired upon the happening of this Condition. Thus where a purchase has been made with the *pactum reservati dominii*, the effect is to give rise to a *Conditio Suspensiva*. Such a suspension comes into force *ipso jure* upon sale taking place. Tradition, therefore, does not affect the Transfer of the Property until the Vendor has been satisfied. As all depends upon the *justa causa* (the intention to transfer or to withhold the Property), and the remaining part of the legal transaction does not in this case in any way apply, the motive becomes immaterial. A payment may be made unduly, or as it is expressed, *indebite;* nevertheless, the *Traditio* is held to be *ex justa causa;* a *Mutuum*, for instance, may have been in contemplation, whilst the recipient understood a Gift to have been intended, nevertheless the Property passes.* It is, however, absolutely necessary that the intention should be directed to the Thing intended to be delivered, and that there should exist an accord, or agreement of intention between the parties. The transferor must have intended to convey the Property to the transferee.† It is not necessary that he should know to whom the Transfer is to be made, for Transfer to an unknown Person, *incerta persona*, is valid in law. It is also held that there may be a Tradition of a *Jactus*

Acquisition by Deputy.

* Evidently Remedies exist to prevent the receiver from improperly enriching himself. It is otherwise where the transferor or transferee contemplated a transaction that in no wise purported to be a Transfer of Property, in which case it does not take place.

† Error as to the identity of the object prevents the Transfer of the Property.

missilium, which may thus be acquired by proxy. As regards Acquisition by deputy, it may be remarked that it suffices when the intention of the transferor is directed to the *Dominus*, even though the substitute may prove faithless. If he direct his intention to the Representative, the *Dominus* does not acquire the Property immediately, but first mediately, after a second Transfer.

In certain cases an Acquisition may be made by a party who had no intention of acting as the Representative of another. In consequence of this principle, certain Persons whose money has been spent in the purchase of Property may claim by the *Vindicatio* the Thing purchased with their means. Thus Wards and Soldiers, and Married Women who have given money to their husbands, and subsequently revoked the Gift, may claim by the *Vindicatio* the Things purchased with their money, in the event of the husband becoming insolvent, or when he has bought Property with money belonging to his wife's Dower.

Fructuum Perceptio.

C. The *Fructuum Perceptio*, Persons to whom the Owner of Property has granted its Fruits in consequence of some Obligatory transaction, or Real Right, but who only retain the Property in Detention; as, for example, Farmers, or Lessees, or Usufructuaries, acquire the Fruits only by Perception, or by the positive act of taking Possession.

Usucapion

D. *Usucapion* consists in the acquisition of Property by a Person who has possessed the same as his own for a given length of time, under certain rightful

Conditions. These may be Ordinary or Extraordinary.* The requisites of an Ordinary Usucapion are, *a*. Possession during Three years for Moveable things, whilst for Immoveables Ten to Twenty years are required, according as the parties reside in the same *(inter præsentes)* or in different Provinces *(inter absentes)*. It is not necessary that the Possession should be held by the Person himself, or by his Representative during the whole of the time, as Derivative Acquisition is allowable, and the Possession of the predecessor who was *in conditione usucapiendi* may be included *(accessio possessionis)*.† *b*. Possession must be founded upon a

Ordinary Usucapion: Its requisites.

* A mode of obtaining Property by Prescription existed even according to the older Roman Law. It was termed Usucapion, and belonged to the *jus civile*, and gave rise to Quiritarian Ownership. Hence, it follows that aliens, *peregrini*, could not obtain Property in this way, nor did land, situated in the Provinces, admit of this institution. These limitations gave rise to a new kind of Prescription, originating in the Prætorian Law, and designated *longi temporis Præscriptio*. It was primarily only available as an Exception, by means of which the Possessor of a thing excluded the Proprietary Action; but at a later period he acquired the *actio in rem*. These two institutes Justinian combined, as in his time the distinction between Quiritarian and Bonitarian Property had ceased to exist. It is now termed Ordinary Usucapion. To complete this he added the Extraordinary Usucapion, which required 30 years' Prescription. Thus the Ownership *in Bonis* was completely abolished, so that all *dominium* became, through the legislation of Justinian, "*ex jure Quiritium.*" It was a remarkable alteration in the law, for it had the effect of extending Quiritarian Ownership to provincial land, and let in a *peregrinus* or an alien to that privilege which had before been the exclusive advantage of the Roman citizen, namely, to hold Property "*ex jure Quiritium.*" (See Gaius, p. 246—280, note *u*., Tomkins and Lemon's edit.) In order to complete his reform, Justinian, by Novella 119, c. 7, ordained that the Prescription of 10 or 20 years should only be allowed where the true Owner was aware of his Right, and of its Transfer to the *bona fide* Possessor; otherwise the Prescription did not mature until after a Possession of thirty years.

† The seller who rescinds a Contract of Sale, and receives Property in consequence of a *Conditio Resolutiva*, may avail himself of the period of time the Property was held by the third party. Equally so, he who has held *Precario* after the Restitution has been completed. It is, of course, understood that the Usucapion of the Testator is continued in the Heir.

justus titulus; that is, upon some occurrence or event which would produce the conviction in a Person that he was the Owner. The *titulus* must be *justus*, that is, an event *per se* must have occurred sufficient to pass Property (*pro soluto, pro emptore, pro donato, pro herede, pro suo*, etc). This event must also be *verus*, that is to say, the legal transaction upon which this condition is based must have been actually concluded. Further, the event must be what is called *purus*, that is, the transaction must not depend upon a *Conditio Suspensiva*. *c.* The Possessor must, by a *justus titulus*, have the conviction of being the *dominus (bona fides)*. This honest belief must be founded upon probable error (*error facti probabilis*), and must have existed from the very commencement. In the acquisition of Property by a Representative, and in those cases where without the knowledge of the Principal no Property can be acquired, Acquisition depends upon the *bona fides* of the Representative. Hence it is said, when *ignoranti possessio per alium acquiritur*, all hinges upon the *bona fides* of the Representative. *d.* The Thing must be capable of Usucapion.

Things incapable of Usucapion.

Things incapable of Usucapion are: *Res extra commercium*, Dotal goods during the continuance of Marriage, Immoveable Property of Minors, Property of the Crown, that of the *Fiscus*, Charitable Trusts, Property belonging to a Municipality,* *Res furtivae, Res vi possessore,*† and *Res a malæ fidei possessore abalienatae.*‡ Further, Things

* The *Vitium* is extinguished as soon as the Property ceases to belong to such persons.

† The *Vitium* is extinguished when the thing reverts to the Possession of the Owners.

‡ Extinction of the *Vitium* in this case is effected by the acknowledgment of Notice of Alienation by the Owners, and of the Right to alienate.

that have been given *contra legem repetundarum* to the President of a Province,* Things which have reverted to the children of a first Marriage in consequence of a second one, Boundary lands. Things the alienation of which is prohibited, cannot be held by Usucapion, even though the permission of the party subject to the limitation be obtained.

Requisites for Extraordinary Prescription.

The requisites for Extraordinary Prescription are: *a. Bona fides*, but without a *justus titulus*; *b.* Possession during a period of thirty years. Forty years' Possession, however, is required where forty years' Prescription is needed to bar an Action; but this Prescription is excluded where no thirty years' Prescription is allowable.† But Things excluded from the Ordinary Usucapion may be acquired by the Extraordinary Prescription. One of the conditions of the Ordinary, as well as of the Extraordinary Usucapion, is, that the *Usucapiens* shall have continued in uninterrupted Possession of the Things of which he intended to become the Proprietor (*continua possessio*). An interruption of the Possession is termed "*Usurpatio.*" Causes of interruption, or *Usurpatio*, are: Discontinuance of Possession, *Mala fides superveniens*, Loss of the capacity to hold Property, Loss of capacity of Usucapion. The bringing of an Action does not cause a *Usurpatio*, but merely renders a subsequent Usucapion inoperative.

Usurpatio.

There is in such a case no interruption of the time of the Prescription, but only a Suspension:

---

* This *Vitium* ceases as in the case of *Res Furtivae*.

† Things belonging to Wards, Things of such a character that, on Action brought the *impedimentum juris* is raised. Hence Dotal Goods, *tigna ædibus alienis injuncta*, Things belonging to a *peculium adventicium regulare*.

1. When a thing liable to be held by Usucapion passes to a privileged person. Suspension of the time of Prescription.

2. When an *impedimentum juris* hinders the Owner from following up his legal remedy. In these instances it is usual to say that the *Prescriptio dormit.*

II. *Obtaining the Ownership of Property without Acquiring Possession thereof.* Ownership without Possession.

A. *Acquisition of Fruits by Separation.* Separated Fruits are regarded as possessing an independent existence. The Owner acquires in them, from the moment of their separation, a new Property. He is, however, limited in this Acquisition by the Right of the *Emphyteuta,* and the *bonæ fidei* Possessor. The Acquisition, however, by the *bonæ fidei* Possessor is a point in dispute. The following propositions are, however, true:—

1. That the *bonæ fidei* Possessor acquires the entire Ownership of the separated Fruits, not the accessions, at the very moment of their separation.

2. This Ownership is not beneficial, and does not protect against Restitution, should the Owner obtain by means of the *Vindicatio* the Restitution of the principal Thing with its Fruits.* Fruits become actual profits only on being consumed, sold, or altered in shape, or where the Possessory Action has been forfeited.

B. *Acquisition by the joining of one Thing with another when the union is so intimate that the Thing blended loses its independent existence.* When the Acquisition of Ownership by Combination.

* He has no *Vindicatio* as regards the Fruits, but must sue for the Principal, when the Judgment may be that he shall obtain this with the Fruits.

Things of several Owners are combined in such a manner* so as to sustain similar relations to each other, *Confusio* or *Commixtio* arises, and a change of Ownership takes place if they cannot be severed, a Joint Ownership is created.† But when the Things are severable, each party retains his separate Ownership.‡ When, however, the Things are not relatively equal, but possess the relation to each other of Principal and Accessory, in this case the Owner of the Principal Thing also acquires the Accessory Thing.§ Such an integral combination is presumed, for if this be not the case, the Owner of the Accessory Thing may proceed with the *Actio ad exhibendum*, and with the *Vindicatio*. In Moveables the accessory quality is determined by deciding which Thing imposes the Condition and which is conditioned;‖ which is the Dominant and which the Servient Thing; which the ornamental, or the larger, or the smaller. In the case of Immoveables, that which is to be deemed the Accessory Thing can hardly be a matter of doubt. There are three cases in which Moveables attach to Immoveables:

Moveables attaching to Immoveables.

1. *Inaedificatio*. The building erected upon a plot of ground belongs to the Owner of the ground, whether it has been built with his own materials or with those belonging to a third party.¶

* By Agreement, or by Accident.

† It must be so, for the Combination becomes a Specification.

‡ It is different where moneys have been mixed. Where such cannot be recognised, those that have been added are regarded as Accessions.

§ Of course, not without having to make Compensation.

‖ According to Justinian, the picture is regarded as the Principal object; the board and canvas are only Accessories.

¶ When buildings have been erected upon a man's own lot, but with the materials owned by a third Person, the Proprietor of such materials has the

2. *Plantatio.*

3. *Satio.* Where the plant in the former case, and the seed in the present, take root, they belong in both instances to the Owner of the soil. A tree growing on the confines of land belongs to the adjacent Owners *pro indiviso;* when, however, it is felled they take it *pro diviso.* Four cases exist in which Immoveables are added to Immoveables: **Immoveables attaching to Immoveables.**

1. *Per Alluvionem,* gradual deposits made by the washing away, and slow sediment of the earth.

2. *Per Avulsionem,* that is, by the carrying away of one portion of the bank of a river, and its deposit upon another part of the river side.

3. By the formation of an island in a *flumen publicum.**

4. In consequence of a river deserting its former bed.†

According to the damage sustained, several Remedies are given for the enforcement of the Rights of Property. For cases of complete violation, the *Rei Vindicatio* is provided. This is an Action in which the Plaintiff seeks to obtain the judicial acknowledgment of his Right of Property, and the Restitution of the same *cum omni causa* against a third party in Possession. It is necessary that the party bringing the Action should be the Owner of the Property, but not in Possession, and that the Defendant should be the non-Owner in **Remedies. The *Rei Vindicatio***

Actio de tigno juncto. Where the materials belong to a man, but the ground does not, in this instance the *malæ fidei* Possessor has only the *Jus tollendi,* but not the *Jus retinendi.* He may, however, use the *Vindicatio* to recover his Property after the demolition of the building. The *bonæ fidei* Possessor has a claim for compensation.

* The river is to be divided by an imaginary line in the middle, and the ground apportioned according as it is situated either on the one side or the other of this line.

† Here the Properties advance and meet in the middle.

Possession of the Property sought to be recovered by the *Vindicatio*. The Plaintiff has to prove that he had at one time acquired the Property, not that he is the present Owner. Should he lose the Ownership during the course of the Action, he is at once non-suited; should he acquire the Ownership in the course of the Action, he will then succeed with the *Vindicatio*. The Person in Possession of the Property, and hence suable, is he who possesses the *facultatem restituendi*. The *Fictus Possessor*, that is, he who holds himself* out as Possessor *(qui liti sese obtulit)*, and he who fraudulently *(dolose)* gives up or surrenders Possession, are in the same position.† The bare or merely natural Possessor may, if he please, name his Principal *(laudatio* or *nominatio auctoris)*, and thus rid himself of the *Vindicatio*. The *Vindicatio* proceeds for the Restitution of the Thing, *cum omni causa*. The Things sued for, however, must have an independent existence; if not, the *Actio ad exhibendum* must invariably be employed in the first instance, always presuming that a severance *salva re* is possible. Still, a *Universitas* may likewise be vindicated.‡ Where Restitution is impossible, and the fault rests with the Defendant, the estimated amount of damage must be made good. By the expression "*omnis res*" is to be understood, all things that belong to the Property claimed, as well as all Accessions and benefits that would have accrued to the Plaintiff had no Action been brought. To these especially belong

Liability of the Defendant

* It is only the Possessor of the Thing itself who can be sued, not the Surrogate, or the Person substituted.

† After the *Fictus Possessor* the *Verus* may also be proceeded against.

‡ The Defendant may, however, prove that each separate part or Thing is his Property.

the Fruits. The *malæ fidei possessor* has to surrender all that he has received or might have received.* The *bonæ fidei possessor* is answerable for such only as are existing at the time of the bringing of the Action; after Action is brought, his position is similar to that of the *malæ fidei possessor.* The Defendant rebuts the *Vindicatio* by the Plea that he has a Right to possess the Property by virtue of a *jus in re,* or by a Right arising out of some Obligatory Relation *(exceptio rei venditæ et traditæ).*† Or the Defendant sets up a counter Claim, demanding compensation for the price paid, or for Outlays incurred. The first is generally disallowed, but Outlays are recoverable. A distinction, however, must in this case be made between the *bonæ* and the *malæ fidei possessor.*

The *Publiciana in rem Actio.*

The *Publiciana in rem Actio* has the same object as the *Rei Vindicatio.* Of Prætorian origin, it aims at the recovering of a Thing acquired *bonæ fidei.* It is founded upon Possession leading to Usucapion. The requisites for the *Actio Publiciana* are the same as those required in the case of Usucapion, that is to say, Things susceptible of Usucapion, *justus titulus, bonæ fidei* juridical Possession. He who has been in Possession under these qualifications, and has lost his Possession, may have recourse to the *Publiciana Actio,* and by a fiction of law his Usucapion is regarded as completed. But his Right extends only against the party who cannot prove a *justus titulus,* hence not against the

* *Post litem contestatem* he is also liable for *casus* or accident.

† For example, a person who is not the Owner sells and conveys Property; subsequently he becomes the Proprietor, and endeavours to obtain it by means of the *Vindicatio.*

Owner;* so likewise the Action does not lie against one who possesses *ad usucapionem*. The Action is for Restitution, *cum omni causa*, and in this it resembles in all respects the *Vindicatio*.

In cases where the Possession is not invaded, but where the free exercise of Ownership only is interfered with, the *Actio Negatoria* lies for the Recognition of natural liberty, for Restitution, for Compensation in Damages, and for Security or Bail against any future disturbance. Ownership lies at the very root of the Action, the Plaintiff must prove this; whilst on the Defendant rests the burden of proving the validity of any Servitudes which he may claim.

Destruction of Ownership

Ownership may be extinguished either by physical or juridical destruction; by the Property passing to a third party; or by abandonment on the part of the Owner. With domesticated and wild animals, Ownership is forfeited whenever they stray away so far that they lose the *consuetudinem revertendi*.

SECTION XXIII.—*Of Emphyteusis and Superficies.*

Von Vangerow, ss. 358—362.
Arndts., ss. 195—200.
Puchta, ss. 174—177.
Gai. Comm., III., 145.
Glück VIII., 378 et seq.
Dig. si ager vectigalis, id est vect., etc. (6, 3).
Cod. de jure emphyteuticario (4, 66).
,, de fundis patrimonalibus, etc. (11, 61).
Dig. de superficiebus (43, 18).

her Real Rights.

AMONG Real Rights, Emphyteuses and Superficies

* Except where the *Vindicatio* of the true *dominus* is barred by an *Exceptio* or Plea.

approximate nearest to Ownership. These legal Institutes very much resemble one another.

1. Emphyteusis had its origin, not in the Praetorian Law, but in the *Jus civile*. It is an assignable, inheritable Real Right in a certain tract of land, capable of yielding Fruits, by virtue of which, and in return for the payment of a yearly *Canon*, as it is termed, or Quit-rent, the holder, during the continuance of his Right, possesses absolutely the entire use, and also the Fruits thereof. The Emphyteuta holds legal Possession of the land, and his Right is a Real Right, for the protection of which the Actions are applicable, to which an absolute Owner is entitled. Whenever the Emphyteuta desires to sell his Right he must give notice to the Owner. The *Dominus* may object to a sale when made to an improper Person; and further, in case of sale, he has the Right of pre-emption. Should he, however, decline to purchase, he has the Right of claiming what is denominated the *Laudemium*, that is, the *Quinquagesima*, or fiftieth part of the purchase money. The Emphyteuta is liable, in addition to his Canon, or Rent, for the payment of all rates, taxes, and other burdens. An Emphyteusis is created by Contract, namely, the *Contractus Emphyteuseos;* by Bequest; possibly also by Prescription. It is terminated by the destruction of the *Ager Emphyteuticarius;* by Merger and Consolidation; by the Expiration of the time for which it was constituted; when the Emphyteuta dies, leaving no heir; by Prescription and Renunciation; finally, by Penalty upon the Emphyteuta, for allowing the ground to deteriorate; by Non-payment of the Canon for three years, and of taxes for two years;

Emphyteusis: Definition.

by Non-payment of the *Quinquagesima*, or by Neglect of the duty of Denunciation.

Superficies: Definition.

2. *Superficies*, which is of Prætorian origin, is that Real Right in a building upon the ground of another, empowering the party entitled to the absolute use of the same, and to the protection afforded by the Actions applicable to Ownership. As the rule, the Right is not granted, as in the case of Emphyteusis, *in perpetuum*, but for a fixed period of time. It may be originated by Contract, by Inheritance, by Testamentary Disposition, or by Prescription. There exists, however, no special distinctive Contract for *Superficies*. The legal transaction may be consummated by Purchase, or by Lease, or by way of Donation. Hence the explanation why a *Superficiarius*, as he is termed, may sometimes have to pay the purchase money, at other times merely an annual *solatium*, or even nothing at all. The grounds for the extinction of the Right of the *Superficiarius* are the same as those of the Emphyteuta, with the exception that no forfeiture can take place.

SECTION XXIV.—*Of Servitudes or Easements.*

Von Vangerow, ss. 338—357.
Arndts, ss. 175—194.
Puchta, ss. 178—192.
Gai. Comm. (Tomkins and Lemon's edit.), p. 234, note *m*.
Savigny Syst. II., 110. Recht des Besitzes, ss. 45, 46.
Glück, IX., 1, et seq., 387; X., 1, et seq., 207.
l. 15, pr., Dig. de servit. (8, 1).
l. 27, ,, de servit. præd. urb. (8, 2).
l. 1, Dig. de usu et usufr. leg. (32, 2).
Instit. de servitutibus prædiorum (2, 3).
Dig. de servitutibus (8, 1).

Dig. de servitutibus prædiorum urbanorum (8, 2).
" " " " rusticorum (8, 3).
" communia prædiorum tam urbanorum, etc. (8, 4).
Cod. de servitutibus et aqua (3, 34).
Instit. de usufructu (2, 4).
Dig. de usufructu et quemadmodum quis utatur, fruatur (7, 1).
Cod. de usufructu (3, 33).
Vat. Frag., s. 41, et seq.
l. 13, Dig. quib. mod. usufr. vel usus amitt. (7, 4).
Dig. de usufructu earum rerum, etc. (7, 5).
" de usu et habitatione (7, 8).
Instit. " " (2, 5).
Cod. de usufructu et habitatione rel. (3, 33).
l. 32, de donat. (39, 5).
l. 19, pr., Dig. si serv. vind. (8, 5).
Dig. si ususfructus petatur, etc. (7, 6).
" si servitutus vindicetur, etc. (8, 5).
l. 11, s. 1, Dig. de Publ. act. (6, 2).
Dig. de itinere actuque privato (43, 19).
" quibus modis ususfructus vel, etc. (7, 4).
l. 6, Dig. de serv. præd. urb. (8, 2).
l. 16, Cod. de usufructu (3, 33).

THE fundamental notion contained in the term Servitude is by no means clear, and consequently there has been much discussion as to its meaning. Many jurists have regarded it as impossible to give an exact definition of Servitudes, and have held that of them only a negative notion can be formed:—That a Servitude is that *jus in re aliena* which is not a Mortgage, nor an Emphyteusis, nor a Superficies, and so on. Servitudes are the most ancient of the *jura in re aliena;* and every Servitude gives a *jus in re aliena* to a certain definite Person, or to a distinctly defined plot of land. It differs from an Obligation, as although this may give as full a Right to the use of a Thing or

Fundamental notion of a Servitude.

Difference between an Obligation and a Servitude.

a Claim, every Servitude gives a Right in the Servient Tenement itself, a *jus in re.* An Obligatory Right is only available against the Person bound, or his Singular Successor; but a Servitude is more than this, it is a *jus in re.* It is also a *jus in re aliena*, and gives the Person or Thing entitled a kind of Dominion over the Servient Tenement. The Mortgagee or Pawnee can take the Thing pledged and sell it, but neither the one nor the other has the least Dominion over the Thing itself. A most marked feature of every Servitude is that it is absolutely untransferable, and in this respect again it differs from Mortgage, Superficies, and Emphyteusis. As to the general nature of a Servitude, Pomponius well observes, "*Servitutem non ea natura est, ut aliquid faciat quis*, veluti viridia tollat, aut ameniorem prospectum præstet, aut in hoc, ut in suo pingat, *sed ut aliquid patiatur, aut non faciat.*"* Thus Servitudes are to be regarded as limitations to the full exercise of the use of Property; and they admit of no marked and definite character, as in the case of Emphyteuses and Superficies, but are simply Rights in the Property of a third party, for the benefit of a given individual subject, such subject being either a Person *(Servitutes personarum)*, or an individual Thing *(Servitutes prædiorum)*. The most general and fundamental principles of Servitudes are the following: (1) *Servitus in faciendo consistere nequit.* (2) *Servitus servitutis esse non potest.* (3) *Nemini res sua servire potest.*† (4) Whatever the Servitude may be, it must

View of Pomponius

Fundamental principles of Servitudes.

* l. 15, s. 1. Dig. de servit. (8, 1).

† It follows from this that a *prædium commune* cannot be burdened with a Servitude.

give to the subject benefited a legal interest. A peculiar characteristic of Servitudes is the quality which they possess of inseparability from the subject to which they are attached. As a consequence of this it follows: (1) That they are non-transferable to another Subject; (2) That even the use of the Right is untransferable; (3) Servitudes are absolutely indivisible, and therefore cannot be acquired in part or forfeited in part.

Personal Servitudes different kinds.

When the Subject for whose advantage a Servitude has been granted is a given human being, the Servitude is termed a Personal Servitude. The Romans mention four kinds of Servitudes of this nature, viz.: *Usus*, *Ususfructus*, *Habitatio*, *Operae*. Still the number of such Servitudes is unlimited, for even Real Servitudes may be constituted as Personal ones, but the above-named four are essentially and only Personal Servitudes. *Operae (servorum, animalium)* and *Habitatio* are, as far as they are based upon ancient Roman usage, as particular Servitudes, now obsolete.

Definition of *Usus*.

Usus is a Personal Servitude; and it consists in the Right to the natural Use of a thing by some definite individual, and the family circle of which he constitutes the head. When the Servient Thing cannot be used without the enjoyment of the Fruits, the Person entitled to the *Usus* is allowed to take the Fruits. But since he posseses only the Right to the natural Use, he is not permitted to barter the Fruits; nor can he allow another to have the enjoyment of the *Usus*. Exceptions, however, to the non-transferability of a *Usus* may arise by means of Testamentary Disposition. When the *Usuarius* himself resides in the house, he may let the

Property; and where a *Usus* is devised to a Lessee, he also may let Property that has been thus left. There are other exceptions limiting the *Usus;* when, namely, the Use is confined to a special custom, or to some particular mode of exercising the *Usus.** The *Usuarius* becomes answerable for *omnem diligentiam;* he must *finito usu* render back the Thing held; he must find Security, and whenever he takes the Fruits he is liable for repairs and taxes. The Owner has no power to limit the *Usus.* Thus he cannot impose onerous or injurious Servitudes, and he can only reap those Fruits which the *Usuarius* does not take.

Liability of the *Usuarius.*

Definition of *Ususfructus.*

When the *Usus* is added to the *Fructus,*† that is, when the Rights to the natural and the juridical Fruits coalesce, the union is termed a *Ususfructus*:—"*Est jus alienis rebus utendi fruendi salva rei substantia.*" The Usufructuary has a Right to the Fruits from the moment he takes Possession of them or gathers them. When the Owner has not separated the Fruits at the time of the commencement of the Usufruct, the Usufructuary takes them. If, however, at the termination of the Usufruct the Fruits have not been gathered by the Usufructuary, the Owner acquires them. But in the case of the *Fructus civiles,* when they equal in value the *natural* Fruit (for example, Rent), they are considered as gathered the instant that the *Fructus naturales* are collected. Otherwise they are divided according to the separate days, and all that falls within these special days, from the commencement to the termination of the Usufruct, belongs to the Usufructuary. The

Who has a Right to the Fruits?

* This is especially the case where Real Servitudes are granted as Personal ones. For example, Common of Pasturage.

† No special Servitude of *Fructus* exists.

Usufructuary may dispose of the Thing, but he is prohibited from altering or allowing it materially to deteriorate. The exercise and benefit of the Usufruct (not the Right) may be conveyed to another. All Accessions, and also those Things which possess no independent existence, as well as Appurtenances, are, in like manner, subject to the Usufruct. The duties of the Usufructuary require that he should exercise due care *(diligentiam)*, and he is also held answerable for *omnem culpam*. He must pay for all ordinary repairs, undertake to discharge all taxes and burdens, and restore the Thing upon the termination of the Usufruct. For the security of the Owner the Usufructuary must give the *Cautio Usufructuaria*, which, with but few exceptions, must not be a Personal, but a Real Security.* The object of a Usufruct can only be, strictly speaking, *res quae usu non consumitur*. A Usufruct may, however, be granted on incorporal and consumable Things by analogy, in which case it is named a *Quasi Ususfructus*. The analogy applies to the inception, the termination of the Right, and also to the *Cautio Usufructuaria*. Where the Servitude applies to *res consumtibiles*, the Usufructuary becomes the Owner of the same. Upon the termination of the Usufruct the Usufructuary must return a similar quantity of the Thing consumed, or Things of the same quality and value. Hence he incurs all risks. A Usufruct of Rights and *Nomina*, as they are termed, or Debts, is invariably a *quasi* Usufruct; for Rights are not Things.†

Power and Liability of the Usufructuary.

Object of a Usufruct.

* As in the case of the *Ususfructus paternus*, when it is certain that the Usufructuary acquires Ownership, and in the case of a Waiver.

† When the party entitled is limited to the enjoyment of Interest only, no Usufruct arises.

Predial Servitudes

Where the benefit to be derived, and for which the Servitude has been created, attaches to Land, the Servitude is termed *Servitus prædii.* The governing principles in Predial Servitudes are the following:—

Advantage must be to the *Prædium dominans.*

1. The advantage must accrue to the Dominant Land. Beyond the actual requirements of the *Prædium dominans*, no Predial Servitude can possibly be created. Thus the Matter and Substance of an Easement are limited to the positive requirements of the Thing. How far this requirement may extend is determinable by the nature and character, or peculiarity of the Land. It is evident that these fundamental rules must exercise an important effect upon the Matter of Predial Servitudes. It is in this influence that the interest lies which arises from the division of Servitudes into *Servitutes prædiorum rusticorum*, and *Servitutes prædiorum urbanorum.* The latter are those Servitudes which attach to Buildings; *Servitutes prædiorum rusticorum* refer to different lots of Land only. The requirements of these two kinds of Land are very different. Thus, when certain privileges are found to be equally applicable as to their Matter, to both classes of Easements, it necessarily follows that in such cases they partake of a different character.*

The *perpetua causa* must be in the Servient Land.

2. The advantage which would accrue to the Dominant Land, must be rendered to it by the Servient Tenement in consequence of the inherent nature possessed by, or residing in the Servient Land. This property is designated its *perpetua causa;* it may reside in the Land itself, as in the case of a Right of Way,

* For example, Right of Way.

or it may be Things appertaining to the Land which are denominated, *Res soli*, as Water, Earth, Minerals, &c.

3. The *prædia* must be, as it is termed, "*vicina*," or near at hand; otherwise, the exercise of the *jus in re aliena* would not be a *direct* benefit to the Dominant Land. It must be a *prædia vicina.*

4. Predial Servitudes are indivisible, and hence cannot be partially acquired, used, or lost. Are indivisible.

5. The constituted Easement becomes a constituent element in the *prædium dominans*, and no Alienation, Mortgage, or Lease, can take place apart from the Dominant Tenement itself. Real Servitudes are either *continuæ* or *discontinuæ*, according as their exercise consists in an unbroken permanent use, or condition; or in the performance of some isolated acts by the party entitled. Are constituent elements in the *prædium dominans.*

The following are *Servitutes Prædiorum Rusticorum:* Kinds of *Servitutes Prædiorum Rusticorum*

1. Right of Way, or *Iter*, entitling to the use of a foot-path; a path for cattle, or *Actus*; a Right to drive a vehicle, or *Via*.

2. Water courses, *Servitus aquæ ducendæ*, the Right of conducting water by means of channels, from the Servient to the Dominant Land.* *Servitus aqnæ hauriendæ*, or the Right of entering upon the Servient Land to fetch water.†

3. Pasturage, *Servitus silvae caeduæ. Calcis coquendæ, cretae eximendæ, arenæ fodiendæ, lapidis eximendi*, and *glandis legendæ*.

---

* *Aqua aestiva* limited to the summer season; *Aqua quotidiana*, where no such restriction is imposed.

† The Right of watering cattle upon the ground of a stranger is termed *Servitus pecoris ad aquam appulsus.*

Kinds of *Servitutes Prædiorum Urbanorum*

The following are denominated *Servitutes Prædiorum Urbanorum* :—

1. Right of lights and prospect. *Servitus altius non tollendi, Servitus ne luminibus officiatur, Servitus ne prospectui officiatur, Servitus luminum.*

2. The *Servitus oneris ferendi** and *Tigni immittendi.*

3. The *Servitus projiciendi* the Right to project a beam into the vacant space of a neighbour. *Servitus protegendi*, the Right of projecting the roof into the vacant area of a neighbour. *Servitus stillicidii*, the Right of allowing rain water to drop on to a neighbour's land, or, as it is termed, "Right of drip." *Servitus fluminis*, the Right of discharging rain water collected in a gutter on the land of a neighbour. *Servitus fumi immittendi*, or the Right of conducting smoke through a neighbour's flue. *Servitus cloacæ mittendæ*, the Right of carrying sewage over the Servient Land; the Right of placing a privy against a neighbour's wall. Some Servitudes are the exact negatives of those just mentioned, having for their object the freeing from some restriction or other, such as: *Servitus stillicidii, Servitus fluminis non recipiendi, Servitus altius tollendi, Servitus officiendi luminibus.* Here the annulling of a *Servitus urbana* is regarded as a Servitude.

Servitudes are created by Agreement.

Servitudes are created as follows :—

1. By Agreement. The Person *constituting* the Servitude must be the Owner,† and have the power of Disposition. The grantee in Personal Servitudes must

---

* The Owner of the Servient Tenement in this case must keep it in a state of repair.

† When the grantor is only an Emphyteuta, or Superficiary, or Temporary Owner, he has only power to grant an Easement within the limits of his Right.

possess the legal capacity to acquire. In Predial Servitudes, a *prædium vicinum* is needed. Whether actual Tradition must accompany the grant is a matter still held in dispute.*

2. By Testamentary Disposition. By Testament.

3. By Judicial Decree, in a *judicium divisorium*, for the purpose of the adjustment, or for the constitution of an Easement which is absolutely necessary for the enjoyment of the Property (necessary Right of Way). By Judicial Decree

4. Usufruct, however, only arises *ipso jure*.† By Usufruct.

5. By Usucapion, when during ten or twenty years, as the case may be, the Right has been enjoyed, *nec vi, nec clam, nec precario*, provided that the Ownership may be acquired during that period. By Usucapion.

Servitudes cease:

1. By the expiry of the period for which they were created, or during which they may be lawfully enjoyed, or by the happening of the Condition upon which they were made to depend. How Servitudes cease.

2. When the Right of Revocation of the grantor is terminated.

3. By *Confusio* (Merger), which is designated in Personal Servitudes "*Consolidatio*."‡

---

* Von Vangerow and legal practice favour the rule. Puchta considers it not necessary, but advantageous, because Tradition gives rise to the *Actio Publiciana*.

† The Usufruct of the father in the *Adventicia*, the *Conjux binubus*, who sacrifices the *lucra nuptialia*; the party who does not bear the guilt of the dissolution of Marriage, when the Ownership of the forfeited goods goes to the children; the poor widow who competes with her own children for the *virilis portio*.

‡ But in the case of Real Servitudes, the Acquisition by the co-Proprietor shall not affect the *Praedium serviens:* and if the event which accompanies the *Confusio* becomes annulled, the Servitude revives.

4. By Renunciation or Disclaimer.

5. By the destruction of the Dominant Thing, be it either a Person or Land.

6. By the destruction of the Servient Tenement (*res serviens*). In the case of Personal Servitudes, by changing the condition of Things; for example, altering an open space or area into Buildings. By the demolition of a Building.

Non-user. 7. By Non-user for the space of ten years, to which, however, in the case of *Servitutes praediorum urbanorum* must be added that of the *usucapio libertatis*; that is, the Possession of the *res serviens* must remain free and unmolested for the period of ten years.

It is immaterial upon what grounds the *Usus* has been discontinued, and on the other hand, it is equally immaterial by whom the Servitude is exercised. The exercise of a Right, unless coupled with the intention to use it, is regarded legally in the light of Non-user. In Predial Servitudes, which entitle the Possessor to modes of enjoyment, *non usus* is construed into a discontinuance of the Easement; in the case of those belonging to a Corporation, discontinuance is presumed upon removal to some other locality. *Non usus*, in the case of Negative Servitudes, consists in the permission of the exercise of the forbidden Right, without any hindrance by the party whose interest is invaded. In Ususfructus, a partially exercised Ususfructus is maintainable only in part. The *alternis annis legatus* does not, however, expire by *non usus*, because the *dies cedens* revives with every new year.

Legal Remedies for Servitudes. For the protection of Servitudes the following Remedies are provided:—The *Actio Confessoria et Publiciana*, which are petitionary Remedies, and the *Interdicta Retinendæ et Recuperandæ possessionis*, which are possessary proceedings. In addition to these some others exist, of which mention has been already made. The *Actio Confessoria* is a real Action, which is employed for the compulsory acknowledgment of the Servitude, Compensation for Damages, and in the event of continued disturbance, the *Cautio de non amplius turbando*. The Plaintiff is the person entitled, even though he may be in Possession. In Personal Servitudes he must prove his Right to the Servitude;* in Predial Servitudes he must, besides this, prove his Ownership in the *praedium dominans*. The *Actio Publiciana* has the same effect as the *Actio Confessoria*, with the exception that in lieu of having to furnish proof of Ownership, the Plaintiff has only to prove the *Traditio ex justa causa*.

SECTION XXV.—*Of Mortgage or Pawn.*

Von Vangerow, ss. 368—392.
Arndts, ss. 364—392.
Puchta, ss. 193—217.
Glück, XIV., 85, 246; XVIII., 161, 393, 428; XIX., 223, 382.
Dig. lib., XX. Cod. VIII., 14—36.
s. 7, Instit. de actionibus (4, 6).
l. 5, s. 1; l. 14, s. 1, Dig. de pignoribus, etc. (20, 1).
l. 19, Dig. de P. et H. (20, 1).
l. 6, pr., l. 8, s. 5, l. 21. Dig. de pignor. act. (13, 7).
l. 1, Cod. si propter public. pensitationes, etc. (4, 46).
l. 28, Dig. de jure fisci (49, 14).
Nov. 97, c. 3.
l. 66, pr., Dig. de evictionibus (21, 2).

* Or that he is within the *Nexus*, in which an *Actio Confessoria* lies (Emphyteuta, etc.)

Dig. de Salviano interdicto (43, 33).
Gai. Comm. IV., s. 147. s. 3, Instit., de interd. (4, 15).
l. 1, Dig. de Salv. interd. (43, 33).
l. 19, Cod. de usur. (4, 32.

Mortgage in Ancient Rome.

Fiducia and *Pignus*

In the ancient Roman Law there were two distinct kinds of Real Security, which were designated as "*Fiducia*" and "*Pignus.*" In the case of *Fiducia*, the Property itself was given as a pledge; whilst in that of *Pignus*, all that was pledged was the Possession of the Thing and not the actual Property. In this most ancient kind of Mortgage there was always an implied Contract for the reconveyance of the object pledged. The Agreement was entered into between the Debtor and the Creditor *cum fiducia sive fiduciæ causa*, that the latter after the extinction of his Claim should remancipate the Property which he had received as a Pledge.* *Fiducia* was effected by means of a *Mancipatio*, or the form of transfer known as *In Jure Cessio*. In this mode of Mortgage the Fiduciary Pact or Agreement *(pactum fiduciæ)* so bound the Mortgagee that when the debt was paid he was bound to reconvey the Property to the original Owner. This the Creditor might do by a *re-Mancipatio* or a *re-In Jure Cessio*. There arose co-existent with *Fiducia*, that form of Mortgage designated as "*Pignus*," in which the Debtor simply gave the Creditor Property to hold in Possession until the debt or claim of the latter was satisfied. These forms of Security lasted for several centuries; but neither of them fully satisfied the claims of Justice, or sufficed to meet the requirements of either Creditor or Debtor. The *Fiducia*

The *Fiduciary Pact.*

Disadvantages of the ancient modes of Mortgage.

* See Gai. Comm. IV., 62, and note 9, Tomkins and Lemon's Edit., p. 689.

involved great inconvenience, and was a crying wrong to the Debtor, as the Creditor could alienate the Property pledged to him at any moment, leaving to the Debtor merely his Right arising out of the Obligation, and the *Actio fiduciæ* which Gaius refers to as a "*bonæ fidei judicium,*"* whilst the unfortunate Debtor lost his Property. The *Pignus* was of more advantage to the Debtor; but the Creditor was placed under a disadvantage, as he had no Right of Property, but merely a *jus distrahendi*. In the sixth century of the Roman State, or at the beginning of the seventh, through the intervention of Prætorian Law, an amelioration took place by the passing of the Servian Law (*Serviana Actio*). This enabled the Mortgagor to proceed by an *Actio in rem*, against any third Person who might be in Possession of the mortgaged Property. At first this Action was only employed for the recovery of the Property of a farmer *(colonus)* given as Security for his Rent *(pro mercedibus fundi)*. Afterwards, however, under the name of *Quasi Serviana*, it was extended to all kinds of Mortgages. In giving an account of the introduction of this Action, Justinian says: "The Servian Action and the *Actio Quasi Serviana* both took their rise from the jurisdiction of the Prætor. By the Servian Action a suit may be commenced for the stock and cattle of a farmer, which are obligated as a pledge for the Rent of the ground which he farms of his Landlord. The *Actio Quasi Serviana*, is that by which a Creditor may sue for a Thing pledged or hypothecated to him, and in regard to this Action, there is no difference between a *Pignus* and an *Hypotheca*, though

The Servian Law: its original application.

Justinian's account of the Law.

* Gai. Comm. IV., s. 62.

in other respects they differ; for by the term *Pignus* is meant that which has actually been delivered to a Creditor, especially if the Thing is a Moveable; and by the word *Hypotheca*, we comprehend what is obligated to a Creditor by a nude Agreement only, without delivery.*

Hypotheca of Greek origin.

The form of Mortgage denominated *Hypotheca* was derived from the *jus gentium*, and, as the etymology of the name imports, from Hellenic sources. In *Hypotheca* the Creditor was not *Dominus*, nor necessarily Possessor, but still he had a *jus in re aliena*, which he might urge in a suit against any third Person. The Property thus pledged did not become a Servient Property, but it was bound as a *res obligata;* and hence the maxim, "*Res non servit sed obligavit.*"

When *Fiducia* ceased.

After the introduction of the *Hypotheca*, the ancient *Fiducia* fell into disuse; but only gradually, for it continued more or less till the times of the Empire. We find, indeed, traces of it in the Imperial Constitutions, which prove that a long period elapsed before it entirely vanished from the legal institutions of Rome. As, however, a *Fiducia* required recourse to be had to a *Mancipatio*, or the *In Jure Cessio*, it must have quite disappeared in the times of the Emperor Justinian, when these ancient forms of Transfer were abolished. The *Pignus*, as a mode of Mortgage, continued, but it became modified so as to render it agreeable to the new institution known as *Hypotheca*. Originally, as we have already stated, *Pignus* entitled the holder to the mere Possession, but in its changed form it became so extended as to resemble *Hypotheca*,

Pignus made to resemble *Hypotheca*.

* s. 7, Instit. de actionibus (4, 6),

giving the holder all the Rights of a *Creditor Hypothecarius*, who was entitled to an *Actio in rem.*

Distinction between.

The term *Pignus*, in its recent and most extensive signification, must be understood as also including *Hypotheca;* but in its stricter acceptation it is used to denote that species of Mortgage which arises when the thing pledged is also delivered to the Mortgagee. A Creditor may very often have an opportunity to detain an *Hypotheca*, but such detention has not the effect of changing this kind of pledge into a *Pignus*. The Detentor may become the *natural* Possessor of the thing pledged, without obtaining the *Possessio civilis*. There is one passage in the Digest which would seem to indicate that no distinction exists between *Pignus* and *Hypotheca*.

Marcianus explained.

Marcianus says, "Inter pignus autem et hypothecam tantum nominis sonus differt." * In this extract, however, the writer only intends to say that both kinds of Mortgage equally give to the Mortgagee a Real Right in the Thing pledged. Both kinds of Creditor have a similar Real Right. That this is the correct view is proved by the title to the Law, "Marcianus libro singulari *ad formulam hypothecariam*." But in other respects there is a great difference, for the *Creditor Hypothecarius* is only a Detentor, and as such is not entitled to the Interdicts.

Remedy given to the *Creditor Hypothecarius.*

To realise his pledge he must have recourse to the *Hypothecaria actio*, or to the *Pignoraticia (in rem) actio*. The procedure is like a *Vindicatio pignoris*, and lies against the Mortgagor himself in Possession, and also, with certain restrictions, against the *Fictus* Possessor.

The *Formula Hypothecaria.*

The *Formula hypothecaria*, a knowledge of the construction of which is of

* l. 5, s. 1, Dig. de pignor. (20, 1.)

the utmost importance for a right conception of the Roman Law of Mortgage, was essentially composed as follows:—"Iudex esto. Si paret, eam rem, qua de agitur, ab es, cujus in bonis tum fuit, Aulo Agerio pignoris nomine obligatam esse pro pecunia, quam ille Aulo Agerio ex mutuo dare oporteret, eamque pecuniam solutam non esse, neque eo nomine satisfactum esse, neque per Aulum Agerium stare, quo minus solvatur satisve fiat, nisi arbitrio tuo Numerius Negridius Aulo Agerio restituat aut pecuniam solvat, quanti ea res erit, tanti Numerium Negidium Aulo Agerio condemna, si non paret absolve."

Definition of Mortgage.

Mortgage, or Pawn, may now be defined in every case as the Real Right of Property in the goods of a third Person, by virtue of which the Creditor possesses the Right of Detention of the thing pawned, on account of his claim or demand. The Creditor has a Right of Sale in case of need, in order to satisfy his demand. This Right is secured to him because his Right is a Real Right entitling him to the Thing pledged.*

Principal kinds at the present time.

The principal divisions of Mortgage in the Modern Roman Law are the following:

1. *Pignus*, which is a Mortgage coupled with a transfer of the Possession; and Hypotheca, without the transfer of Possession.

2. *Pignus Generale* and *Speciale*, comprising the whole estate of the Mortgagor, or only a part of it.

3. *Pignus Publicum* and *Privatum*, that is to say, a *Pignus* judicially executed, and one not judicially declared.

4. *Pignus Necessarium* and *Voluntarium*, or compul-

* Not an *Obligatio rei*, but a Real Claim, as Von Vangerow maintains.

sory and voluntary, the former being made by order of the Court, the latter voluntarily.

Mortgage presumes a Claim.

A Mortgage presumes a Claim, or Demand, for the satisfaction of which the Pledge has been given. It is immaterial what the Claim may be, as a Natural Obligation suffices to support a Mortgage. But where no Claim can be maintained, a Pledge or Mortgage becomes impossible. The Mortgagor may obtain the Possession of his Property, *ipso jure*, on the ground of the invalidity of the Claim; and by pleading its invalidity *ope exceptionis*, he is able to set up his *Exceptio* or Plea against the Action given to the Mortgagee. Everything may be pledged *quod emtionem venditionem recipit*. Things denominated *Res corporales et incorporales* may be also mortgaged. Hence *Res incorporales* are capable of being pledged. In the first place, however, the pledging of Servitudes must be considered. The Pledge of a Real Servitude is in the very nature of things impossible, as the Servitude cannot be severed from the Land; but the separate Mortgage of the enjoyment of the Usufruct is allowable; not, however, that of the *Usus*. A Servitude that has not been granted may be conceded by way of Pledge; that is, the Mortgagor may concede the Right to the Mortgagee to constitute a Usufruct until his Claim is satisfied. The *Servitutes rusticorum constituendæ* may be pledged; that is, the Creditor may obtain the Right to grant a Servitude to a third party. He does not, however, himself acquire the Servitude. In the case of the Mortgagee of a "*Chose in action*," the Creditor may give notice to the *debitor debitoris*, upon which the Debtor must pay him. If at the time of the

What Things may be mortgaged.

mortgaging of the *Chose in action* a Right of Mortgage was in existence, it continues valid as an additional Security. Every *Pignus nominis*, or Mortgage of a debt, implies and contains a *Subpignus*. Things *in esse* and also *in posse*, part of an Estate (Special Pledge), or the entire Estate (General Pledge), and even the Mortgage itself, may be mortgaged.

Further Requisites.

In addition to the existence of a Claim or Demand, and an object to be pledged, the general conditions or requisites necessary to originate a Mortgage, must also exist in each particular case. These may arise:

Pignus voluntarium.

1. By the voluntary act of the party (*Pignus voluntarium*).

Judicial Decree.

2. By a Judicial Order or Decree.

Pignus necessarium.

3. By operation of Law (*Pignus necessarium*).

A Mortgage can only originate in one of these causes. It cannot arise from Succession; but on the contrary, Succession presupposes its existence. The Possession of this Right always presupposes the Possession of the Obligation, to satisfy which the Pledge or Mortgage has been given. So intimate and close is the connection of Mortgage with Obligation, that it has been said a Mortgage is founded upon Private Disposition.

Two kinds of Voluntary Mortgage.

There are two kinds of *Pignora voluntaria*, namely, those which arise by Agreement (*Pignus conventionale*), and those which are originated by Testament (*Pignus testamentarium*).* The requirements for such Mortgages are: Ownership on the part of the Mortgagor, added to the Right of Disposition. The Property also of a third Person may be pledged in the event of

* The *Pignus testamentarium* has, however, no preference over that which existed *inter vivos*.

the Pledgor becoming the Owner of it;* or upon the Owner consenting, or upon his subsequently ratifying it, or where the Pawnor is the *bonæ fidei* Possessor of the Property at the time of payment.†

The second mode of creating a Mortgage is by Judicial Order or Decree. Of this there are two kinds: Two kinds also by Judicial Decree.

1. The *Pignus prætorium*, which takes place as the result of a *Missio in possessionem*, dating not from the Decree ordering the surrender of the Possession, but from the date of the actual Possession itself.

2. The *Pignus in causa judicati captum*, which is granted to enforce a Judicial Sentence, and which dates from the time of the enforcement of the Distraint.

The third mode of creating a Mortgage is by Legal Prescript. This combines *ipso jure* with the Obligation or Claim from the very moment that the latter comes into existence. But it is only an *Hypotheca* which can be created in this particular manner. Legal Mortgages, that is, those which arise by operation of Law, are of two kinds; they are either those which comprise *the entire Estate* of the Debtor, or those which attach only to certain particular Things. Entitled to a general Legal Mortgage are: Mortgage by Legal Prescript. Who are entitled to it:—The *Fiscus*.

1. The *Fiscus*, for all taxes resulting from Obligations due to him, a rule which holds good especially against the Comptrollers of the Taxes. This Right is

* When this has not been stipulated for, the Pledgor acquires the Property, and the Creditor at the time of making the Pledge has acted in good faith, in this case the Creditor has given to him the *Utilis actio hypothecaria*, and also *Justae exceptiones*.

† The Creditor has the protection of the *Actio hypothecaria*, as the *bonæ fidei* Possessor and the Pledgor are protected by the *Actio Publiciana*.

also possessed by the Prince and his Consort, and likewise by Municipalities.

Infants, Minors, Lunatics.

2. Infants, Minors, and Lunatics have the same upon the Estates of their Tutors or Curators, for all Obligations arising out of the *Tutela* or the *Cura*. This Right of Mortgage also appertains to these Persons where the Mother has discharged the duties of Guardianship, and in the case of her marrying again before rendering the accounts required by Law, and surrendering the Property. This Right further extends to the Property of the Stepfather.

Children of a first Marriage.

3. The Children of a first Marriage have a Mortgage upon the Property which reverts to them upon their Parent marrying a second time.* So also the Children upon the Estate of their natural Father, for the *bona materna* and *materni generis* entrusted to his administration on their behalf.

Wife and her Heirs for her *Dos*, etc.

4. The Wife and her Heirs likewise possess a Mortgage on account of her *Dos*, and also for the *Paraphernalia* to the extent that such may have entered into the Estate of the Husband, reckoning from the date of its receipt; and further, the *Donatio propter nuptias*, on account of commencing from the date of its settlement.

The Husband for the promised *Dos*.

5. The Husband upon the Estate of the Person whose duty it is to constitute or settle a *Dos*, either because he is liable by operation of Law, or because he has agreed so to do.

The Heir, etc., of deceased Husband or Wife.

6. The Heir or Legatee of either the deceased Husband or Wife, upon the Estate of the Survivor,

* The Right of Mortgage does not first attach from the date of the second Marriage, but from the time that the *lucra* are acquired by the *parens*.

where such Estate has been devised upon the Condition of the Survivor not marrying again.

The Church on the Property of the Emphyteuta.

7. The Church has a Mortgage upon the Property of the Emphyteuta for any possible deterioration.

Special Rights of Mortgage, and by whom possessed.

Special Rights of Mortgage are possessed:—

1. By the Lessor of a *Praedium rusticum* on the Fruits of the same, even where they have been raised by a sub-Lessee; but the Claim is restricted to the Fruits, and for Obligations arising out of the Lease.

The Lessor upon the *invecta* etc.

2. The Lessor of a *Praedium urbanum* has a Mortgage upon the *invecta* and *illata* of the Lessee, brought upon the Property by him, *ut ibi perpetuo sint*; and also in respect of Obligations arising out of the Contract of Lease. In sub-letting, the first Lessee has a *sub-pignus* over the Things mortgaged to the sub-Lessee, which remain mortgaged to him for the amount of the rent of the sub-Lessee.

The lender of Money for a building.

3. He who furnishes money for the erection of a house has a Mortgage upon the building, and also upon the ground on which it is erected, provided the money has been actually expended in the erection.

The Ward.

4. The Ward has a lien upon the Property of his Guardian, or on that of any third Person, when it has been acquired with the Ward's money, unless he should prefer to proceed by the *Vindicatio*.

The Singular Successor, etc.

5. The Person entitled to a Singular Bequest, and the Universal Legatee, have also a Mortgage upon the Estate inherited by the Person burdened with the Legacies; and when several Heirs are thus charged, each of them must bear the burden *pro rata* to their respective shares in the Property.

The sphere of the operation of a Mortgage embraces,

A Mortgage embraces the Thing and its Accessions and Fruits.

according to the nature of the Thing pledged, not only the Thing itself, but also all its Accessions.* It likewise comprehends the Fruits, if at the time of their severance they become the Property of the Mortgagor or his Heirs, whether they be tacitly or expressly mortgaged or not. A General Mortgage of the Mortgagor's Property comprehends not only his entire present Estate, but also all his future acquired Property.† It comprises all Singular Things, in the same manner as if they had been specially pledged, and the Mortgage is not annulled by their Alienation. The above also holds good in the case of a mortgaged *Universitas;* and it is only as an exception that the several Things comprised in the General Mortgage can be alienated; namely, in the case where the *Universitas* requires the Alienation of such perishable goods or articles as would be depreciated in value by keeping; for example, Things in a warehouse. Hence, the Thing pledged is answerable wholly and indivisibly for the Obligation, even though the Obligation itself may be divided.‡

Extent of a Mortgage.

As regards the extent of Mortgage, it comprises, according to its nature, the entire Obligation for which it has been given, with all the Accessions

* This Puchta denies.

† From this general rule must be excepted those Things which are actually indispensable to the Debtor, or such as are of especial value to him, such as Household Furniture, Orders, Decorations, &c. The General Mortgage dates from the moment of the Acquisition of the Property, and it comprises all the several Things of which the Property is composed.

‡ If a Creditor dies, leaving several Heirs, each becomes Mortgagee; and the Thing is held to be mortgaged to each. If a Mortgagor dies leaving Heirs, the Thing mortgaged continues chargeable for the amount, until all the Heirs have paid.

thereto; provided the liability was even potentially present at the time of the giving of the Mortgage. Hence, the Thing mortgaged is liable for Interest, Outlays, Costs of Suit, Interest arising from Delay, and Penal Stipulations; if such were antecedent to the Agreement giving rise to the Mortgage; indeed even for Obligations for which the Mortgage has not been given, the Creditor who is in Possession of the Thing mortgaged has, as against the Debtor claiming delivery of the Thing, the *Exceptio doli;* that is to say, he may retain the Thing mortgaged as long as other and further Claims due to him remain undischarged. This Right, however, he possesses only as against the Debtor, not as against a co-Mortgagee, neither before nor during Bankruptcy.

The Matter or contents of a Mortgage.

The Matter of a Mortgage essentially contains the *jus distrahendi.** In order, however, that Sale may be made, the Obligation must have become due.† Further, there must be non-fulfilment on the part of the Debtor; notice of the same in the case of private Sales; two years' notice is required in Sales made by order of a Court; two months must elapse, and finally, there must be observed priority in the Claims of the Creditors. The *Creditor posterior* has no Remedy except that of the *jus offerendi.* According to the Roman Law, Private Sale was allowable; according to the

* By Modern Law, a *Pactum de non distrahendi* has only the effect of rendering it necessary to ask the Creditor three times for payment before Distraint.

† Not, however, liquid, as it is termed, or actually payable, though it is beyond doubt that Sale by the Judicial Decree of the Court will be suspended where objection is raised to the Obligation itself. A Private Sale is void where no Claim or Obligation exists.

German Law, Sale by order of the Court is the rule. Private Sale must be made by the Creditor *bona fide;* that is, the Creditor must act for the greatest possible interest of the Debtor. Hence, he is not allowed to sell to a *persona supposita.*

Effect of *Distractio* or Sale.

A *Distractio*, or Sale, once made has the following effect:—

1. The Property passes to the Purchasers, just as if the Mortgagor himself had made the Sale; hence, with all the burdens which by virtue of the Mortgage legally attach thereto, Rights of Mortgage excepted.

2. As the Creditor only sells *Procuratoris nomine*, he does not warrant Title.*

3. As the rule, *Distractio*, once made, is irrevocable.

4. When a larger amount is realised than will satisfy the Creditor, the Debtor is entitled to the surplus; if less, the Debtor continues liable under the Obligation for the deficiency.

Dominii impetratio.

When the *Distractio* has been unsuccessfully attempted, and the Debtor has received a second notice requiring him to pay, the Mortgage Creditor may himself obtain the Ownership of the Thing mortgaged *(dominii impetratio).* He takes, however, in the first instance, only a Revocable Ownership of the Property, subject to a biennial redemption by the Debtor.

The essential character of every Mortgage, of

* The Purchaser may obtain from the Vendor the cession of the *Actio pignoraticia contraria*, to enable him to resist the Mortgagor in any Action he may bring. It was forbidden by Constantine that a *lex commissoria*, that is, a conditional Agreement, should be made between the Mortgagor and the Mortgagee, that in the event of the former delaying to discharge his Obligation, the Mortgage Property should at once fall to the Ownership of the Mortgagee.

which mention has been already made, is the *jus distrahendi*. This may, without doubt, be qualified by Agreement between the parties. Thus it may be varied as to the mode in which Sale shall be made; or again, it may be agreed that the Fruits of the Property, which properly speaking belong to the Mortgagee, shall be received by him in lieu of Interest *(Pactum antichreticum)*. It is, however, expressly forbidden that the mortgaged Property in the event of default of payment on the part of the Debtor shall, without anything further being done, go to the Creditor *(Lex commissoria)*. The above conditions, however, which are a departure from the general principle regulating Mortgages can only take effect when it has been specially agreed between the parties that such shall be the case.

The *jus distrahendi* may be qualified by Agreement.

There is also established a legal modification of the strict rule. It is ordained that a Mortgage Creditor, having two Rights, the *pignus nominis*, and a *subpignus* shall possess two Remedies by which he may obtain the satisfaction of his Claim. He may sell his Right, or he may exercise it himself. He may exercise the Right arising from a *Chose in action* which has been mortgaged to him; that is to say, he may take steps against the Debtor of his Debtor, provided the time for enforcing his Right of Mortgage has arrived, and the Mortgage Debt is due.* The mortgaged Right of Mortgage becomes available when the time for the exercise of the Right of Mortgage has arrived, and when, moreover,

The Mortgagee may sell his Right, or he may exercise it.

* The Mortgage Creditor may retain the Thing pledged, if by doing so, he can satisfy his Claim out of it. If the Thing mortgaged does not consist of money, the *pignus nominis* becomes changed into a *pignus corporis*.

the time for the exercise of the mortgaged Right of Mortgage has matured.*

Claims of several Mortgagees.

The application of the above principles gives rise to but little difficulty where the thing is mortgaged to one Creditor only. But the important question may arise: How is it when Property is mortgaged to several Creditors at the same time on account of different Obligations or Claims; when it is not adequate to satisfy all the several Claimants? In this case a conflict of interests arises, and the question then to be decided is, who takes by priority? According to the Roman Law, two priorities are known, namely, *Privilegium* and *Seniority*. Preferential Mortgages are possessed by the *Fiscus* for all arrears of unpaid taxes; also by the wife, and *her* children, for her *Dos;* also to the Creditor who has lent money to be expended in the repairs or restoration of a Thing *(versio in rem)*. Among these privileged Creditors, again, some take priority over others; for instance, the *Fiscus* for arrears of taxes, and the Creditor who has given money to pay for a substitute in the Militia, when he himself has reserved such priority of Mortgage by an instrument in writing, such writing being duly attested and signed. All other privileged Creditors take precedence according to their respective priorities in point of time. Where no privilege decides, priority is determined by *time* alone; hence the maxim, "*Prior tempore, potior jure.*"

Two priorities *Privilegium* and *Seniority*.

The maxim *Prior tempore etc.*

For the proof of priority in time, as against the Mortgagor himself, a private written instrument will suffice; but as against other Mortgage Creditors there

* The Mortgage is not chargeable in favour of a second Creditor, for a larger amount than that claimed by the first Creditor.

must be some public Instrument, or other means of proof. As in a privileged Mortgage proof of priority in time is in no wise necessary, it possesses a preferential Right over those which are founded on some public Instrument, but which are not privileged. The prior Creditor has the Right to be satisfied in the first instance; he sells first, and the Creditor taking after him cannot distrain without his consent. But he may acquire this Right of Alienation by placing himself in the position of the prior Mortgage Creditor. This may be accomplished as follows:—

1. By satisfying the prior Creditor, in which case he steps *ipso jure* into the place of the satisfied Mortgagee, and this even though it be contrary to the will of the prior Mortgagee; but he only succeeds to the extent of the Claim of the first Creditor or Mortgagee* (*Jus offerendi* and *succedendi*). Of several Persons entitled to the exercise of this Right, he who is first entitled precedes all the others. When several Rights of Mortgage exist in the same Person, it is necessary to make a tender for all, for if this were not done, he might again immediately use his *Jus offerendi*. The *Jus offerendi et succedendi.*

2. The Person who lends money to the Debtor for the purpose of satisfying a previously existing Mortgage Creditor, reserving, however, the Mortgage to himself.

3. When several Things have been pledged, and one Mortgagee permits the sale of the Property pledged to

---

* He acquires for himself this advantage: he may effect the sale of the Mortgaged Property whenever he thinks best, and at the time most favourable to his own Claim. His own Claim continues unaltered, he has only acquired the Right of determining the time and place of Sale.

him, that another Mortgage Creditor may be paid off with the proceeds; in this case the former Creditor who has allowed the Property to be sold takes the place of the satisfied Creditor.

4. The purchaser of a Thing pledged to several Mortgagees, which the Debtor has sold to satisfy a Mortgage Creditor, acquires as his security the Rights of the satisfied Creditor.

5. In the case of the *Successio in sui ipsius loco* by means of a *Novatio*.

6. When with the assignment of the Obligation the Right of Mortgage is also transferred.

7. When the Mortgage Creditor brings his Action against a third Person in Possession of the Thing pledged, and the latter satisfies the Claim of the Creditor, he may demand the assignment of the Mortgage.

Remedies of the Mortgage. The legal Remedies for the protection of the Mortgage give to the Mortgagee the Right to the exercise of the *Jus distrahendi*. This is given in order to secure the main object aimed at, or contained in the Mortgage. In other words, the law will aid him to retain the Possession of the Property mortgaged if he happens to hold it as a *Pignus*, or help him to obtain Possession if he should simply have the Property as an *Hypotheca*. The Creditor who enjoys the actual *Pignus*, or the Thing in Possession, has the *Interdicta retinendæ* and *recuperandæ Possessionis*. The Mortgage Creditor who has the *Hypotheca* has for his legal Remedy the *Actio hypothecaria*. These Remedies are available against third parties in Possession for the delivery of the Thing pledged, and also if it should be needful, *cum omni* *causa.** The Plaintiff must prove the making of the Mortgage in his interest, and that the Property pledged was *in bonis* of the Mortgagor. The Pleas in answer to the Plaintiff's declarations in this Action are:

Pleas of the Mortgagor.

1. The Plea that the Property is mortgaged to the Defendant himself. The Plaintiff must in this case prove his superior Title.

2. The Plea on the ground of necessary and useful outlays.

3. Several Pleas arise out of the *Beneficium cedendarum actionum.*

4. The *Præscriptio temporis,* which is available when a third party has been in Possession for thirty years, or when the Debtor and Mortgagor have been in Possession for forty years.

5. The Plea of the *Excussio personalis.*

General and Special Mortgage.

The party attacked, the Defendant may demand that the Plaintiff should look to the Debtor and his Sureties for the satisfaction of his Claim; or he may require that the Plaintiff himself shall seek satisfaction in the first instance from some other Property. This he may demand when to a Special Hypothecation a General Mortgage has been superadded (as for example, a house, and all the goods), because a General Hypothecation is presumed to be subsidiary to a Special one.

Interdictum Salvianum.

The *Interdictum Salvianum* aims at altogether a different object to that pursued by the *Actio hypothecaria,* which we have just explained.† It does not seek to determine the Rights of Mortgage, its purport being only to give

* By satisfying the Plaintiff (*Jus offerendi*) he relieves himself from the Action.

† It is an *Interdictum adipiscendæ possessionis.*

the Possession to the Plaintiff. To effect which it is sufficient to prove the fact of the Mortgage having been made. This Interdict is allowed to every Mortgage Creditor, but can be employed only against the Mortgagor.

Remedy for a Mortgaged Right.

A question still remains to be answered: What Remedy has a Creditor in case of a mortgaged Right? In the case of a *Pignus nominis*, he has a *Utilis actio in personam;* in the case of a *Subpignus*, a *Utilis hypothecaria.*

Extinction of a Mortgage: by satisfaction, etc.

The modes or grounds for the extinction of a Mortgage are very various. Two, however, must be mentioned as especially characteristic:

1. The extinction of the Obligation, which takes place when the Creditor is either satisfied, or by his own will or fault remains unsatisfied.

By Sale, etc.

2. By Sale on the part of the Mortgage Creditor.

Other grounds of extinction may be mentioned, as Renunciation, Confusion,* the Expiration of the Term for which the Mortgage was made, or the happening of a *Conditio resolutiva*, or the physical or juridical Destruction of the Thing pledged,† or Prescription, if made by some one who only possessed a revocable Ownership, when the Ownership of the same terminates.

---

* Confusion is not allowed *aequitatis causa* to take place in some instances; for example, where the Creditor purchases the Thing pledged from his Debtor, that an antecedent Mortgage Creditor may be discharged.

† It revives, if the Thing be resuscitated.

BOOK THE SIXTH.

THE LAW OF INHERITANCE.

SECTION XXVI.—*Introduction.*

Von Vangerow, ss. 898—404.
Arndts., ss. 468—610.
Puchta, ss. 446—565.
Gai. Comm. II., 97—289.
Instit. II., III. 1—11.
Glück XLIII., 40 et seq.
l. 1 pr., Dig. de divis. rer. (1, 8).
l. 22, Dig. de fidei, et mandat. (46, 1).
l. 193 de R. J.
l. 151 de V. S.
Gai. Comm. IV., 16, 17.
s. 4—8, Instit. de Con. pos. (3, 9).

Ulpianus observes: " Hereditas enim non heredis personam, sed defuncti sustinet, ut multis argumentis juris civilis comprobatum est."* To which Julianus adds: "Hereditas nihil aliud est, quam successio in universam jus, quod defunctus habuerit." †

Introductory.

THE principle which pervades the entire system of the Roman Law of Inheritance is known as that of direct Universal Succession. In the Laws of the Twelve Tables the exact and fundamental notion implied by the term *Hereditas* comes out fully; and for more than

* l. 34, Dig. de adquir. rer. dom. (41, 1).
† l. 62, Dig. de R. J. (50, 17).

a thousand years it appears to have been always present to the mind of the Roman Jurist. The principle referred to may be explained as follows:—Upon the death of a Man, it is only the physical Being that dies, not the legal or juridical Person, entitled to the Property of the *Defunctus*. The surviving juridical Person attaches to another individual capable of sustaining it, another *Träger*, as the Germans express it, with whom it at once unites. Such a legal Person possesses all the Rights enjoyed by the *Defunctus*, or as it is usually and properly expressed, *he represents him*. That the Successor to the *Defunctus* should obtain *ipso jure* all the Property of the deceased is only a consequence that springs from the peculiar relation which he sustains.

Fundamental Principle of Inheritance.

Thus the essence of Succession consists in this, that there is no change whatever in the legal subject, but only a change in the individual to which that subject becomes attached. Hence it is incorrect to speak of the *transmission* of the Property of the *Defunctus* to a new subject. For example, an Obligation is absolutely untransferable, and by its very nature is confined and fixed to the contracting parties themselves; but whilst this is the case, the Heir steps into the Possession of all the Obligations belonging to the deceased, both *active* and *passive*, that is to say, inherits all his Claims and becomes chargeable with all his Liabilities. The Heir also, in a certain sense, steps into the *bona fides* and the *mala fides* of the deceased, as the *mala fides* of the *Defunctus* is never changed into *bona fides* in the Heir.

Essence of Succession.

Again, this idea of direct Universal Succession is not so narrow that only one Person may be the Successor of the *Defunctus*. The Heir is not always

Several Heirs may succeed to one *Defunctus*.

limited to one Person, or as it is expressed, he is not always *Heres ex asse*, but the Succession may be continued in a plurality of Persons, or there may be what we term co-Heirs *(Heres ex parte)*. A Testator may make A his Heir for the $\frac{1}{100}$th part of the *Hereditas*, and B for $\frac{99}{100}$ths, and each of these Heirs will be a Universal Successor. A Succession in *Universum jus*, and in *Totum jus*, it must be evident, are quite different ideas. A Person who succeeds to the least part of the Estate of a *Defunctus* as a co-Heir, has a Right on all the corporal and incorporal Property of the *Defunctus*, and is also held liable in regard to all the Claims against his Estate. The Universal Successor in Roman Law, and the Modern Heir to the whole of a man's Estate are quite different ideas.

How Succession may originate: by Testament or by Law.

Succession to the Inheritance may originate in two different ways. It may be either derived from a Testament, in which the Testator expresses his own will in regard to the Succession, and in which case we speak of a Testamentary Succession *(Testamentaria Hereditas)*; or in the event of his failing thus to appoint, the Law steps in and provides a Legitimate Succession *(Legitima Hereditas)*. The Heir who is appointed steps into the place which, in the event of a Testament having been made, would have been occupied by the *Heres testamentarius*.

The *Bonorum Possessor* is now regarded as the Universal Possessor.

When we come to the later development of the Roman Law we find a distinction existing between the Universal Successor and the *Bonorum Possessor*. In the earliest times of Rome this distinction was one of great importance, but at the era of the classical Jurists it had ceased to be so, and the *Bonorum Possessor* came to be as much regarded the Universal Successor as the *Heres* who obtained the *Hereditas*.

We are now in a position to understand the following statements.

When the physical Personality of a human Being ceases to exist, his juridical Personality does not become extinct. When death ensues the legal Personality of the deceased is regarded as continuing to exist in the Inheritance, and under these circumstances the Inheritance is said to be an *Hereditas jacens*. It is in consequence of this continuance of the juridical Person that the Rights of the deceased are maintained, and also that his Property is regarded as a totality.

Hereditas jacens.

Exception when the Rights are of a personal nature.

There is, indeed, one exception to this important principle which occurs in the case of those Rights which are of a supremely personal nature; that is to say, those Rights which are inherent to the individual natural person. Such, for example, as Rights of Family, Ususfructus, etc. The Property of the *Defunctus* passes as a totality to certain Persons, and according to legal prescription. For this purpose, a *Successio in universitatem* is ordained, for a Singular Succession would not suffice to accomplish the complete transmission of the Inheritance. It would not, for instance, pass the Obligations. It is to this taking of the Property of another that the term "Succession" is applied; and it is further denominated a "*Successio in universum jus Defuncti.*" The Property thus passed to the survivors is called the Inheritance or *Hereditas;* and it is termed by the Germans "*Erbschaft.*" The Successor is termed the Heir *(Heres);* whilst his Right to succeed is termed

Succession.

his Right of Inheritance, and by the Germans "*Erbrecht*" or *Hereditas*, in that sense of the word which denotes Right of Succession. The Heir always represents the Person of the Testator, for he has suffered himself to be invested with the Personality of the *Defunctus* so far as regards his Property relations. Hence, the Inheritance is a Right in the Person of the Testator or *Defunctus*, which has passed from him to the Heir. As the rule, a certain period of time, of shorter or longer duration, elapses between the death of the Testator, and the *Adition*, or entrance of the Heir upon his Inheritance: hence, the question must arise, Who is the party to be clothed with the legal Personality of the *Defunctus*; or, as the Germans express it, "Who is to be the *Träger* during this intermediate period of time?" In the absence of a natural person, a juridical Person must be found to accept the Inheritance, and such a juridical Person is created in the Person of the *Hereditas jacens*. This juridical Person, for the interval, is regarded as the Owner of the Things constituting the Inheritance. Thus the *Hereditas jacens* may acquire Rights, and may also incur Liabilities; but only under circumstances in which no special act of the Will is required; for it is manifest that the *Hereditas jacens* is possessed neither of Capacity to act nor organs or means of action. The fiction of the Personality of the *Hereditas jacens* ceases the very moment that the Heir has entered upon the Inheritance. But even after the *Adition* of the Heir, the juridical Person of the *Defunctus* must be still considered as residing in the Inheritance. The Heir is, however, always considered as the Representative of

The *Hereditas jacens* is a juridical Person.

the juridical Person of the *Defunctus*, and even when in point of fact, a commingling of the Property of both has taken place, yet, in point of law, the Estate of the deceased is always considered as distinct from the Property of the Heirs.

Hereditas and *Bonorum Possessio.*

The modern Roman System of Succession has emanated from an amalgamation of the strict rules of the Civil Law with the body of rules established by the Praetorian Law. The Law of Inheritance recognised by the *Jus civile*, was termed *Hereditas;* whilst the Law of Inheritance introduced by the Praetorian Law, was denominated the *Bonorum Possessio.*

Peculiarities of the Praetorian Law.

The tendency of the Praetorian Law manifestly led to an extension of the circle of Persons entitled to inherit, which in the *Jus civile* was an exceedingly narrow one, so as to make the Roman Law of Inheritance in some degree co-ordinate with the altered views of the times. The Praetorian Law recognised, indeed, none as *Heredes* who were not such according to the *Jus civile;* but it promised to others, who were not *Heredes*, a *Bonorum Possessio*, or in other words, the Possession of the Heritable Property, if they chose to make *Adition*, or entrance, upon the Inheritance. If they did this, they obtained the Right to avail themselves of the *Interdictum quorum bonorum*, and the legal Remedies appertaining to the Inheritance were available both for and against them, as *Utiles actiones*. The *Bonorum Possessor* was in *heredis loco*. The *Bonorum possessiones* gradually developed into a complete system of Inheritance, but only with reference to the *Hereditas* strictly so called. As the *Jus civile* conveyed the Inheritance, sometimes by Testament, sometimes *ab intestato*, sometimes against the Matter of the Testament; so the Praetor granted the *Bonorum Possessio*, sometimes *secundum tabulas*, sometimes *contra tabulas*, sometimes *ab intestato*. The Praetor also received into his system of Succession the rules of Succession employed in the Civil Law. The Heirs by the Civil Law could avail themselves of the *Bonorum Possessio*, and thereby acquire the benefit of the *Interdictum quorum bonorum*. The order of Succession in which the Heirs by the Civil Law and the Heirs by the Praetorian Law were to be called, was clearly defined. The effect of the *Bonorum Possessio* was different, according as the place of the Heir by the *Jus civile* was prior or collateral or after the place of the Praetorian Heir. In immediate connection with this subject stands the division into the *Bonorum possessio cum re* and the *Bonorum possessio sine re*. Until the time of Justinian, the two systems of Succession stood in marked contrast to one another. This contrast continued even in the time of Justinian, and is presented in the Institutes, the Digest, and the Codex, although previously the Imperial reforms of the Civil Law had been undertaken in the spirit of the Praetorian Law. By the alterations of Justinian made by the Novellæ 115 and 118, the *Bonorum Possessio* has ceased to be an independent system of Inheritance; and in most cases, where formerly only a Praetorian Inheritance was given, at present an Inheritance in accordance with the Civil Law rule is granted. Hence, the advantages of both were combined. Thus the acquisition of the Rights of Inheritance, as a general rule, is now determined in accordance with the

Bonorum Possessio, secundum or *contra tabulas*, or *ab intestato*

Law of Inheritance altered by Justinian.

principles of the *Hereditas.* Only in exceptional cases, where the *Bonorum Possessio* remains, and where it creates an intermediate Possession of the Inheritance, are the principles of the *Bonorum Possessio* applicable. Of this we shall speak more hereafter. The requisites now for a Succession to an Inheritance are:

Requisites for a Succession to an Inheritance.

1. The death of a Person capable of holding Property, even when the Estate consists merely of Debts.

2. The Right of Succession may be as it is expressed purely *passiva;* or the Right to succeed to the Inheritance of a certain Person.

3. Acquisition.

Respecting the second and third prerequisites, it will be necessary, specially, to allude. The Right to succeed to an Inheritance, also requires two further Conditions: Capacity to inherit and Citation. Persons capable of Inheriting or capable of Succession are all natural Persons, but not indeed all juridical Persons. The Capacity to inherit may be granted by legal enactment, or by special concession. By legal Enactment, Churches, Communities, and Charitable Corporations, are capable of inheriting. It is also necessary that this Capacity to inherit should exist in the natural or legal Person at the time of Citation to the Inheritance. The call to the Succession may take place either by virtue of the last Will of the *Defunctus* which has been made for that purpose, in which case, the expressions *Testamentum, Testamentaria hereditas* are applied to the Inheritance; or by legal Precept, where no Testament exists. The latter mode of Succession is denominated *Hereditas legitima,* or intestate Succession.

The *Hereditas* is either *testamentaria* or *legitima*

According to German Law, Succession may take place in consequence of a Contract entered into between the parties; that is to say, by the stipulation of one Person in regard to the Inheritance of another. Such an Agreement, however, is not to be confounded with a Contract between two parties to succeed to the Estate of a third Person; for a Contract of this nature is null and void. As the Heir succeeds in *omne jus defuncti*, Heirs succeeding by Intestacy and by Testament cannot concur together. This is in accordance with the fundamental maxim of Inheritance, "*Nemo pro parte testatus, pro parte intestatus, decedere potest.*" The parties are entitled to obtain the Delation, or Right of Inheritance, immediately after the *Defunctus* deceases. The instant of his death is also the moment of time at which the Delation of the *Hereditas testamentaria* takes place, as soon as it is certain that the *Defunctus* has died intestate, that is to say, without having made a valid Testament. The Delation may be made at several distinct periods of time. This, however, can only take place when the entire body of Persons to whom the Delation of the Inheritance appertains, is no longer existing. The period of the second and third Delation and so on, is the dissolution of the first and second, and so it proceeds. But the Delation only gives the possibility of becoming the Heir. The actual Acquisition of the Inheritance *(adquisitio hereditatis)* takes place regularly by a distinct act of volition on the part of the Heir, which act is presumed by his Entrance upon the Inheritance. Such Heirs are designated *Heredes extranei*, in contradistinction to the *Heredes necessarii*, who only exceptionally, and because they have stood in the

Succession according to German Law.

Intestate and testamentary Heirs cannot concur.

power of the deceased acquire the Inheritance *ipso jure* at the very moment of the Delation.

When the Inheritance has been acquired, it is in accordance with principle acquired for ever. Hence the maxim, "*Semel heres, semper heres.*"*

Legacies: of two kinds till Justinian.

Benefits to non-Heirs at the cost of the Inheritance are termed Legacies. The Roman Law recognised two kinds: Legacies by the Civil Law, and the Praetorian *Fideicommissa*. Justinian has set aside both distinctions and instituted one form of Legacy in their place. But even at the present time, the terms Legacy and *Fideicommissa* are used, though in a different sense. By the expression *Fideicommissa* is to be understood a Thing bequeathed, or devised, which being transmitted through a third Person comes to the Person benefited. By the word Legacy is now implied every other kind of bequest. Each Legatee is termed a Singular Successor. Nevertheless, the objects of a Legacy can not only be separate Things belonging to the Estate, but also certain parts of the same, or, indeed, the whole of the Property. In the latter two cases, it is usual to speak of a Universal *Fideicommissum* or Testamentary Trust.

Section XXVII.—*Of Succession by Intestacy.*

Von Vangerow, ss. 405—426.
Arndts., ss. 478—481.
Puchta, ss. 458—460.
Gai. Comm., III. 1—87 (Tomkins and Lemon's edit.), pp. 431—481.
Mühlenbruch, in Glück's Comm., XXXV., 219; XXXVII., 356.

---

* From this fundamental maxim it follows that no one can be made Heir by a *Conditio resolutiva*.

Instit. de hereditatibus, quae ab intestato deferuntur (3, 1).
" de legitima agnatorum successione (3, 2).
" de SCto Tertulliano (3, 3).
" de SCto Orphitiano (3, 4).
" de successione cognatorum (3, 5).
Dig. si tabulae testamenti nullae extabant, unde liberi (38, 6).
" unde legitimi (38, 7).
" " cognati (38, 8).
" " vir et uxor (38, 11).
" de suis et legitimis heredibus (38, 16).
" ad SC. Tertull. et Orphit. (38, 17).
Cod. unde liberi (6, 14).
" " legitimi et unde cognati (6, 15).
" de suis et legitimis liberis et ex filia nepotibus ab intestato venientibus (6, 55).
" ad SC. Tertull. (6, 56).
" ad SC. Orphit. (6, 57).
" de legitimis heredibus (6, 58).
" communia de successionibus (6, 59).
Nov. 118, Nov. 89, c. 12.
Dig. de successorio edicto (38, 9).
Cod. " " (6, 16).
Dig. unde vir et uxor (38, 11).
Cod. " " (6, 18).
Dig. si a parente quis manumissus sit (37, 12).
Cod. si liberalitatis imperialis socius, etc. (10, 14).
" de hereditatibus decurionum navic., etc. (6, 62).

JUSTINIAN, in his Novellæ 118 and 127, introduced important reforms into the Law of Succession by Intestacy; and in these reforms the principle of Cognation lies at the basis. Succession by Intestacy occurs when a Person has died intestate; that is, when he has either made no Testament at all, or left one that is invalid. The Heirs by Intestacy of the deceased are: Intestate Succession reformed by Justinian.

1. The natural Relations, or *Cognati*, whose Relationship arises from legitimate Marriage. When there has Heirs by Intestacy are: the *Cognati*.

been no Marriage, so far as regards the Mother, Children springing from the union stand on an equal footing with legitimate Children; but such is not the case as regards the Father and the Paternal Relations. It is only the *incestuosi* that have no Capacity for Succession in regard to their Mother and the Maternal Relations. Illegitimate Children, however, are entitled to receive one-sixth of the Property left by the Father, and he the same from them, when neither a Wife of the Father nor Children born in wedlock exist. Children conceived in a putative Marriage, as also those who, though they were born illegitimate, have become subsequently legitimised, rank equally with Children born in wedlock. The Child not conceived at the time of the death of the *Defunctus* can never be entitled to take by Intestacy, because at that time no cognate Relationship existed between him and the *Defunctus*. Entitled by Intestacy also are:

Relatives by Adoption.

2. Relatives by Adoption; though here certain distinctions must be made. Those who have been wholly adopted, and those who have been arrogated, are capable of inheriting as regards the adoptive Father and his Agnates, and, on the other hand, may be inherited by them. To this rule there is, however, an exception in the case of those who have been arrogated during their Minority. The Property of such must be surrendered to their respective families. He who has been *ab extraneo* adopted *(in Adoptione minus plena)* inherits from his adoptive Father, but not from his Agnates, and he himself is not inherited either by the latter or the former. He who has been adopted by a woman, inherits from his adoptive Mother, but not

from her Relatives. In all these cases it is tacitly presumed that the bond of Adoption has continued to the day of the death of the *Defunctus*.

The *Adoptatus* and the *Arrogatus* inherit their natural Father in the First class.

How, it may be asked, is the Law as regards Inheritance in the case of Relatives of the full blood? In the case of the *Adoptio minus plena* this remains untouched in conformity with the ruling doctrine; so also in the *Adoptio plena*. Accordingly, the *Adoptatus* and the *Arrogatus* inherit from their natural Father in the First class. Puchta, however, takes a different view. According to him, Adoption makes no alteration in the relationship of the Child to the Mother, but it does to that of the Father. The *Arrogatus* and *plena Adoptatus*, he thinks, inherit from their natural Father in the Fourth class. The correctness of the common view is shown by the 118th Novella, which ordains, that all the agnate and cognate Descendants shall take the Inheritance in the First class. On the other hand, those whose natural Parents concur with the adoptive Father succeed to the Inheritance of the adoptive Father.

Brothers and Sisters inherit the *Adoptatus*.

As regards Brothers and Sisters of the full blood, they inherit the *Adoptatus*, just as if no Adoption had taken place. Brothers and Sisters created by Adoption succeed in the Third class, with the *consanguinei* or *uterini* of this class. Equally so the *Adoptatus* inherits from Brothers and Sisters related to him by the full blood, or those related to him by Adoption. Entitled, further, by Intestacy are:

Husband or Wife are entitled to Intestate Succession

3. The surviving Husband or Wife, when the Marriage has been dissolved by death. In such a case, if no other Relatives exist, there arises what is

denominated the *Bonorum Possessio unde vir et uxor.* Apart from this general Law of Succession, there exists also a Succession for the poor Widow. She takes one-fourth of the Inheritance, if there are less than four Children; she takes the *virile* portion when there are four or more Children. Of this portion she has only the Usufruct; if, however, the Children are her own, she takes concurrently with them.

The *Ordo succedendi:* Five classes

Amongst those who in the former paragraph are entitled to succeed *ab intestato*, an order of Succession has been established by Law *(Ordo succedendi).* There are Five classes.

The First class.

In the First class, the Persons entitled to the Succession are the Descendants of the *Defunctus;* and also the *Posthumi descendentes.* In this class the proximity of the Grade does not count, even a more distant one is called to the Inheritance, if between him and the *Defunctus* no Delation intervenes. In this case there exists, as it is termed, a Right of Representation, or to use the expression preferred by Von Vangerow, "a legal Substitution." That the Father is entitled to the Usufruct of the Property which the Children inherit from the Mother, that he enjoys the Usufruct of a *virile* portion of the Property of the emancipated Children as a *Praemium emancipationis*, does not prove that the Father succeeds in the First class, for in these instances he is not at all to be regarded as the Heir.

The Second class.

To the Second class belong those Ascendants who are entitled to the Succession; but in this class, the nearer Grade excludes the remoter one, even though the class should belong to another line of Ascent. Further, and equally with these the Brothers and Sisters of the full blood, and again, the Sons and Daughters of these, on their demise, rank in the Second class. The Brothers and Sisters of the full blood take the place of their deceased Parents, but not the Grandchildren.

Accordingly, Ascendants succeed with their Brothers and Sisters, and further, with Brothers and Sisters together with Brothers' and Sisters' Children, and with Brothers' and Sisters' Children alone. This is so since the date of the 127th Novella. Formerly, according to the 118th Novella, the Children of Brothers and Sisters did not inherit jointly with their Ascendants. Brothers and Sisters of the full blood take the place of their deceased Parents.

In the Third class, Brothers and Sisters of the half-blood succeed whether they be *consanguinei* or *uterini*, and are called to the Succession at the same time, and together with the Sons and Daughters of deceased Brothers and Sisters of the half-blood. The Third class.

In the Fourth class, stand the other collateral Relatives, those who do not belong to the Second or Third class, and this without distinction whether they be of the half or of the full blood, but with a preference for the nearest Degree. The Fourth class.

In the Fifth class, the surviving Husband or Wife succeeds by virtue of the *Bonorum Possessio unde vir et uxor*. The Fifth class.

Speaking generally in respect to the Five classes enumerated above, the following principles apply:

1. Each prior class takes precedence of the succeeding one, and excludes the latter class. Prior class preferred.

2. In many classes the proximity, that is, the Degree or Grade of a Person, or of several Persons, gives him or them a preference over others of the same class. Prior Grade usually preferred.

Such is the case in the Second class as regards the Ascendants, and also in the Fourth class.

Successio graduum et ordinum

3. A *Successio graduum et ordinum* takes place in those cases where the Delation to the Inheritance has been without result;* if this be so, it is repeated (Successive Delation). In the first instance the Inheritance is offered to the succeeding Grade of the same class (where the preference of the Grade decides), and after that to the succeeding class. The division of the Inheritance amongst several Persons who have been called to the Succession is made as follows:

Division of an Inheritance among several Persons.

Successio in capita or *in stirpes*, or *in lineas*.

Either as many portions are made as there are Persons entitled to inherit, which is termed *Successio in capita;* or the Estate is divided into as many portions as there are Stems in the Persons constituting the Succession. In this case it is termed *Successio in stirpes*. Again, it may be that two portions are created (*Successio in lineas*), of which one goes to the paternal Ascendants, who again subdivide the portions allotted to them, *in capita*, or by heads. The division by heads takes place in the case of Descendants of the first Degree.

Reservation of the triple portion.

Second and following Degrees divide the Estate *in stirpes*.

If, however, the Wife of the *Defunctus* is pregnant, a triple portion is reserved in order to meet the possible Claim against the Estate, in the event of her having three Children at the same birth. In the case of *descendentes* of the Second and the following Degrees, the division of the Estate is made *in stirpes*, where such Persons are called to the Inheritance alone, or where

* In other words, where no one has become the Heir, whether it be with or without the will of the Delator. Successive Delation is, however, excluded, where the Delator has already acquired, and equally so where a Transmission occurs.

they are entitled to the Succession with Descendants of the first Degree.

In the case of several Ascendants of equal Grade, but belonging to the paternal and maternal Lines; there takes place when they inherit alone, once for all, a *Successio in lineas;* but when they concur with Brothers and Sisters, or Brothers' and Sisters' Children, a *Successio in capita.* The one nearest in Grade excludes all the others. Where several are equally near, and of the same Line, they divide not according to Lines, but *in capita.* In the same Line the division does not take place by Lines. Those that are of an equal Grade share *in capita.*

Ascendants of equal Grade succeed *in lineas* or *in capita.*

Nephews, when they stand alone, in accordance with the decision of the Diet at Spiers, in the year 1529, succeed *in capita*, where they concur with others *in stirpes.* The mode of partition is determined according to the time of the Delation. Manifold Relationship entitles, in the case of the *Successio in stirpes*, and also *in lineas*, to a proportional increase or multiple portion, but this never occurs where the division is *in capita.*

Nephews succeed *in capita* or *in stirpes.*

SECTION XXVIII.—*Of Testamentary Succession.*

Von Vangerow, ss. 427—466.
Arndts., ss. 483—505.
Puchta, ss. 461—484.
Gai. Comm. II., 97, 119 (Tomkins and Lemon's edit.), pp. 293—313.
Glück XXXIII., 347; XXXIV., 26, 53 et seq., 149 et seq.; 1, 10, 39; XL., 109, 188, 248 et seq.; XLI., 229, 254; XXXV., 50. Mühlenbruch, in Glück, XXIX., 117; XXXVIII., 118, 168, 214; XXXIX., XLII., 19, 130 151, 245; XLIII., 370, 381, 390 et seq.

Savigny Syst., II., 204; III., 226 et seq.
Instit. quibus non est permissum facere testamentum (2, 12).
Dig. qui testamenta facere possunt, etc. (28, 1).
Cod. " " " vel non (6, 22).
Instit. de heredibus instituendis (2, 14).
Dig. " " (28, 5).
Cod. " " et quae personæ heredes instituі non possunt (6, 24).
Cod. si quis aliquem testari prohibuerit vel coëgerit (6, 34).
Gai. Comm, II., 117, 193 et seq.
Dig. de conditionibus institutionum (28, 7).
Dig. de conditionibus, etc., quae in testamento scribuntur (35, 1).
Cod. de institutionibus et substitutionibus sub conditione factis (6. 25).
Cod. de conditionibus insertis tam legatis quam fideicommissis et libertatibus (6, 46).
Dig. testamenta quemadmodum aperiantur, inspiciantur et describantur (29, 3).
Cod. quemadmodum, etc., inspiciantur et describantur (6, 32).
Dig. de SCto Silaniano et Claudiano, quorum testamenta ne aperiantur (29, 5).
Cod. de his, etc., at SC. Silanianum (6, 35).
Dig. de tabulis exhibendis (43, 5).
Cod. " " (8, 7).
Dig. de rebus dubiis (34, 5).
Cod. de verborum et rerum significatione (6, 38).
Instit. de testamentis ordinandis (2, 10).
Dig. qui testamenta facere possunt et quem, etc. (28, 1).
Cod. de testamentis et quamadm. test. ord. (6, 23).
Instit. de heredibus instituendis (2, 14).
Dig. " " (28, 2).
Cod. " " (6, 24).
Instit. de vulgari substitutione (2, 15).
,, de pupillari substitutione (2, 16).
Dig. de vulgari et pupillari substitutione (28, 6).
Cod. de impuberum et aliis substitutionibus (6, 26).
Gai. Comm. II., 179, 180.

l. 9, Cod. de impub. et al. substit. (6, 26).
Instit. quibus modis testamenta infirmantur (2, 17).
Dig. de injusto, rupto, irrito facto testamento (28, 3).
Instit. de militari testamento (2, 11).
Dig. de testamento militis (29, 1).
Dig. de bonorum possessione ex testamento militis (37, 3).
Cod. de testamento militis (6, 21).
l. 31, Cod. de testamento (6, 23).
Nov. 107, c. 1.
l. 8, Cod. qui test. fac. poss. (6, 22).

THE Testator has the power to exclude from the Inheritance the regular legal Succession, by the nomination of one or more Heirs. Such a nomination is revocable up to the very moment of his death. According to the Roman Law a declaration of a last Will must be made in a definite form, namely, by Testament. By this is understood that legal transaction by virtue of which a direct Heir is appointed. It is only in a Testament that a direct Heir can be nominated. Other Testamentary Dispositions may be made by Codicil; but the appointment of the Heir constitutes an essential characteristic of a Will. The last Will may, however, contain other Testamentary Dispositions besides the appointment of an Heir; for example, it may contain Legacies and the appointment of a Tutor.

Power of a Testator.

Definition of a Testament.

He who desires to make a Testament must possess the Capacity required to do so. This Capacity is termed the *Testamenti factio activa.* The expression *Testamenti factio*, it is to be noted, has three significations, namely:

Testament factio activa.

1. The Capacity to make a Testament.

2. The Capacity to take beneficially under a Testament which is termed the *Testamenti factio passiva.*

Testamenti factio passiva.

3. The Capacity to act as a Witness at the making of a Testament.

Incapable Persons.

Incapable are Minors, Lunatics, Spendthrifts, Deaf and Dumb Persons; not, however, those who are only Deaf, or those who are only Dumb; Children under the *potestas*, except in regard to the *peculium castrense vel quasi*. The required Capacity must have existed at the time of the making of the Testament, otherwise the Will is invalid, and subsequent Ratification does not repair the flaw. But where a Person at the time of the making of the Will possesses the *Testamenti factio*, but loses it subsequently, the Will remains in force, unless, indeed, he has lost his Right by a *Capitis deminutio*. The reason for this exception lies in the Rule of Law that the *filius familias* cannot die *testatus*.

Formalities in making a Testament.

As regards the formalities that must be observed in the making of a Will, it may be observed that Testaments are either such as have been made under public authority, termed *Testamenta publica;* or private Testaments, *Testamenta privata*. A Testament is regarded as of public authority when it is made:

How a *testamentum publicum* is made.

1. Either by means of a protocol in Court, in which case it is said to be *Testamentum apud acta conditum;* or,

2. By the delivery into Court of the Testamentary document for safe custody, which is termed *Testamentum judici oblatum;* or,

3. By the delivery of the Will to the Regent, when it is called a *Testamentum principi oblatum*.

How a *testamentum privatum* is made: *Ordinary* requisites.

For the execution of a private Testament several formalities are needed. The *ordinary* and the *extraordinary* form must be distinguished. To the *ordinary* formalities in the making of a private Testament belong:

Septem testes, rogati, voluntarii, idonei.

1. The calling together of *Septem testes, rogati, voluntarii, idonei*. The witnesses are said to be *rogati* when they are made acquainted with the functions they

will be required to discharge; *voluntarii* when they are present without constraint; *idonei* are such as possess the *Testamenti factio*, who are not of the female sex, nor are the instituted Heirs, nor under the *potestas* of the Heir; nor Persons under the *potestas* of the Testator; nor Deaf, Blind, Insane, nor Dumb Persons, nor Minors.

Unitas actus.

2. *Unitas actus*, that is, the testamentary Witnesses must be assembled at one and the same place with the Testator; the execution of the Will must not take place on two different days of the calendar, nor be interrupted by any other business. In the case of a written Testament, the document must be submitted to the Witnesses, and must be subscribed by them, and sealed with a proper seal.

Testamentum holographum and *allographum.*

A Testament that is written by the Testator himself is said to be *holographum;* and when written by another person for the Testator, it is termed *allographum.* The Testament written by the Testator's own hand need not be signed by him, when it is declared in the Testament that it is in the Testator's own writing. When not in his own handwriting it must be signed by him.

Testamentum nuncupativum.

The Testament may also be submitted to the Witnesses sealed, but in this case the Testator must declare that the document contains his last Will; he must sign his name upon the outside of it and over it, and the witnesses must append their signatures and affix their seals. In the case of a verbal Testament (*Testamentum nuncupativum*), the Testator must declare in the presence of the Witnesses, and in intelligible language, the entire Matter of the Will. Upon doing this the formalities necessary are concluded. It is also regarded as a verbal Testament if after the verbal declaration it is reduced to writing, in order to facilitate the proof. In such a case it is said to be "*Testamentum nuncupativum in scripturam redactum.*"

Extraordinary forms of private Testaments.

The *extraordinary* form of a private Will consists either in the increase, diminution, or alteration of the above formalities. *Increased* formalities occur in the case of the Will of a Blind Person, or of a Person who cannot write. In the latter case an eighth Witness is called in, who subscribes the Will for the Testator.

Testament of a Blind Person.

The Testament of a Blind Person necessitates the presence of a Notary, or eighth Witness, by whom the last Will is then written; or if it has been already written, it is merely read; upon which he and the Witnesses subscribe and seal the Record. All these forms must be observed in the presence of the Testator and of the Witnesses. *Fewer* formalities are required:

Will of a Soldier.

1. In the case of the Will of a Soldier, executed on the field, in which case certainty of intention suffices. Such a Testament is valid for one year after his honourable discharge from service.

Testamentum tempore pestis conditum.

2. In the case of a *Testamentum tempore pestis conditum*, the Witnesses need not be in immediate contiguity with the Testator.

Testamentum ruri conditum.

3. In the case of a *Testamentum ruri conditum*, in case of necessity five Witnesses suffice, of whom one may subscribe for all where the others cannot write.

Altered formalities in a *Testamentum parentum inter liberos.*

As to *altered* formalities, these occur in the case of the execution of a written Testament by which Ascendants appoint *only* their Children as Heirs; in which case there is no need of Witnesses, but the names of the Children and their portions must be described by words. A Testament of this kind can neither contain bequests to strangers, nor can it annul an already existing valid Will. From this *Testamentum parentum inter liberos* must be distinguished the *divisio parentum inter liberos*, by means of which, the Ascendants predetermine the intestate portion of the Inheritance to be given to a Child.

The Heir must possess the *Testamenti factio passiva.*

The essential Matter of a Testament consists, as already mentioned, in the naming of a direct Heir, or, as it is expressed, the *Heredis institutio*. But the institution of an Heir, presupposes the fitness of the party instituted. He must possess the *Testamenti factio passiva*; that is to say, the fitness of being thought of as Heir at the time of the making of the Testament. A later Acquisition of this fitness does not suffice, not even in conditional institution. The only exception to this rule is in the case of Wills made by Soldiers.

Distinction between Incapacity to acquire and Incapacity to inherit.

Incapacity to acquire is something different from Incapacity to inherit. The question as to the fitness to acquire arises at the moment of the Delation. If the Person instituted was not capable of acquiring the Property at the time of the making of the Testament, but has become so at the time of the Delation, he acquires the Inheritance. The restriction imposed upon the Husband or Wife remarrying, involves a partial Incapacity, since, if the Husband or Wife remarries he or she cannot take more than the least portion given to a Child of the first Marriage. Similar is the limitation of the Concubine and her Children, where legitimate Children exist; they are not permitted to receive jointly more than one twelfth part, and the Concubine herself is not allowed to take more than one twenty-fourth part of the Estate.

The Testator must possess *complete consciousness* and *free will.*

That a Will may possess legal validity, it must have been executed during *complete consciousness.* It must also have originated in the *free will* of the Testator. Where the Testator has been coerced, either to make or alter a Will, the compulsory Disposition is voidable and the Property reverts to the Fiscus. But where the Testator has been prevented from executing a last Will and Testament, Infamy results to the party preventing it, and his portion reverts to the Fiscus.

Error or Fraud vitiates Testament

Where error controlled the Will of the Testator, and where, but for such error, a Disposition would not have been made, the error cancels the Testament. This rule is not contradicted by the maxim "*falsa causa non nocet,*" for, should it be proved that the ground or reason the Testator had held as true, was false, the Testamentary Disposition becomes void; for example, if the Testator institutes A as Heir, and it can be proved that he had only instituted him because he believed him to be his illegitimate Child, whilst A is not his illegitimate child, the Testament becomes void. The same rule applies in the case of Fraud.—

Testament void on account of *Motive.*

Void on account of the Motive are: the Nomination of the Regent *litis causa,* and also *captious* Dispositions, that is, Dispositions made with the Condition that the party benefited shall also institute the Testator or some one else at some future time in his Testament. The invalidity of this Disposition has its cause in the immorality of the Motive. On the other hand, Dispositions made to prejudice the Heirs, termed *legata pœnae nomine relicta*, are not invalid according to the Justinian Law. Thus, Legacies may be left which the Heir is bound to pay in the event of his failing to discharge certain burdens imposed upon him. That a Testament may be legally valid, certainty of Intention is necessary. There must be what is termed *certum consilium*. Hence, a Testamentary Disposition cannot be left to the choice of a third Person. The *tempus solutionis*, however, may be left to the choice of a third Person. A Testament may be also made dependent upon the accidental performance of another, or upon his *bonum arbitrium*. The well-known example is that of "*Si Titius in Capitolium ascenderit.*"

Legata pœnae nomine not now invalid.

The Testator may also name several Heirs, and the choice of *the* Heir may be left to a third Person. If the election is not made, all are called to the Inheritance. But as the Person nominated is, nevertheless, in all these cases, considered as having been nominated under the Will of the Testator (which is in accordance with the general rule); these instances cannot, strictly speaking, be regarded as exceptions. Conditions must generally be dealt with in Testaments as in other transactions. The following, however, is important and peculiar; namely, *Conditiones resolutivæ*, *impossible Conditions*, and those which offend against propriety and good morals, are considered as never having been inserted. They have, however, the effect of annulling another legal transaction. Again, those that are *relatively impossible* are invalid, that is, impossible at the time of the making of the Testament. If they become impossible at a later period the intended beneficiary receives nothing. Those that are *partially*

A Testator may nominate several Persons as his Heirs.

Effect of Conditions in a Testament.

impossible from their very inception only avail as partially inserted. Those that have become *subsequently impossible* are regarded as having been originally inserted. As offending against propriety and *bonos mores* must be reckoned the Condition not to marry; not to change one's Domicil; to have an illegitimate child; to have a child by a woman, whom a man cannot marry. In the interpretation of the conditional institution of an Heir, the leading principle is "*Primum locum voluntas defuncti obtinet.*"

A Condition not to marry, &c. *contra bonos mores.*

The *voluntas defuncti* is to be regarded.

Conditional institution of an Heir.

This maxim holds good particularly where, in the institution of an Heir, several Conditions occur; or if the institution occurs once conditionally, and at another time unconditionally, here the unconditional institution absorbs the conditional one, and the several Conditions are regarded as alternatively added. The Condition attached to a Legacy is not regarded as added to the institution of the Heir. When any one appoints his Child to be his Heir, and imposes upon him the Restitution of the Inheritance to another, the Condition is supplemented to the extent that the Child is considered as having no Descendants. By a Condition the Delation of an Inheritance is deferred till the time of the completion of the Condition. Now, as regards the time of the fulfilment, it matters not in the case of a Condition which is independent of the will of the party benefited, what the time of its accomplishment may be, the Condition may already have been fulfilled even during the life-time of the Testator. But when an act of the Will of the Party benefited is needed to call the Condition into existence; and the Testator desired this act of the Will to take place (*ut testamento pareatur)*, in this case, the act must occur after the death of the Testator. It is somewhat different, if it be material to him what result ensues. In this case, that which we expressed in the previous paragraph holds good.

In some cases, a non-fulfilled Condition is considered as fulfilled. When, for instance, something has to be given to a third Person, and he refuses acceptance; when a *Conditio potestiva*, which one has agreed to perform, becomes, by some chance, impossible. Pending the contingency of the Condition, the Heir cannot touch the *Hereditas*, but he may accept the *Bonorum Possessio contra tabulas*. He must, however, provide Security, the so-called *Cautio Muciana*. This Security must be given to the co-Heirs, and to the substituted Heirs, but not to the intestate Heirs.

A Condition sometimes considered as fulfilled.

Cautio Muciana.

For the fulfilment of this Obligation the Heir who has been instituted under a negative *Conditio potestiva*, or as it is termed, a *Conditio non faciendi*, and, indeed, under such a Condition as first becomes operative after the death of the Legatee, is entitled to the benefits and advantages already mentioned as appertaining to the *Bonorum Possessio contra tabulas*. The institution of an Heir, where the element of Time is introduced, becomes only then operative when the *dies* is *incertus*. A *dies certus*, whether it be *a quo* or *ad quem*, avails as if it had not been inserted. The *dies a quo* not, because the Heir may admit or recognise the *bonorum possessio secundum tabulas;* the *dies ad quem* not, because the rule prevails, *Semel heres, semper heres*. The institution of an Heir with a *Modus* has this peculiarity, that the beneficiary need not fulfil the *Modus* where the fulfilment

The insertion of a *dies a quo* or *ad quem* inoperative.

Institution of an Heir with a *Modus*.

lies solely in his own interest; but the Judge may insist upon its fulfilment when public interests are involved, with this modification only, that is to say, co-Heirs have the Right of insisting upon the fulfilment of the *Modus*. Finally, as a third condition for the legal validity of a Testament, the Intention to make a Will is necessary, and the Intention to accomplish this must be clearly expressed. The declaration of the Intention must also be commenced and completed by means of speech. Again, the legal, and what are termed autonomic forms—that is, such forms as the Testator imposes, must be observed. For example, the Testament must be deposited in Court, when the Testator has declared this to be his wish.

The Intention of the Testator to make a Testament must be evident.

A Testament would be imperfect in which no Heir had been instituted, or which failed to contain all those things that were certainly intended by the Testator. The expressions employed in a Will are immaterial, and it is not necessary to use the word Heir. The Testator may even reserve the designation of the Person who is to be his Universal Successor for another occasion. When this is done the Will is termed a *Testamentum mysticum*. Where the declaration of the Intention is so unintelligible that it conveys no meaning, or one evidently different to that which the Testator intended to convey, the Testament becomes void. Exceptionally, however, the use of an erroneous surname, or a faulty description, a *falsa demonstratio*, as it is termed, does not invalidate, for if the Intention of the Testator can be ascertained with certainty it does not vitiate the Testament. Certainty of the Intention is guaranteed by the Prescript

Testamentum mysticum.

of the *Senatus Consultum Libonianum.* According to this Law, all Dispositions in favour of the party who writes the Testament, or in favour of any one through whom the writer acquires, shall be void, except in the case where the writer is the sole Heir by Intestacy of the Testator. *S. C. Libonianum.*

As the Testator may, at the same time, not only institute one Person, but several, to the Inheritance, the question arises, how great the share of each shall be. When the Testator does not determine the Portions, the Heirs inherit in equal shares. But there may be a tacit Disposition of the Portions of each by the mode of nomination, as when there is the conjunction of several Heirs. Those mentioned in one phrase, or grouped together under a collective name, become entitled to one Portion only. As an example of more than one Persons mentioned in the same phrase, take the following:—"A shall be my Heir; B and C shall be my Heirs;" here A takes half, and B and C take the other moiety. Again, for an instance of those mentioned in one phrase, take the following:—"A and the sons of B shall be my Heirs;" here A takes one half of the Inheritance. When the Testator has instituted the Heirs, either all or some of them, to definite parts of the Estate, the so-called *Heredes in certa re,* all the Persons instituted must be considered as actual Heirs. There is, however, a difference of opinion amongst Jurists upon this point. Some are of opinion that the *Heres ex re certa,* who has been instituted with the Heir for an uncertain Portion or a quota, should be regarded as a Legatee. According to this view he would not have the *Actio familiæ herciscundæ,* and would have to

Portion of each Heir when there are several.

Heredes in certa re.

Inadequate determination of Portions.

allow the deduction of the *Quarta Falcidia.* When the Testator has determined the Portions of each Heir, but not in an adequate manner, it is necessary to distinguish the cases where he has divided too much or too little. In the first instance the Portion accruing decreases; in the latter case the Portions increase *pro rata.* Where only some of the Heirs have Portions given to them, and others are instituted to undefined Portions, in this case when the defined Portions do not exhaust the Inheritance, the residue goes to those instituted Heirs whose Portions have not been defined. But should the defined Portions exhaust the Inheritance, in such a case each Portion is reduced by one half, and the residue thus artificially created is assigned to that Heir whose Portion was not defined.* If the Testator has referred to some other mode of division, the question arises, whether he has intended this Appointment as a Condition, or not. In the first case, if he has intended the Institution as conditional, the rules and principles of conditional Institution apply; in the latter case, where the Apportionment should have been made, and has not been made, the Inheritance is divided equally. When the Testator merely hints at a certain Appointment, which cannot be discovered, the Institution to the Inheritance becomes void.

Testamentum reciprocum.

Several Testators may make their last Testamentary Dispositions in one Testament *(uno actu).* But this as the rule is only allowable when one Testator appoints

The Rule "*Ex asse fit dupondium.*"

* The Romans regarded the entire Inheritance as an *As,* and divided it into parts. Hence they said, "*Ex asse fit dupondium,*" or "*tripondium,*" that is to say, out of the usual fraction of 1-12th into which it was divided, 1-24th or 1-36th is made, as the case may be.

another, in the event of his prior death, to be his Heir. Such a Disposition is called a *Testamentum reciprocum*. Each Testator, however, may revoke his Will at pleasure, but it is presumed that each of the Joint Testaments shall only continue valid when the other has not been revoked. Such a Testament is called a *Testamentum correspectivum*. The Testator cannot bind his Will, for if he could do this it would no longer be a Testament, but a Contract. Thus the Testator cannot be bound to revoke. But the Testator who may choose to revoke his Testament, after he has inherited the Estate of the other Testator, must surrender the Inheritance of the deceased Testator to his intestate Heirs. Exceptionally, however, the Testament of the one party continues in force, though the other has been destroyed; and this is the case when its dissolution has taken place either on account of the Incapacity of the other party, or in consequence of the failure of the party benefited by the Testament.

Testamentum correspectivum.

The Dispositions which can only occur in a Testament are Disinherison and the Substitution of a direct Heir. Substitution, however, may be made in the case of Legacies, but this may also be inscribed in a Codicil.

The subject of Disinheritance will be treated in the next paragraph. Here only thus much should be remembered, that the express exclusion of any one from the Succession, who would otherwise have been the Heir, must be understood as indispensable. A Testator may institute a Person as his Heir, and then threaten him with Disinherison under certain circumstances. Or a Testator may, and this, indeed, is the principal case, disinherit his *Heredes necessarii*.

Substitution of an Heir.

By Substitution is understood the Appointment of an Heir, under the Condition that the Heir first appointed cannot or refuses to inherit. This is termed "*Vulgaris Substitutio.*" He who has power to make a Will, can also substitute; and he who can be instituted as the Heir, can also be substituted as such. One Person may be substituted for several, or several Persons may be substituted for one. In this case, when the Substitute is to enter, all the other Heirs must have failed; that is to say, they must be precluded from becoming Heirs. The order in which they are precluded is immaterial: hence the rule, "*Substitutus substituti censetur esse substitutus instituto.*" From this rule, also, it follows that he who is substituted for a co-Heir, when all the co-Heirs fail, not only receives the portion of the substituted Person, but also that of the instituted Person who has preceded him. Further, a reciprocal Substitution of several co-Heirs is allowable. This is denominated *Substitutio reciproca sive breviloqua*, which greatly resembles the *Jus accrescendi*, but is not identical with it. It is similar to this extent, that the Person instituted, when he has entered, cannot refuse the substituted Portion, and when he has not entered, he cannot acquire the substituted Portion. It is, however, different, in as far as the rule "*Portio portioni accrescit*" does not hold, from which it follows, that to the Heir only, not to his Heirs, the Portion that has failed accrues. In computing the *Quarta Falcidia*, the Heir must bring into hotchpot his Portions obtained, both by Substitution and Institution. As the ordinary, or vulgar Substitution is really the conditional

Substitutio reciproca sive breviloqua.

Institution of an Heir, it takes place where the *primus* does not become the Heir. But the party transmitting must invariably precede the Substitute, because the Delation, as will be hereafter seen, is not vacant.

The Substitution fails when the *Institutus* becomes the Heir, even if he himself, at a later period, allow Restitution to take place; when the Substitute dies before the *Institutus;* when a Transmission intervenes; when the Substitute, in the case of *Substitutio reciproca*, becomes the Heir, but not as the *Institutus*. In the case of Children who are minors under the immediate *potestas* of the Testator, the Testator can substitute an Heir for the *filius familias*, if, at a future time, the Child should become an Heir, but should die during his Minority. This is termed a "*Substitutio pupillaris.*" The Testator who wishes to make a pupillary Substitution, must necessarily name an Heir for himself. He may institute his Child, or a stranger. He may thus disinherit the Child, and yet name a Substitute in his place. But in this case he cannot impose Legacies on the Substitute. This is in accordance with the maxim "*Pater semper suo legat.*" Hence, the Father makes two Testaments, one for himself and one for his minor Child. He may make one in writing, and the other by word of mouth; or he may combine the two in one document. In the latter case, he need only once observe the prescribed formalities; in the former case, he must observe them twice. Similarly, when he makes two documents, his own Testament must, in point of time, precede the other Testament. The Testament for the *Suus* is always valid as an adjunct to the paternal Testament, and it possesses this

When Substitution fails.

Substitutio pupillaris.

The maxim "*Pater semper suo legat.*"

The Testament for the *Suus* an adjunct to the paternal Testament.

peculiarity that it stands or falls with it. Again, the Father is not restricted in his choice of pupillary Substitutes, provided they only possess the *Testamenti factio passiva*. He is, moreover, not bound to regard the *Heredes necessarii* of the Child, nor his own. The pupillary Substitute is the Heir of the Minor, not of the Father. It matters not from what source his Property has been derived. Likewise, both Inheritances may be joined in one Person, namely, in that of the Pupil, or in that of the Substitute. This takes place because the Pupil becomes the Heir of the Father, or because the Father has nominated the Substitute as his Heir. When this occurs, they have to be considered as inseparable, and as one. From this it follows:

Restrictions on the Substitute.

1. The Substitute cannot sever the paternal Inheritance from the pupillary Inheritance, when the Pupil has become the Heir to the Father.

2. When the Substitute has been nominated Heir to the Father, he cannot enter upon the Inheritance of the Father, and disclaim that of the Pupil.

3. When the Substitute has become Heir to the Father, the pupillary Inheritance reverts to him of itself. When the Father, in the case when he is not bound so to do, institutes his *Suus* as his Heir, the pupillary Substitution may then be combined with the vulgar Substitution; indeed, this Canon will be presumed when the Testator has not expressly declared the contrary to be the case. This is denominated *Duplex Substitutio*. But the pupillary Substitute of the pupillary Substitute, is not the pupillary Substitute of the Person to whom the latter is pupillary Substitute. The reason for this lies herein: that in the

Duplex Substitutio

case of several pupillary Substitutions, the object of the second is quite distinct from that of the first. For example, to the minor Son of A, the minor Son of B is substituted; to the latter, X is substituted; here X appears only as the pupillary Substitute of B.

When pupillary Substitution expires.

Pupillary Substitution expires when the Minor comes of age, or if he die during the lifetime of the Father,* or, pass from under his *potestas*, when the paternal Testament becomes void.

Substitution for insane Children.

In analogy to pupillary Substitution, Justinian introduced the Substitution for insane Children. Every Ascendant shall be empowered to nominate a Substitute for an insane Descendant, to whom he has left, at all events, his Legitimate Portion, provided that he makes his selection from the Children of the insane Person, or if he have none, then from the Brothers and Sisters of the insane Person. This is termed Quasi pupillary Substitution. Quasi pupillary Substitution is, indeed, the institution of an Heir, but it only affects that Property which the *furiosus* receives from his Father. According, however, to the constant practice, the Substitution extends to the entire Inheritance. Where several Ascendants dispose of the same, according to Puchta, the Disposition of that one prevails whose parental Right dominates. The great difference between pupillary and Quasi pupillary Substitution is self-evident. Quasi pupillary Substitution expires when the *furiosus* dies during the lifetime of the Testator, when he becomes *sanae mentis*, or has only lucid intervals, or where the paternal Testament fails.

Quasi pupillary Substitution.

* But where the Child has been instituted, this Institution is upheld as a vulgar Substitution.

Recitatio of a Testament.

A Testament which has been made in writing is, according to Roman Law, submitted to the inspection of the Court for the purpose of the Judicial recognition of the testimony respecting the Seal. The Testament is then opened and read. This is termed the *Recitatio*. According to Modern Law the concurrence of the Court is made to depend upon the intention of the Testator, or of the parties interested. Those who are to execute and carry into effect a Testament, that is to say, the Father, or the Authorities, or the Law, or the parties interested, are designated the Testamentary Executors.

Testamentary Executors.

Invalid Testament.

In concluding this section, it is necessary to make some statement as to the Invalidity of a Testament. A Testament is either invalid from its inception, or it becomes so subsequently. A Testament is invalid from its inception:

1. By reason of some defect in its form, in which case it is a *Testamentum injustum, sive non jure factum.*

2. In consequence of some defect in the Institution of the Heir, because the Testator at the time of the making of the Testament did not possess the *Testamenti factio activa.* The Testament is then said to be *Testamentum nullum* or *nullius momenti;* and by the Ancient Law it was invalid by the Preterition of a *Suus.*

Grounds of subsequent invalidity.

A Testament becomes subsequently invalid:

1. When the Testator becomes *alieni juris;* hence, if he suffers a *Capitis deminutio*, his Testament becomes a *Testamentum irritum.*

2. When the instituted Heir declines the Heirship, or cannot accept it. This may occur when the instituted Heir dies, or loses the *Testamenti factio passiva*, or when the Condition interpolated in the Will defeats

the Institution of the Heir. When this takes place neither the co-Heirs nor the substituted ones can enter, and there results what is termed a *Testamentum destitutum*.

Testamentum destitutum.

3. When the Testament has been broken, whether this happens because, subsequently, a *Praeteritus Suus* arises, either by Conception in Wedlock, Adoption, Arrogation, or by Legitimation, or because the Testator himself revokes his Testament. In this case it is termed *Testamentum ruptum*.

Testamentum ruptum

Again, a Testator may revoke his Testament by the making of a new and valid Testament, even when the Revocation of the former one is not expressly stated. The exceptions to this rule are:

A Testator may revoke his Testament by making a new Will.

a. Even the incompleted Testament shall operate to produce a *Testamentum ruptum* when the nearest Heirs by Intestacy having been passed over in the first Testament, are instituted in the second.

b. When the Testator destroys the second Testament with the avowedly declared intention of restoring the first Testament.

c. When the Testator, under the erroneous impression that the Heirs in the first Testament have failed, makes a second one, the Institution of the Heirs in the first Testament continues in force. When the Testator, in the second Testament, desires the validity of the first, it continues operative as a Codicil. Moreover, by the mere Revocation of a Testament ten years old, before the Court, or in the presence of three Witnesses, and further, by its physical destruction.

A Testament becomes subsequently void:

4. When it is *Inofficious*. A Testament which is

invalid from its very inception, or which has subsequently become so, is either void or voidable.

Testaments which are void.

Void Testaments are:

1. The *Testamentum injustum.*

2. The *Testamentum irritum.* In order that this may take place, it is necessary that the Testator should have regained his lost *status* before death.

3. The *Testamentum destitutum.*

4. The *Testamentum ruptum*, unless, indeed, the *Heredes necessarii* have ceased to exist before the death of the party leaving the Inheritance.

Voidable Testaments.

Voidable Testaments are:

1. Testaments made under Coercion.

2. The Inofficious Testament. When a Testament becomes invalid, as the rule, Succession by Intestacy follows; but when an Inofficious Testament becomes only in part void, in this case (see the next Section), the Succession that takes place is partly Testamentary, partly that by Intestacy. A voidable Testament may be made to convalesce by the recognition of the parties interested, not so the Testament that is actually void. The void Testament only acquires stability when the parties interested therein concur by an Agreement, in which case, there is a *Venditio hereditatis*. Any different mode of acknowledgment contains only the repudiation of the Person recognising it, and the other Heirs who become Claimants to the Inheritance by Intestacy are not excluded thereby.

Section XXIX.—*Of Necessary Succession.*

Von Vangerow, ss. 467—489.
Arndts., ss. 591—607.

Puchta, ss. 485—495.
Gai. Comm., II., 115, 123, 124, 127, 134, 137; III., 71.
Glück, VI., 560 et seq.; VII., 1—490; XXXV., 76—119.
Mühlenbruch, XXXV., 119, 133, 301; XXXVI., 1, 38; XXXVII.; XXXVIII., 1—117.
Instit. de exheredat. liberorum (2, 13).
Dig. de liberis et postumis heredibus instit. vel exheredandis (28, 2).
Cod. de liberis præteritis vel exheredatis (6, 28).
" de postumis heredibus instituendis vel, etc. (6, 29).
l. 29, Dig. de liber. et postum. hered. etc. (28, 2).
Dig. de bonorum possessione contra tabulas (37, 4).
Cod. " " " " etc. (6, 12).
l. 12, pr., Dig. de inj. rupt. irrit. fact. testamento (28, 3).
Dig. de inofficioso testamento (5, 2).
Instit. de " " (2, 18).
Cod. " " " (3, 28).
Nov. 115, c. 3, 4; 123, c. 19.
Cod. de inofficiosis donationibus (3, 29).
" " " dotibus (3, 30).
Nov. 53, c. 6.
" 117, c. b.

The Testator is placed under certain restrictions.

THE Testator is, as regards the Persons to whom he leaves his Property by Will, not absolutely unrestricted. He must, according to Legal Prescript, pay regard to certain Relatives in a particular manner. There are three rules he is bound to consider:

1. He must remember certain of his Relatives.

2. Again, for Others he must make provision.

3. Others he is required to institute, when none of the grounds of Disinherison laid down by the law are stated to exist.

In consequence of these principles a Succession sometimes takes place even against the Will of the *Defunctus*, and it is to this Succession that the phrase

A Testator must not pass over his *Sui*, his *Emancipati*, nor his *Heredes necessarii*.

"Necessary" is applied. The first limitation of the Testator, namely, that he must remember certain of his Relatives is one that is purely formal. He is required either formally to institute, or formally to disinherit his *Sui*, his *Emancipati*, and his *Heredes necessarii*. If he pass over the former, the Testament becomes null and void. When he passes over the latter, the *Bonorum Possessio contra tabulas* takes place. But the *Sui*, as well as the *Emancipati* are entitled to the *Bonorum Possessio contra tabulas*. The latter operates by displacing the Institution of the Heir, and by establishing the Claim of the Persons called under the *Bonorum Possessio*, not, however, of all the Heirs by Intestacy. In this case the Testament is not absolutely annulled, but the beneficiaries in it are displaced so far as their Rights are incompatible with that of the necessary Heirs. When several Persons are called, the order of Succession is the same as that by Intestacy. Exceptionally, also, not only the *Liberi praeteriti*, but also the *Instituti* have the *Bonorum Possessio contra tabulas;* when, for instance, another necessary Heir is passed over, and is thus in the position to make use of the *Bonorum Possessio (Commisso per alium edicto)*.

The *Legitimate Portion*.

The second restriction imposed upon the Testator is that he is bound to make provision for certain Persons; this, indeed, is a material restriction. The portion of the Estate applicable for this purpose is termed the *Legitimate Portion (Portio legitima)*, and those entitled are termed, "Persons entitled to the Legitimate Portion." These are:

1. The Descendants of the Testator, to the extent

that they would have inherited from him *ab intestato*. Those, however, who have been arrogated and those adopted from an Ascendant are not entitled, as far as regards the natural Father; nor those adopted *ab extraneo*, as far as regards the adoptive Father.

Entitled to it are the Descendants of the Testator.

2. The Ascendants of the Testator in the absence of Descendants and under similar conditions.

His Ascendants.

3. The Brothers and Sisters of the full blood and half blood on the Father's side, when the Testator has instituted a *Turpis persona*. This rule does not include the *Liberi uterini* and Brothers' and Sisters' Children. A necessary Heir who has been excluded by this Order of Succession, is not necessarily so for ever, for those preceding him may fail in consequence of Renunciation; or upon being nonsuited in the Testamentary Suit, termed the *Querela*, upon which the Delation to the Inheritance is repeated. The "Plaint of an inofficious Will," as the *Querela* has been termed, may fail on account of the Person who institutes it having been legally disinherited. The amount or extent of the Legitimate Portion varies according to the number of Persons who would have inherited the *Defunctus ab intestato*. If there are four or less, the Legitimate Portion is one-third of the Portion by Intestacy of the necessary Heirs; when there are five or more, it amounts to the half of that Portion. In computing the Legitimate Portion it is necessary to pay regard to the value of the Estate of the *Defunctus*, as only the net value of the Estate is taken into consideration. In respect to the number of persons, according to which it has to be computed (as all the intestate Heirs, and those also who have been disinherited are to be

His Brothers and Sisters

Amount of the Legitimate Portion.

reckoned), the calculation must be made with reference to the time of the death of the *Defunctus*. For the Bequest of a Legitimate Portion no special form is prescribed. This, however, is understood, that it must be left, as it is expressed, *sine gravamine;* that is, no Condition must be imposed, and there must be no restriction as to Time or Mode. A *gravamen* is indeed considered as if it had not been written. When more than the Legimate Portion has been left, the *gravamen* is allowed to burden the surplus. The invalidity of the *gravamen* is set aside by the acceptance of the party burdened, and the acceptance is brought about by the granting of a surplus subject to the Condition that one submits to the *gravamen*. This is what is termed the *Clausula Socini*. All that the Testator *mortis causa* has left to the Party entitled must be included in the calculation of the Legitimate Portion. That, however, which has been given *inter vivos*, as the rule, is not included. This is the case:

The *Clausula Socini.*

Gifts *inter vivos* not included in the Legitimate Portion.

1. When it was so stipulated at the time of making the Gift.

2. When it was given as a *Dos*, or a *Donatio propter nuptias*.

3. When it has been given for the purchase of a Post *(militia)*.

Not included in this calculation is also that which the Person entitled has not received directly from the Testator *(ex substantia)*, but has obtained by the failure of another, as in the case of Substitution or Accretion. If the Testator has failed in fulfilling his duty by passing over Persons whom he ought to have remembered, or by Disinheritson of Persons whom he ought to have

The *Querela inofficiosi testamenti.*

made provision for, this does not invalidate his Testament, but the parties entitled may, after his death, attack it by means of the *Querela inofficiosi testamenti*. The *Querela* is based upon the fiction, that the Testator was insane, "*Quasi non sanæ mentis fuerit testator.*" It proceeds for the destruction of the Testament and the Delation of the Succession by Intestacy. After the *Querela inofficiosi testamenti* has been instituted, it is thought that during the Process another suit cannot be brought for the recovery of the Inheritance. The Plaintiff is the Person first entitled *in concreto* to the Legitimate Portion. The Action passes only to the Heirs when it has been commenced, that is, when preparatory steps have been taken. Nevertheless, Descendants may transmit it to their Heirs, if they have died *deliberante herede scripto*. When a Transmission does not take place, for example, when a party entitled repudiates, what is termed Accretion ensues. When all the first Delations fail without giving rise to any Transmission, a new Delation is commenced. From this it follows, that the Testator must make provision for the next Persons entitled to the Legitimate Portion, if he has disinherited the first in a legal and proper manner. The Defendant in the *Querela* is the party who has entered upon the Inheritance by virtue of the Testament, and likewise the Universal Fidei-Commissary, to whom Restitution has been made. The effect of the Action is the Rescission of the entire Testament with all its Contents, against which the *Clausula codicillaris* does not protect. This effect of the Rescission of the Testament may in part take place:

The Defendant in the *Querela*.

1. When the suit has been brought or has succeeded

nly against one of several Heirs. It is only the nstitution to the Inheritance that concerns him and he Legacy that depends thereon, that are rescinded. For example, a Brother brings a suit, and there are instituted in the Testament partly *personæ turpes*, partly *honestæ*; or there is found amongst the instituted Heirs, an Heir by Intestacy, who is instituted only for his Intestate Portion.

2. When the Portion of the Plaintiff does not amount to the whole of the Inheritance. For example, a Brother and a Nephew of the full blood exist; as only the Brother of the full blood is entitled to the Legitimate Portion, he can proceed only for a partial Rescission. The Portion that would go to the Nephews remains with the Testamentary Heirs.

3. When of two parties entitled to a Legitimate Portion, one succeeds and the other fails. These rules are consequences of the principal rule, that no one can claim more than his Intestate Portion by Intestacy.

The *Querela* is barred after the expiration of a *Quinquennium*, or period of five years; or by the death of the party entitled when the proceedings have not been prepared or commenced; further, by express or tacit Renunciation. For example, by the acceptance of Legacies, purchased from the Heirs. A Renunciation during the lifetime of the Testator is impossible. Finally, when the Testament does not appear as a violation of duty in consequence of the improper conduct of the necessary Heir; when the *Defunctus*, by immoderate donations amongst parties living, or by an *immodica* , has violated the Legitimate Portion, whether intentionally or not. In these instances, the *Querela inofficiosæ donationis vel dotis* may be instituted.

The *Querela* is employed as a Plea, when an Action is brought upon the promise of a Donor. The violation of the Legitimate Portion must exist at the time of the making of the Gift, and also at the time of the death of the Testator. The Plaintiffs are the same Persons as those entitled to institute the *Querela inofficiosi testamenti*. The Defendants are the Donee and his Heirs. This Action does not lie against third Persons. By means of the *Querela*, the Donation is so far rescinded as may be necessary for the supplementing of the Legitimate Portion, but not the whole of it; and in the case of several successive Donations, commencement is made with the last. The reasons for setting it aside are the same as those laid down for the *Querela inofficiosi testamenti*. When something has been left to the Person entitled to a Legitimate Portion, but not the whole of the Legitimate Portion, the *Querela inofficiosi testamenti* does not apply, but instead of it, the *Actio ad supplendam legitimam*. This Action partakes of the nature of the Action by which a certain devised Property is claimed; thus it is sometimes the Action to recover a Legacy, sometimes the *Actio familiæ herciscundæ*, sometimes the *Hereditatis petitio*. The Action also passes to the Heirs, and neither the acceptance of the Property left, without reservation, nor the expiration of a period of five years prevents its being employed.

The *Querela* may be employed as a Plea.

The third limitation has been introduced by Justinian in the 115th Novella. It consists in this:—Descendants shall either institute their Descendants who shall be entitled to the Legitimate Portion, and Descendants their Ascendants similarly entitled; or

The Rule as to the *Querela* introduced by Justinian.

if a lawful ground exists for Disinherison, disinherit them with a statement added containing the reasons. Hence there can be no Preterition, no Disinherison without a declaration of the grounds upon which it is made; and the instituted Heir must prove the ground of the Disinherison. The Institution may be in any form the party chooses, as long as it is direct. If the Persons instituted have too small a share assigned to them, they have the Right to sue for the deficiency; if they have been instituted under a Condition, the Condition is struck out.

Grounds upon which Parents may disinherit their Children.

Parents may disinherit Children on the following grounds:

1. When they have been guilty of some outrage towards their Parents.

2. When they have in some other way caused them a gross injury.

3. When they bring a criminal charge against them, treason excepted.

4. When they associate themselves with poisoners.

5. When they attempt the life of their Parents.

6. When they have had sexual intercourse with the wife, or bride of the Father.

7. When they have caused the Parents a heavy pecuniary loss by Denunciation.

8. When a male Descendant refuses to become Bail for the person or debt of his imprisoned Ascendant.

9. When Children prevent their Parents from making a Will.

10. When they join a band of jugglers or stage-players against the wish of their Parents, provided that the Parents do not themselves carry on such an occupation.

11. When a Daughter, who is a Minor, abandons herself to an immoral course of life; and when a Daughter of full age pursues a like improper course, having refused a decent Marriage.

12. When the Descendant has neglected an insane Ascendant.

13. When the Descendant has failed to ransom his Ascendant from imprisonment.

14. When a Child becomes heretical, whilst his Ascendant remains orthodox.

When Descendants may disinherit.

Descendants may disinherit their Ascendants where they find the latter placed similarly as described in the paragraphs numbered 3, 5, 6, 9, 12, 13, 14. In the violation of the grounds for Disinherison, analogy is not excluded. The above-named legal Prescripts entail the invalidity of the Institution of the Heir as a consequence, without however vitiating the other Testamentary Dispositions. As to the legal Remedy by which the invalidity may be tested, a controversy exists. According to Von Vangerow, a *Querela* of nullity must be instituted. Puchta rejects this notion, and makes the following distinctions: If there has been formal failure, that is, if no grounds have been set forth for the Disinherison, only a declaration of the necessary Heirs is required, that they intend to avail themselves of the Necessary Succession. Thus there is an analogy to the *Bonorum Possessio contra tabulas*. When the failure has been made in some material point, as an invalid reason assigned for the Disinherison; in such a case the Heirs possess the *Querela inofficiosi testamenti*. The *Querela*, according to Modern Law, operates as the Rescission of the Institution of the Heir.

Rule laid down in the Novellæ as to Necessary Heirs.

What relation, it may be asked, does the Modern Law assume as set forth in the Novellæ in respect to the Earlier Law bearing upon the Necessary Heirs. As regards Brothers and Sisters, the Law contained in the Novellæ ordains nothing new. The Descendants and Ascendants, however, by the Novella 115, are made Necessary Heirs on account of Preterition. Thus the *Sui* and the *Emancipati* are no longer exclusively such. It is a disputed point whether the results of the Ancient Law come into operation at the present time, when an unallowed Preterition according to the Ancient Law has preceded. According to Von Vangerow the Institution and Disinherison of the *Sui* and the *Emancipati*, and the operative legal Remedies to be employed, are all required to be determined according to the principles of the Ancient Law.

Von Vangerow's view.

According to this view the following must be considered as valid Law:

1. When the Testator has neither formally instituted nor disinherited his *Sui* or *Emancipati*, either the Testament becomes null and void, or the *Bonorum Possessio contra tabulas* takes place.

2. When he has disinherited the same without the introduction of any lawful grounds of Disinherison, the *Remedium* according to Novella 115 steps in.

3. When the Testator has passed over other Descendants or Ascendants, again the *Remedium* according to Novella 115 becomes applicable.

Puchta's view.

According to Puchta, the Prescripts contained in the Novellæ take the place of the Prescripts of the Ancient Law. As a result of this, there would be at present no distinction between the *Sui* and the *Emancipati* and the other Ascendants and Descendants. In case of Preterition, the law laid down in the Novellæ applies to all these Persons. The law in force would be this:

1. The Testator must either institute the Persons named as Heirs, or he must disinherit them upon some specially adduced lawful grounds for Disinherison.

2. The burden of the proof of this lies upon the instituted Heir. In addition to Disinheritance as a punishment, *Exheredatio bona mente* is likewise allowable. For instance, a person disinherits his spendthrift Son, but institutes his Children as Heirs, and provides sufficiently for the maintenance of his Son. In such a case, all that is required is, that the good intention of the Testator should be adequately expressed.

3. The violation of these Prescripts involves the invalidity of the Institution of the Heir, without, however, invalidating the other Dispositions.

4. The invalidity is not an absolute nullity, but only a rescissibility.

5. The invalidity is brought about sometimes by the declaration of the Necessary Heirs that they intend to avail themselves of the Necessary Succession, sometimes by the *Querela inofficiosi testamenti*.

6. The Heirs by necessity succeed thereupon *ab intestato*.

7. Also partial exclusion necessitates the naming of a ground for the Disinherison.

8. As regards Brothers and Sisters, the Ancient Law remains in force.

Section XXX.—*Of the Dissolution of the Delation.*

Von Vangerow, ss. 490—496.
Arndts., ss. 501, 502, 508, 519, 520.

Puchta, ss. 495—506.
Gai. Comm. II., 199, 205, 215, 223.
Mühlenbruch XXXVIII., 466 et seq.; XLIII., 103 et seq., 109, 143 et seq., 243.
l. 18, s. 1, l. 19, Cod. de jure delib. (6, 30).
l. un. Cod. de his, qui ante apertas tabulas, etc. (6, 52).
l. un. s. 5, Cod. de caduc. tollendis (6, 51).
Dig. de acquirenda vel omittenda hereditate (29, 2).
Cod. de repudianda bonorum possessione (6, 19).
" " vel abstinenda hereditate (6, 31).
Cod. quando non petentium partes petentibus accrescant (6, 10).
Cod. de caducis tollendis (6, 51).

Grounds for the dissolution of the Delation.

A DELATION is dissolved when the Acquisition does not take place. The grounds for the dissolution are: The death of the party entitled to the Delation, or the Renunciation of the same; intervening unfitness to acquire; the unworthiness of the party to whom the Delation is made; and the Rescission of the Testament. The Delation cannot be annulled by a *Conditio resolutiva*. The *Clausula privatoria* is no *Conditio resolutiva*. It is either:

1. Disinherison, which must take place at the time of the Institution of the Heir; or,

2. A conditional Appointment of a Universal Fideicommissum.

SECTION XXXI.—*Of the Acquisition of the Hereditas, and of the Bonorum Possessio.*

Von Vangerow, ss. 497—518.
Arndts., ss. 506—520.
Puchta, ss. 496—505.
Gai. Comm. II., 153—158, 161—163, 166—169.
Glück VII., s. 562 et seq.; XI., 1 et seq.; XXXVIII., 330 et seq.

Mühlenbruch XXXVI., 140 et seq.; XLI., 277 et seq., 355 et seq.; XLII., 289 et seq., 325 et seq., 445 et seq.; XLIII., 124 et seq., 150 et seq.
Savig. Syst. IV., 451 et seq.
Instit. de heredum qualitate et differentia (2, 19).
Dig. de acquirenda vel omittenda hereditate (29, 2).
Cod. de jure deliberandi et de adeunda vel acquirenda hereditate (6, 30).
l. 14, Dig. de suis et leg. her. (38, 16).
l. 6, s. 5, Dig. de acqu. vel om. her. (29, 2).
l. 30, s. 10, Dig. de fideic. libert. (40, 5).
l. 7, s. 1, Dig. h. t. (29, 2).
l. 59, s. 6, Dig. de hered. inst. (28, 5).
Dig. de jure deliberandi (28, 8).
Cod. " " (6, 30).
l. 3, s. 7, Dig. de bon. poss. (37, 1).
l. ult. Cod. qui admitti ad bonorum poss. (6, 9).
ss. 9, 10, Instit. de bon. poss. (3, 9).
l. 22, Cod. de jure deliberandi (6, 30).
Nov. 1, c. 2, compare with s. 6 Instit. de hered. qual. et differentia (2, 19).
Dig. de separationibus (42, 6).
Cod. de bonis auctor. jud. possid., etc. (7, 72).
s. 5, Instit. de oblig. quae quasi ex contr. (3, 28).
Dig. de hereditatis petitione (5, 3).
" si pars hereditatis petatur (5, 4).
" de possessoria hereditatis petitione (5, 5).
" de fideicommissaria hereditatis petitione (5, 6).
Cod. de petitione hereditatis (3, 31).
Gai. Comm. IV., 133, 134.
Dig. quorum bonorum (43, 2).
Cod. " " (8, 2).
Cod. de Edicto D. Hadriani tollendo et quemadmodum, etc. (6, 33).
Dig. de bonorum possessione furioso, etc. (37, 3).
Cod. de curatore furiosi vel prodigi (5, 70).
Dig. de ventre in possessionem mittendo, etc. (37, 9).
" si ventris nomine muliere in possessionem, etc. (25, 5).

Dig. si mulier ventris nomine in poss. (25, 6).
Dig. de Carboniano Edicto (37, 10).
" " " (6, 17).
l. 20, Dig. de inoff. testamento (5, 2).
Dig. familiæ herciscundæ (10, 2).
Cod. " " (3, 36).
Cod. communia utriusque judicii, tam familiæ, etc. (3, 38).
Dig. de collatione (37, 6).
Dig. de dotis collatione (37, 7).
Cod. de collationibus (6, 20).
Nov. 18, c. 6.
Dig. de hereditate vel actione vendita (18, 4).
Cod. " " " (4, 39).

Sui and *Extranei heredes.*

I. Acquisition of the Hereditas. It is necessary to distinguish between the *Sui heredes* and the *Extranei heredes*. All Children who are in the *potestas* of the Testator are *Sui heredes*. The *Sui heredes* acquire the Inheritance *ipso jure*, and they are, according to the *Jus civile, Heredes necessarii;* except, indeed, when the Testator has, by instituting them under a *Conditio potestiva (si voluerit)*, made them *Heredes*. By the Praetorian Law these Heirs obtained what is denominated the *Beneficium abstinendi*, by which they can free themselves, if they are so minded, from the Inheritance. This *Beneficium* passes to the Heirs. It is lost by Merger. Such abstinence from the Inheritance may, however, be set aside. All Heirs that are not *Sui* are

Heredes voluntarii.

Extranei, and all *Extranei* are *Heredes voluntarii*. To effect the Acquisition of the Inheritance by a *Voluntarius*, Entrance upon it is always necessary. For an Entrance upon the Inheritance there must be a Power to will, and a Capacity to dispose. Thus, in the case of an *Impubes*, a *Minor*, a *Prodigus*, the co-operation of a Guardian is required. In the case of a *Filius familias*, who is an *Infans*, the Father enters, otherwise both together; upon which the Inheritance belongs to the *peculium adventicium*. If the Father refuses his co-operation, the Inheritance becomes a *peculium adventicium irregulare*. When the Son refuses to co-operate, the Father may enter for himself. There must also be three months' knowledge of the Delation, and Entrance must be strictly in conformity with its provisions. Thus a conditional or a deferred Entrance is void. The time of Entrance is, only as the exception, not optional with the Heir. It is not optional:

Time of Entrance sometimes not optional with the Heir.

1. When the Testator has named a certain period in his Testament.

2. When the necessary Heir wishes to institute the *Querela inofficiosi testamenti*, the instituted Heirs must enter within six months, or within one year, according as they are present or absent from the country. When they have not entered, they are treated, after the expiration of this time, as if they had done so. If the Heir delays to enter, the parties interested, namely, the Heirs of the Substitute and the Creditors, have the Right to compel him to petition for a period for deliberation, termed the *spatium deliberandi*. Such a respite of time the Judge is not allowed to extend beyond a period of nine months. What has been said in the former paragraph applies also here. The Heir who enters upon the Inheritance during this time is not regarded as such; but he is bound, in order to avoid future Liability, to make an Inventory. Should he not make an Inventory, and subsequently refuse the Inheritance, he is exposed to the Oath of Discovery by the parties interested; if, however, he enters, he

cannot deduct from the Legatees the *Quarta Falcidia*.

What constitutes an Entrance upon an Inheritance.

The Entering upon an Inheritance consists in the declaration of the Heir that he intends to accept the Inheritance which has fallen to him. If this is made expressly, it is termed *Aditio hereditatis;* when it takes place tacitly, it is termed the *Gestio pro herede.* The acceptance cannot be made by Substitution. He who is entitled to acquire the Inheritance, and he only, may also refuse it. The Renunciation, or Repudiation, as it is termed, of the Inheritance must necessarily be *post delatam* and *ante aditam hereditatem.* Partial Repudiation, as also the Revocation of the Renunciation, are inadmissible.

Acquisition of the *Bonorum Possessio.*

II. ACQUISITION OF THE BONORUM POSSESSIO. This always presumes a judicial act. In the Acquisition of the *Bonorum Possessio edictalis* merely *agnitio* is needed; in the *Bonorum Possessio decretalis,* a *petitio* is likewise required. This *petitio* must be accompanied by a substantiation of all the circumstances alleged. The *Bonorum Possessio edictalis* is that for which the requisites have been narrowly defined by Edict; *Bonorum Possessio decretalis* is that the obtaining of which depends upon a *causae cognitio.* This declaration must be made by the *Liberi* and *Parentes* within a year, by other Heirs within a hundred days. It may also be made by a Representative.

The object of the Acquisition.

The object of the Acquisition is the Property devised or given by the Will. The several Portions of an Inheritance are inseparable; so that in the Acquisition of one Portion there is involved the Acquisition of

Jus accrescendi.

the other. In consequence of this arises the *Jus accrescendi*; when one of several co-Heirs fails, the Portion which then becomes vacant accrues to the Heirs who remain, in proportion to their respective shares. Hence the maxim, "*Solo concursu partes fiunt; cessante concursu partes cessant.*" The *Jus accrescendi* arises *ipso jure*, so that a Portion that has become vacant need not be specially entered upon (*Portio portioni accrescit*). This rule does not apply when the vacancy arises by the *in integrum restitutio*, or by Disclaimer. It only, indeed, occurs in the case where the Heir who has failed lacks the Right of Transmission, and no Substitution has taken place. By Substitution the Testator may indirectly prevent the *Jus accrescendi* taking effect; he cannot absolutely exclude it. It occurs equally in the case of Heirs by Testacy and by Intestacy. In Succession by Intestacy the *Jus accrescendi* rests upon the following grounds:

Grounds of the *Jus accrescendi* in Intestate Succession.

1. The vacant Portion accrues to that Person who would have received it, if the party failing had not been present from the very commencement.

2. It accrues in proportion to the shares.

3. Thus, when the parties succeed *in capita*, it accrues *in capita*. The *Jus accrescendi* takes precedence of the *Successio graduum*.

4. The occurrence of the *Jus accrescendi* does not change the mode of the Delation. For example: A man dies leaving a Brother, one Nephew of one and two Nephews of another deceased Brother; the Brother falls away before the Acquisition of the Inheritance. Here the former mode of Delation continues, namely, the *Successio in stirpes*.

In Succession by Testacy, the *Jus accrescendi* rests upon the following principles:

In Succession by Testacy.

1. The Portion of the party failing accrues to the other party entitled with him.

2. The Portion of several Persons entitled conjointly failing, accrues to the others who are entitled conjointly, whether these are conjoined *re et verbis*, or only *re conjuncti*. The *verbis tantum conjuncti* have no preferential claim on the *Jus accrescendi*. By the expression *re et verbis conjuncti* is to be understood those Heirs who, in the same sentence, are called to the same *quota* of the Inheritance, or Thing devised, without any designation of the parts. *Heredes conjuncti* are Heirs who have been instituted to one and the same *quota*, but in different sentences or propositions in the Will. *Verbis conjuncti* are those Heirs who are called in the same proposition to the same *quota* or the same Thing, but with the addition also of the determinate part.

3. When several Heirs are instituted for distinct Portions, others without such Portions, and one of the latter fails, the question arises whether those instituted *sine parte* were conjoined with one another, or whether they come to the Inheritance *separatim*. In the latter case, the Portion that falls in accrues to all.

4. *Portio regulariter cum onere accrescit*. Those cases are excepted where the Portion burdened is considered from the first as not written. In the case of the Testament of a Soldier, the *Jus accrescendi* does not occur, unless the Testator has expressly desired it.

When an acquired Inheritance is lost

The Inheritance once acquired is lost again:

1. When any one avails himself of the *Beneficium abstinendi*.

2. When any one permits himself to be barred from

entering upon the Inheritance by the *in integrum restitutio.*

3. When the Testament is rescinded.

SECTION XXXII.—*Of the Acquisition of the Inheritance by some one else than the Person Delated.*

Von Vangerow, vol. II. p. 24, s. 3.
" " s. 491.
Arndts, ss. 512—516.
Puchta, ss. 502—504.
Mühlenbruch, XLIII., 143 et seq.
l. 18, s. 1, l. 19, Cod. de jure delib. (6, 30).
l. unica " de his qui ante apertas tabulas etc. (6, 52).
l. unica s. 5, " de caduc. toll. (6, 51).

AMONG the grounds for the dissolution of the Delation must be mentioned the death of the Delatee. Hence the maxim, "*Hereditas nondum adita non transmittitur ad heredes.*" An exception, however, to the rule occurs in cases of Transmission, as they are termed. In four cases there exists a Transmission of the Delation; that is to say, a Succession thereto. This is something quite different, indeed it is the very opposite, to Successive Delation. Successive Delation is regarded as a new Delation, whilst in a Succession to a Delation, the older one is sustained. Transmission takes place in the following instances:

Dissolution of the Delation by death.

Transmission.

Successive Delation.

1. When the Person, the Delator, has died without having entered by reason of an *impedimentum juris.* For example, an instituted Heir dies, but without having entered, because he has been prevented by the *Edictum Carbonianum,* or by a well-founded *impedimentum facti;* as, for instance, *absentia reipublicæ causa.*

In these cases his Heirs are relieved by the *in integrum restitutio (Transmissio ex capite in integrum restitutionis)*.

2. When an Inheritance has been delated to an *Infans*, and the Father has neglected to enter, he may, after the death of the Child, still enter for himself. This is called *Transmissio ex capite infantiæ.*

3. When a Descendant has been instituted in a Will; and dies *ante apertas tabulas*, leaving Descendants, these are held to be entitled to enter upon the Inheritance (*Transmissio Theodosiana*).

4. When a Person is called to the Inheritance by Testament or *ab intestato*, but dies without entering thereupon, his Heirs are allowed to enter upon the Inheritance any time within the space of a year from their having notice of the Delation (*Transmissio Justinianea).*

That a *Suus* when he dies, without having entered upon the Inheritance that has been left him, should transfer to his Heir the Right subsequently to acknowledge the Inheritance, forms no exception to the rule, because he is *Heres necessarius* and acquires *ipso jure*. There is no *Transmissio ex jure suitatis*.

Section XXXIII.—*Effects of the Acquisition of the Inheritance.*

Von Vangerow, ss. 501—517.
Arndts., ss. 521—540.
Puchta, ss. 496—506.
[See Authorities given under Sect. XXX.]

The general Rule.

The general effect of the Acquisition of the Inheritance is to transfer all the Property relations of the Testator to the Heir. Only those legal relations which had reference to the physical existence of the Testator are not transferred. Hence, Personal Servitudes, certain Actions, and certain Obligations do not pass. The effect of Transmission is as follows :

1. That all those legal relations that existed at that time between the Testator and the Heir become confounded, that is, they merge into one another.*

2. That the Creditors of the Testator and the Heir himself have to look to the entire Property.

3. That the whole of the heritable Estate passes to the Heirs.

A modification of these general principles is made in favour of the Heirs by the *Beneficium Inventarii*, and is introduced for the benefit of the Creditors of the Inheritance by means of the *Beneficium separationis Bonorum*. The *Beneficium Inventarii* consists in this: The Heir who actually enters upon the Inheritance, and who commences to execute within thirty days a formal Inventory before a Notary and witnesses shall not suffer any injury by his *Adition* upon the Inheritance, or as it is expressed, he may "*Sine omni damno discedere.*" He must actually enter, as the Petition for time in order that he may deliberate is not regarded as entering upon the Inheritance. Again, according to the modern practice the Heir must notify the Court

The Beneficium Inventarii.

* Confusion plays an important part in Roman Law. Here we see that it arises when there is a collision of Rights in the same legal Subject. It arises in Obligations whenever the Claim and the Liability unite in one and the same Person. When this takes place so that the Creditor and the principal Debtor become one and the same Person, the entire Obligation is extinguished. Again, if the principal Debtor and the accessory one happen to coalesce in the same individual, or if the latter becomes identical with the Creditor, the accessory Obligations are extinguished. (*See* on this Gaius in note l. 4, p. 535, Tomkins & Lemon's edit.)

of his intention to make an Inventory; upon which the Inventory is made and furnished by the direction of the Court. The Inventory must be completed within sixty days, at the most within a year, and must also be subscribed within that time. The Heir who avails himself of the Inventory is not liable beyond the amount of the Inheritance. In paying the Creditors he has no need to consider the Priority of the Creditors, but he pays them as they come. At the present time a judicial division is customary, and it is made according to the analogy of proceedings in Bankruptcy. The Heir may, in lieu of payment, hand over the appraised Goods; indeed even the mortgaged Goods at their taxed value. The costs of the making of the Inventory and the Administration are, however, first deducted. During the making of the Inventory, the Heir cannot be molested by any Creditor. By virtue of the *Beneficium Inventarii*, any *Confusio* or Merger is kept *in suspenso*. Such is the effect of the *Beneficium Inventarii*.

Limits the Liability of the Heir

Beneficium Separationis.

Beneficium Separationis consists in the following: That the Creditors of the Inheritance and the Legatees may claim that the Estate shall be exclusively employed to satisfy their Demands. Each separate Legatee and Creditor may demand separation, until, but not after the lapse of five years; further, when the Property belonging to an Inheritance and a man's own have become mixed; and finally, when the parties entitled to the Separation have conducted themselves as the Creditors of the Heir.

It is also a result of the Acquisition of the Inheritance, that the Heir is bound to observe *rite* the final Disposition of the Testator. The Law refers this

Obligation to a quasi Contract, which is accepted by the fact of the Entrance upon the Inheritance. The charge which gives rise to an Obligation binding the Heir, must yield to another Person a Right of Claim; it must not be *contra bonos mores*, nor be unintelligible: hence, what are termed *Nuda praecepta* have no obligatory effect. Should the Heir delay the fulfilment, he is judicially admonished; proceedings are then stayed for a year; after the lapse of which time he is declared *indignus*, and his Portion is forfeited to his Substitute, or to his co-Heirs or Legatees; failing these, to the Intestate Heirs; finally, to the *Fiscus*. These, then, are required to discharge the burdens imposed. Other important consequences of the Acquisition of an Inheritance are the Obligations which arise between the co-Heirs. These create:

Obligations of the co-Heirs.

1. A *Communio*, which, in respect to the *corpora* and the *jura in re*, is a *Communio pro indiviso*—except, indeed, in the case of a Mortgage, which is *in solidum*. In respect to the Obligations, it is held to be *Communio pro diviso*, except in the instance of indivisible Obligations, which pass actively and passively *in solidum* to the Heir. Arising out of the *Communio* is the Obligation to allow the division to be made, and the Liability for mutual performances towards one another. This includes compensation for Outlays, and for Injuries arising from *dolus* or *culpa*. For the fulfilment of these Obligations, either of both together, or of each by itself, the *Actio familiæ herciscundæ* lies. It is what is denominated a *duplex judicium*. The proper Plaintiff is the acknowledged co-Heir, or those who are *in heredis loco*, as the

Communio

The *Actio familiæ herciscundæ*.

Universal Trustee; the *Impubes arrogatus*, in respect of the *Quarta divi Pii;* or the destitute Widow. Should the Defendant dispute the Capacity of the Plaintiff to the title of co-Heir, he is then compelled to resort to the *Hereditatis petitio*. Exceptionally, namely when the Plaintiff is the Possessor, in which character he cannot institute the *Hereditatis petitio*, the decision given in the *Actio familiæ herciscundæ* will likewise decide upon the Exception or Plea incidentally raised. If one of the co-Heirs is ignored by the *judicium*, then the whole *judicium* becomes void. In dealing with the *Judicium familiæ herciscundæ*, the judge must dissolve the *Communio* and undertake the division. Either the particular Thing is actually divided, or the several Heirs take separate Things by lots; or the separate Things are sold, and the proceeds handed to the Heirs. The Records which refer to separate Things, those Heirs receive who take these separate Things. Records that refer to a Property that has been divided, that Heir takes whose Portion is the largest. In the case of equal Portions, who shall take the Records is determined by Agreement or by Lot, or the judge decides. In regard to the division of an Inheritance, the *judicium* contains the *adjudicatio;* actual direction to take the Property; and the *condemnatio*, which can never again be attacked, if once it has acquired legal force. The suit for the division of the Inheritance can only be once employed, for by separation the *Communio* ceases. Should separate Things remain undivided, it is necessary as regards these that the *Actio communi dividundo* should be brought.

Who take the Records.

Liability to Collate.

2. The Liability to Collate. This is employed for

the adjustment of the Estate, and takes place where an Heir surrenders to the heritable Estate constituent parts of his own Property, in consequence of judicial coercion, and in order that they may be divided as a portion of the Goods of the Inheritance. This occurs in the case of joint Inheritance by several Descendants, when one of them has acquired something from the common Parent during his lifetime for some business purpose. They may jointly inherit in consequence of a Testament, or *ab intestato*. All the Descendants of the Testator are bound to collate, as far as they belong to his next nearest Heirs by Intestacy, and actually succeed as his Heirs. By the refusal, however, to accept the Inheritance, the Liability to collate is avoided. Again, the Descendants of more remote Grades are bound to collate when the intervening Persons fail. They confer or bring into hotchpot that which they have themselves received, and what their *Praedefunctus parens* had received, and would have been bound to contribute; provided that they have inherited from the intervening Person, and have received, as it is termed, the *Conferenda*. Entitled to demand Collation are those Persons, and only those that will be benefited by Collation taking place. Thus those *Extranei* are not entitled who may possibly succeed with the parties entitled to the Collation. Collation does not take place where the Testator has thought fit to exclude it. The Things brought into Collation are: The *Dos*, *Donatio propter nuptias*, marketable Militia, Gifts which were made coupled with the Condition of Collation at the time of their delivery or when any other Descendant has already brought into Collation a *Dos*

Who may demand Collation.

Things brought into Collation.

The object may be collated *in natura*, or its value given.

or a *Donatio propter nuptias.* The party bound to collate has the option whether he will give the object to be collated *in natura* or contribute its value. When the value of the Thing to be collated has not been determined, substantial Security must be given. A point in dispute is, whether the *Beneficium inventarii* does not protect against the risk of contributing more than the value of the Inheritance. Von Vangerow affirms that it does, but this Puchta denies. The duty to collate becomes extinguished by Disclaimer of the Inheritance, by Restitution after Adition, and by Accidental Destruction of the object to be collated. Finally, as to the effect of the Acquisition of an Inheritance, reference must be made to the legal Remedies, denominated *Petitoria* and *Possessoria.* The legal Remedy termed *Petitoria* is, indeed, the *Hereditatis petitio* in which the Plaintiff demands the acknowledgment of his Real Right in the Inheritance and the condemnation of the Defendant. The Plaintiff is the Heir, whether Testamentary or *ab intestato*, Civil or Praetorian Heir, direct or fideicommissary Heir, *heres ex asse*, or *heres ex parte*, that is to say, the sole Heir, or he who is Heir with others. The Defendant is:

The *Petitoria* and *Possessoria* Remedies.

The Plaintiff.

Who is Defendant.

1. He who possesses *pro herede;* that is under the impression that he is the Heir, also the Universal Trustee and the purchaser of the Inheritance.

2. He who possesses *pro possessore*, the *Praedo;* that is, any one who takes Possession of the Inheritance without a true title and *mala fide*.

3. The Heirs of a *pro herede*, or of one *pro possessore possidens.*

4. The Fictus Possessor.

5. He who possesses as Surrogate of the Inheritable Property; here the maxim introduced by the *Senatus Consultum Juventianum*, "*Pretium succedit in locum rei, et res in locum pretii*" applies. The evidence the Plaintiff has to adduce has reference to the following points:

S. C. Juventianum.

What the Plaintiff must prove.

1. As to the death of the Testator.
2. As to the Delation of the Inheritance.
3. Further, that the object sued for belongs to the Inheritance.

A Written Testament is proved by publishing the Testamentary Record. Should the Testament, after the death of the Testator, be destroyed, its contents may be proven by other means; if destroyed before his death, it will be necessary to prove that the Testator did not know of its destruction, and that he did not intend it. Verbal Testament is proved by depositions on Oath of the seven Witnesses, who must therefore be all living at the time of its probate. The object of the suit is the surrendering of the Property belonging to the Heir, *cum omnis causa*, also the Surrogate of such Thing, that is to say, that which stands in the place of another Thing. This distinguishes the *Hereditatis Petitio* essentially from the *Rei Vindicatio*.

How a written and a verbal Testament are proved.

As regards the Fruits, it is necessary to distinguish between the *bonæ fidei* Possessor and the *malæ fidei* Possessor. The latter is answerable for all Fruits before the *litis contestatio* or issue, *fructus percepti* and *percipiendi*, also for *omnis culpa;* he is likewise answerable for *casus* for all Fruits gathered subsequent to the time of the *litis contestatio*. The *bonæ fidei* Possessor is liable for all the *fructus percepti* before the *litis*

As to Liability for Fruits.

contestatio, from which he has derived any benefit; and from and after the date of the *litis contestatio*, for *fructus percipiendi* and *omnis culpa*. How is it in regard to the counter Claims of the Defendant? He has a Claim for Compensation and for all Expenses should he have been a *bonæ fidei* Possessor. The *malæ fidei Possessor* claims the *impensæ necessariæ*, and *utiles*, should these have improved the Property. The *pro herede possidens* may deduct a debt of the Testator's which is owing to the Possessor; the *Praedo*, however, must first surrender and subsequently make good his Demand. Whatever the Possessor has paid to the Creditors of the Inheritance, or to Legatees, he may deduct therefrom should he have been a *bonæ fidei Possessor*. The *Praedo*, only when he has found Security; but whatever has been paid to the Heir cannot be reclaimed. Pending the litigation respecting the Inheritance, neither the *petitor* nor the *possessor* can institute a suit on account of the Inheritance against third parties; but a third party, as a Creditor or a Legatee, may sue them because they claim to be Heirs.

Claims of the Defendant.

Possessory legal Remedies of the Heir

The following are the possessory legal Remedies by means of which the Heir sues for the Inheritance:

Interdictum quorum bonorum.

1. The *Interdictum quorum bonorum*. This is a summary legal Remedy to obtain the Possession of the Inheritance without deciding the legal question itself. The Plaintiff is he who claims the *Bonorum Possessio*; the Defendant he who possesses or possessed *pro herede*, or *pro possessore*, and has wrongfully surrendered. The recognition or agnition of the *Bonorum Possessio*, and the truth of the Claim upon which it rests must be proved.

2. The *Remedium ex lege ultimatum, Cod. de edicto Divi Hadriani tollendo.* He who has been instituted Heir by a Testament having no visible defect, may by virtue of the *Remedium** obtain the Detention of the Inheritance should no other Person under a special title as *pro emptore*, or *donatore*, possess the Inheritance, or provided that an opponent does not produce an equally perfect Testament, or provided the time of Prescription has expired.† *The Remedium de edicto Divi Hadriani.*

3. The *Bonorum Possessio ex edicto Carboniano.* When the minor Child of a Testator has his descent and his Right to the Inheritance of the Testator disputed, he may nevertheless obtain Possession as though no dispute had arisen, and the definitive decision as to the matter in dispute must be deferred until his majority, except when the invariably preceding *causæ cognitio* proves that the Child has been substituted. Until then the Child has the Possession, and receives only Alimony. The administration passes to that party who finds Surety. When the *Impubes* does this, it is for his advantage since it has the effect of making him Defendant in the Action. When neither side will provide Security, a Curator named by the Court takes Possession. On the arrival of the majority of the *Impubes*, the *Bonorum Possessio ex edicto Carboniano* terminates. *Bonorum Possessio ex edicto Carboniano.*

4. The *Missio in possessionem ventris nomine* consists in this, that the pregnant Widow may claim a provisonal decree entitling her to the Possession of the Inheritance in the name of her unborn Child. She has the Right of Detention and receives Alimony; the *Missio in possessionem ventris nomine.*

* He is *in possessionem missus*, but does not receive Possession proper.

† Other objections are rejected *ad separatum*.

administration, however, is conducted by a *Curator ventris*. Where the pregnancy of the Woman, or the character of the Descent of the *Nasciturus* is disputed, a *causae cognitio* is instituted.

Bonorum Possessio furiosi nomine.

5. The *Bonorum Possessio furiosi nomine*. The insane Person, *Suus heres*, acquires the Inheritance left him, *ipso jure;* but in the case of an *Extraneus heres*, the Curator must take cognisance. Should the *Furiosus* die insane, the Inheritance, in the event of there being no Quasi pupillary Substitute, passes at the very moment of his death to the nearest intestate Heirs of the *Defunctus*.

SECTION XXXIV.—*Of the Alienation of the Inheritance.*

Von Vangerow, ss. 517, 518.
Arndts, s. 540.
Puchta, s. 521.
Glück, XVI., 309 et seq., 341 et seq.
Dig. de hereditate vel actione vendita (18, 4).
Cod. " " " " " (4, 39).
l. 2, pr. Dig. h. t.
l. 2, Cod. h. t.
l. 5, Cod. h. t.
l. 16, pr. Dig. de pact. (2, 14).

The Alienator remains Heir.

AN Inheritance that has been acquired may be alienated. But even after Alienation the Alienator remains the Heir, and the recent Acquirer can only exercise the Right of a third Person, that is, of the Heir. He has, however, as against the Debtor, the *utiles actiones*, and the *Hereditatis petitio* may be instituted against him. The Inheritance passes as it is: hence the Vendor does not warrant against Eviction, nor against latent defects. Should the *Jus accrescendi* arise, the purchaser takes the accruing Portion, unless the intention of the contracting parties demonstrates that it was not so intended. Obligations and Rights that have been extinguished by Merger, or Confusion, the Purchaser must make good to the Vendor, or reinstate him in the same position. As for example, in the case of Servitudes.

SECTION XXXV.—*General Rules regarding Legacies.*

Von Vangerow, ss. 519—547.
Arndts, ss. 541—579.
Puchta, ss. 522—552.
Gai. Comm. II., 191—193, 198, 199, 201, 202, 209, 216, 235, 236, 238, 239, 241, 242, 243, 244, 245.
Glück, XVIII., 259; XLIV., 1, et seq., 311 et seq.; XLV.
Instit. de legatis (2, 20).
Dig. de legatis et fideicommis. XXX.—XXXII.
Cod. " " (6, 37).
" de fideicommissis (6, 42).
" communia de legatis et fideicommissis, et de in rem missione tollenda (6, 43).
Ulpianus, XXIV., XXV.
l. 8., Dig. si quis omissa causa testamenti ab intestato (29, 4).
l. un., s. 11, Cod. de caduc. toll. (6, 51).
Instit. de codicillis (2, 25).
Dig. de jure codicillorum (29, 7).
Cod. de codicillis (6, 41).
l. 32 (ult.), Cod. de fideicommissis (6, 42).
Dig. quando dies legator. vel fideicomm. cedat. (36, 2).
Cod. quando dies legati vel fideicommissi cedit. (6, 53).
Dig. " " ususfructus legati cedat. (7, 3).
l. 1, Cod. comm. de legat. et fideic. (6, 43).
Dig. ut in possessionem legatorum s. fideicommissorum causa esse liceat (36, 4).
Cod. ut in possessionem legat. s. fideic. causa mittatur, et quando satis dari debeat. (6, 54).

Dig. ut legatorum s. fideicommissorum causa caveatur (36, 3).
Dig. quod legatorum (43, 3).
Cod. " " (8, 3).
Instit. de lege Falcidia (2, 22).
Dig. ad leg. Falcidiam (35, 2).
Cod. " " " (6, 50).
Dig. de his quae pro non scriptis habentur (34, 8).
" de regula Catoniana (34, 7).
Instit. de ademtione et translatione legatorum (2, 21).
Dig. de adimendis vel transferendis legatis (34, 4).

Only one kind of Legacy in ancient Rome.

In ancient Rome, before the time of the Emperors, there was only one kind of *Legatum;* but under the Empire there arose a second species denominated *Fideicommissum.* The latter mode of Bequest had existed during the period of the Republic; but it possessed no legal validity. It was simply what the term etymologically implies, a charge imposed upon a man's conscience. In the time of Augustus, however, it became a legal Institute, and from the reign of this Emperor till that of Justinian, *Legata* and *Fideicommissa* existed side by side with each other; the former as Legacies given by the *Jus civile*, and the latter as compulsory Bequests made by virtue of the *Jus gentium.* Like other legal Institutions of Roman Jurisprudence, *Legata* as based upon the *Jus civile* were regulated by strict and precise forms, but while this was the case they had a free and enlarged sphere of operation. On the other hand *Fideicommissa*, though less strict in their form of inception, were far more limited in their scope and operation.*

In regard to *Legata* by the Ancient Law, they were required to be inserted either in a Testament or in a

* Gai. Comm., Tomkins and Lemon's edit., pp. 367—374, 405—410.

confirmed Codicil, and further, it was only the *Heres scriptus* not the *Heres legitimus* that could be burdened with Legacies. In this early period as we learn from Gaius, there were four kinds of these strict *Legata*, "Legatorum utique genera sunt *quattuor* aut enim *per vindicationem* legamus, aut *per damnationem*, aut *sinendo modo*, aut *per praeceptionem*."* In regard to *Fideicommissa*, the rule originally was, that they might be made in any form; at a later period, however, they came to be inserted in an unconfirmed Codicil; but no *verba sollennia* were required, and every Person competent to take Property from the Testator might be burdened with *Fideicommissa*. For the realization of a *Fideicommissum* there could be no *Vindicatio*, no *Condictio*, but simply a *Persecutio*, which took place by means of a *cognitio extraordinaria*. Finally, there was not required for a *Fideicommissum* the *Testamenti factio*, either *activa* or *passiva*, whilst for a Legacy both of these qualifications were absolutely indispensable.

The distinctions between *Legata* and *Fideicommissa* abolished by Justinian.

The marked distinctions subsisting between *Legata* and *Fideicommissa* had in many respects been taken away long before the time of Justinian. *Legata*, through the Senatus-consultum Neronianum and the legislation of Constantine which abolished the necessity for *verba sollennia*, came much nearer to *Fideicommissa*, whilst the requirements needed for *Fideicommissa* brought them into much closer resemblance with *Legata;* so that, at the time of Justinian the gap that divided the two kinds of Bequest had been greatly narrowed. The final step which abolished all distinction, was taken by this Emperor, an account of which will be

* Gai. Comm., II., s. 192.

The Institutes quoted.

found in the Code.* In the Institutes, Justinian remarks, "Observing that the Ancients confined Legacies within strict rules, but accorded greater latitude to *Fideicommissa* as arising more immediately from the wishes of the deceased, we have thought it necessary to make all Legacies equal to Gifts in Trust, so that no difference really remains between them."† It was in this way that a perfect *exequatio* took place, resulting in the production of only one kind of Bequest. The new institution deriving its elements from the principles regulating both *Legata* and *Fideicommissa*. It is quite erroneous to suppose that either the one or the other of the older modes of Bequest prevailed as the rule "*id quod pinguior est*," controlled the new institution. For example, according to the theory of *Fideicommissa* we have stated, that the only Remedy originally provided was a *Persecutio;* but as in a *Legatum* the Ownership was transferred, the Legatee was entitled to the proprietary Actions. Now, in the Modern Roman Law, when Property is left *precative*, the theory of *Legata* is held to apply. By the Ancient Law the *Jus accrescendi* did not apply to *Fideicommissa;* but now, since the more favourable view is always to prevail, such Bequests are entitled, just as much as *Legata*, to the *Jus accrescendi*. The ruling principle is, that the Bequest, of whatever nature it may be, is to be construed so as to confer the greatest benefit on the Person entitled. In the thirty-first and thirty-second Books of the Pandects we find both kinds of Bequests are treated under the same Rubric, "*De legatis et fideicommissis*."

The *Jus accrescendi* now applicable to *Fideicommissa*.

* l. 2, Cod. Comm. de leg. et fideicomm. (6. 43).

† s. 3, Instit. de legatis (2, 20).

A Legacy is defined as the Appointment of a Singular Succession in the Estate of a *Defunctus*. The Persons that present themselves to our notice in every Legacy are: The Testator, the *Oneratus* or Party burdened, and the *Honoratus* or Beneficiary. In the first place it is to be observed that every Person who intends to make a Bequest must possess the *Testamenti factio activa*. The Persons who may be charged with Legacies are:

Definition of a Legacy.

Who may be burdened with a Legacy.

1. The Heirs and the Person who stands *in heredis loco*.

2. The Person who has been remembered by the Testator *conditionis implendæ causa*.

Whilst, however, the Persons just mentioned may be burdened with Legacies, the following exceptions must be carefully noted:

Upon what a Legacy cannot be imposed.

1. The Legitimate Portion cannot be burdened.

2. Upon that which is given no burden can be imposed. A Thing can only be burdened when it is required to be surrendered in consequence of a sum of money having been given, and when the sum of money has been accepted under this understanding.

3. The Pupillary Substitute can only be burdened, in as far as he, or the *Impubes*, is instituted Heir in the paternal Testament.

To the question, who is burdened in a concrete case? it may be said in reply generally, that the Heirs are answerable *pro rata*. Such is the case when the Testator has not specially indicated them, or has only burdened some one, but not all, and has not in any exact mode determined their respective relations. When, on the other hand, he has mentioned all the Heirs

The burden falls upon the Heirs *pro rata*.

separately, and has named them as being burdened, the burden has to be divided *in capita* or by heads.

Who is the *Honoratus*.

The *Honoratus*, or Beneficiary, may be any Person who is possessed of the *Testamenti factio activa*. The Parties burdened are liable *in solidum* in the case of objects that are indivisible, and those alternatively burdened are regarded as Correal Debtors. The *Honoratus* in a concrete case is the party upon whom the Testator, by an expressed intention, has conferred a benefit; and even the Heir himself may be benefited by the bequest of a Legacy. When the Testator has named certain Persons in his Will as those who are to be burdened with the Legacies, it is

Prelegacy.

an ordinary Testament. Should he, however, not have named such *Onerati*, the notion of a Prelegacy arises. But as the Heir cannot pay himself a Legacy, he only takes the Portion which the co-Heirs contribute as Legatee; and the Portion by Confusion or Merger falls to him as Heir. This latter Portion he must reckon in the *Quarta Falcidia* and *Trebelliana;* he must also, when he, as *Fideicommissarius*, restores the Inheritance, restore this Portion; and should he have co-Legatees, the same accrues to the co-Legatees. Should the Prelegatee not acquire the Inheritance because he disclaims it, or because he abstains from it as a *Suus*, or because he has lost his Portion on the ground of some indignity, he then acquires the whole of the Prelegacy. Should, however, the Prelegatee die before entering upon the Inheritance, or after the time that the Legacy has been acquired, he only transmits to his Heirs the Portion that does not become merged. These rules are, according to Von Vangerow, to be laid down only as presumptions of the Condition, *Si heres non fuerit*. By the Disclaimer of the Inheritance this Condition is fulfilled; but when the Prelegatee dies before the Acquisition of the Inheritance, he is said to have died *pendente conditione*, and hence he loses the conditioned Portion accruing to the Prelegatee. The Action by which the Prelegacy is enforced, is the *Actio familiæ herciscundæ*. The Person making the Bequest may also so dispose that several Persons shall take the same object, one after the other. Such a Legacy is termed a Successive Legacy; and when this Disposition has been made in favour of the family of the founder, it is termed a Family *Fideicommissum*, or a Family Testamentary Trust. Belonging to the family are the Descendants of the Person to whom the Legacy is bequeathed, whether they be those of the Testator himself, or of any other Person; and only failing such Persons, the Sons-in-law and the Daughters-in-law succeed. The number of cases of Restitution may be limited; but when they are unlimited in number, the Legacy is termed a *Fideicommissum perpetuum*, or a Family Testamentary Trust *in perpetuity*. This is what is now understood in Germany by a Family *Fideicommissum*. The order of the Succession to a Legacy may be predetermined by the founder. When he has not defined it, the choice is given to each successive Legatee to appoint a Successor from the parties entitled, and should they fail to do so, the Intestate Heirs succeed. Several Persons who are equally nearly related to the Testator take the Family Testamentary Trust jointly, and the division is made *in capita* when the founder has not otherwise appointed. Should a

The Action for the Prelegacy.

Successive Legacy.

Fideicommissum perpetuum.

Succession to a Family Testamentary Trust.

Possessor undertake to alienate, the next nearest Persons entitled step into his place. When the parties so agree, the *Fideicommissum* is destroyed; but when only a part of those entitled have thus agreed, in this case those only who concur sacrifice their Right. In the case of involuntary Alienation (Bankruptcy), the parties entitled must allow the purchaser to remain in Possession until the death of the vendor.

What Things may be the object of a Legacy.

Every kind of Thing whatever may be the object of a Legacy, provided that it is not a Thing *extra commercium*, and that it does not belong to the Legatee at the time of the making of the Bequest. Things may be *extra commercium omnium*, or *extra commercium legatarii*. It does not damage the Legacy if they stand only *extra commercium onerati*. The exceptions to this rule are the following:

1. When a Thing is bequeathed subject to a Condition, and *pendente conditione* it is brought *in commercio*.

2. When the Legatee *pendente conditione* has lost the Ownership of the Property.* When the Legatee does not acquire the Thing in consequence of the rule cited, he cannot claim its estimated value.

How Legacies may be made.

Dispositions, as above explained, may be made:

1. By Testament.

2. By an informal Declaration addressed to the party burdened, the so-called oral *Fideicommissum*, which must be verified by a confirmatory Oath. In the first place, the Legatee cited takes the Oath of Calumny; then the party burdened swears the Oath of Delation. No other modes of proof exist.

---

* His Ownership, for example, might be only a *Dominium revocabile*.

3. By Codicil. By a Codicil is to be understood a Testamentary Disposition, in which no direct Heir is appointed. That it may have legal efficacy, the observance of Testamentary solemnities is required; but five Witnesses suffice. No special form is needed for the *Codicilli testamento confirmati*, because these are regarded as integral portions of the Testament which confirms them. Testamentary privileges are also available for the Codicil. As Witnesses for its execution, even Legatees may be called. But sealing the document by the Witnesses is not required, nor the signature of the Person who makes the Codicil. Thus there exists a manifest difference between a Testament and a Codicil, equally as regards their matter and their form. Hence it may happen that a Testamentary Disposition which is invalid as a Will, may be valid as a Codicil. In order, however, to effect this, it is necessary to employ the Codicillary Clause. If this is done, a Codicil may exist even in the case where the Testament becomes void by reason of the omission of the Necessary Heirs.

Definition of a Codicil: Requisites for it.

Difference between a Testament and a Codicil.

In reference to the Acquisition and the Payment of a Legacy, the Romans employed two expressions. They say "*Dies legati cedit*" when they wish to denote that the time of the Acquisition has arrived; they say "*Dies legati venit*" when they wish to express that the time for its Payment has come. The Legacy is regularly acquired at the moment of the death of the Testator, save when a highly personal Right is the object of the Legacy, or when the Legacy is conditional. Should the Legatee die *pendente conditione*, the Legacy becomes void. On the other hand, should he

Dies legati cedit and *venit.*

A void Legacy.

once have acquired the Legacy, he then transmits it to his Heirs.

The above rule suffers no exception where the Institution of an Heir is conditional, or the Legacy is imposed or charged upon a Substitute, or a pupillary Substitute. The time of a Legacy becoming due is, as the rule, the period of the *Hereditas adita:* except in the case of a Conditional Legacy, for in this case the rule is *Pendente conditione dies legati nec cedere, nec venire potest;* except also in the *Legatum sub die certo;** and in the case of a Legacy where another Person is burdened as the direct Heir.† The Acquisition of the Legacy takes place *ipso jure*, but it may be excluded by Repudiation. But neither Agnition, that is, Acceptance, nor Repudiation can take place before the arrival of the *dies veniens*. Again, neither partial Agnition nor partial Repudiation is admissible. Further, Repudiation once made cannot be revoked.

When the Legacy becomes due.

There is neither Agnition nor Repudiation before the *dies veniens*.

The Acquisition of a Legacy is something quite different to the Acquisition of the Right which constitutes the object of the Legacy. When this is:

1. Property, or a *Jus in re*, found in the Estate of the Testator, or in that of the party burdened, the Legatee acquires the Property intended for him, or the *Jus in re*, at the very moment that the *dies legati venit.*

2. If it be an Obligation, the Legatee is regarded from that moment as the Assignee. Between the party burdened with the Legacy and the Legatee there exists a *Quasi* Contract which renders the *Oneratus* liable for the performance, and makes him answerable

* The *dies cedens* is not deferred.

† The party burdened, Substitute, etc., must first receive his Portion.

for *dolus* and *culpa lata*. Fruits and Interest must be accounted for and paid, except in the case of *Legata ad pias causas*, from the time that the *Oneratus* is chargeable with delay *(mora)*.

For the enforcement of his Claim the Legatee has the following Legal Remedies: Remedies of the Legatee.

1. In the case of a bequeathed *Species testatoris propria*, the Legatee has an *Actio in rem*. *Actio in rem.*

2. On the ground of a *Quasi* Contract he has an *Actio in personam*, the so-called *Actio ex testamento*. *Actio ex testamento.*

3. Since the Beneficiary has a Mortgage on the Estate of the *Oneratus*, he has also a Right to avail himself of the *Actio hypothecaria*. *Actio hypocario.*

4. He has further the Right to demand the Security, known as *Cautio legatorum servandorum causa*, when immediate performance is unnecessary. Security need not be given when the Parents or the Fiscus are burdened, nor if the parties charged be exempted by the Testator. Should default be made in providing Security, the Beneficiary is entitled to enter upon the Goods inherited by the *Oneratus*, and should the *Oneratus*, notwithstanding such entry, and after the lapse of a period of six months, still be in default, a *Missio ex secundo decreto* takes place, which comprises the Estate of the *Oneratus* himself, and further permits the Perception, as it is termed, of the Fruits. *Cautio legatorum, &c.*

On the other hand, the *Oneratus* has the following Rights: The Rights of the *Oneratus*.

1. He may claim Compensation for expenses.

2. He may claim that all Real Rights that have become extinct by *Confusio* shall be resuscitated.

3. That the *Honoratus* shall find Security when the

Legacy has been bequeathed subject to a negative *Conditio potestativa*, or *ad tempus*.

Interdictum Quorum Legatorum

4. He has the *Interdictum Quorum Legatorum* against the Legatee, who, before the Heir takes Possession of the object, himself seizes the Possession of it. This Interdict also lies against his Successor, as also against the party who has entered, but who refuses to relinquish the Detention, though the ground upon which the Detention was based has ceased to exist.

The *Quarta Falcidia.*

5. He has the important Right of the *Quarta Falcidia.* It is an established rule that the Testator shall not bequeath, as Legacies, more than three-fourths of his Property; that one-fourth, termed the *Quarta Falcidia*, shall be deducted from the Legatees *pro rata*, and remain for the benefit of the Heir. The Right to this deduction appertains to every direct Heir; not, however, to the Legatee, nor to the Universal Testamentary Trustee (*Universalis fideicommissarius*). In the case of several Heirs, each must preserve intact his Fourth of the Inheritance. The problem, how to compute this fourth part where several Portions unite in one and the same Person, is to be solved as follows:

Computation of *Quarta Falcidia.*

1. When the union has been produced by accident, as when one co-Heir inherits another, a Fourth is deducted from each Portion.

2. When the union has been so brought about that several Portions are bequeathed to the Heir, by the side of each other, conditionally and unconditionally, the Fourth part is deducted from the combined Portions.

3. The same rule holds good when the combination is consequent upon a vulgar Substitution, for this is to be regarded as a conditional Institution.

4. When the union has been brought about by a pupillary Substitution, it is necessary to distinguish: *a*. Whether Legacies are imposed upon the instituted Pupil and the Substitute, or upon the Pupil alone, or upon the Substitute alone; in these instances, the Fourth is deducted from the *paternal* Inheritance; *b*. Should the Pupil be disinherited, and the Substitute instituted, the Fourth is still deducted from the *paternal* Inheritance; *c*. When to a Pupil his co-Heir has been substituted, and Legacies have been imposed on the latter as *Substitutus* or *Institutus*, in this case the Fourth is deducted from the combined Portion ; *d*. If Legacies have been imposed upon the Pupil and the co-Heir in a similar case, it depends whether the co-Heir has been burdened as a *Substitutus* or as an *Institutus*. In the first case, the Legacies are computed together, and in respect to that which has been imposed upon him as *Substitutus;* the freely instituted Portion is also liable to contribute. The Legatees, however, of the Pupil cannot take any advantage of this Portion. In the second case, when the Portion of the Pupil has been overburdened, the Fourth is certainly deducted from this, and when the Portion of the co-Heir is overburdened, a summation of the Legacies of the Portions is made. The Necessary Heir is permitted by the Canon Law first to deduct the Legitimate Portion, then from the remainder to deduct the Fourth part.

The Persons from whom the Fourth part is deducted are the Legatees, the Testamentary Trustees, and the Donees *mortis causa*. Donations, however, made *inter vivos* are exempted. The computation of the Fourth From whom the *Quarta* is deducted.

must be made at the very moment of the death of the Testator, and in the following manner:

The Property left must be valued in money.

1. The Property left by the *Defunctus*, after deducting debts, must be valued in money. Things according to their ordinary value; Obligations that are doubtful in consequence of Insolvency, etc., are set apart, but the Heir must find Security. In the case of Obligations already due, Interest for delay is to be deducted.

Legacies also must be valued.

2. The amount of the Legacies must be similarly valued. Conditional Legacies, however, are not reckoned; Legacies due, according to their present value; in like manner, Rent charges for life. In the case of other Rents, the Capital has to be reckoned at an Interest of four per cent.

3. The Heir must include in the Fourth that which he has received *titulo universali;* hence he is not required to bring Legacies into the account.

Remedies available for the Heir.

4. The deduction takes place *pro rata*. The Heir is entitled at once to make the deduction. Should he, however, have omitted to do this, and thus have paid too much, he can avail himself of the *Condictio indebiti*, the *Interdictum quod legatorum*, the *Actio de dolo*, an *Actio in factum*, in order to protect himself.

When the *Quarta Falcidia* is not deducted.

The Falcidian Fourth is generally not deducted:

1. In the case of the Testament of a Soldier.

2. When the Testator forbids the deduction.

3. When the Heir loses the deduction by his failing to make an Inventory.

4. When the Heir renounces or disclaims it.

In some Special Legacies.

The Fourth is not deducted in the following instances of Special Legacies:

1. In the case of *Legata ad pias causas*.

2. In that of *Legata debiti.*

3. In the case of a Legacy that is calculated upon a Legitimate Portion.

4. When a Bequest is made of a Thing of which the Alienation is prohibited. When privileged and non-privileged Legacies concur, the Heir may in regard to such, look to the latter should the former not yield what he demands.

A Legacy fails either for intrinsic reasons or because the Testament in which it is created falls to the ground. In the following cases, however, the Legacy is upheld although the Testament fails: When a Legacy fails.

1. When the instituted Heir *in fraudem legatorum* disclaims the Testamentary Inheritance. The Disclaimer of the Inheritance resembles the non-fulfilment of a *potestative* Condition, the non-Agnition of the *Bonorum Possessio.* Whenever the party disclaiming an Inheritance subsequently acquires it, or a part of it, but by a different title; for example, as Heir by Intestacy, or when he has received a price for his Disclaimer, the Legatee may bring an Action against him, or against any third Person in Possession. A Legacy is upheld if the Heir disclaims *fraudulently.*

2. When the Testament has been made by the Testator under the erroneous belief that he had no Heirs by Intestacy, and the Testament on account of such error becomes void.

3. When the Inheritance as a *vacans* reverts to the *Fiscus.*

4. When the Testament remains in force by way of Codicil, and the Codicillary Clause has been added to it.

The other reasons which render a Legacy invalid are

Other reasons which make a Legacy void.

either such as have existed from the very commencement, or such as have arisen subsequently. A Legacy is void from the commencement, when some essential requirement was wanting at the time it was made.

The rule of Cato.

In this case the important rule of Cato applies, "*Quod ab initio vitiosum est, tractu temporis convalescere nequit.*" In other words, the Testament that would have been invalid if the Testator had died immediately after its execution, remains invalid even if the Testator should die at a later period, and the original grounds for the invalidity of the Testament should have ceased to exist during his lifetime. Suppose, for example, the Testator had bequeathed *pure*, a *Res extra commercium*, and at a later period this fatal defect in the Legacy was remedied. The rule, however, does not apply to Conditioned Legacies, nor to Legacies the *dies cedens* of which first occurs at the moment of Entry upon the Inheritance.

Subsequent Invalidity.

Invalidity which takes place at a subsequent period may have its cause:

1. In an *Ademtio*, that is, in the Revocation of the Legacy, which may be informal, or even conjectural, in the case of the Alienation of the Thing bequeathed after animosity between the Testator and Legatee has arisen.

2. In a *Translatio*, that is, in some alteration made with the Legacy, whereby, indeed, the requisites of the *datio* alone could have been fulfilled. This may take place in various ways; as, for example, the Legacy may be given to a third Person, or another object may be substituted in its place, or its performance may be imposed upon some other Person.

3. By the failure of the *Oneratus*, or rather when

the Portion burdened passes to another in consequence of the *Successio ordinum et graduum*.

4. By the failure of the Beneficiary, in consequence of his death before the *dies cedens*, or upon his becoming incapacitated, or because he has repudiated the Legacy, or the *Conditio* becomes *deficit*.

5. In a change that has been effected in the object left as a Legacy; as when the object physically perishes, or becomes *extra commercium*, or suffers a Specification. If this emanates from the Testator, it becomes a *quaestio facti*, whether the Legacy has expired or not.

6. In the case of a *Concursus causarum lucrativarum;* that is, where the Legatee receives the devised object from another quarter *ex lucrativa causa*.

Thus when a Legacy fails from one cause or another, the Substitute obtains it; if there be neither a Substitute nor a *Collegatarius conjunctus*, it remains with the *Oneratus*. Should there, however, exist a *Conjunctus*, the *Jus accrescendi* takes place. This Right is only possessed by the *Re conjuncti*, and they possess it in the following manner:

1. *Re et verbis conjuncti;* as, "I bequeath to A and B the *fundus*." These have the preference before mere *Re conjuncti*, but must bear the *Onus* with the accruing Portion.

2. *Re conjuncti* acquire *ipso jure*, and they need not undertake the *Onus* of that which fails.

SECTION XXXVI.—*Of Particular Kinds of Legacies.*

Von Vangerow, ss. 548—555.
Arndts, ss. 568—579.

Puchta, ss. 529—532, 549.
Gai. Comm. (see previous section).
Savigny Syst., II., 106, et seq.
s. 6, Instit. de legat. (2, 20).
l. un. s. 11, Cod. de caduc. toll. (6, 51).
l. 11, Dig. de usufr. accres. (7, 2).
s. 4, Instit. de legat. (2, 20).
Dig. de optione vel electione legata (33, 5).
" de tritico, vino vel oleo legato (33, 6).
" de annuis legatis, et fideicommissis (33, 1).
" de alimentis vel cibariis legatis (34, 1).
" de instructo vel instrumento legato (33, 7).
" de peculio legato (33, 8).
" de penu legata (33, 9).
" de supellectili legata, (33, 10).
" de auro argento mundo ornamentis unguentis veste vel vestimentis et statuis legatis (34, 2).
" de usu et usufructu et reditu et habitatione et operis per legatum vel fideicommissum datis (33, 2).
" de servitute legata (33, 3).
" de usufructu accrescendi (7, 2).
" quando dies ususfructus legati cedat. (7, 3).
s. 1, Instit. de usufructu (2, 4).
l. 2, 3, Dig. quando dies legator. (36, 2).
Dig. de dote praelegata (33, 4).
" de liberatione legata (34, 3).

Legacy of a particular Singular Thing.

1. THE Bequest of a particular Singular Thing, or *Species*, must now be considered. When such a Thing is bequeathed, it must be ascertained, (1) whether it belongs to the Testator, in which case it becomes the Property of the Legatee on the arrival of the *dies veniens*, with all the Real Rights and Burdens imposed upon it; (2) If it be the Property of the *Oneratus*, an Obligatory relationship arises between the Legatee and the Heir; (3) If it belong to the Legatee, the Legacy is void; (4) If owned by a third Person, the Legacy is

valid, provided the Testator knew this, and the *Oneratus* is obliged at the very least to give to the Legatee the appraised value. If the Testator did not know this, the Legacy becomes void.

2. The Bequest of a *Universitas*. Such a Bequest comprises all those Things which at *the time of the death of the Testator* constituted the sum total of his Property and includes all his active and passive Obligations. A Legacy of this kind is not rendered void by the partial destruction of any of the Things which constitute the *Universitas*. Bequest of a *Universitas.*

3. The Bequest of a Quantity takes place even though none of the Property named exists as part of the Inheritance. In the case of an indefinite Bequest, all that is found in the Inheritance belonging to the class to which the thing mentioned belongs is to be considered as bequeathed. Bequest of a Quantity

4. The Bequest of a *Genus* takes place when the Thing bequeathed is only described by its kind. Such a Legacy is invalid: (1) When no Property of the *Genus* bequeathed can be found in the Inheritance; (2) When the *Genus* has been too generally described. As the rule, the Legatee has an option, but he cannot select the best Thing. He can only do so when the Testator has expressly given him the Right of Selection. On the other hand, the Heir is at liberty to do so when the Testator has given him freedom of choice to select not the worst Thing. When several Heirs or Legatees are entitled to enjoy the Right of Selection, and cannot agree as to the Person who is to select, the Lot must be had recourse to in order to decide. If in accordance with the Will of the Testator a third Person be Bequest of a *Genus.* Right of Selection.

empowered to select, and he should fail to do so or die within a year, the Right of Selection, subject to the above limitation, passes to the Legatee. The selection once made is final. Should the Thing selected be claimed and recovered by Judicial Sentence, the Legatee, although he may have made selection, has again the Right of choice; and when the Heir has chosen, he is entitled to be indemnified against Ejectment from the Possession *(Evictionem praestare)*.

Bequest of an *Alternativum*.

5. The Bequest, termed by the Germans an "*Alternativum*," has much resemblance with the *Legatum generis*. The same principles apply that control the Selection, and the rule is also applicable, that Things left as Legacies need not be absolutely part of the Inheritance. Each of the objects named is *in obligatione*. From this it follows, that where the Legatee has received one of the Things left him during the lifetime of the Testator as a Present, he may still claim the other on the ground of the Bequest. But after choice has been made, the Things not selected are removed beyond the range of this Obligation.

Bequest of Rents.

6. The Bequest of Rents, that is, periodical revenues *(Legatum annuum, menstruum)* has this peculiarity, that each period of time is regarded *legally* as though it were a Legacy existing by itself. From this it follows that only the first period is viewed as an unconditional Legacy; all the subsequent ones are made subject to the Condition that the Legatee is alive. Hence each of these Legacies has its own *dies cedens*. This is not the case *naturally*, for a Bequest of Rents is acquired forthwith, just as when a round sum is bequeathed at once, the payments only being deferred for given periods of time.

7. The Bequest of Alimony comprises food, the cost of education and means of support. When the amount or quantity is not determined, and a dispute arises, the Judge must decide, *ex æquo et bono*, paying regard to all the circumstances connected with the case. The Judge is required to take into consideration how much the Person named, or an equally nearly related Person has formerly received from the Testator, or what is the relative position of the Legatee to the Inheritance. Legacies of Alimony are analogous to Legacies of Rents, and are conditional, that is to say, a new *dies cedens* occurs with every one. But they possess the peculiarity, that they are particularly favoured beyond all other Legacies. They may be left to those incapable of taking other Legacies; and when they are bequeathed until Majority, it is understood that they are to be enjoyed until the *pubertas plena*, namely, eighteen or fourteen years. They are also exempt from the deduction of the *Quarta Falcidia*.

Bequest of Alimony.

Legacies of Alimony favoured.

8. The Bequest of a *Dos*. When the amount is doubtful, here again it must be determined *ex æquo et bono*. When it is bequeathed to the Husband, it is regarded as the constitution of a *Dos*, but if it be left to the Wife, it is not so. In the case of Marriage not ensuing, the Legacy becomes void, except when the Husband bears the blame. When the Marriage is concluded, after its dissolution the Wife takes the *Dos*. In the above case the Legacy is either the Bequest of an object for a given purpose, or a direction to the *Oneratus* to give a *Dos* to the future Husband of the Legatee.

Bequest of a *Dos*.

9. The Bequest of Obligations. This may be (1)

Bequest of Obligations.

Legatum nominis.

Legatum nominis, that is, the Bequest of the Claim which the Testator or his Heir is entitled to make upon another Person, which is only valid when a *nomen*, as it is expressed, actually exists. It holds good when reimbursement has taken place after the Testator's death, and the Capital goes to the Heir, or when the Testator has received the same without the *animus adimendi*. It is no *Legatum nominis* when the Testator bequeaths a certain object, which he may claim out of an alternative Obligation. Here the Heir must prosecute the Debtor, and if he gives up the object bequeathed, the Legatee takes it; but if the Debtor gives the other object, the Legatee receives nothing. When in the case of such an Obligation, a Legatee is named for any object, he either receives the object or its estimated value. (2) *Liberatio legata*, that is, the Bequest of an Obligation which is due from some one to the Testator, or his Heir, or a third Person, which Legacy presumes the existence of an Obligation. It should, however, be observed that Sureties, but not co-principal Debtors, may rely on the *Liberatio*. (3) A *Legatum debiti*, that is to say, the Bequest of that which the Testator already owes to the Legatee, provided that some advantage results, is equally valid, even when no *debitum* exists, as long as a certain sum is named. The *Dos* may also be bequeathed in the same form as an Obligation. *Dos praelegata*, or *relegata*, corresponds to *Legatum debiti*, whereby time for Restitution and Right of Retention, except on account of *impensae necessariae*, fall to the ground.

Liberatio legata.

Legatum debiti.

Bequest of Real Rights.

10. The Bequest of Real Rights. It is only the Legacy of a Usufruct that presents anything peculiar. Here the

dies cedens and *dies veniens* always exist; and when a Legacy is made for given periods, several Legacies are called into existence. Repetition takes place if the Testator bequeath the Property "for a lifetime," and if a loss should take place during the lifetime of the Legatee. Where to one Legatee a thing is bequeathed, and to another Legatee the Usufruct, the two Legatees divide the Usufruct between them. The *Jus accrescendi* is quite peculiar in the case of a Usufruct. It even accrues on one side to the co-Legatee who has fallen away, and on the other side, not only when the co-Legatee *ante diem cedentem* falls away, but also when that event takes place *post diem cedentem*, in accordance with the rule, "*Quia usufructus non portioni sed homini accrescit.*" The *Cautio usufructuaria* cannot be remitted.

SECTION XXXVII.—*Of the Universal Fideicommissum, or Universal Testamentary Trust.*

Von Vangerow, ss. 556—560.
Arndts, ss. 580—588.
Puchta, ss. 553—557.
Gai. Comm. II., 247 et seq., 254.
Instit. de Fideicommissariis hereditatibus (2, 23).
Dig. ad Senatus-consultum Trebellianum (36, 1).
Cod. " " " (6, 49).

Definition of a Universal Fideicommissum.

BY a Universal Fideicommissum, or Universal Testamentary Trust, is understood the charge or direction to the Heir *(Fiduciarius heres)* to restore the whole, or a part of the Inheritance to a third Person, called the *Fideicommissarius heres.* This direction takes place in the form of an ordinary Bequest. The efficacy of the Universal Testamentary Trust, as also that of the ordinary Legacy, depend upon this, that the party burdened, the *Oneratus*, becomes the Heir. The Entrance, however, upon the Inheritance is by the

S.C. Pegasianum.

Senatus Consultum Pegasianum no longer in the option of the Heir, and the Beneficiary may compel the *Oneratus* to enter upon it. If the Institution of the Heir be conditional, the Heir may be compelled to fulfil the Condition, if it be a *potestative* one, and easy of performance. If Representation is allowable, the Testamentary Trustee may fulfil the Condition. By compelling the *Oneratus* to enter upon the Inheritance, the Testamentary Trust and the other matters contained in the Testament are sustained. The Liability of the Person burdened passes to his Heirs. Should, however, he or his Heirs be compelled to enter upon the Inheritance, they take no benefit under the Will, and sacrifice the Right of deducting the Falcidian Fourth; but they suffer no disadvantages by their Entrance upon the Inheritance. When the Heir has entered upon the Inheritance, he becomes the real Heir, with all the consequences resulting from his Entrance upon the Estate. Thus he becomes Owner, Creditor, Debtor. He is only restricted in the case of Alienation. This, in unconditional Testamentary Trusts, is at once void; in conditional ones, it becomes void upon the happening of the Condition. Alienation is allowed:

When the Testamentary Trustee may alienate.

1. When the Testator permits it.

2. When the Parties interested consent.

3. When it takes place because the things are perishable.

4. When it takes place to pay the Debts of the Inheritance.

When the Fiduciary Heir has to restore the whole of the Inheritance, he is liable for *dolus* and *culpa lata;* when he is only liable for partial Restitution he is bound to *diligentia in suis rebus*. The time of Restitution is, when the originator of the Testamentary Trust has not determined otherwise, the time of the Entrance upon the Inheritance. The form by which Restitution is made, is a simple declaration of the Fiduciary, that he restores, or tacitly acquiesces in the taking of Possession on the part of the *Fideicommissarius*, or *cestui que trust*, as he would now be called. The Restitution is considered as completed when the Trustee desires to withdraw from the duty imposed, or dies without Heirs.

Time and Form of Restitution.

The subject-matter of the Restitution includes everything which was under the control and Disposition of the Testator. But in no case can that be regarded as belonging to this category which the Fiduciary has received not as Heir, but which he has obtained *conditionis implendae causa*, either as a Gift *inter vivos*, a Legacy, a Prelegacy, or as Fruits. In respect to the *Jus accrescendi* there is a difference of opinion. When the Testamentary Trust is limited to *quidquid ex hereditate, supererit*, that is, to that which at the time of the death of the *Fideicommissarius* still remains, he may consume three-fourths of the Inheritance. Moreover, the *Senatus Consultum Pegasianum* ordains that the Heir who is required to restore the whole or a part of the Inheritance, may make a similar deduction to that which is permitted to the Heir who has been overburdened with Legacies. He may likewise retain one-fourth part of the Inheritance for himself, which fourth part is called *Quarta Trebellianica*. This rule

Subject-matter of Restitution.

S. C. Pegasianum.

Quarta Trebellianica.

was introduced by the *Senatus Consultum Pegasianum.* Justinian, however, who amalgamated this *Senatus Consultum* with the *Senatus Consultum Trebellianum,* retained the name of the latter law. The principles of the Falcidian Fourth apply also in this case. After Restitution made, the *Fideicommissarius* is regarded as the Heir, and becomes answerable as such; but the recipients of Legacies are not liable to him beyond the amount which they have received. The making of an Inventory by the Heir avails as against Creditors; but he himself has not the *Beneficium Inventarii.* The heritable Property passes into his Ownership, and the Obligations, active and passive, are transferred to him. Nevertheless, the following distinctions must be made:

The *Fideicommissarius* is regarded as Heir.

When the Fiduciary is liable.

1. When the Fiduciary restores all without deduction, the Creditor of the Inheritance and the Legatees must look to the *cestui que trust.*

When not.

2. When again the Fiduciary deducts the Trebellian Fourth,* and restores the other portion of the Estate, he is, as regards the Fourth, free from Liability.

3. When the Fiduciary is required to make only partial Restitution, he still continues answerable for the portion which remains in his hands, except the Fourth.

4. When the Fiduciary restores more than he ought to, he still continues liable as regards the overplus.

SECTION XXXVIII.—*Of Gifts in Contemplation of Death.*

Von Vangerow, ss. 561—563.
Arndts, ss. 589—590.

* This is at once deducted from the particular Legacies and from the Universal Trust.

Puchta, ss. 72, 552, 463.
Savigny Syst. IV., s. 170.
Dig. de mortis causa donationibus (29, 6).
Cod. de donationibus mortis causa (8, 57).
s. 1, Instit. de donat. (2, 7).
Nov. 87, praef.

Donationes mortis causa resemble Legacies and Contracts.

DONATIONS made *mortis causa* occupy a position midway between Legacies and Contracts; they contain a pecuniary benefit like Gifts, but are only perfected when death ensues. It is in this latter respect that they resemble Legacies. In respect to such Gifts the following differences must be noted:

1. The *Mortis causa donatio* is an Agreement.

2. It is not a Gift taken out of the Inheritance, and the fate of the Inheritance does not affect it. From which it follows that the Entrance upon the Inheritance is of no importance whatever as far as concerns a *Donatio mortis causa*.

3. It does not require for its validity either the *Testamenti factio activa* or *passiva*.

4. It excludes all idea of the existence of an *Oneratus*.

5. He who attacks a Testament as being invalid or inofficious in Form, and does so without succeeding, sacrifices the Legacies bequeathed to him, but not the *Mortis causa donatio*.

6. When the Gift *mortis causa* happens to be an Annuity, or a yearly Rent, it is regarded as a simple Gift.

Points of resemblance between *D.m.c.* and Legacies.

The Revocation of a Legacy does not involve the Revocation of a *Mortis causa donatio*. *Mortis causa donationes* have the following in common with Legacies:

1. A Legacy must be made before five Witnesses;

otherwise it would be construed as a mere Gift. According to Puchta, every *Mortis causa donatio* must be made before five Witnesses.

2. The party benefited must also be *capax* at the time of the Acquisition of the Gift, namely, at the period of the death of the Donor.

3. These Gifts are also liable to the deduction of the Fourth.

4. The Donees yield the precedence to the Creditors of the Inheritance.

5. The Legitimate Portion is likewise deducted from the *Mortis causa donationes*.

SECTION XXXIX.—*Of Bona Vacantia and Ereptoria.*

Von Vangerow, ss. 252, 564, 565.
Arndts, ss. 424, 520, 607, 608, 609.
Puchta, ss. 562, 563, 564.
Cod. de bonis vacantibus et de incorporatione (10, 10).
Dig. de his, quae ut indignis auferantur (34, 9).
Cod. " " quibus ut " " etc. (7, 35).

When an Estate is *Bonum vacans*.

AN Estate is *Bonum vacans* when no Person, or no further Person, is called to the Inheritance. Should such a case arise, the *Fiscus* at once becomes entitled to the Inheritance. The *Fiscus* enters upon the *Universitas*, and he becomes entitled as the Universal Successor. He acquires all the Obligations, both active and passive, and thus becomes liable for all the Debts, and must likewise pay all the Legacies. Should he, however, avail himself of the *Beneficium inventarii* he ceases to be liable beyond the value of the Estate. If the *Fiscus* sells the *Bonum vacans*, the party to whom he sells enters into the same legal relations as the *Fiscus*.

An Estate is said to be *Bonum ereptorium* when it has been forfeited by the Heir, or by the Legatee on account of some Unworthiness. Neither the *Hereditas*, nor the Legacy, regarded as such, becomes invalid; on the contrary, they are deemed valid, but the Devise or the Bequest is taken away. The grounds upon which this is done are what are termed "Grounds of Indignity," namely:

When an Estate is *Bonum ereptorium*

"Grounds of Indignity" affecting the Heir and the Legatees.

A. *Those that concern the Heir and the Legatees.*

1. Causing the death of the Testator by *dolus* or *culpa*.

2. Neglect of duty in not judicially prosecuting the murderer of the Testator.

3. Hindering the Testator from making or altering his Testament.

4. Undertaking the Liability (especially during the lifetime of the Testator) of paying a Legacy to a Person incapacitated.

5. Raising of a *controversiae status* against the Testator.

6. Stipulating without the knowledge or the consent of the Testator in respect to the Inheritance.

7. Attacking, or aiding to attack his last Will as *inofficious*, or forged.

8. Continuing an illicit intercourse with the Testator.

In all the above cases the forfeited Property goes to the *Fiscus*.

9. Refusing a Guardianship on account of which one has been remembered by the Testator. The benefits in this case go to the co-Heirs, or the *Oneratus*.

10. Omitting to educate, when the Testator has left the Property to a party for that purpose.

11. Failing to bury the Testator, when the party has been remembered by the Testator for that purpose.

12. Neglecting the Obligation to discharge certain imposed duties.

Those which concern the Heirs only.

B. *Those which concern the Heirs only.*

1. Concealment of the Goods belonging to the Inheritance in order to injure the Legatees.

2. Some Error of the Testator in regard to the paternity of the instituted Heir.

3. Declaration of the Testator that he does not wish to retain the instituted Heir as his Heir. This may be evidenced by erasure of the Heir's name.

In the above three cases the Ereption is in favour of the *Fiscus*.

4. Neglecting to redeem the Testator from captivity, when the Person knows that he is to be his Heir.

5. Refusal to take care of an insane or idiotic Testator.

6. Omitting to fulfil the duty of petitioning for a Tutor.

7. By unworthy conduct, both Brothers and Sisters may lose the Inheritance.

Those which concern the Legatee only.

C. *Those which concern the Legatee only.*

1. Concealment of the Testament.

2. When the abstraction of the goods belonging to the Inheritance is combined with the loss of the value of the goods so abstracted. In these instances, the *Oneratus* receives the things abstracted. In order that in any concrete case the principles of Indignity, Ignominy, or Unworthiness may apply, it is necessary, when they refer to an Inheritance, that Delation should have taken place; and when they concern a Legacy, that the

Legacy should have been acquired. When the *Indignus*, notwithstanding his Indignity, has entered, such Entrance is not without effect, for Merger or Confusion will take place, and other Rights become extinguished. The *Ereptor*, as he is termed, acquires *ipso jure* the Rights which the *Indignus* would have acquired; he takes his place in every respect, and hence he is bound to accept the burdens imposed upon the Inheritance.

SECTION XL.—*The Quarta Divi Pii.*

HE who has been arrogated during Minority, when the *Arrogator* emancipates him, or disinherits him without sufficient cause, has a Claim upon the Fourth Portion of the Estate of the Arrogator. This is termed the *Quarta Divi Pii.* The Obligation may be enforced against the Inheritance, and against the Heirs by means of a personal Action which passes to the Plaintiff's Heirs; provided he has survived the death of the Arrogator. Should the Arrogator have made Alienations *inter vivos* in order to diminish the Right of the Person arrogated, the latter has the *Actio Quasi Faviana* or *Calvisiana*, according as the Arrogator has died with or without a Testament. These Actions lie against the receivers, should they still have anything, for Restitution, or for the balance required to make up the Fourth.

BOOK THE SEVENTH.

OBLIGATIONS.

SECTION XLI.—*Of the Nature and Matter of Obligations.*

Von Vangerow, ss. 566—710.
Arndts, ss. 201—392.
Puchta, ss. 218—410.
Gai. Comm., III., ss. 88—225 (Tomkins and Lemon's edit.) pp. 481—580.
Savigny, 1, 4.
Instit. de obligationibus (3, 13).
Dig. " " et actionibus (44, 7).
Cod. de oblig. et actionibus (4, 10).
l. 14, s. 4, Dig. de fideijussoribus, etc. (46, 1).
l. 85 de V. O. (45, 1).

The notion implied in every Obligation.

THE notion implied in every Obligation is the following: It is that legal relation subsisting between two Persons by which one is bound to the other for a certain performance. Thus Justinian says: "Obligatio est juris vinculum, quo necessitate adstringimur alicujus solvendæ rei secundum nostræ civitatis jura."* It is the Right to the performance of something on the part of a third Person; or, as the Germans express it, "Ein Recht der fremden Handlung." The expression now employed in correct German to denote an Obligation

* Pr. Instit. de obligationibus (3, 13).

is the following, "Ein Recht der Forderung," or a Right or Claim; that is, an Obligation is the Right to claim or demand something from another. It is a bond of Law which binds us "*alicujus solvendæ rei;*" or, as it is stated by Paulus, "Obligationum substantia non in eo consistit, ut aliquod corpus nostrum aut servitutem nostram faciat, sed ut alium nobis adstringat ad dandum aliquid vel faciendum vel praestandum."* The Persons who are united by such a *vinculum juris* are called the Debtor and the Creditor. Thus there must be in every Obligation two Persons bound, the Debtor who is bound to a *solvere*, a *dare*, or a *facere*, as the case may be, and the Creditor who possesses the Demand or Claim.

Definition of Paulus.

The Debtor and Creditor.

It is further to be observed that while the legal relation thus created is called, in its totality, an Obligation, it would be erroneous to suppose this to be the only meaning of the word, for the *passive* relation sustained by the Debtor to the Creditor is likewise called an Obligation. Again, the phrase "*Obligatio nobis acquiritur*" presents to our consideration an Obligation from an *active* point of view.

The term Obligation applied to the *passive* relation of the Debtor.

Sometimes, also, the term "*Obligatio*" is used for the *Causa obligationis*, and the Contract itself is designated an Obligation. There are passages in which even the Document which affords the proof of a Contract is called an Obligation. Such applications, however, are but a loose extension of the term, which, according to its true idea, is only properly employed when it is used to denote the debt relationship, in its totality, *active* and *passive*, subsisting between the Creditor and the Debtor.

Extension of the term *Obligatio*.

* l. 3, Dig. de obligationibus et actionibus (44, 7).

An Obligation differs from a Real Right.

An Obligation differs entirely from what is termed a Real Right; that is, a Right in which the Thing itself is the object of the Right. In all Real Rights we do not sustain any relation to a Person; but the Thing itself, the object of the Right, stands related to us. There are apparent Obligations in which there seems to be a *nexus* between a Person and a Thing; as, for example, when a house or a farm is rented, when there is a *jus utendi fruendi*, or a Usufruct. But to suppose that such a *nexus* constitutes an Obligation would be quite erroneous. The Person who rents a house has no *jus habitandi*, and the farmer has no *jus fruendi*. The hirer of a house possesses the Right to claim that the party who rents to him shall allow him to dwell in the house he has rented, but he has no *jus habitandi* in the strict sense of the term. In every case that could be suggested involving a legal Obligation, it would be found that the Person never stands in any relation to the Thing itself. The *juris vinculum* is always between the Debtor and the Creditor.

Thus, we may briefly state that Obligations mediate the Exchange of Things between Persons. This legal relationship binds one Person (the *Debitor*) to render to another Person (the *Creditor*) the performance of something involving pecuniary value; for example, Property, Possession, User, Labour, &c. The Romans gave to these different classes of performances three distinctive terms, namely, *dare, facere, praestare*. *Dare* is used in reference to Quiritarian Property or Quiritarian Servitudes; *facere* signifies every other performance not included in the former, for instance, Service;

The meaning of *dare, facere, praestare*.

praestare refers to any performance involving compensatory Damages.

It is worthy of note that considerable differences exist amongst civilians as to the precise definition to be given to these words. Puchta, in his Lectures on the Modern Civil Laws (vol. ii., p. 3), takes a different view to that given by Möhler; he says that *dare, oportere*, mean granting an Easement or Servitude, and that *praestare* means any other performance, which also may be termed a *facere*. Puchta's view.

The object of an Obligation, or Claim, consists in the doing of something, a Feasance; or the not doing of something, a non-Feasance. But the transaction must possess for the Creditor* some pecuniary interest affecting his Property; moreover, it must be something physically possible, and it must also be lawful; further, it must not only be an act permissible, but it must not entirely depend upon the will of the Person rendered liable.†

The subject-matter or object of an Obligation must not be wholly undetermined, though it may be more or less uncertain. The Obligation proceeds for a *certum* where the *quid, quale, quantum*, or, in other words, where the object has been individually determined and The subject-matter of an Obligation must be more or less certain.

---

* When the Creditor has no pecuniary interest depending upon the performance, the Debtor may or may not perform his promise. It is otherwise when a pecuniary value is created by a Condition. A value of affection is also sufficient to sustain an Obligation.

† An Obligation may be made conditional upon the will (*arbitrium*) of a third party, so that until his election is made, no Obligation will exist. It is different in the case of the *arbitrium boni viri*. This may be left to the Debtor, and, as the rule, is presumed to be so left. As the *bonus vir* may be replaced, the Obligation does not become invalid, because no election has been made by this third party. Purchase and Hire are, however, excepted from this Rule.

brought under the Dominion of the Creditor. This rule, however, does not include fungible Things, because with *res fungibiles* it does not depend upon the individual Thing; and the *Obligatio* is *certa*, when the fungible Things are definitively determined, both as regards quality and quantity. Every *Obligatio* is *incerta* which does not proceed for a *certum:* for example, the Claim of Interest; or of a special individually determined Thing, but one which is not subject to the Dominion of the Creditor; or of an alternative object. When there are alternative objects, both are held to be *in Obligatione;* but only one *in Solutione.* From this it follows, that if one of the objects is destroyed by accident or *casus*, the Debtor is not discharged; he is only discharged when all the objects are destroyed, and the Debtor is only exceptionally permitted to give the worth of that which is less in value. Where the loss has been caused by the fault of the Creditor or of the Debtor, it depends who had the choice of the Things. As the rule, the Debtor has the choice (not so in the case of Legacies, where the Legatee elects) and he enjoys this Right until it is exercised; that is, until payment of the Debt, when nothing has been determined as to the Right of election or choice. Election may, however, be conceded to the Creditor by special Agreement, in which case the Creditor renders his choice valid by means of an Action. The Right of election passes both in the case of the Creditor and Debtor to their Heirs. If the Right of election has been conceded to a third party, the whole *Obligatio* is regarded as an *Obligatio conditionalis*. Thus, such Obligations are uncertain (*incertæ*), for by their very nature they are inchoate.

Of alternative objects both are *in Obligatione*, one *in Solutione*.

The object of an Obligation gives rise to a further classification; for an Obligation is, according to its subject-matter, divisible or indivisible. It is divisible when it is directed to the creation of a juridically divisible object of Property, as, for instance, the Ownership of a certain particular object. It is indivisible if it is directed to a Servitude, or if its aim is directed to some completed act or omission, a *facere* or a *non facere*, regarded as a whole. This classification is in so far of importance, as only divisible Obligations may be separately demanded, separately performed, and separately extinguished; whilst by transmission to several Heirs, they become divisible into separate and distinct Obligations. A similar effect takes place, in part, in the case of those Obligations that have for their object a *genus*, or to satisfy which an alternative object may be selected. Otherwise, the Debtor might first give half of one Thing, and then, at a subsequent period, half of another. When he, in the first instance, gives half of one Thing, and subsequently gives the whole of another, he may reclaim by the *Condictio* the half first given.

An Obligation is divisible or indivisible

Further, it is of importance to determine whether the performance of an Obligation is to be by a Money payment; or by Compensation for Damages; or by payment of Interest; or by payment as a Penalty.

Performance of an Obligation by a money payment, etc.

1. Where payment is to be made in a sum of Money, and a change takes place in the Mint value, What, it may be asked, is the effect? Where the Mint value is changed, the number of the coins to be given in payment is varied, not the sum; but the

Exchange of Mint value.

variation in the exchangeable value of money produces no effect. Where the particular kind of money was indicated in which payment was to be made, as, for instance, Sterling money, or United States Gold, and the particular kind has subsequently been withdrawn from currency; the metallic value is, without doubt, the amount due to the Creditor. In the absence of any stipulation as to payment in any particular kind of money, the Debtor may pay in any money that is acknowledged to be current at the time.

Mediate and Immediate object of an Obligation

2. The pecuniary value of a transaction, which is in other respects only the mediate object of an Obligation, may become its immediate object. It may become both the principal object of the Obligation, as in the commission of a forbidden act, and also the subordinate object, as in the case of delay in the performance of the principal object. Again, the principal object in a Claim, or upon which the Claim is based may lose its Property value, as when the Thing to be given ceases to exist. The term Pecuniary Value has been used to designate *quanti res est*. The determination of this value depends upon the object that is to be valued, whether it be a *thing* or a *transaction*, and the particular circumstances which determine its value to the Creditor. The mere value of a Thing as an article of sale, the *verum rei pretium*, must be taken into consideration when the value is either not at all the object of the Obligation,* or if such should be the case, is yet brought into notice not on account

Pecuniary Value, or *quanti res est*.

---

* For example, the *Quarta Falcidia* is to be calculated. In this case the Testamentary Goods must be first valued as an element of the inheritable Property.

of any presumption of damage. On the other hand, special circumstances must come into consideration, the *æstimatio ejus quod interest*, when the value is the object of a Claim or Obligation in consequence of some damage done.

Measure of damage: *damnum emergens; lucrum cessans.*

The amount of a Person's interest, regarded as the subject-matter of an Obligation, is the difference between the value of the Property after the happening of the damaging circumstance, and the value the Thing damaged would have possessed, without the intervening injury; it may be that the deterioration of the value of the Property is immediate, or that it is a *damnum emergens;* or it may be that some future benefits are diminished, or that there is what is denominated a *lucrum cessans.* To claim the actual value due to a Person is understood to mean the claiming of the adjustment of these differences. The principles applicable for computing such values are the following: *a* It is only the actual interest possessed in the Property that can be made the subject of a Claim.* *b.* It is only injuries resulting from damaging events that are taken into consideration.† *c.* Damages which arise out of a connection of individual circumstances are allowable only in the case of *damnum emergens.*‡ In determining the value of a *lucrum cessans,* only the gain resulting from the Thing itself ought to be estimated, the *utilitas*

---

* The value of affection is not taken into consideration.

† For example, non-delivery of forage and consequent death of cattle; Sale of a diseased animal and consequent infection of a whole herd.

‡ For instance, a Creditor is liable to a third Person for the delivery of a certain Thing under a penalty, and the Debtor makes default. The Debtor, in consequence of his default, becomes liable for this penalty.

*circa rem ipsam.** *d.* In estimating the local rate of Interest (that is, the difference arising from the fact of a payment being made at a place other than it ought to be), all the special circumstances must be taken into consideration. *e.* Interest must never exceed the *alterum tantum* of the original value of the thing as an article of sale, unless the Claim, as in Actions arising from Delicts, proceeds from its very inception for Interest. The *Juramentum in litem*, by which the Plaintiff determines his Claim, has already been mentioned.†

Interest not to exceed *alterum tantum* of original value.

Definition of Interest.

3. Moreover, Interest itself may become the subject-matter of an Obligation. By Interest is meant the equivalent which the Debtor owes to the Creditor for the use of a certain quantity of a Fungible Thing, payable in a Thing of a like kind. The quantity upon which Interest is payable, is called the Capital, or *Sors*. Where there is no Capital, no Interest can possibly be claimed. The foundation of the Obligation to pay Interest may be referrable to some legal transaction, which is termed "*Usurae ex obligatione;*" or it may arise from some Judicial Prescript, in which case it is called "*Usurae officio judicis praestandae.*" Such legal Interest is termed "*Usurae ex mora;*" ‡ Interest upon the purchase-money due, which must be paid from the time that the buyer is put into Possession of the goods purchased; Interest

Obligation to pay Interest.

* As, for example, money due by way of Interest, not possible gain, resulting from speculation.

† In this case the Creditor himself fixes the amount claimed. In the cases included under the rules laid down above in paragraphs *a* to *e*, the Judge must determine the amount upon the Plaintiff establishing his proof.

‡ These include Interest, which the Fiscus and Minor may demand upon every Claim that will bear Interest, the liquidation of which has been delayed, although not as *mora*.

on money belonging to a third party appropriated to one's own use, without his consent; Interest upon Capital, the Property of a third party, the administration of which has been entrusted to one who has left it unemployed by neglect: in these cases the Obligation to pay Interest constitutes a part of the principal Debt, or Claim; but the Interest can only be sued for with the Capital itself. Hence, if the principal Claim be excluded by Prescription, the Interest is likewise barred. When the Liability for Interest rests upon a legal transaction, the Right to sue for Interest may give rise to a distinct Action, or it may be only possible to sue for it in connection with the principal Debt, according as the Obligation to pay it has come into force either by a separate Agreement, such as a Testamentary Disposition, or by judicial recognition. Where Interest is payable under an Agreement, the rate will be determined by the Contract itself; where the Interest is legal, it is fixed in part by the Legislature. A maximum rate of Interest of Six per Cent. was adopted by the Romans. With the Germans Five per Cent. is the legal rate. But *personæ illustres*, or nobles, can only stipulate for Four per Cent.; merchants may charge Eight per Cent., and in some instances* even Twelve per Cent. is allowable. There are also further restrictions to be noticed. *Anatocismus*,† or Interest upon Interest, is forbidden. *Usuræ*

Rate of Interest.

Anatocismus.

* In the case of the *Contractus trajecticii* and also for Loans of Money for *Usuræ rei judicatæ.*

† Compound Interest is not allowed; nor the adding of Interest to the Capital, which is termed *Anatocismus conjunctus;* nor even that the same shall bear Interest, as new Capital, which is denominated *Anatocismus separatus.*

ultra alterum tantum is also forbidden; that is, arrears of Interest exceeding the amount of the Capital itself cannot be recovered. Usurious Interest may be refused; it cannot be reckoned in with the Capital Debt, and if it has been paid, it may be demanded back.

Penalties may originate Obligations.

4. Finally, Penalties sometimes constitute the subject matter of Obligations. A Penalty is the loss which a wrong-doer is subjected to beyond what would be actually required for Restitution. This loss also occurs apart from any Compensation for Damages, and as a legal consequence only, in the case of Delicts (Torts); it arises in the case of Torts at times, in conjunction with compensatory Damages; at times in Obligations which are based upon Contracts. It may also in some cases be determined by Agreement, when it is designated Conventional Penalty. By the latter is to be understood every loss or Damage stipulated for by Agreement, which either of the contracting parties may sustain by the entire default of the other party to meet his Obligation, or by his failing to fulfil it in a proper manner. An Obligation, for the enforcement of which a Penalty is stipulated, is either of such a nature that its non-fulfilment would of itself produce legal consequences, as for instance a promised yet non-performed delivery, or such as where the fulfilment is secured by a stipulation that Damages shall be obtained in the event of non-fulfilment. In either case it must be treated as an independent promise to be adjudged under certain Conditions.

Definition of Conventional Penalty.

Promise not to play music in a house.

The promise not to play music in a house is, for want of an appreciable consideration, not obligatory. The adding of a penal sum sanctions such a promise, which in itself would not be binding. A Condition must neither be immoral nor impossible. Whenever a Condition takes place by the act of the party who has imposed the Conditional Penalty, as for instance when an act is not done which should have been done, or a delivery not made which ought to have been made, then the Conventional Penalty lapses.

Action upon a Condition involving Penalty.

The Action is brought upon the Condition taking effect, either, as the case may be, for default of the observance of the Condition, or for its improper or only partial fulfilment, when the sum stipulated for is by way of a pure Penalty. But when it is to be regarded as an arbitrary estimate of damage for the breach of an Agreement, the Penalty agreed upon may be sued for, or, in the alternative, the performance of the Agreement may be demanded. If, however, it be an arbitrary estimate of damage for improper, or faulty, as for instance delayed fulfilment, an Action lies to compel the performance of the Obligation, and also for the Conventional Penalty, or for satisfaction to the extent of the interest involved.

Hitherto the subject-matter of Obligations has been treated of; firstly, of the immediate object, or the transaction; then of the performance, or the mediate and pecuniary value. According to the kind or species of pecuniary value, Obligations were formerly termed divisible or indivisible, determinate or indeterminate. Then again, certain performances have been referred to, to which particular principles were deemed to be applicable.

Subjects of Obligations.

The question now is, who or what are the subjects of an Obligation? and what influence do they exert upon the Obligation itself?

Bilateral Obligation

The subjects or parties to an Obligation are the Creditor and the Debtor. Where both parties possess this character, that is, when each party is Debtor and each Creditor, as in the case of a Contract of Sale, the Obligation is said to be *bilateral*. Where this is not the case, as where the immediate and essential Matter of a Contract is to give a Right to one party, and to impose a corresponding duty upon another, a Contract is termed *unilateral*. The bilateral character of an Obligation is of importance in a twofold view: *a*. When in the *Contractus claudicantes*,* the party not liable, himself decides in favour of the existence of a concluded transaction such a Person becomes bound to its complete performance; *b*. He who sets up a Claim based upon a bilateral Contract, admits that he is himself liable. In consequence of this it follows that a contracting party who claims without having performed his part, may be rebutted by the Plea denominated the "*Exceptio non adimpleti contractus.*" It must then be determined either by Law,† or by the terms of the Agreement, who has the first duty to perform. The party who sets up the *Exceptio* must prove the existence of his counter Claim. The Plaintiff must prove the possible performance that may be demanded from him.

The *Exceptio non adimpleti contractus.*

There may be several Debtors and several Creditors.

In an Obligation there may be merely one Creditor and one Debtor opposed to each other, or there may be several Persons on either side. This may happen in the following way:

* These are Agreements in which, on account of special circumstances, only one of the contracting parties is bound. For example, if the Pupil, without the authority of his Tutor, has concluded a Contract.

† In the single instance of Letting, when the Lessor has to perform his part first.

a. There may appear to be but one existing Obligation, whilst there are really several distinct and independent Obligations* which simply concur in their common origin. Several Obligations.

b. The apparently single Obligation may contain, from its very inception, several Obligations which concur with one another at one particular point, namely, in their subject-matter. Such an Obligation is said to be made *in solidum.* Each separate Creditor may demand the same and also the entire object, and each Debtor is liable for the performance of the entire Obligation; but the object can only be demanded once, and the Obligation need be only once performed. Obligation *in solidum.*

c. When there is really only one Obligation, whilst there is a plurality of subjects on the one side or the other, or perhaps upon both sides, as the case may be, the object nevertheless being identical, such an Obligation is termed a *Correal Obligation.* When there are several Correal Creditors, or several Correal Debtors, these Obligations are distinguished into *Correales obligationes activae* and *passivae.* Every *Correus* is either wholly a Creditor or wholly a Debtor. From which it follows that whatever a Correal Creditor does with the Obligation, has the same effect as if each several Creditor did it; what a Correal Debtor does, holds good for all the remaining ones. But when the Action proceeds to the *litis contestatio* against one of the Debtors, it does not destroy or annul the Obligation as far as the other Debtors are concerned. The Correal Debtor Correal Obligation

* For example, a Creditor or a Debtor dies leaving several Heirs. Another instance is the following: Where a Delict or Tort has been committed. The Penalty affects every wrong-doer, and every Person injured may claim Compensation.

may be sued by a Creditor, and he need not demand the whole Debt from him. Puchta and Arndts think, though Von Vangerow is of a different opinion, that by means of the *Exceptio divisionis*, introduced by an *Epistola divi Hadriani*, Correal Debtors bound *in solidum* may obtain a division of the burden imposed upon them, though not when they have become such by Delict, or by Testamentary Disposition. But when a Debtor has paid the whole Debt, he has not *ipso jure* a Right of contribution as against the others;* but he may demand the assignment of the Action from the Creditor, and by this means he may recoup himself. Similarly the Creditor who receives the whole payment need not pay anything to the other Creditors, unless there be a special Agreement binding him to do so. A Correal Obligation is extinguished whenever the ground, or cause of extinction, strikes at the object of its existence. If it only invades the relationship of the subject to the Obligation, it has the effect merely of destroying the relation of the several subjects to the Obligations.† In the Obligation *in solidum*, of which mention has already been made, the grounds of extinction only annul or cancel the Obligation when they carry with them the complete satisfaction of the Creditor.‡ When one Debtor has satisfied the entire Obligation, he may demand contribution from the others, and that even without any special ground of Obligation; because in satisfying his

Exceptio divisionis.

* To obtain this there must be some special foundation for the Obligation, as, for instance a *Societas*, or a *Mandatum*, &c.

† For example, in the *pactum de non petendo*.

‡ This holds good when there are several Debtors as well as when there are several Creditors, for here each Creditor has a special Obligation in regard to which he himself only has power to dispose.

own Obligation, he has also discharged all the collateral Obligations. An interruption in the time of Prescription affects only the party with whom it has been interrupted. The guilty act of one Debtor affects that Debtor only. In Correal Obligations, the converse of the above holds good, because in these Obligations but one Obligation exists; though, as already observed, each of the several Creditors or Debtors acts as if he were the only party to the Agreement.

In Correal Obligations only one Obligation.

It is not every Obligation that is protected by a legal Remedy. Those Obligations which have not such protection are termed *Naturales obligationes;* others are denominated *Civiles.** A *Naturalis obligatio* has its origin either in some imperfect and informal inception, as would be the case if forms prescribed by law have been neglected, or on account of the disqualification of a *Filius familias* in the case of a loan. Again, a Natural Obligation may arise in consequence of some partial or incomplete solution (Prescription, Competency). It would, however, be quite erroneous to suppose that a *Naturalis obligatio* is devoid of all legal effect; for it may serve as the foundation or basis† of some other legal transaction; and to the extent that the Debtor has discharged his Obligation, so far he is entitled to the *Soluti retentio;* or a Natural Obligation may be made available by way of Plea.

Naturales obligationes.

---

* At first, by the expression *Naturales obligationes* was understood those which were *honorariæ.* These Obligations were first made actionable by the *Praetorian Edict.*

† Mortgage, Suretyship, Novations, are transactions of this kind.

SECTION XLII.—*Of the Exercise of Obligations.*

Von Vangerow, ss. 574—575.
Arndts, ss. 218—228.
Puchta, ss. 238—248, 280.

Wherein the exercise of Obligations consists.

THE exercise of Obligations consists in the realisation and the acceptance of their fulfilment. The object of the fulfilment is the subject-matter, or object of the Demand. Hence the maxim, "*Aliud pro alio, invito creditori, solvi non potest.*" For the immediate object of the Obligation there is substituted a money value, when the performance agreed upon becomes impossible, or when the Creditor renounces his Right thereto. As the rule, the time of performance and the creation of the Obligation are synchronous.* Frequently, however, the period is deferred, either by private Agreement or by some Legal Prescript, or by the nature of the performance itself. Where any doubt exists, the Debtor may satisfy the Claim against him sooner than the period when it would actually become due. When the Debtor pays at an earlier period, with the concurrence of the Creditor, a Debt not bearing Interest, he has a valid Cláim for Discount *(Rebate, Interusurium).* He deducts such a sum from the Claim of the Creditor as leaves a balance which, if put out at Interest for the interval falling between the day of payment and the day the Debt would become due, would realise at that time the exact amount then due. The amount deducted constitutes what is denominated *Interusurium*, or Discount.

Time of Performance.

Discount.

* For the existence of the Obligation the Romans employed the expression *dies cedit;* for the period of its enforcement, *dies venit.*

Place for Performance.

The place for the performance of a Contract is the place fixed by the terms of the Agreement. When the Debtor makes default, the Creditor may sue in any competent Forum having jurisdiction at the place of performance, or at the place of Action brought, and in the latter instance also for the *interessi loci*.* When several places are alternatively named, the Debtor has the Right of election until Action brought; from the commencement of the Action the Right of election passes to the Creditor. Where no place of performance is named, the Debtor must deliver any object he may be bound to restore at the place where it was received. If it be a *Species* or a quantity taken from a certain ascertained stock, it must be rendered where the stock is situated. Other objects may be delivered at any suitable place. Where no place is named for the performance, if the character and essence of the Contract depend upon the place of performance, the Obligation becomes void.†

Exceptions to the above Rules.

There are, however, exceptions to the above rules.

The fulfilment of an Obligation may be modified:

Aestimatio.

1. As to its value. Where the original subject-matter of the Obligation cannot possibly be performed, and the Debtor is not wholly discharged on account of the impossibility of performance, the Creditor, in this instance, must be satisfied by Compensation in Damages, (*Æstimatio*). Further, when a Debtor, owing a sum of money, is without funds on the pay-day, not by any fault on his part, *sine culpa*, and the Creditor demands

"Beneficium dationis in solutum.

* As long as *Actiones stricti juris* were in force, this was effected by the *Actio arbitraria de eo quod certo loco.*

† For instance, the promise to build a House where it may suit the party making the promise.

payment, the Debtor has the Right to discharge the Debt by rendering his most valuable Effects, such Effects to be appraised by the Court, upon Surety being given against any Action to recover the Property.* The Creditor on his part is bound to take such Things in lieu of payment. To this mode of solution the expression "*Beneficium dationis in solutum*" is applied. Finally, we may refer to the case of an Inheritance. The Debtor can never compel the Creditor to accept an Inheritance, but the majority of the Creditors may compel the minority to accept. Notice must be given to all the Creditors. The majority is determined not by the number of the Creditors, but by the value of their respective Claims. The dissentient Creditor looks to the Sureties, the Mortgagee to his Pledge, and only the concurrent chirographic Creditors are bound.

Beneficium competentiæ.

2. Another modification of the fulfilment of an Obligation consists in regard to the time of performance. The performance is suspended where the Debtor avails himself of the so-called *Beneficium competentiæ*. In some instances, indeed,† the Creditor must be satisfied with what the Debtor can spare, and he is required to wait his time for the payment of the residue (*Condemnatio in quantum facere potest*). The Debtor must submit a statement of his Property; then his personal

* In actual Eviction, the Creditor may become the Purchaser, or consider the Obligation not as discharged.

† The *Exceptio competentiæ* is allowed between Husband and Wife, Parents and their Children, Brothers and Sisters, Partners, the Father-in-law and the Son-in-law, on account of the promised *Dos;* the Donor against the Claim of the Donee; Soldiers; in some cases it also extends to a *Filii familiæ;* the Debtor who has assigned his Goods to his Creditors, in respect of after acquired Property. The *Exceptio* is essentially personal, and goes neither to an Heir nor to a Surety.

requirements must be taxed or ascertained, *ne egeat.* Competency touches only the execution, it does not lessen the Obligation, and may be brought forward at the time of execution. Fulfilment is further suspended by Delay *(Moratorium)*, a privilege granted by the Regent, affording protection to a Debtor for five years before his Creditor can proceed against him for his Debt.* The performance of the Obligation may also be suspended. The majority of the Creditors have the Right of imposing this upon the minority, extending, but not exceeding the respite beyond a period of five years. Finally, fulfilment is postponed by means of the *Cessio Bonorum.* The Debtor who, without any default on his part, becomes insolvent, may avert the disgrace of a Bankruptcy by assigning all his Property to his Creditors. The Sale of his Effects takes place not in his name; he cannot be arrested, and should he acquire Property hereafter, he may plead, as against a suing Creditor to whom he still remains liable for the balance of his Claim, the *Exceptio competentiæ.* The *Cessio Bonorum.*

When several Creditors collide or clash in their Demands, and the Debtor becomes insolvent, the relationship arising from Bankruptcy ensues. All Creditors who wish to participate in the distribution of the existing assets of the Bankrupt Estate must become parties to the Bankruptcy. This satisfaction must be sought by them in common, and no longer separately. They become parties to the Bankruptcy by Edictal Citation. The effect of Bankruptcy upon Bankruptcy. Its effect.

* The Debtor must, however, find Sureties for the due payment at the termination of the time. The *Moratorium* binds only those Creditors who were such at the time when the *tempus respirationis* was given.

a Debtor is, that he loses all Right of disposal, not, however, the Ownership of his Property; and that the management of his Estate is given to the Assignee in Bankruptcy. Of Creditors in Bankruptcy, we must distinguish between those entitled to the *Vindicatio*, who are denominated "*Separati ex jure dominii*," that is to say, those who claim certain specific Things found in the Bankrupt's Estate as their own particular Property;* and those who are termed "*Separati ex jure crediti*," who rank as Creditors in the Bankrupt Estate, but who sever a portion of the Bankrupt's Estate to the exclusion of all others, whereupon a special Bankruptcy takes place as regards the portion thus severed.†

Collocation of Creditors in Bankruptcy.

The Creditors in a Bankruptcy proper rank as follows:

1. Those who are absolutely privileged Creditors; as, for instance, Creditors claiming for expenses incurred by the last illness of the *Defunctus*, Wages of servants, and Fiscal dues.
2. Preferential Mortgage Creditors.
3. Simple Mortgage Creditors.
4. Privileged Chirographic Creditors.‡
5. Simple Chirographic Creditors.

---

* By means of the *Rei Vindicatio*, *Hereditatis petitio*, *Actio commodati*, *Actio in rem scripta*, &c.

† For example, Creditors having a claim against the Inheritance may avail themselves of the *Beneficium separationis*. Trade Creditors, again, exclude other Creditors by means of the *Actio contributoria*.

‡ There are, however, Claims which have a preference "*Privilegium exigendi.*" This *Privilegium exigendi* attaches either exclusively to the Person of the Creditor, as, for instance, to the *Fiscus*, to Municipalities, to the Ward, to the Wife; or it is included in the Obligation itself, such, for instance, as Funeral expenses, Costs for the reparation of a building in ruins, Outlays for the purchase of a ship, for Money deposited with a Banker, or Money Dealer, without Interest.

SECTION XLIII.—*Of the Origin of Obligations.*

Von Vangerow, ss. 595—615.
Arndts, ss. 229—248.
Puchta, ss. 249—285.
Gai. Comm., Tomkins and Lemon's edit., pp. 530—538, III., ss. 163—168.
Savigny Oblig., I., 267, 381; II., 284.
Glück IV., 108, 529; XVI., 91; XVII., 19; XVIII., 76 et seq.
Savigny Syst. des heut. röm. Rechts Bd. II., 272; III., 263, 307.
Pagenstecher de literar. obligatione.
Instit. de verborum obligatione (3, 15).
" de inutilibus stipulationibus (3, 19).
Dig. de pactis (2, 14).
" de verborum obligatione (45, 1).
Cod. de pactis (2, 3).
" de comprehenda et committenda stipulatione (8, 38).
" de inutilibus stipulationibus (8, 39).
Dig. de praescriptis verbis (19, 5).
Cod. de rerum permut. et praescriptis verbis (4, 64).
l. 57, Dig. de oblig. et act. (44, 7).
l. 9, " de contrah. emt. (18, 1).
Cod. ut actiones et ab heredibus et contra heredes incipiant (4, 11).
" si quis alteri vel sibi sub alterius, etc. (4, 50).
" inter alias acta vel judicata, etc. (7, 60).
Instit. per quas personas nobis obligatio acquiritur (3, 28).
Dig. de evictionibus et duplae stip. (21, 2).
Cod. de evictionibus (8, 45).
l. 2, Cod. de rescindendae vend. (4, 44).
l. 35, pr. Dig. de contr. emt. (18, 1).
l. 6, pr. Dig. de lege commissoria (18, 3).
l. 17, fin. Cod. de fide instrument. (4, 21).
Instit. s. ult. de verb. obl. (3, 15).
l. 12, Cod. de contr. v. comm. stipul. (8, 38).
l. 115, s. 2, de verb. obl.
Dig. de pollicitationibus (50, 12).

Modes of the origin of Obligations.

OBLIGATIONS are created in various ways. The mode of their origin exerts an influence upon the very Matter of the Obligation. The different modes of the origin of Obligations are the following: Legal Transactions, Forbidden Acts, and States or Plights.

I. Legal Transactions. It must be ascertained in the first place, before all other considerations, whether the creation of an Obligation was intended by the parties, or whether either of the parties intended merely some lawful aim, without intending to create an Obligation.* According as this is the case or not, the distinction is made between Agreements and *Quasi* Contracts.† Agreements constitute the most frequent mode of origin for Obligations. By these are to be understood, that accord of the several Persons, namely, the contracting parties, by virtue of which one party promises something; whilst the other party accepts the promise. Hence it follows, that there must be several Persons; there must also be Concurrence of Will *(Consensus)*; and the declaration of this Concurrence, Promise, and Acceptance. It is only by exception that a mere Promise, a *Pollicitatio*, engenders an Obligation.‡

Agreements.

* For instance, Acceptance of a Tutorship, Entrance upon an Inheritance, *Negotiorum gestio*.

† The parties to the Transaction are bound *quasi ex contractu* just as if the Legal Transaction were a *Contractus*.

‡ This is the case in the following circumstances:—

1. In the case of a *Pollicitatio* made to a *Respublica*.
2. In the case of a Promise to a Church or Charity.
3. In Dotal Promises.
4. In what the Germans denominate "Auslobung," that is, a distinct Promise made to the public in general. Until its completion, however, the Promissor may retract. But as soon as a third party has once accepted, and the Promissor wishes to recall his "Auslobung," he must pay all the expenses that have been incurred by his proffer.

For the declaration of the Will various forms are prescribed, upon which depend: Forms necessary for the declaration of the Will.

1. The validity of the Contract; (for example, judicial insinuation or publication.)

2. Its enforcibility.

According, to Roman Law, indeed, a mere *Pactum*, a mere Agreement, a Declaration of the Will, expressed in any terms, created no actionable Obligation; but only those Agreements which were made in specially imposed forms, gave rise to binding Contracts. The forms thus observed converting a mere Agreement into an Obligation, *causæ obligationum*, are the following:

1. *Res*. The performance of an act lays the foundation for some counter performance on the other side. *Causæ obligationum: Res.* There are two classes of Obligations which stand *in re*. In one class, the reciprocal performance which may be demanded is not stipulated for, but must be rendered, since, by an act of ours, or without our act, an object would become transferred to the Property of another, which he would hold illegally.* In the other class, reciprocal performance can be claimed, because by the performance on the one part, performance on the other has been promised. Contracts that have been created in this manner are termed *Real Contracts*. When the Actions that arise out of these Contracts have special names given to them, they are termed Nominate Contracts, *Contracta Nominata*. Nominate Contracts. Such are: *Mutuum*, *Commodatum*, *Depositum*, *Pignus*. When the Actions have

* In the performance of an innominate Real Contract, *Contractum innominatum*, as long as the reciprocal performance has not been completed, the Plaintiff, instead of suing for the performance of the Contract, may proceed by the *Condictio causa data, causa non secuta*. In other cases there is given to the Plaintiff the *Condictio indebiti, ob turpem causam etc.*

Innominate Contracts. no special name given them *(Actio praescriptis verbis)*, such Real Contracts are called *innominate*. They are the following: *Do ut des, Do ut facias, Facio ut des, Facio ut facias*.

Other forms are:

Stipulatio. 2. *Verba*, Words spoken in which the Agreement is clothed. The most important case by far of the *verborum obligatio*, is the *Stipulatio*.

Writings. 3. *Litteræ*, that is written words in a given form. Such must not be confounded with acknowledgments for Debts, which are proofs, but not *causae obligationum*.

In some instances:

Consensus and *Consensual* Obligations. 4. By mere *Consensus*, by accord without form, an Agreement is converted into a binding Contract. The consent in this case is the *causa civilis*. There are four Consensual Obligations: *Emtio venditio, Locatio conductio, Societas*, and *Mandatum*.

The *causae civiles* heretofore enumerated, are in the present day not necessary to make Agreements actionable. Stipulations and Literal Contracts have now become obsolete. At the present time Consensual Agreements are the rule. When an Agreement has been concluded, it becomes valid the very moment the parties to it are in accord upon all essential points.

Acts not binding. Non-obligatory are:

1. A Proffer until it be accepted.*

2. Negociations, or preparatory acts, unless the several provisional points are settled by Special Agreements *(Pacta præparatoria)*. Thus the first point may be determined, namely, that an Agreement shall be made,

* It may be asked, how is it in the case of proposals made to parties at a distance? Before the Absentee has received the proposition, Revocation is allowed, and that whether the Revocation becomes known to the absent party before or after his acceptance.

(Pacta de contrahendo); from which there arises a Right of Action for its performance, or for Damages resulting on account of its breach. Written drafts of concluded Agreements, to which some more solemn form has been added, are deemed perfect and conclusive, when the form happens to be merely arbitrary and is added only for the sake of proof. When the form is one prescribed by Law, the Memoranda made by the parties about to enter into a Contract and termed by the Germans "*Punctationes*," are merely preliminary drafts; possibly also *Pacta de contrahendo*, if the legal form operates only to consolidate the security of the transaction. Otherwise, the perfection of an Agreement depends upon its nature.*

Arrha, or Earnest-money.

To give additional validity and force to the performance of Agreements, irrespective of Suretyship, the Renunciation of Exceptions, or Pleas, the Promissory Oath and Judicial Confirmation; Earnest-money, denominated "*Arrha*," and the so-called *Constitutum* are employed. *Arrha* is either given as the proof of a concluded Contract and becomes returnable upon its performance, or it partakes of the nature of a conventional Penalty when the bargain is made simultaneously with the *Lex commissoria;* or it partakes of the nature of a forfeitable Deposit, upon the loss of which either party may withdraw from the Contract *(Arrha pœnitentialis)*. The *Constitutum* is the promise of the performance of an existing Obligation by means of a new Agreement. The Action arising from this is

Arrha pœnitentialis.

Constitutum.

* At Auction every bid constitutes a separate Contract, subject to the Condition that no better Contract shall be made within a given time.

termed "*Actio constitutoria.*"* The *Constitutum* presumes an existing Obligation, but not necessarily one existing between the two Promissors. A third party may have been constituted in lieu of a Debtor *(Constitutum debiti alieni)*, who henceforth is to be bound to another Person constituted as Creditor. The performance of the *Constitutum*, not the *Constitutum* itself, annuls the original Obligation. When no time is fixed, the Judge determines the time of performance, which must be a period of not less than ten days.

An Agreement binds the Heir. The effect of a concluded Agreement is that the Promissor is bound to the exact performance of his Promise, or Undertaking. This effect passes to the Heirs, but the Agreement in other respects does not affect third parties. From which it follows that no one can make a promise for a third party, nor accept a promise for a third Person. This rule does not now hold good in Modern Law, for an Assignment, or Cession, may be presumed by a fiction of Law.

An Obligation must have a material basis, or *causa*. If, moreover, an Agreement is to be effective as an Obligation, it is absolutely necessary that it should be founded upon an adequate material basis or *causa*. In other words, the Promise must intend some lawful object; it may be the exercise of an act of liberality *(Donatio)*; or the fulfilment of a

---

* The advantages of the *Constitutum* are the following:

1. It is an acknowledgment of the Obligation on the part of both the constituents.

2. It also renders possible the transformation of the Obligation in respect of Time, Place, Object, or Subject.

3. The possibility of imposing a Liability, or of creating a Right for a third party.

4. The possibility of obtaining an Action in the case of *Obligationes naturales*.

pre-existing Obligation,* as in the case of the *Constitutum* just explained; or some Compensation, as, for instance, conventional Penalty; or some pecuniary benefit received. An Agreement entered into, without actual *causa*, that is, without an adequate material consideration, is destroyed by the *Condictio sine causa*, and by an *Exceptio* or Plea. Again, an acknowledgment of Debt, without a material *causa*, is called *Cautio indiscreta*, and has no efficacy as evidence.

Aleatoriae, or Wager Contracts.

The effect of an Agreement made by way of wager, and upon which profit and loss to one party or the other is made contingent upon the taking place of certain unknown events, is peculiar. The peculiar Matter of the Contract is termed *Alea*, and Agreements resting on such grounds are designated *Aleatoriae*, or Wager Contracts. Transactions of various kinds may be concluded in this manner.

Two kinds of Wager Transaction must be here distinguished:

Insurance, Lotteries, etc.

1. Those where the hazardous business serves another purpose, such as Insurance, Lotteries, the Sale of Things to be hereafter acquired.†

Wagers and Gambling Transactions.

2. Those where the hazardous business is in itself the object, such as Wagers and Gambling Transactions.

Transactions of the first kind are absolutely binding.

---

* He who promises, or to whom a Promise is made, is regarded as the *Procurator*. In the first case, when a Promise is given, a declaration is made to warrant the performance if the third party should make default. In this sense must be explained the Promise that a third party will perform.

† It is termed a *Pactum spei*, where the Expectancy constitutes the subject-matter of the Agreement, in which case the existence of the Thing is uncertain. It is denominated *Pactum rei speratae* if the Thing is the subject-matter whilst the quantity of the Thing is uncertain. In the first case, reciprocal performance is required even when nothing results; in the latter it is not so.

The latter kind create no binding Obligation, for the desire to wager is held to be no juridical *causa*, and losses paid may be recovered by means of the *Condictio indebiti* any time within fifty years.

Forbidden Transactions.

II. Forbidden Transactions. These, in as far as they give rise to an obligatory relation* are designated Delicts. The objective presumption of a Delict is the commission of a legal wrong; the subjective presumption is the intentional guilty violation of a lawful Right, which is *Culpa* in its most extended signification.

Culpa lata.

Dolus.

When the intention of the wrong-doer has been directed towards the producing of the wrongful and illegal act, there is said to be *Dolus;* but when the intention has not been directed to the illegal consequences, whilst yet these might have been foreseen on the part of the wrong-doer, the wrong perpetrated is designated *Culpa*.

Standard whereby to measure *Culpa*.

The standard to measure the conduct of a Person acting is that of a *Bonus pater familias* placed in similar circumstances. He who has acted as such bears no blame; that is, no *Culpa* can attach to his conduct.

The consequences of a Delict.

The legal consequences of a Delict are:

1. Liability for compensatory Damages when the Delict has caused a pecuniary loss.

2. Punishment, public or private. Private punishment still exists, though it is administered less often than under the Roman Law. Punishment and compensatory Damages may be simultaneously demanded; likewise, several punishments arising out of separate Delicts against the same object. When private and

* That is, as the source of independent Obligations in contradistinction to modifications of existing Obligations, (*Vide* § 10).

public punishment concur, both may be demanded, if the wrongful acts or Delicts are different in their characters.

III. Condition or Plight is the cause or origin of Obligations to this extent, that a Person who finds himself* in a certain state may, without any act on his part, become liable for the performance of an Obligation.

SECTION XLIV.—*Of Representation in the inception of Obligations.*

Von Vangerow, ss. 608, 653, 661.
Arndts, ss. 245—248.
Puchta, ss. 273—279.
Gai. Comm. IV., ss. 70—75.
Savigny Oblig. II., 33 et seq.
Glück, XIV., 235 et seq.
Instit., ss. 1, 2, quod cum eo, qui in al., etc. (4, 7).
Dig. de exercitoria actione (14, 1).
Dig. de institoria actione (14, 3).
Cod. de institoria et exercitoria actione (4, 25).

Representation extends the effect of an Obligation.

PRIMARILY, the effect of obligatory acts extends only to the parties concerned in the transactions. By Representation this operation is extended to others. The relation of Representation, in consequence of which one may by the act of another enter into legal relations, is either one originated by necessity; that is, based upon the control that the Constituent exercises over the Representative: or it is voluntary; that is, dependent upon office or appointment. The Obligation always passes through the Representation.

* For instance, one who is a joint-Owner, or a co-Heir, or the Relative of another.

Persons who acquire by Representation. Those who acquire Obligations by necessary Representation are:

The Heir. 1. The Heir, by reason of his relation to the Testator or *Defunctus*, into whose Personality he is considered to enter.

The *Pater familias.* 2. The *Pater familias*, through the *Filius familias*, by virtue of the *Patria potestas*. Such an Acquisition generally takes place when the Son acquires *ex re patris*. The Father acquires as if he had himself contracted. But as the Son has actually contracted, it depends upon his knowledge whether error shall void the Contract; or whether, from the want of knowledge of some given circumstances, a Claim shall arise.*

Authorization by Mandate. The principal case of Acquisition by *Voluntary Representation* is, that of authorization by Mandate. The Mandatary is the contracting party, and he acquires a Right in the first instance only for himself. His Person comes into question where a question arises of mistake or of ignorance. When a Claim arises because he has acted without knowledge of a certain circumstance, such want of knowledge is to his advantage, whilst knowledge militates against him. The *Dominus* is not benefited by his own ignorance,† nor injured by his knowledge.‡ Thus, in the first instance, the contracting *Procurator* always acquires the Right, but the Obligation passes by a real or fictitious *Cessio* or Assignment to the *Dominus*. These principles as to the *Procurator* are also applicable in the case of official

* For instance, Eviction on account of defects in a Thing.

† Except in the case of a collusive understanding between the *Procurator* and the Debtor.

‡ Except where the *Dominus* has given the special order.

Representation, such as the Representation of a Judicial Person and of Guardianship. Even without office or authorization, the fact of a party having in certain instances concluded a Contract for the benefit of another, leads to the same result as if he had concluded the transaction as a party duly authorized, so that the *Dominus* has an *Actio utilis*. When an Ascendant grants a Dowry *(Dos)*, and has stipulated for its Restitution either to his Daughter or her Children, the latter have conceded to them a *Utilis actio*. When one Person delivers the Property of another to a third party, either for his use or to take care of it, stipulating that it shall be returned to the Owner; the latter has the Right to avail himself of the *Actio utilis commodati vel depositi*. If the Donor burdens the Donee with the Condition of making over the Property to a third Person, the latter has an *Actio utilis*. When an alienating Mortgage Creditor has reserved to the third party the Right of redemption, this party may avail himself of an *Actio in factum*.

The Testator may bind the Heir.

The following Persons are bound by their necessary legal relations:

1. The Heir by the Testator.

The Father may be bound sometimes by his Son.

2. In certain cases the Father by his Son.* The cases are: *a*. If the Father has ordered his Son to do certain things, or if he has subsequently ratified his acts, he becomes liable *in solidum* to the *Actio quod jussu*; *b*. When the Father has induced his Son to act to the prejudice of a Creditor, the Creditor may institute

* Not always, but only in special instances. The Actions are denominated *Actiones adjecticiæ qualitatis*. (See Gaius, note *w*, p. 694. Tomkins and Lemon's edit.)

against him the *Actio de eo quod malo dolo patris captus fraudatusque actor est; c.* When the Father derives a pecuniary benefit by the transaction of his Son,* he is liable to the extent of the advantages he has obtained, and may be sued by the *Actio de in rem verso; d.* When a Father has given a *Peculium* to his Son, the Creditors may sue the Father for one year after the termination of the *potestas* by the *Actio de peculio*, claiming the whole amount, deducting, however, what the Father (or any other Person for whom he is answerable) may owe him, and adding that which may have been lost by his *Dolus; e.* If a part of the *Peculium* is employed in trade, with the Father's knowledge and consent, those Creditors who have become such relying upon this fact, have the Right of being preferentially satisfied out of that portion of the *Peculium*. Should the Father oppose this Demand, the Creditors may proceed against him by the *Actio tributoria*, a procedure more advantageous than the *Actio de peculio*, because the trade Creditors have a Right of severance, whilst, on the other hand, the Father possesses no such preferential Right. In these five instances the Father is liable for the business Obligations of his Son.

The *Actio tributoria:* its advantage.

There are, however, two other cases in which third parties are equally liable, who are represented by voluntary Representation. When, for instance, a trader employs a trade manager for his business, he becomes answerable *in solidum* for the business transactions of his manager, whether such manager were

Trade manager.

* The Action presumes a direct Acquisition, not an intermediate one by means of the *Peculium*. Not, however, only the absolute increase belongs to this, but also the savings made by a Creditor.

instituted by necessity, or has been instituted by a voluntary act. The Actions against traders are the *Actio institoria*, when the Factor has been named; and the *Actio exercitoria*, when a *Magister navis* has been appointed.

Actions against traders.

These Actions presume some business transaction of the trader, which either he or his Substitute has concluded, by virtue of a Procuration *(Procura)*.* In lieu of suing the principal trader by the Actions just named, the Creditor may proceed against the trade manager, even though the latter has not contracted in that Capacity. If the Creditor elects to pursue the principals, and there are several of them, they are severally answerable, *in solidum*. The Liability of the principal trader is not restricted in the case of Voluntary Representatives to these two instances, but at present it comprehends all transactions concluded by the *Procurator* in virtue of his authority. In the latter case, the *Actio quasi institoria* must be employed.

The *Actio quasi institoria*.

Again, juridical Persons, and also Persons who are under the *Tutela* are answerable for their Officers and Guardians. The principal *Dominus* is not liable for the illegal and prohibited acts of his business manager, beyond the pecuniary benefit he may have derived from his acts.† But mere gain is not in itself a sufficient ground to create a Liability. There must be some additional reason to render the party who has received the benefit liable. There is no

* An Alteration, a Revocation must be notified if it will affect a third party.

† It is different in the case of the *Actio exercitoria* and *institoria*. In these Actions the principal is answerable for the modification of the Obligation by illegal acts. Delicts also give rise to Liabilities.

Actio de in rem verso utilis. But an *Actio negotiorum gestorum* lies against the party benefited; provided the presumption necessary for the instituting of this Action is found to exist, such presumption being that of not merely having made a pecuniary gain.

Section XLV.—*Of the Alteration of existing Obligations.*

Von Vangerow, ss. 588, 637.
Arndts, ss. 249—253.
Puchta, ss. 263—272.
Gai. Comm., III. 207.
Glück, XVI. 239 et seq., 271 et seq.
Dig. de pactis inter emtorem et vend. (18, 1).
" de in diem addictione (18, 2).
" de lege commissoria (18, 3).
Cod. de pactis inter emtor. et vend. (4, 54).
Dig. de (usuris et fructibus etc. et de) mora (22, 1).

The primary intention of an Obligation may undergo a change.

The primary intention of an Obligation, even during its continuance, may undergo a change. The Matter which it contained at the commencement of the transaction may become modified in its nature. The grounds for this may be:

By Agreement between the parties.

1. Agreement between the parties. Agreements of this kind, which enlarge the original Matter of an Obligation, are termed "*Pacta adjecta.*" Such do not create a new Obligation, but only enlarge or extend an existing one. Of this kind are: *a.* The *Addictio in diem*, by which the contracting parties stipulate that the Contract shall become void upon better terms being obtained from a third party within a given time. The Condition, which in a case of doubt must be taken to be

a *Conditio resolutiva*,* becomes inoperative the moment more advantageous terms are offered and accepted. But the first Contractor can secure to himself the Contract by his Acceptance of the same Conditions. *b*. The *Pactum displicentiæ*, a different kind of *Pactum*, by which one or both parties reserve to themselves a Right of *pœnitentiæ* for a certain time, in cases of doubt as to the time, for sixty days. *c*. A third kind of *Pactum* is the *Pactum commissorium (Lex commissoria)*, by which it is stipulated that the transaction shall become void upon one of the contracting parties making default in point of time. The defaulter must give back what he has received, but he cannot claim that which he has rendered.

Pactum displicentiæ.

Lex commissoria.

2. Wrong, by *Dolus*, by *Culpa*, by *Mora*, by Refusal, and by Denial. Firstly, it is necessary to deal with wrongs arising from *Dolus* and *Culpa*. *Dolus* and *Culpa* are the subjective presumptions of an unlawful transaction. Illegal acts not only create new Obligations, but they change and modify those which already exist. This happens when an Obligation arising out of a corresponding Obligation is violated by the activity or non-activity of the party *(in faciendo* or *in non faciendo*). For fraudulent breach, the party charged must invariably answer, as a *Pactum de dolo non praestando* is no answer to an Action.

Wrongs arising from *Dolus*, *Culpa*, etc.

Culpa is divisible into two degrees: *Culpa lata*, or that absolutely heedless conduct, *id non intelligere quod omnes intelligunt;* and *Culpa levis*, the neglect which a *diligens Pater familias* similarly situated would

Culpa lata and *Culpa levis.*

* The principles applicable to a *Conditio resolutiva* thus become applicable. Hence all the effects of the Contract are cancelled, and that retrospectively.

have avoided. Generally speaking, there are no greater and lesser degrees of *Culpa*. It is true that, in some legal relations, as to the conduct of a Person the measure of care a man would give to his own concerns is applicable; but the *Omissio diligentiæ in suis rebus* is not a special ground of *Culpa*, because the measure of wrong is subjective (relative *Culpa*, or *Culpa in concreto*). It is by the application of this subjective Rule that in any particular case the existence of *Culpa* is proved.

Liability for *Culpa*.

He for whose benefit the Contract has been made is answerable for *Omnis culpa*. A party concluding a transaction for a third Person is answerable only for *Dolus* and *Culpa lata*. To this, however, there are exceptions. In the case of kindly services rendered, and also in the case of a *Precarium*, the Agent is only liable for *Dolus* and *Culpa lata:* but he who has undertaken *voluntarily* the business of another party, is made liable for *Omnis culpa*. In cases where private Rights are intermixed with those of third parties, as with a *Societas*, a *Communio incidens*, Dotal Matters, and in Wardship, only *Diligentia in concreto* is required.

Burden of proof for *Dolus* and *Culpa*.

In regard to the burden of proof for *Dolus* and *Culpa*, it is to be observed:

1. That he who charges with *Dolus* must prove it.

2. When a Claim is based upon the *Culpa lata* of another, it must be proved that the Defendant has acted heedlessly and without reflection, or differently to the manner in which he would have acted in his own business.

3. When *Levis culpa* only is charged, the Defendant must prove that some Accident *(Casus)* has occurred.

4. When *Omissio diligentiæ* is charged, the Plaintiff

has merely to prove the illegal fact. The Defendant, however, may show that Accident *(Casus)* has been the cause, or that he would not have acted differently in his own affairs.

Mora. A second kind of breach of an Obligation, effecting also a modification of the Liability itself, arises from what has been already denominated as *Mora* (Delay). By *Mora* is understood the illegal delaying of the performance of an act which a party is bound to discharge. It is termed *Mora solvendi*, when the Debtor makes default in point of time. This kind presupposes that the Demand is due, that the Debtor has been in default,* and that he has been warned by the Creditor for the non-fulfilment.† Generally, the effect of *Mora solvendi* is, that the Debtor must make good any Damage the Creditor has sustained by the *Mora*. From this it follows that he is liable also for Accident *(Casus)*, and there is a perpetuation of the Obligation; unless, indeed, he can show that the loss would have occurred without the *Mora*, and that it would necessarily have affected the Creditor. Further, Fruits and Interest have to be accounted for from the moment the *Mora* arises.

Mora solvendi.

Mora is denominated *Mora accipiendi* when the Creditor on his part makes default in regard to the time of his Acceptance. The presumption is, that performance has been tendered *rite*, as it is termed,

Mora accipiendi.

---

* It is questionable whether *Culpa* is claimed or not.

† In some instances, Interpellation is unnecessary. There is a *Mora in re* in contradistinction to *Mora ex persona* where such is demanded, namely, in Obligations arising out of Delicts, in the case of the absence of the Debtor, for Debts owing to a Minor, and where a *dies certus solutionis* is fixed. The last case is, however, disputed; but it is held in practice.

that is, in the proper manner, and that the Creditor wrongfully refused to accept. From that instant the Debtor is answerable only for *Dolus* and *Culpa lata*, and if the risk has not already passed to the Creditor it passes to him from that moment. The Creditor is bound to make good to the Debtor every damage arising from Delay on his part.

That *Mora*, both as regards the Creditor and the Debtor, terminates on the destruction of the Obligation is manifestly self-evident. What is termed the purgation of *Mora* is very characteristic. Any subsequent *Mora* annuls the former; and by the performance of that which is due, with that which has been added by *Mora*, the *Mora* is entirely extinguished. *Mora accipiendi* and *Mora solvendi* cannot co-exist.

Purgation of *Mora*.

Effect of Denial or Refusal.

Lastly, an Obligation may become modified by Denial or by Refusal. By Refusal to give or satisfy a Legacy left *ad pias causas;* by Refusal of Restitution in the *Actio quod metus causa*. The Penalty incurred in the first instance is tenfold; in the second, quadruple. By Denial in the *Actio legis Aquilae;* in the *Actio depositi miserabilis;* in Actions upon an acknowledgment of debt; the subject-matter of the Obligation is increased twofold. Hence the maxim, "*Lis inficiando crescit in duplum.*"

Accident.

3. Accident *(Casus)*. An Obligation may become void, or may be modified, that is, increased or decreased, by Accident. When, during the interval of time between the inception and the completion of an Obligation, the subject-matter or object has increased, the question arises: For whose benefit are the *Commodi rei*, as they are termed, or the Increments?

They belong to the Creditor;* but he takes them only in as far as they arise out of the very Thing itself; such, for instance, as Fruits and Accessions.† Advantages accruing to the benefit of the Debtor from other causes, by the Sale of a Thing, by the unlawful act of another, out of which a Claim arises, go to the Debtor, when the *periculum*, or risk, is likewise with him.

Section XLVI.—*Of the Assignment or Transfer of Obligations.*

Von Vangerow, ss. 574, 576, 577.
Arndts, ss. 254—259.
Puchta, ss. 280—285.
Glück, XVI., 379 et seq., 458.
Dig. de hereditate vel actione vendita (18, 4).
Cod. " " " " " (4, 39).
l. 3, Cod. de novat. (8, 42).
l. 1, Cod. de O. et A. (4, 10).
l. 16, pr. Dig. de pact. (2, 14).
l. 5, Cod. quando fiscus (4, 15).
l. 22, Cod. mandati vel contra (4, 35).

Obligations not transferable.

Properly speaking, Obligations are not transferable; a Contract cannot be assigned, because the Obligation cannot be severed from the original parties. But to meet the absolute necessity that exists under certain circumstances to make an Assignment, the exercise of an Obligation is made transferable.‡ The Debtor may nominate a Substitute to discharge the

* The Creditor would have been liable for the loss if it had occurred within this time. "*Commodum ejus esse debet cujus periculum.*"

† Interest on amounts due for Hiring and Rent excepted, so far the Debtor is liable for any Claim for Damages made by an ejected Lessee.

‡ A less available mode is by Delegation, because the pre-existing Obligation is rendered void, and the assent of the Debtor becomes necessary to enable a new Creditor to take the place of the former one.

Obligation to the Creditor; who may appoint a Substitute or Representative to make the Claim for him. When the Substitute either pays, or undertakes the management on his own account, he is called a *Procurator in rem suam.** The act by which, on the part of the Creditor a *Procurator in rem suam* is appointed,† is termed "*Cessio*" or "Assignment." This is accomplished either by the legal Transfer of a business, denominated "*Cessio voluntaria;*" or by legal Prescript, termed "*Cessio necessaria,*" when a Person acquires thereby the independent right of converting the Obligation of a third Person for his own benefit. According to Modern Law, a *Cessio* is regarded as complete if the *justa causa præcedens*, as, for instance, the legal Transaction or the legal Precept‡ is adequately present to make it valid.§ The assent of the Debtor is not needed. Assignment is allowable in all Claims, even in those which are not actionable.‖ But as only the Obligation, not its legal cause, passes by the Assignment; it follows as a matter of course, that the Assignee does not acquire the relation of the Mandatary, or of the Lessee; but

Procurator in rem suam.

Cessio, or Assignment: *voluntaria* and *necessaria*.

The Assignee only obtains the Right of Action.

---

* *In rem suam* because he employs the Obligation for his own benefit, not for the benefit of the Creditor.

† As a Sale, Gift, &c.

‡ For example: he who is compelled to pay a Debt which is not his own, or only such in part, has the *Beneficium cedendarum actionum.* He must, however, ask for the Assignment before Payment, because after Satisfaction the Obligation becomes discharged. The party completing a transaction by a voluntary Representative, has the Right to obtain from him an Assignment or Cession of the Action arising from the business. And similarly in other cases.

§ In other words, if the *justa causa praecedens* be present, a Mandate is presumed. Nevertheless, the Mandate always forms the basis of the Assignment. For example: A is bound to assign to B. This suffices for B, he has thus his *Legitimatio ad causam.*

‖ In the latter case it is made valid by Plea; for example, in Compensation.

only the Right of Action residing in the Person of the Transferor, namely, the *Actio mandati locati, etc.*

Herein there exists no exception to this rule. On the other hand, the following Rights and Obligations are not assignable: Non-assignable Actions.

1. Public Actions, and *Actiones vindictam spirantes;* because such Actions do not exist as Property prior to the *Litis contestatio*, and are non-transferable after the *Litis contestatio*, as they are *Actiones litigiosæ.*

2. Obligations which presume a strictly non-alienable quality in the Person of the Creditor: such as Obligations for Servitudes, Alimony, and the appointment of Personal Servitudes.

3. Assignment to one having Dominion over the Assignor is prohibited.

4. Obligations due to Wards cannot be assigned to their Guardians.

5. The Claim of a Jew upon a Christian cannot be assigned by the Jew to another Christian.

6. Litigious Claims are non-assignable.

The *Lex Anastasiana*, which forbids an Assignee who has acquired a Right by purchase to recover more than the price he has paid, is only a limitation of the general rule regulating Cession. The burden of proof as to the amount paid falls upon the Assignee.* The *Lex Anastasiana.*

Assignment, or Cession, finds its expression in three ways: Effect of Assignment.

1. In regard to the relation between the Assignor and Assignee. This relationship arises out of the *justa* As to Assignor and Assignee.

* Those Obligations are excluded which are employed in common for the purpose of currency, as Bills of Exchange; and Obligations which are made in lieu of payment; or consequent upon a distribution of the Property of a *Communio;* or in Satisfaction of a Creditor by the Possessor of a Pledge.

causa praecedens. Generally, the Assignor is bound to warrant the existence of the Claim, unless it is assigned as a disputed Claim, or is ceded from mere motives of liberality. The Assignor is only exceptionally answerable for the goodness of the Claim.*

As to Assignee and *Debitor cessus*.

2. In regard to the relations subsisting between Assignee and *Debitor cessus*, the Assignee is a Procurator. Hence it follows that the Debtor can make use of all Exceptions or Pleas which he could have employed against the Assignor, prior to his entering into the special relation with him, as well as those given to him against the Assignee. It follows, further, from this, that the Assignee is entitled to enforce every Right of preference possessed by the Assignor, provided they are not processual,† and that from the legal benefit at the time of the Assignment, a confirmed Right has already proceeded *in concreto*.‡ Hence, finally, it follows that the Assignee cannot avail himself of his *own privilege* in regard to the assigned Obligation. But as the Assignee exercises indeed the Right of a third Person, though for his own advantage, it follows that he may avail himself of privileges which relate only to the enforcement § and enjoyment, but do not touch the nature of the Obligation.

* He is answerable: 1. If he has collusively prevented the liquidation. 2. If he has induced the Assignee to accept it by means of deception. 3. When the Assignment is made in lieu of Payment.

† Such processual Pleas must be excluded as have their foundation only in the Person of the Assignor, not affecting the Person of the Assignee; as for instance, the Liability of a foreigner to find Security.

‡ As an example, it may be mentioned that the *Fiscus* has, without Agreement, the Right to claim Interest. If he assigns his Right, the Right of claiming Interest passes to the Assignee up to the time of Assignment. The *Privilegium exigendi causa* also passes.

§ To these belong those of Process.

3. In respect to the relationship between Assignor and *Debitor cessus*. After the Cession or Assignment the Assignor continues to be the Creditor until the Assignee has contested the Claim with the Debtor to the *Litis contestatio;* or until he has given him notice *(Denunciatio)* of the Assignment. As to Assignor and *Debitor cessus.*

SECTION XLVII.—*Of the Dissolution of Obligations.*

Von Vangerow, ss, 616—622.
Arndts, ss. 260—277.
Puchta, ss. 286—302.
Gai. Comm. III., 168—170, 172, 176, 177, 179.
Glück XV., 59 et seq.
Instit. quibus modis obligatio tollitur (3, 29).
Dig. de solutionibus et liberationibus (46, 3).
Cod. de " " " (8, 43).
Dig. de compensationibus (16, 2).
Cod. de " (4, 31).
Dig. de novationibus et delegationibus (46, 2).
Cod. de " " " (8, 42).
Dig. de pactis (2, 14).
Cod. de " (2, 3).
Dig. de acceptilatione (46, 4).
Cod. de " (8, 44).
Instit. ss. 3, 4, de excep. (4, 13).

OBLIGATIONS are dissolved *ex professo:* *Ex professo.*

1. By Payment, that is, the tendering of that which is due to the Creditor, or to his Mandatary, or to the so-called *Solutionis causa adjectus,** or to the *Creditor* By Payment.

* The *Adjectus* acquires no actual Obligation. He cannot at any time bring Suit, neither can he dispose of his Claim. But the Debtor may pay him, and the Creditor cannot prevent this. This marks the distinction between an *Adjectus* and a Mandatary.

creditoris when it is done for the purpose of satisfying the Obligation.*

The Debtor only is liable to pay, but any third party may become entitled to claim. Whether a third Party may claim Compensation, depends upon whether the Claim has been assigned by the Creditor to the Claimant before Payment, or whether the requisites for the Mandatary Action, or the *Actio negotiorum gestorum* exist or not. Finally, there must be on the part of the Debtor and Creditor Capacity to make the Disposition: thus Payment to a Ward is only valid when made with the approval of the Guardian;† and a Ward can only make a valid Payment with the consent of his Guardian.‡

Capacity to pay or to accept Payment.

Proof of Payment.

He who maintains Payment, must prove it. This proof may be given by various kinds of evidence; as by Witnesses on Oath; but more especially by the production of a Receipt, or *Apocha (Apocha non alias, quam si pecunia soluta sit).* A Receipt granted by a private Person is evidence after thirty days. Until then the *Exceptio non numeratae pecuniae*, may be pleaded. It is erroneous to say that, after that time no rebutting evidence may be adduced, as it is only denial on Oath that is forbidden. Payment may be also presumed, rendering any proof unnecessary; as by cancelling the account; or by returning it to the Debtor. The Receipts for the last three Payments that have become due

Apocha.

* Everything must be measured by the fundamental principle of *negotiorum gestio.* Hence, Payment, when such is prohibited, or when it is made without benefit to the Creditor, does not discharge the Debtor.

† But on proof of the *versio in rem,* release or discharge takes place.

‡ Except where the Ward has paid the same as the Guardian would have paid.

furnish presumptive evidence that the previous Demands have been satisfied.

2. By Deposit and Dereliction. Where a Debtor cannot pay his Creditor, because he refuses to accept or is unable to accept in consequence of absence, the Debtor may deposit in Court the amount due. He may even go so far as to abandon the Property when Deposit is impracticable, as in the case of wine sold without the casks; or when by retaining the goods damage might ensue; or where notice has been disregarded. Such Deposit and Dereliction, or Abandonment, take the place of Payment. The Deposit may be reclaimed by the Debtor, until accepted by the Creditor. When this is done, the Obligatory relation revives, as though it had never been discharged.

By Deposit and Dereliction.

3. By Novation, or the Dissolution of an Obligation by the substitution of a new one in its place. According as the Dissolution has its origin in an act of the will, or in some act which has immediately this effect, such as *Litis contestatio*, or a Judgment; *Novatio* is termed *voluntaria* or *necessaria*. *Novatio* is also divided into *simplex* and *qualificata*, according as the object or the subject is changed. The latter in which the subject is changed is either *expromissio*, when the Debtor is changed; or *delegatio*, when the Creditor is changed. The change of the Creditor is not valid without his consent; that of the Debtor may or may not be coupled with his consent. Consent is obtained in the form of a Mandate: the Creditor authorises another Person to become the Creditor; the Debtor empowers another Person to become the Debtor. The Person making the request is termed "*Delegans;*" the Debtor under

Novation.

Voluntaria* or *necessaria.

Simplex* and *qualificata.

the new Obligation is named "*Delegatus;*" the Creditor under the new Obligation is termed "*Delegatarius.*" The two last mentioned must have contracted with each other, for then only is a *Novatio qualificata* possible.

The requisites of a Novation.

The requisites of a Novation requiring special mention are: *a.* Two valid legal Obligations; the prior one which is to be changed, and a new one which is to produce the Novation:* *b.* A subject entitled *Cui recte solvitur, is etiam novare potest.* The exceptions are *solutionis causa adjectus;* the *Filius familias* in regard to Claims arising out of the *Peculium;* the party authorised to receive Payment: *c.* The *Animus novandi* which need not be expressly declared, but must not be presumed. Where the *Animus novandi* is defective, the *Obligatio posterior* is either a mere *addendum* to the Contract, or an independent Obligation which the Creditor may claim to have fulfilled in lieu of the prior Obligation, with all its accessories, Interest, Pawn, and Guaranteeship. This is manifestly of importance in Correal Obligations. When a Right attaches to the former Obligation, and it is intended to transfer it, it operates just the same under the new Obligation as under the old.

Release.

4. By Release. The Creditor may, by Agreement, release his Debtor, in whole or in part.†

* When the original Obligation is conditional, the new one is so likewise. When the new Obligation is conditional and the Condition is still extant, a valid Obligation is in force. If the Condition fails the prior Obligation remains in force.

† The Roman Law acknowledged two transactions of this nature: a solemn one, the *Acceptilatio*; and an informal one, *Pactum de non petendo.* The former operates *ipso jure*, destroying the Obligation; the latter *ope exceptionis*, and absolves the Debtor. It discharges him, his Sureties, and his Heirs if concluded *in rem;* it discharges the Debtor only when made *in personam.* In Correal Obligations it operates subjectively only.

5. By *Contrarius consensus* or *Mutuus dissensus*. This solution takes place only when the Obligations arise out of mutual consent, and only as long as the Obligation still rests on the mere *Consensus*. Such a union of will operates *ipso jure*. When the Obligation is no longer dependent upon mere Contract, the union between the parties constitutes a new Agreement. *Contrarius consensus, or Mutuus dissensus.*

6. By *Transactio*, or as the Germans term it *Vergleich*. By this is understood an Agreement by virtue of which two or more Persons convert a disputable, uncertain legal relation, in which they find themselves, into a certain and definite one, by a mutual relaxation of their Claims and Demands. On the part of the Persons themselves, *Transactio* presupposes a Right of Alienation. In regard to the object, a *Res dubia* is required. Hence, *post rem judicatam* no *Transactio* is possible.* It is also necessary that the object should be subjected to the private Disposition of the parties.† Should there be error in one of the points, which the parties to the Agreement did not consider doubtful at the time, the *Transactio* becomes utterly void. *Transactio*, when legally made, has the same effect and operation as *Res judicata*. It binds, however, only the parties privy to it; still the claims of Creditors upon the Estate of the deceased are dependent upon the quota of the Inheritance as determined by the *Transactio*. *Transactio*

7. By Oath. The parties may agree that the matter in dispute between them shall be determined by affirmation on the oath of one of them. In regard to both By Oath.

* For the same reason *Transactio* of a Testamentary Disposition *ante apertas tabulas* is void.

† Hence, there can be no *Transactio* for the Dissolution of Marriage. *Transactio* can be only permitted after *causae cognitio* by a Judge.

the subject and the object, the same rules apply as those applicable in *Transactio.* The same remark holds good in reference to its scope and operation. An Oath operates only upon the parties to the Agreement.* An Oath tendered to a Person may be taken or refused. The party proposing it, however, cannot retract if it has been once accepted.

By Arbitration.

8. By Arbitration. This is an Agreement by which two or more Persons bind themselves to submit their disputes or differences to the decision of a third Person, who is called a Referee or an Arbitrator. The effect is, that neither side can pursue their Remedy *aliunde*, and that submission to the award becomes compulsory. For this purpose, an *Actio* and an *Exceptio* are allowed. The requisites for an Arbitration are: (1.) Election of a fit Arbitrator; thus, no Insane person can discharge the duty. (2.) Acceptance and performance of the duties by the Person elected. The grounds giving rise to the dissolution of an Arbitration are numerous, namely, *Contrarius consensus*, Death, Hostility, Lapse of Time.

By a *Conditio resolutiva.*

9. By the arrival of a *Conditio resolutiva*, of a fixed limit of time.

By Prescription.

10. By an extinctive Prescription.

By *Res judicata.*

11. By *Res judicata.* Final judgment dissolves an Obligation; but *Res judicata* can only affect the parties privy thereto. It can only be employed by way of *Exceptio*, and can never be made the cause or basis of an Action.

* Save in cases of Correal Obligations, with co-principal Debtors and Sureties; with the *Successor in rem in peculium;* for and against the Son and the Father; and in the case of a Representative empowered to take an Oath.

12. By Notice. As the rule, notice is inadmissible. It is, however, allowable in Mandates, Partnerships, and certain cases of *Locatio conductio*. By Notice.

There are some occurrences which only effect the Solution of an Obligation as a consequence. Such are the following: Solution as a consequence.

1. Set-off, or Compensation. By this is meant the deducting of one Demand from another directly opposed to it. This appears as a fictitious reciprocal Payment. The Requisites are: *a.* Two valid Claims, which, however, need not be connected with each other;* *b.* Such Claims must be Obligations of the Plaintiff and the Defendant;† *c.* Compensability of the object, which can only be possible in the case of fungible Things. The Claim for a *Species* can never be made the object of a Compensation, or Set-off; that of a *Genus*, rarely.‡ *d.* That the counter Claim be liquid, or certain; the rule of Law being, "*Liquidi cum illiquido nulla compensatio,*" that is, the existence of the Claim and its subject-matter must have been determined; *e.* That the counter Claim be due, though the time for Payment having matured does not furnish an impediment. Set-off never takes place by itself *(ipso jure)*, the special act or Agreement of the parties is always needed; or, if Action be brought, there must be the citation of the other party. Set-off.

---

* The exceptions to this are: 1. In *Cessio* or Assignment. 2. In *Correi Socii.* 3. In Suretyship.

† The Debtor must have the choice and the Right to demand something of the same *Genus* from the Creditor.

‡ If a much longer period of time is needed to determine this than to prove the case, then the Defendant is postponed *ad separatum.*

Then, however, the two Obligations become retrospectively extinguished, in whole, or in part, according to their extent.*

Omission of Set-off by error or intention.

Where an allowable Set-off has been omitted in error, the *Condictio indebiti* is permitted; if intentionally neglected, the counter Obligation must be sued for separately. When the Set-off has been disallowed by the Judge, it is of importance to ascertain whether he disallowed it on account of some informality in the form of the Compensation, or if the Obligation itself was disallowed. In the first instance, the separate Obligation still remains enforceable; but in the latter, not.

Merger, *Confusio.*

2. Merger, *Confusio*. This takes place where an Obligation and a Liability merge in one and the same Person. If *Confusio* takes place: *a*. Between a Creditor and the principal Debtor, the entire Obligation becomes extinguished; *b*. When this occurs between the principal, and the party accessorily liable, or between the latter and the Creditor, then the accessory Liability becomes extinguished; *c*. When this happens between the correal Debtor or the correal Creditor, the Creditor has the Right of election.

Concursus causarum lucrativarum.

3. The *Concursus causarum lucrativarum*. When a party entitled to a *Species* for some pecuniary reasons, receives this *Species* on account of some other pecuniary reasons, the Obligation becomes discharged.

Impossibility of performance.

4. Impossibility of performance. This, when purely accidental, avoids the Obligation either in whole or

---

* In this sense, according to the authorities, Compensation operates *ipso jure:* properly it only acts *ope exceptionis*. Otherwise Obligations, and counter Obligations, could not co-exist. It could not be left to the choice of the Creditor, either to avail himself of the Compensation, or to pursue his separate Right.

in part *(Casus a nullo praestatur)*. But the question arises, Who is to bear the loss, who is to sustain the risk? In unilateral Obligations, this always falls upon the Creditor. In bilateral Obligations, where a particular thing has to be done, the risk also falls upon the Creditor. For example: in a Sale the Purchaser obtains no performance from the Debtor, but must still perform his part, and bear all the risk. There is, however, an exception to this in the case of alternative Obligations where, before performance, all the Things contracted for must have perished; and in Contracts for a *Genus*. For the maxim is, "*Genus perire non censetur.*" In bilateral Obligations, when the Obligation is that of Contract for the use of a Thing, the risk remains with the Debtor, because here the Liability is reproduced at every moment of time. The Debtor is not bound to pay Interest, but he obtains no mutual performance of the Obligation. The same holds good in bilateral Obligations for Servitudes.*

5. The Dissolution of the interest of the Creditor in the matter; for without some interest no Obligation can exist. **Dissolution of interest.**

6. Destruction of the principal Obligation, which discharges all those Obligations that are accessory. **Destruction of the principal Obligation.**

7. Forfeiture by way of Penalty. In any case of unlawful Self-help; unlawful Assignment;† by Conceal- **Forfeiture as a Penalty.**

* But the party who has contracted for Service, and who is prevented from obtaining the performance, must nevertheless, on his part, render counter performance.

† In the case of the Assignment, or Cession of Obligations against those under the *Tutela;* Assignment to one having control over another; Assignment of Claims of Jews against a Christian and to another Christian.

ment of Debts existing between the Ward, and the intended Guardian, on entering upon the office of Guardianship. In these instances all Obligations become extinguished.

By Death.

8. By Death. There are Obligations which are essentially personal in their nature, and are made solely in reference to a Person. These, it is obvious, are extinguished by Death.

Section XLVIII.—*Of the Division of Particular Obligations.*

Von Vangerow, s. 623.
Arndts, s. 278 et seq.
Puchta, s. 303.
Gai. Comm. III., 90, 91.
Glück XI., 464.
Instit. quibus modis re contrahitur obligatio (3, 14).
Dig. de rebus creditis si certum petetur, etc. (12, 1).
Cod. de rebus creditis (4. 1).
Cod. si certum petatur (4, 2).

The classification of Obligations.

The foundation for the classification of Obligations is derived from their origin. Accordingly, they are divisible into Obligations arising out of Contracts, or Quasi Contracts; out of Delicts or Quasi Delicts; or *ex variis causarum figuris*. Obligations arising out of Agreements become divisible into Unilateral, or such as require that one party should be a Debtor, and the other the Creditor; and Bilateral, or such as by their nature require that each party to the Contract should be, at the same time, both Debtor and Creditor. Unilateral Obligations again may be of such a nature that reciprocal Liability is impossible (limited, unilateral Agreements); or such that a counter Claim may be possible.

SECTION XLIX.—*Of Limited Unilateral Obligations connected with Business.*

Von Vangerow, ss. 639, 648, 650.
Arndts, ss. 279—283, 289, 290, 314.
Puchta, ss. 304—318.
Gai. Comm. III., 90, 91.
Glück VI., 106 et seq., XVIII., 51 et seq.
Instit. quibus modis re contrahitur obligatio (3, 14).
Dig. de aestimatoria (19, 3).
" nautae, caupones, stabularii ut recepta restituant (4, 9).
" furti adversus nautas, caupones stabularios (47, 5).
" de extraordinariis cognitionibus (50, 13).
" de proxeneticis (50, 14).
l. 22, de praescript. verb. (19, 5).
(See also authorities to previous section.)

1. To the class of limited unilateral Obligations belongs the form of Loan termed "*Mutuum.*" This is a real Contract, the essence of which is, that a party delivers over to another a quantity of fungible Things, with the intention of transferring the Property, and with the understanding that the receiver shall return the same quantity of a similar kind, *tantundem ejusdem qualitatis.* Only an Owner possessing Capacity to alienate has power to transfer the Property, and to bestow it as a *Mutuum.* Exceptionally, a *Mutuum* arises *ex post,* when the recipient subsequently acquires the Ownership of the Property, whether by *Commixtio*, or by *Praescriptio*, or by *bona fide* Consumption. It is also necessary that the Creditor should transfer the Property. Up to the time of the transfer of the Property, the *Vindicatio* lies against the receiver; after that event, the *Condictio.* There are, however, several exceptions to this rule: *a.* The Creditor *Mutuum.*

may request his Debtor to make Payment to some future *Mutuum* Debtor; *b.* The Creditor may agree with his Debtor that, for reasons agreed upon between the parties, the Debtor shall retain Things due on some other legal *causa*, as a *Mutuum; c.* The Creditor may deliver any kind of Property whatever to a third party, requesting him to sell it and to keep the proceeds of the Sale as a *Mutuum (Contractus mohatrae).** The Liability to return the Things borrowed at a specified time arises from the nature of the Contract of *Mutuum* itself.

The *Condictio ex mutuo.*

The Creditor has the *Condictio ex mutuo.* This Action cannot be employed by a Person who has lent money to a *Filius familias* without the consent of his Father. In such a case the Plaintiff would be met by the *Exceptio Senatus Consultum Macedoniani*, which both the Father and the Son are entitled to plead.† But when Payment has been made, the *Condictio indebiti* does not avail.‡ The Father has, however, the *Vindicatio*, when the Son has paid with the Father's money.§ The *Exceptio Senatus Consultum Macedoniani* is not allowed where the Donor has been only guilty of excusable error; or if the Property was lent in a case of inevitable necessity; or if the assent of the Father has been obtained; or when the *Filius familias* has become a *Pater familias*, and has acknowledged the Debt. The risk passes to the Debtor immediately

* Compare "Glossarium ad scriptores mediae et infimae Latinitas," v. *Mohatra* quo, inquit Escobarius, *quis, egens pecunia, emit pecunia credita* a mercatore merces *summo pretio*, et *statim ei pecunia numerata pretio infimo revendit.*"

† So also the Surety, if he has his Remedy against the *Filius.*

‡ For a *Naturalis obligatio* still remains.

§ The pieces of money must be still *in natura*, or have been expended *dolo malo* by the Creditor.

upon his receipt of the *Mutuum*. This rule, however, is liable to an exception in the case of the *Pecunia trajectitia (foenus nauticum)*, and the *Pecunia quasi nauticum*, where the Creditor takes the risk of dangers of the seas or other perils. *

The acknowledgment of a Loan made in writing may be disputed for two years from the date of its execution; either by an Action claiming the Restitution of the Loan, or by the Plea of *Non numeratae pecuniae*, or by Protest. After the expiration of two years; or if the Receipt has been admitted; or after giving up all opposition to the Demand, the Receipt or acknowledgment becomes conclusive evidence of the Debt. Counter proof is, however, admissible.

The acknowledgment of a Loan may be disputed.

Finally, Interest does not necessarily attach to a *Mutuum*, unless it be by Agreement.

2. *Contractus aestimatorius*, called by the Germans "*Trödelvertrag.*" This Contract takes place when a Thing is given to a third party, subject to a Condition either to render the value of the Thing, or to give back the Property itself. The recipient is bound to perform the Obligation in one way or the other, but he obtains no Ownership in the Property. He incurs no risk unless he has expressly undertaken it, or by his obtrusion has done so constructively. Whatever the Person who has taken the Contract from the Seller obtains over and above the stipulated *pretium*, belongs to the former.

The *Contractus aestimatorius*.

3. The *Receptum nautarum cauporum stabulariorum*. A Ship-master taking charge of goods or passengers;

Receptum nautarum cauporum stabulariorum.

* On account of the risk undertaken, Interest over and above the legal rate may be claimed.

an Innkeeper receiving persons and their luggage; and a Stable-keeper who stalls cattle; are all answerable for the deterioration of the goods or the animals entrusted to their care, or if the Property confided to them be stolen. The party liable can only excuse himself by showing that the damage was occasioned by a *vis major*, or that the loss has resulted from some intrinsic fault in the Things he had in charge. The ground of his Liability lies in the implied Contract arising out of the reception of the charge. The party injured sues by means of the *Actio de recepto*. Proof must be furnished of the Illation, as it is called, or the bringing in of the Thing; of damage; and of the robbery: a proof so difficult that it is frequently fatal to the Action.

Performance of services.

4. *Performance of services*, which arises when one person renders to another person services which are ordinarily performed only for reward. The party rendering such service may claim remuneration even without having stipulated for it. It is, however, not every service for which remuneration can be demanded without an Agreement. The ground of the Obligation rests upon the tacit understanding that the party deriving a benefit is understood to have agreed to recompense the service. Such services are those rendered by Artisans, Teachers, Advocates, Physicians, Scriveners, Accountants, Brokers, and Factors or *Proxenetæ* as they are termed.

SECTION L.—*Of Unilateral Reciprocal Business Obligations, with possible Counter Claims.*

Von Vangerow, ss. 629—631, 659, 664.
Arndts, ss. 284—288, 291—299.

Puchta, ss. 319—330.
Gai. Comm. III., 206, pp. 525—530; III. 62, and note 9. (Tomkins and Lemon's Edit.)
Glück V., 318; XIII., 426; XIV., 1; XV., 137, 239.
Dig. commodati vel contra (13, 6).
Cod. de commodato (4, 23).
Instit. de mandato (3, 26).
Dig. mandati vel contra (17, 1).
Cod. " " (4, 35).
Dig. depositi vel contra (16, 3).
Cod. " " (4, 34).
Dig. de pignoratitia actione vel contra (17, 3).
Cod. " " (4, 24).
Dig. de negotiis gestis (3, 5).
Cod. " " (2, 19).
l. 3, pr. Dig. de O. et A. (44, 7).

The Debtor may claim by the *Actio contraria.*

ALTHOUGH in a Unilateral business Obligation, only one party appears as Debtor, it is yet possible in certain legal relations that a counter Claim may arise on the part of the Debtor. The Action given to the Debtor to enforce this counter Claim is called the *Actio contraria*. The Obligations in which *Actiones contrariæ* may occur are the following:

Loan, or *Commodatum.*

1. Loan or *Commodatum.* This is what is termed a *Real Contract*, and is entered into by the making of a gratuitous Bailment of an unconsumable Thing, for a certain use, coupled with the stipulation to return the same Thing after it has been used. The receiver, *Commodator*, is answerable for all neglect, for *Omnis culpa;* and as far as the loan has been made for his benefit he is liable for *Culpa lata;* to the extent that it is made in the interest of the Bailor, or if made for mutual benefit for *Diligentia in suis rebus.* When the Bailee exceeds the limits of use agreed upon, he becomes

guilty of a *Furtum*, and becomes liable for Accident (*Casus*). After completed use, the Thing must be returned. The *Actio commodati directa* lies to compel the fulfilment of this Agreement. The Bailor must allow the Bailee to employ the Thing for the use agreed upon. This distinguishes the *Commodatum* from the *Precarium*. He must refund all outlays or expenses incurred for the preservation of the Thing lent, and is held answerable for *Dolus* and *Culpa lata*. The Bailee has the *Actio commodati contraria* for the enforcement of these Liabilities.

Actio commodati directa.

Mandatum

2. Mandate or *Mandatum*, called by the Germans, *Bevollmächtigungsvertrag*. This is a consensual Agreement, by which a Person named the *Mandatarius*, or *Procurator*, promises gratuitously* to do some lawful act for the *Mandans*. The object of the Mandate must be of some value to the *Mandans*, or to a third party.

Kinds of Mandates: *generale* and *speciale; simplex* and *qualificatum;* expressed and implied.

There are several kinds of Mandates: *a.* in regard to its object, a Mandate is either *generale* or *speciale*, according as it refers to a class of transactions, or only to one in particular. *b.* As regards the Person, a Mandate is either *simplex* when made for the benefit of the *Mandans*, or *qualificatum* when made for the benefit of a third party;† it is a Cession when the *Mandans* relinquishes an Obligation, to which

* At the present time a Mandate is admitted, even though it be assured by a special remuneration (Glück, XV., p. 290.)

† The *Mandatum qualificatum* is a form of Intercession. It consists in this, that some one requests another to conclude a legal transaction on credit with a third Person. The Surety is the Mandator, the Creditor is the Mandatary. It is a marked characteristic of the *Mandatum qualificatum*, that it takes precedence of the principal Obligation.

he is entitled, from a third party, for the benefit of the Mandatary *(Procurator in rem suam)*; it is an *Assignatio* when the Mandatary receives an order to obtain Payment from a third party.* *c.* The Mandate is, in respect of its form, either expressed or implied. The latter is specially understood to be the case when any one has knowingly and tacitly allowed a third Person to transact his business for him.

Assignatio.

A Mandate is at first a Unilateral Transaction. The Mandatary is bound to perform the business he has undertaken *rite*, and, indeed, personally, unless it is understood that the Performance is to be left to some third party. The Mandatary is answerable for *Omnis culpa.* He must render an account, and surrender that which he has come into Possession of by the execution of the Mandate. He is answerable for Damages, Neglect, and Injury; and especially for Interest, in case of undue Delay. The *Mandans* must make good all Outlays incurred by the Mandatary, in the execution of the Bailment, and he must indemnify him against all Damage sustained in carrying out the Mandate; he must liberate him from all Liability incurred in accepting the Mandate; and, finally, he is answerable for *Omnis culpa.*† To enforce these Obligations, the *Mandans* has the *Actio mandati directa*, the Mandatary the *Actio mandati contraria.*‡

Liability of the Mandatary

A Mandate is terminated either by Death or Revocation. It expires upon the death of either the

Termination of Mandate

* Assignation is only a Mandate; Cession is Payment.

† He is not, however, answerable for Accident *(Casus)*.

‡ Mention has been already made of another operation of a Mandate, namely, the founding of a representative—relationship.

Mandans or the Mandatary, unless extended to their Heirs.*

Depositum. 3. Contract of Deposit *(Depositum).* This is a Real Contract, and arises whenever a Depositor entrusts a third party, called the Depositary, with a Moveable Thing to take charge of *without* Compensation. Liability of the Depositary The Depositary, by his acceptance of the Thing, makes himself answerable for its safe custody, and for *Dolus* and *Culpa lata.* He is bound to return the Thing on demand. He can neither set up the plea of Retention, nor that of Compensation; nor can he plead that he is discharged under an Agreement. When there are several Depositaries, each is answerable *in solidum:* the Heirs of a Depositary *pro rata.* If, however, the Thing is indivisible, and held by one only, he must give Security.

Actio depositi directa and *contraria.* The Action against the Depositary is the *Actio depositi directa.* The Depositor must pay all charges incurred in the preservation and Restitution of the Thing deposited; also for Damage which the Depositary has sustained by the fault *(Culpa)* of the Deponent. For this purpose the *Actio depositi contraria* lies.

Special kinds of Deposits. Finally, several special kinds of Deposits may be mentioned in this place: *a. Depositum miserabile,* a Deposit which has been made in a time of special calamity. The Depositary who denies the receipt of the Deposit, is condemned in double the amount. *b.* The *Depositum irregulare,* which takes place when Money or other fungible Things are deposited in such a manner that they are retainable, not *in specie,* but

* When the Mandatary did not know of the death of the *Mandans,* it is regarded as if the *Mandans* had been still alive.

in genere. The Depositary becomes Owner, the risk is transferred to him. An Obligation to pay Interest may be created by a *Pactum adjectum*, which may be enforced by the *Actio depositi* (not *mutui*). It is erroneous to suppose that the fact of allowing the Depositary to employ the Money always converts a *Depositum* into a *Mutuum*. On the contrary, this depends upon the intention of the parties. A *Depositum* may however be converted into a *Mutuum* if the parties so choose.

c. Sequestration. The custody of a Thing in dispute is sometimes entrusted to an uninterested third party, called the *Sequestrator*, to be handed back to the party succeeding, after the termination of a Suit. Sequestration is either made by the order of a Judge, or by an Agreement between the parties. When the *Sequestrator* has not only the custody, but also the use and employment of Property, the nature of the transaction is changed; it becomes a Mandate or a *Locatio conductio*. From this arise the following Actions: *Actio depositi sequestraria; Actio mandati sequestraria; Actio locati conducti sequestraria.* Sequestration.

4. Mortgage Contract or Pawn *(Pignus)*, consists in this, that one party deposits a Thing with another party as Security for a Claim, with the Condition, that upon discharge of the Debt the Thing pledged shall be returned. The party primarily liable is the receiver of the Thing or the Mortgage Creditor. He is bound to keep the Thing with due care, is answerable for all neglect, for *Omnis culpa*,* and must return the Thing as soon as his Claim shall have been satisfied. The Mortgagor has to refund all expenses incurred for the Mortgage Contract: *Pignus.*

* For *Casus* also where the Thing has been used without permission.

The *Actio pigneraticia directa* and *contraria.*

preservation of his Property, he is answerable for *Dolus* and *Culpa*, and likewise for Eviction. For the protection of these Rights the Mortgagor has the *Actio pigneraticia directa*, the Creditor the *Actio pigneraticia contraria.*

Negotiorum gestio.

5. The *Negotiorum gestio.* This is a Quasi Contract, and consists in the voluntary performance of the business of another *without his request.* From this transaction arises on the part of the Principal, the *Actio negotiorum gestorum directa;* and the *Actio negotiorum gestorum contraria*, on the part of the Agent. The requisites for the first Action are the undertaking of the business of another without his authority.* The second Action requires more to support it: there must have been the actual conducting of the business with a view to an Obligation.† The business must not have been performed against the will of the *Dominus.* The thing done must have been *utiliter cœpta*, that is, begun under circumstances by which there appeared to be a probable advantage to the *Dominus.*‡ The

Liability resembles that of *Mandatum*

Obligation that arises between the Principal and the Agent resembles that between the Mandator and the Mandatary. The *Negotiorum Gestor* is compelled to bring the business he has undertaken to a close, even though the *Dominus* may in the meantime have died; otherwise he becomes liable for Damages and sacrifices any Claim he may have for remuneration.

---

* The *Actio directa* is not excluded if the *Negotiorum Gestor* thought, although in error, that it was a Mandate.

† Hence the same is excluded when the *gestio* is performed as an act of liberality, or in one's own interest; or if under the belief that a Person is conducting his own business.

‡ Under these presumptions an Action lies against Persons incapacitated to act by Law.

Further, he must answer for *Omnis culpa*, except in the two following instances: in an event of great emergency he is held liable only for *Dolus*, and for *Culpa lata;* and in the case of his intermeddling with a Matter in which the *Dominus* himself has not interfered, in which case he is answerable for Accident, *(Casus)*. Finally, the *Negotiorum Gestor* must render accounts; give up that which in the course of his business he has acquired; and even pay Interest either when he has allowed Moneys to lie idle, or has used them for his own benefit. On the other hand, the *Dominus negotii* has also duties to perform. He must repay all necessary Outlays, which the *Gestor* has incurred; he has to indemnify him from any liability incurred. He need not ratify Contracts of Sale; but the third party may bring the *Utilis actio de in rem verso* against the *Dominus*. After ratification the Sale cannot be disputed. For by a ratification the ratifying *Dominus* assumes the position of a Mandatary to the *Gestor* and to the third party.*

Duties of the *Dominus negotii.*

A special kind of *Negotiorum gestio* is the *Unauthorized conduct of the management of a funeral.* The Action given in this case is termed the *Actio funeraria* and it may be rendered available after notice of prohibition, or when the Liability has been incurred in error.

Actio funeraria.

6. *Cura bonorum.* This is the management of a transaction by virtue of some public authority. The authorities may appoint for certain Property which needs Administration, an Administrator, named a *Curator bonorum.* This appointment takes place, *a.* In

Cura bonorum.

* The *Negotiorum gestor* cannot be prejudiced by it. The *Actio mandati* does not lie against him, but only the *Actio negotiorum gestorum.*

the case of Bankruptcy an Assignee of the Bankrupt Estate is appointed: *b*. When the Heirs to an Estate are uncertain, either because the Heir is not yet born *(Curator ventris nomine)*; or because he is not of age and has acquired the *Bonorum possessio ex edicto Carboniano*, and is being proceeded against, but fails to give Security; or because the Heirship is quite a matter of uncertainty; or because several Heirs are still deliberating as to their acceptance of the Inheritance:* *c*. Finally, in the case of the absence of the Heir, and when he has not provided sufficiently for the Administration of the Estate. The *Curator* has no power of Alienation except in case of perishable Goods, and he is answerable for *Omnis culpa*.

Management of Business, *ex officio*.

7. Management of Business by virtue of Office. An Officer is answerable for *Omnis culpa*. An Action is available against the Heirs within ten years; against the Officer for twenty years. When there are several Officers they are answerable *in solidum*, but in the first instance the party causing the injury is held liable.

SECTION LI.—*Of Reciprocal Business Obligations.*

Von Vangerow, ss. 632—638, 640—646, 657, 658.
Arndts, ss. 300—321.
Puchta, ss. 359—374.
Gai. Comm. III., 139—155, pp. 518—524 (Tomkins and Lemon's edit.)
Glück X., 419; XI., 1 et seq., 93 et seq., 119 et seq.; XV., 371 et seq., 450, 460; XVI., 1 et seq., 239, 271; XVII., 1 et seq., 263, 331, 497; XVIII., 112 et seq.
Dig. de rerum permutatione (19, 4).

* In the last case the Nomination of a *Curator bonorum* is in the interest o the Estate generally.

Cod. de rerum permutatione et de praescriptis, etc. (4, 64).
Instit. de emtione et venditione (3, 23).
Dig. de contrahenda emtione, et de pactis inter emtorem, etc. (18, 1).
Cod. " " et venditione (4, 38).
Dig. de actionibus emti et venditi (19, 1).
Cod. " " " (4, 49).
Dig. de periculo et commodo rei venditæ (18, 6).
Cod. " " " (4, 48).
Cod. de fide et jure hastae fiscalis et de adjectionibus (10, 3).
Dig. de pactis inter emtorem et venditorem compos. (18, 1).
Cod. " " " " (4, 54).
Dig. de in diem addictione (18, 2).
Dig. de lege commissoria (18, 3).
Instit. de locatione et conductione (3, 24).
Dig. locati conducti (19, 2).
Cod. de locato et conducto (4, 65).
Dig. de migrando (43, 32).
Instit. de societate (3, 25).
Dig. pro socio (17, 2).
Cod. " (4, 37).
l. 1, s. 1, Dig. de usur. (22, 1).
l. 34, Dig. pro socio (17, 2).
l. 25, s. 16, Dig. fam. erciscundae (10, 2).
l. 3, Cod. communia utriusque judic. (3, 38).
Dig. finium regundorum (10, 1).
Dig. familiae erciscundae (10, 2).
Cod. " " (3, 36).
Cod. comm. divid. (3, 38).
Cod. comm. utriusque judicii tam fam. (3, 38).

THE notion of Reciprocal Business Contracts has been already explained. It is now necessary to refer to the different Obligations belonging to this classification:

1. Barter. This Consensual Contract is that Agreement by which two Persons promise the one to the other to exchange one Thing for another. Here the Price and Thing exchanged are identical. The Property Barter.

passes by delivery even when counter performance has not been made.

Contract of Sale.

2. Contract of Sale. The essence of this Contract consists in this: one party named the *Vendítor*, agrees with a second party called the *Emtor*, to transfer a commodity,* *Merx*, for a given sum of money, *Pretium*. As soon as the consent of the contracting parties has been exchanged in regard to the *Pretium* and the *Merx*, the *Emtio venditio*† or Sale is *perfecta*. Upon the completion of the Contract, the risk, or as it is expressed, the *Periculum rei venditae*, passes to the Buyer. The exceptions to this rule are: *a*. When the Sale has been made conditionally; *b*. When the Sale has been made *ad pondus, ad nummum*, or *ad mensuram*; *c*. When the Sale has been made *ad gustum*, that is, subject to approval. But until the Thing sold is weighed, counted, or measured; or until it is approved of, the risk remains with the Seller.

The *Actio emti* and the *Actio venditi*.

The Liabilities arising out of a Contract of Sale are enforceable by the Buyer by the *Actio emti*; by the Seller by means of the *Actio venditi*. The Purchaser claims delivery of the Thing sold, *cum omnis causa*;‡ the Seller claims the price stipulated for. The purchase money bears Interest from the moment of the receipt of the Thing sold. The Ownership of Commodities sold does not pass at all unless the Goods are paid for, or a *Credit Contract* has been made. A special duty of the Seller is to

---

* *Commodities* are all things corporal or incorporal which may form the subject-matter of a Contract, ready money or cash excepted.

† The Seller bears the *Periculum interitus*, the Buyer the *Periculum deteriorationis*.

‡ That is, with natural and civil Fruits, with Accessions and Rights of Action attaching.

warrant against latent defects. When the Things sold have latent defects, known or unknown to the Seller, two Actions are given to him: the *Actio redhibitoria*, for the dissolution of the Contract; and the *Actio quanti minoris*, for a reduction of the Price. The first is available within six months, the second within a year. The Action is not barred because the Property has been destroyed. Another Liability which the parties to the Contract reciprocally incur, is that of a mutual warranty, *ut rem*, Wares or Price, *habere liceat*. There is also the Obligation to recompense for Eviction.* This may be undertaken by promise, in which case the party evicted sues upon the promise made. Where such is by legal presumption, the Action goes for the amount of Interest in the form of the *Actio emti*. The requirements for the satisfaction for legal Eviction are: *a. Vitium in jure transferentis*, that is, defective Title on the part of the Transferor; † *b. Ablatio rei per judicem*, by which is to be understood, impeachment of the Right in question by judicial decision; ‡ *c. Litis-denuntiatio ad auctorem*, and indeed to the nearest *Auctor*.§ When the Transferor, or *Auctor*, cannot be found, Notice is to be presumed. The Liability to answer for Eviction does not apply, when (not *dolose*,) a *Pactum*

Actio redhibitoria, and the *Actio quanti minoris*.

Eviction.

* Eviction is the disputing by legal Process of the Right to a Thing acquired by a derivative Title.

† For example, the Thing sold was not the Property of the seller. In Real Servitudes, as the Rule, no Claim can be set up for Eviction; in Obligatory limitations none whatever.

‡ The judgment must in this case be in consequence of a *vitium in jure*. Hence there is no Eviction either by the unrighteousness of the Judge or the neglect of the parties.

§ Delay in giving Notice (*Denuntiatio*), according to some jurists, leads to the loss of the Right of recovery. Von Vangerow, however, is of a different opinion.

de non præstando evictione has been made; or when some one has acquired the Property of another with the knowledge of this fact. In addition to the Warranty against Eviction, another Obligation exists, which applies to both parties, namely, Warranty against all *Culpa*. When *Dolus* underlies, the Plaintiff may sue for the dissolution of the Contract. Indeed, even without *Dolus* this Action is allowed, when either side has been damnified* to the extent of half the value, *Laesio enormis;* that is, when the Price paid for a Thing is less by one-half than that which has been given. The Agreement, however, is sustainable when the party accused makes good the difference to the extent of the true value of the Property at the time of the Sale. The Action on account of *Laesio enormis* is excluded by legally valid remuneration; in the case of the *Emptio spei;* in a Compromise *(Transactio);* † and in judicial Divisions. But it is not excluded in the case of Sales by Auction. The Action is maintainable only against the wrong-doer and his Heirs, not against a third party.

Laesio enormis.

Finally, it is necessary to bear in mind the collateral Agreements which may attach to Contracts of Sale, by means of which the Obligations arising therefrom may be extended.

Hiring and Letting: *Locatio et conductio.*

3. Hiring and Letting, or *Locatio et Conductio*, is that Contract, by means of which a Person named the *Locator*, promises to another Person, called the *Conductor*, the use of a Thing in consideration of the

---

* According to Puchta, the Seller only. He also holds that the Action for *Laesio enormis* is confined to Sale only. Von Vangerow extends this Right to Contracts of letting and hiring.

† Except when the valuation of the Thing in regard to which a *Transactio* has been effected, has been made in error.

payment of a sum of Money for Rent *(Merces)*. The Rent must be in Money, though it may be paid by means of a fruit-bearing Thing, or in fruits, if it be so agreed, as long as the *Merx* is *vera* and *certa*. The moment the parties to the Contract agree on the object, and the *Merces*, the Contract is completed. Things consumable *quae usu consumuntur vel minuuntur* are excepted from the *Locatio Conductio*. Otherwise, Things, Rights, Services, are capable of being let and hired.

Accordingly, the following kinds of *Locatio conductio* are to be distinguished: **Different kinds of *Locatio conductio*.**

a. *Locatio conductio rerum*, or the Letting and Hiring of Things corporal and incorporal.

b. *Locatio conductio operarum*, Hire of Work and Service; and *Locatio conductio operis*,* Contract for Works.

Firstly, it is necessary to treat of the responsibilities of the Hirer and Letter of Things. The Letter must give up the Thing for the special purpose agreed upon; vouch the *frui licere*, pay the public rates and taxes, recompense outlays that have been necessarily and properly incurred by the Hirer. On the other hand, the Hirer must pay the stipulated Price, and return the Thing upon the termination of the Hiring.† Both parties vouch against *Culpa*, neither warrant against Accident *(Casus)*. Hence the Letter has not to make Compensation where Accident (*Casus*) has rendered the **Liabilities of Hirer and Letter.**

---

* Here the *Locatio conductio irregularis* may be mentioned. This exists where fungible Things have been given to be worked up or to be transported, without specially stipulating that just the same identical Things should be worked up or transported. This is the only instance of *Locatio conductio irregularis*.

† Even where he finds it impossible, from personal reasons, to use the Thing; unless, indeed, the Letter can let his Thing in some other quarter.

use of the Thing impossible,* but the Hirer, under such circumstances, need not pay the Rent. The Hirer or Lessee has the Right of Sub-letting *(Aftermiethe)*, unless he has specially renounced the Right.

Termination of the *Locatio conductio rerum.*

The *Locatio conductio rerum* terminates on the expiration of the stipulated time. A tacit *Relocatio*, however, is presumed when the Hirer or Lessee, after the expiration of the time of Hiring or Letting, continues with the knowledge, and without the opposition of the Letter, to use the Thing let.† Other grounds for the dissolution of the *Locatio conductio rerum* are: Destruction of the Property, and warning to surrender up Possession, where no time has been stated. Exceptionally, the Contract of Hire is terminated by notice, even when the period of Hiring has been fixed.‡ As the rule, Death is no ground for the dissolution of this Contract.

The maxim "Purchase cancels Hire."

It is also wrong to interpret the maxim, Purchase cancels Hire, "*Kauf bricht Miethe,*" in the sense that Purchase at once terminates the Contract between the Hirer and the Letter. The true interpretation of this maxim is, that the Purchaser of the

* One instance needs special mention: When the Hirer of a Thing yielding Fruits has been hindered by some extraordinary calamity from reaping the Fruits, he is entitled to claim a partial remission of the Rent. But when the term of Lease includes several seasons, the *ubertas* of the one must be taken to compensate for the *sterilitas* of the other.

† In the letting of Real Estate, the time required for notice is one year; in the letting of Houses, Notice to Quit may be given at any time.

‡ This takes place: 1. On the part of the Hirer, when the giving Possession is delayed on account of defects impairing the use, or on account of imminent danger. 2. On the part of the Letter, in consequence of arrears of Rent; on account of his own pressing necessities, though this applies only to Buildings, not to Land; on account of necessary Buildings; and on account of the use of the Thing in such a manner as amounts to a violation of the Contract.

Property need not trouble himself about the Lessee or Hirer.

The second kind of Letting was that of the *Locatio conductio operarum*, and *operis*, according as the mere service or the completing of some Contract or work, *Opus*, had been let and undertaken. Only such services can be the subject-matter of Contract of Hire for which a remuneration is paid. Hence scientific and artistic employment cannot be the object of this Contract. Parties to the Contract are reciprocally liable to each other for *Culpa*. In regard to *Casus*, it is necessary to distinguish between *Locatio conductio operarum* and *Locatio conductio operis*. When, in consequence of Accident, the *Redemtor*, that is, the Conductor (Hirer), is prevented from carrying out the services he has undertaken, he must bear the loss; but he is not bound to answer for consequential damages *(Interesse)*. When the *Locator*, from personal reasons, is prevented accepting the services, he must still pay the wages agreed on, unless the Hirer has obtained other employment. *Locatio conductio operarum.*

But how is it as to the *Locatio conductio operis?* When the *Opus*, by some Accident, has not been completed, the *Redemtor*, or party engaging to do the work, is not liable for the *Interesse*, or consequential damages; but, on the other hand, he cannot claim his Price.

When the *Locator* is the cause of the non-completion of the work, he must pay a proportionable amount. In cases where the *Opus* has been completed, but before acceptance and approval, has perished, the Contractor may claim the Price, on proof of the fitness and completion of the work. He has, moreover, in this case, a stronger Claim for the Price, when the

Locator has caused the loss by his own improper directions. Where it has perished during a period of Delay caused by the *Mora* of the *Locator*, the *Locator* must bear the loss. In regard to the termination of the *Locatio conductio operis*, the only peculiarity is that it is extinguished upon the death of the *Redemtor*.

Actio conducti directa and *contraria*. From *Locatio conductio*, if such be for the Hire of Labour or of Things, arise the *Actio conducti directa* and *contraria*. A peculiar application of the *Actio*

Jettison. *conducti* occurs in Roman Law in cases of Jettison. Should a part of the cargo be thrown overboard, to save the ship from perils of the sea, by means of which the rest of the cargo is saved; the Owner of the Things cast overboard brings the *Actio locati* against the Shipmaster, and he again brings the *Actio conducti* against the Owner of the Goods saved, for repartition of the loss. At the present time an Action lies immediately against the co-contributors, that is to say, against the Owners of the Goods saved, as well as against the Owners of the Ship. The Average, or partition, affects all the Goods, inclusive of those thrown overboard, according to their value. The value of the Things thrown overboard is assessed according to their cost; that of the Things saved is estimated at the market value at the port of arrival.

Partnership: *Societas*. 4. Contract of Partnership *(Societas)*, which is the association of several Persons termed the *Socii*, for the purpose of some lawful common object, such Persons binding themselves to the employment of Things or

* The *Interdictum de migrando*, when the Person who lets stops the *Conductor*, who desires to give up the tenancy, from leaving, even after he has made Payment of what is due.

services in common. The Contract is complete the very moment the *Socii* have notified their assent.

Several kinds of Partnership.

There are several kinds of Partnership: *a.* In regard to its purport or aim, a Partnership is termed either *quaestuaria* or *simplex*, according as the intention is one of gain or not; *b.* In regard to its object, a *Societas* is either *general*, when it comprises the whole Property, present and future; or *special*, when only a part of the Partners' Estate is devoted to the Partnership. A *Societas specialis* is a subordinate kind of the *Societas quaestuaria.* A kind of *Societas specialis* is, for example, the carrying on in common of some business, or some branch of trade, involving the joint Possession of particular Things. In both instances an important question arises, whether the Things contributed by the several *Socii* are, in the absence of any Agreement, to become joint Property *(Societas sortis)*, or merely to be for the joint use *(Societas usus)*. In the case of consumable Things and fungible Things, joint Property is presumed; in the case of Things non-consumable and non-fungible Things, joint use only is presumed.* When the Things are consumable, the enjoyment of the use of another, without the destruction of the existing Ownership, is inconceivable. This, however, is not the case with non-consumables. When a Partnership is established, Liabilities arise between the *Socii*, which are essentially similar. Each of the Partners must contribute the share agreed upon; must pay into a common fund what has accrued to him from

Liabilities of Partners

* To this category belongs the Condition, that if one *Socius*, in consequence of his insolvency, is made a Bankrupt, the others suffer with him in consequence of his Bankruptcy.

the Partnership business; and if it be money, in the event of *Mora*, or if he have applied the money for his own use or benefit; he is bound to pay Interest; he is answerable for *Diligentia in concreto;* must compensate his Partners for necessary and beneficial Outlays, adding Interest. He is even liable for any casual damage which a Partner may have sustained in attending to the Partnership business. For the enforcement of these Rights every *Socius* has the *Actio pro Socio*. The share of Profit and Loss in a Partnership is equally divisible, unless provided for by special Agreement, though the contributory amount may vary.

Actio pro Socio.

Special Agreements between Partners.

By Agreement it may be determined:

1. That a Partner shall sustain no Damage.

2. That one Partner shall have a larger proportion of the Profits than the others. In both these instances, however, he must make good this inequality by doing something more, or otherwise adjust the difference.

3. That one Partner shall take a different share from that taken by another Partner in the resultant Profits in one instance, and a different proportion of the resultant Loss to that which he takes in another.

4. The determination of the proportions of Profit may be left to the arbitrament of one of the Partners, or to an impartial party *(boni viri)*. When Profits only are stipulated for, Loss in the same proportion is implied, and *vice versa*. An Agreement, however, that one of the Partners shall have no gain, but that he shall bear all the losses, is impossible. Such a Partnership is termed *Societas leonina*. For "*Nulla Societas est, quae donationis causa interponitur.*"

Societas leonina.

The *Actio communi dividundo*

For the division of the Profits, and for the determination of the Rights between the parties, there is given the *Actio communi dividundo*.

Relation of Partners to third parties.

What now is the position of Partners as to third parties? When the business is done by all the Partners, each becomes entitled, and is answerable *pro rata* according to his share in the Partnership; unless there be a special Agreement by means of an active or passive Correal Obligation. When the business has been concluded by one or more of the *Socii*, the same being a Partnership matter, the others claim as Assignees. They are all liable, and that *in solidum*, when the contracting party, as their Mandator, or *Institor*, has concluded the business as such. They become also liable *in solidum* by a subsequent ratification of the business. Partners are answerable, but only *pro rata*, when a transaction has been concluded on account of the Partnership, and they have derived a profit thereby. But should the *Socius* have concluded the business in his own name, they do not become liable, even though some advantage may have been derived. Partners are liable for the Delicts of a *Consocius* or Copartner, whenever they knowingly permit the gain arising out of such wrong-doing to go to the Partnership fund.

Dissolution of Partnership does not affect the Rights of third parties. A Partnership ceases:

How a Partnership is dissolved.

1. By the expiration of the stipulated time.

2. Whenever the object has been attained for which the Partnership was formed.

3. On the destruction of the subject-matter or object of the Partnership.

4. Upon the death of one of the Partners, or upon one of the Partners suffering a *capitis deminutio maxima*, or *media*. The Partnership expires even when it has been agreed that the Survivors or their Heirs shall continue; for what subsequently exists is a new Partnership. The Heirs claim all, and pay all they may be entitled to, or answerable for to the date of the death of the *Defunctus* or Testator. The *Actio pro Socio* is given for this purpose. The Heirs are bound to carry on transactions that have been already commenced.

5. Upon the confiscation of the Property or upon the Bankruptcy of a Partner.

A Partner may retire.

6. Upon the retirement of a Partner, which is always allowable, and which cannot be prevented from taking place by a *Pactum, ne abeatur a societate;* or by the *Pactum, ne intra certum tempus abeatur.* But this must not be so construed as to permit a *Socius*, with a wrongful intent, to withdraw at an inconvenient time, without being liable for Damages. The principle regulating such a *Renunciatio* is expressed in the following maxim: *Socium a se, non se a socio liberat;* that is to say, the party thus renouncing ceases to be in a position in which he can derive any benefit, but he still remains liable. He continues liable in the absence of the other Partners, until notice of his Renunciation has reached them.

The maxim, *Socium a se.*

Fellowship: *Communio.*

V. Fellowship or Community of Interest (*Communio*). This exists whenever a real legal relation is sustained by several Persons jointly, *pro indiviso*. In this way Ownership, *Superficies*, and *Emphyteusis*, may be held. On the other hand, *Nomina* are *ipso jure divisa*. In contrast to that Community which is created by

Agreement and is termed a *Societas*, a casual Fellowship or Community may arise, termed a *Communio incidens*. Moreover, the origin of such a *Communio* is immaterial.

Two Obligations arise from this Community: *a.* Upon its Dissolution, there must be Partition; hence the Actions are designated, Actions for Partition *(Judicia divisoria)*; *b.* For the performance of a Personal Warranty, such as for compensatory Damages, Outlays, and the surrender of that which has been acquired in consequence of the Community. Partition of the Property cannot be prevented even by Agreement; but a Clause or Condition, *ne intra certum tempus petatur*, is allowable. Partition may take place judicially or extrajudicially. The latter mode occurs in the case of an impeachable detriment or injury; the former never, except by impeachment of a judicial sentence.

The Clause *Ne intra*, etc.

Three Actions exist to enforce the Obligations arising from a *Communio*. The *Actio familiae herciscundae*, of which mention has been made in the Law of Inheritance; the *Actio communi dividundo*;* the *Actio finium regundorum*. The *Actio communi dividundo* can only be made use of, when neither the *Communio* nor the share is in dispute, unless the Plaintiff be in Possession, in which case he cannot resort to the *Vindicatio*. The Action can neither be employed after Partition has been made, nor for the *Praestationes personales*, as they are termed, that is, those obligatory performances which are engendered by the *Communio;* whilst, on the other hand, the *Communio* remains in force even at the time the Action is being employed for the enforcement of the

The three divisory Actions.

Actio communi dividundo.

* This Action also is used in the case of a Community arising out of a Partnership, as ancilliary to the *Actio pro Socio*.

Actio finium regundorum.

Praestationes. The *Actio finium regundorum* lies for the determination of *praedia rustica*, that is of disputed boundaries between different Owners. It occurs when the boundaries of land are uncertain, or when the neighbouring Proprietors claim different limits. This Action may be instituted by the Emphyteuta, the Mortgage-Creditor, the Usufructuary, as well as by the Owner. It lies not only for the principal object, but also for the performance of collateral Obligations, namely, for improvements involving profit and for compensatory Damages. The *Actio communi dividundo* is an Action for Partition, because the *praedia vicina*, when the original boundaries cannot be ascertained, are regarded as in common, and are therefore liable to be divided equally between the parties. The *Actio communi dividundo* is a *Judicium duplex*, that is to say, both parties are Plaintiffs, and both are Defendants in the Action.

The *Actio communi dividundo* is a *Judicium duplex.*

Section LII.—*Obligations arising out of Delicts and cognate Cases.*

Von Vangerow, ss. 605, 674—688, 692—705.
Arndts, ss. 322—339.
Puchta, ss. 375—387.
Gai. Comm. III., 182—190, 195—200, 202—208; IV., 8, pp. 546—580 (Tomkins and Lemon's edit.)
Glück, III., 485 et seq.; IV., 167; V., 468 et seq. 518; VI., 54; X., 272, 306, 392, 399; XI., 375; XIII., 211 et seq.
Instit. de obligationibus, quae ex delicto nascuntur (4, 1).
Dig. de furtis (47, 2).
Cod. " " et servo corrupto (6, 2).
Dig. de condictione furtiva (13, 1).
Cod. " " " (4, 8).

Instit. de lege Aquilia (4, 3).
Dig. ad legem Aquiliam (9, 2).
Cod. de lege Aquilia (3, 35).
Dig. arborum furtum caesarum (47, 7).
" vi bonorum raptorum (47, 8).
" de incendio, ruina, naufragio, etc. (47, 9).
" de sepulchro violati (47, 12).
Cod. " " " (9, 19).
Dig. de religiosis et sumtibus funerum (11, 7).
" l. 3 pr. de via publica (43, 11).
Dig. de publicanis et vectigalibus (39, 4).
" quod metus causa gestum erit (4, 2).
Cod. de his, quae vi metusve, etc. (2, 19).
Instit. de vi bonorum raptorum (4, 2).
Dig. vi bonorum raptorum et de turba (47, 8).
Cod. " " " (9, 33).
Dig. de dolo malo (4, 3).
Cod. " " " (2, 21).
Dig. de doli mali et met. exceptione (44, 4).
" de calumniatoribus (3, 6).
" ne quis eum, qui in jus vocabitur, etc. (2, 7).
" de alienatione judicii mutandi causa facta (4, 7).
Cod. " " " " " " (2, 54).
Dig. quae in fraudem creditorum facta sunt (42, 8).
Cod. de revocandis his quae in fraudem, etc. (7, 85).
Dig. de extraordinariis cognitionibus (50, 13).
Cod. de poena judicis, qui male judicavit (7, 49).
Gai. Comm. III., 223, 224; IV., 52.
Dig. si mensor falsum modum dixerit (11, 6).
Instit. de injuriis (4, 4).
Dig. " " (47, 10).
Cod. " " (9, 35).
Dig. de libero homine exhibendo (43, 29).
Cod. " " " " (8, 8).
l. 7 pr. dig. de jurisdict. (2, 1).
Dig. de his, qui effuderint vel dejecerint (9, 3).
l. 40, 41, 42, Dig. de Aedil. Edicto (21, 1).
Dig. XLIII., 6 bis. 15.

Dig. de mortuo inferendo et sepulchro aedificundo (11, 8).
" de operis novi nuntiatione (39, 1).
" de remissionibus (43, 25).
Cod. de novi operis nuntiatione (8, 11).
Dig. quod vi aut clam (43, 24).
" de damno infecto et de sugrundis etc. (39, 2).

Unlawful acts creating new Obligations.

In a former paragraph, unlawful acts have been taken into consideration, in so far as they modify existing Obligations. In the present Section it is intended to show how far they go to create entirely new ones. The following belong to this class:

Theft: *Furtum.*

I. Theft *(Furtum)* is the unlawful, intentional purloining of a Thing from a greed of gain. To define it more fully and exactly, "*Furtum est contretatio rei fraudulosa lucri faciendi gratia vel ipsius rei vel etiam usus ejus possessionisve.*" It is said to be "*manifestum*" when the thief is taken before he has had time to conceal the stolen Goods; in other cases it is termed "*nec manifestum.*" By a special Prescript, this Delict cannot be committed by the abstraction of Things appertaining to an Inheritance before the Heir has entered, or before he has taken Possession of the inherited Goods. As between Man and Wife, Theft does not exist in Law, at least as *Furtum* in the strict signification of the term; but there may be what is termed an *Amotio rerum*, and upon this is founded the *Actio rerum amotarum*. Otherwise the legal Remedies for *Furtum* are the *Condictio furtiva* and the *Actio furti*. The latter is a purely penal Action, involving punishment, and has become at the present time obsolete. Not only is the Owner of the Property Plaintiff, but all Persons having an interest in the Theft. The Action lies against the

Amotio rerum.

Actio furti.

Thief and his associates, and when several Persons are implicated *in solidum;* but it does not lie against their Heirs. In the case of *Furtum manifestum*, the Action proceeds for the fourfold; in the *Furtum nec manifestum* for the twofold. The *Condictio* is a *rei persecutio cum omni causa.* Expenses incurred by a Thief are not made good to him; he is answerable for all Accident *(Casus)*, and the value of the stolen Property is calculated at the highest price which the Goods would have fetched if sold at any previous time whatever. The only party entitled to proceed is the Owner, and he must be such at the time of the commencement of the Action. The Defendants are the Thief and his Heirs, not his accomplices. When there are several Thieves they are all answerable *in solidum.*

Condictio furtiva. Liability of the Thief.

II. Injury, or *Damnum.* The principal instance is that of *Damnum injuria datum.* It presumes an unlawful positive and culpable act, causing injury. As to the degree of culpability, *Culpa levis* suffices. The Action which lies is the *Actio legis Aquiliae.* The Owner of the Property is the Plaintiff; hence also any Freeman can bring this Action for wrong done to himself, because he holds himself in his own Ownership. It may also be mentioned that he may sue not only for compensatory Damages, but also for Compensation for suffering endured. But not only is the Owner Plaintiff, but all other Persons entitled to the same Thing, namely, such Persons as might have sued the Owner. The Person who has inflicted the injury is the Defendant. When there are several Defendants they are answerable *in solidum.* The Action goes for Compensation in Damages, and when the Defendant

Injury, or *Damnum.*

denies the Injury, for twice the amount. Hence the maxim, "*Lis crescit contra inficiantum in duplum.*" In the case of damage done to four-footed domestic animals, the value is estimated by the last year's price, or otherwise according to the value during the last month.

Actio legis Aquiliæ.

It is an important question to determine, whether in cases of damages arising out of Obligatory Relations, the *Actio legis Aquiliæ*, is available. It is held that this Action is not excluded, but that an Obligatory Relation exercises upon it a modifying influence. By virtue of an Obligatory Relation, it frequently happens that there is a Right to a transaction which may result in injurious consequences: in which case the transaction is of a culpable character. But, on the other hand, if a questionable transaction is not warranted by an Obligatory Relation, the *Actio legis Aquiliae* applies, even when no Action would arise from the Contract.*

Several special kinds of Damages.

There are several special kinds of damages, namely: *a.* Secret injury to trees, which the Germans call "*Baumfrevel,*" when a Person secretly and dishonestly fells, or carries away the trees of another Person. As a punishment for this injury there is given the *Actio arborum furtim caesarum*, which goes for double *(duplex)* the value; *b. Damnum coactis hominibus datum;* when injury has been caused by a crowd, the *Actio vi bonorum raptorum* lies; *c. Damnum turba datum;* when a riotous mob has caused any damage, an *Actio in factum* lies for double the amount of injury; *d.* When injury is suffered during a time of special calamity, an *Actio in factum* lies for the

* The Depository, for instance, who is only answerable under the Contract of Deposit for *Dolus* and *Culpa lata*, is not for that reason justified, when chargeable with the least oversight or neglect.

quadruple value; *e.* When damage is done to a grave, the *Actio sepulcri violati* can be employed; *f.* Injury arising from the interment of a corpse at a place where it ought not to have been buried, gives rise to an *Actio in factum* to compel removal or for Damages in the form of a pecuniary penalty; *g.* For injury done by altering a public road so as to carry it over private Property; that is, if a Person wrongfully commits an act of trespass by diverting a public road, so as to intrench upon private Property; for this there is given the *Actio viæ receptae; h.* Injury done by farmers of the revenues, for instance, by wrongfully levying customs, entitles the party injured to an *Actio in factum* for twice the amount, if sued for before the lapse of a year; but after that time for the actual amount only; *i.* Damages done by another man's animals. A Delict may be committed even by an animal, in which case its Owner becomes answerable. Against the Owner of an animal which has depastured upon our ground, the *Actio de pastu* lies. For other damages done by animals belonging to a third party, and done, moreover, *contra naturam sui generis*, the *Actio de pauperie* may be brought. This Action lies for injury done not only by wild animals, but also for damage done by domestic animals contrary to their taming. The Defendant is the Owner of the animal at the time of the bringing of the Action. The Action goes for compensatory Damages, or the Defendant may, if he please, by surrendering the animal, free himself from the Liability, unless the animal has died after the period of the *Litis contestatio*. Should the animal, however, die before, he is entirely discharged.

Actio sepulcri violati.

Actio viæ receptae.

Actio de pastu.

Actio de pauperie.

Violence and Menace.

III. Violence and Menace. Wrongs or Delicts may be committed coupled with force, as: *a.* Robbery or Theft accompanied with violence; against this there was originally the *Actio furti, Condictio furtiva, Actio vi bonorum raptorum;** *b.* Dispossession by violence *(Interdictum de vi)*; *c.* Forcible detention of one *in jus vocatus*. When this is done the Plaintiff has against the wrong-doer an *Actio in factum* for that which he hoped to obtain judicially from the party forcibly detained. There are two Remedies given to the Person who has suffered a change in his legal condition by the unlawful use of *metus*, or terror: *a.* The *Actio quod metus causa*, by which the Plaintiff seeks for relief from the injury which he has suffered; *b.* The *Exceptio doli*, which is a Plea employed by a Person to defeat an Action brought against him on the ground of the coercive engagement. Both are *in rem scripta;* that is, are available against every one who may have derived, or endeavoured to have derived, any benefit by means of the *metus*. As against a *bonæ fidei* Owner, the procedure only affects what he may still hold in Possession. Against the *malæ fidei* Owner, it includes also the *Fructus percipiendi*. Heirs are likewise liable to the extent of the *quantum ad eos pervenit*. The Plaintiff is the party coerced, and his legal Successors. The object of the Action is the reinstating of the parties in the enjoyment of their original Rights.

The *Actio quod metus causa*.

Exceptio doli.

Deceit and Fraud.

IV. Deceit and Fraud. Against intentional unlawful injury, when the offence does not partake of the character of any other distinct Delict, for which a special

* This Action is now obsolete. It was limited as to the time *(annalis)*, and went for the fourfold.

Action is given; the party injured is furnished with two legal Remedies: the *Actio* and the *Exceptio doli*. There are two exceptions to these subsidiary Remedies: the *Actio doli* will concur with the *Actio quod metus causa*, and also with the *Actio præscriptis verbis*. The Plaintiff is the party injured and his legal Successors. The Defendant is the party chargeable with the fraud. The Action also lies against his Heirs for the *quantum ad eos pervenit*. It goes for compensatory Damages, but it must be brought within two years, after which period it can only be employed to claim Restitution to the extent of the benefits received. Against Persons occupying what is termed a high position, the *Actio doli* does not lie; but *an Actio in factum* must be brought. Again, *Si duo dolo malo fecerint, invicem de dolo non agent*.

When the *Actio doli* is unavailable.

There are some fraudulent acts, for which the *Actio doli* is unavailable: *a*. The preventing a party to a Suit by some act of deception from appearing in Court. In this case an *Actio in factum* lies for the *id quod interest*. But this Action does not pass to the Heirs, nor does it lie against the Heirs; or, as it is expressed, it is neither *ad heredes* nor *in heredes*. *b*. Fraudulent Sale made to hinder pursuit by legal Process. In this case, also, there lies *intra annum* an *Actio in factum* for Damages, and against the Heirs *quantum ad eos pervenit*. The Sale must be an actual legal Transfer, and not a mere deprivation. This Action will not lie when the Sale has been made on account of death. Moreover, since the development of the principles of the *Ficta possessio*, this Action is not much used. *c*. *Calumnia*, which is the taking of money for the *Calumnia*.

purpose of bringing a vexatious Action, or as an inducement to refrain from an Action. To prevent this, there is given the *Condictio ob turpem causam*, and an *Actio in factum* for the fourfold. Both these Actions must be brought *intra annum*. *d.* Fraudulent Sale by an insolvent Debtor to the prejudice of his Creditors. In this case the legal Remedies applicable are the following: The *Actio Pauliana*, and the *Inderdictum fraudatorium*, which is essentially connected therewith.

Condictio ob turpem causam.

The *Actio Pauliana* and the *Interdictum fraudatorium;* and their requisites.

The requisites for both Actions are:

1. Such an Alienation as consists in the diminution of the indebted Estate. As, for example, the abandonment of a *Jus in re*, a Real Right, in favour of another; or the relinquishment of such a Right by *non usus*. Payment, however, does not belong to this class, even though it be the solution of an *Obligatio naturalis*, or of a debt not yet due; though the *Actio Pauliana* is founded in reference to the *Interusurium*; that is to say, for those benefits which the Creditor would have acquired had earlier Payment been made. On the other hand, the *Actio Pauliana* applies, if, before the commencement of the Bankruptcy, a Mortgage has been given for a debt evidenced by writing; likewise in the case of the *Datio in solutum;* for in both these cases a new transaction is concluded. This is the view taken by Von Vangerow; some jurists are of a different opinion. Other prerequisites are:

2. *Animus fraudandi* on the part of the Debtor.

3. The party to whom the Alienation has been made must also have been a *Particeps fraudis*.

There are, however, exceptions to this:

(1) If the Property has been acquired *ex lucrativa causa*.

(2) When the *Fiscus* has been damnified.

4. The Creditors must be unpaid. Plaintiffs are the unpaid or partially satisfied Creditors and their Successors. The Defendant is the *Fraudator*, whose Heirs and Principal are answerable to the extent of the advantage derived. The Action proceeds for restoring the Plaintiffs to their former state. It must be brought within a year. If brought afterwards, the Damages recovered reach only to the extent that the party has been benefited. It claims also Compensation for the *Fructus percipiendi*. What the Defendant has perchance given for the Thing received, he is entitled to have restored to him, if it be still in existence.

Violation of Official Duties.

V. Violation of certain Official Duties. The Judge who, with *Dolus* or *Culpa lata*, so misconducts a Suit, as to be chargeable with misconduct; or who decides wrongly, and has thereby caused injury; may be sued for Compensation by an *Actio in factum*. This Action is also allowable as a *Utilis actio*, in cases of *Jurisdictio voluntaria*. The Land Surveyor, who *Dolo* or *Culpa lata* measures incorrectly, and has thereby caused a loss, is liable to be sued by an *Actio in factum*, for any damage he may have caused, if no other Remedy be available to the party injured.

Injury to the Person

VI. Injury to the Person (*Injuria*). Strictly speaking, all Delicts that have been committed fraudulently, are wrongs against the Person. The object, however, aimed at in most instances, is not specially to harm the Person, but rather to inflict an injury on a Person's pecuniary Rights.

Definition of *Injuria*.

Now, an act done primarily with a view to the infliction of a wrong upon another, when the intention does not aim at the Property, or recedes from it, is termed "*Injuria.*" Two cases are to be distinguished: (1) *Injuria ex generale edicto*, wilful wrong done with an *Animus injuriandi;* as, for instance, breaking into a dwelling-house; infringing upon personal liberty. (2) *Injuria* in a more restricted sense, denominated *Contumelia;* that is to say, the uttering of derogatory opinions. The Action given is termed the *Actio injuriarum*, and it proceeds for an arbitrary pecuniary Penalty, hence it is also designated *Actio injuriarum aestimatoria.* As this is an Action *vindictam spirans*, it does not go either *in heredes* or *ad heredes.* The more exact consideration, however, of this subject belongs to Criminal Law.

Injuria ex generale edicto.

Contumelia.

Actio injuriarum.

Certain relations involving Debt.

VII. Relations involving Debt for the prevention of future injuries, or injuries already inflicted. To these belong the following: *a.* A series of Regulations made for the protection of public Property, and for its due and proper use. Thus, for the protection of a *Locus sacer* against any Person who attempts to do anything injurious to it, there is given the *Interdictum ne quid in loco sacro fiat.* Again, for the protection of a *Locus publicus*, the party damaged can use the prohibitory *Interdictum ne quid in loco publico vel itinere fiat* against the party causing the injury. For the protection of a public road against deterioration, against impediment thrown in the way of its use, against the prevention of its repair, the *Interdictum ne quid in loco publico vel itinere fiat* is given. For the protection of a public river the following Interdicts are given: The *Interdictum ne quid in flumine publico ripave ejus fiat, quo pejus navigetur; ne quid in flumine publico fiat, quo aliter aqua fluat, atque uti priore aestate fluxit; ut in flumine publico*

Special *Interdicta.*

navigare liceat; and *de ripa munienda* an Interdict against the party preventing repairs to the banks of a river. For the protection of public sewers, against any party causing injury thereto, the *Interdictum de cloacis* may be employed. *b.* The enactments protecting against any one hindering an interment, or impeding the erection of a tomb, are the *Interdictum de mortuo inferendo* and the *Interdictum de sepulcro aedificando.** *c.* Here may be mentioned the rule which ordains that a party injured by new works may prohibit their continuance with the following result: that if the works are proceeded with after the Prohibition, and before the dispute is settled, they must be reinstated in the same condition as they were in at the date of the *Nuntiatio.*

Operis novi nuntiatio.

The effect of the *Operis novi nuntiatio* is to secure the *Interdictum demolitorium*, which requires only proof of the *Nuntiatio* having been made, added to a Right in the ground threatened. The *Operis novi nuntiatio* is a private Act, a Prohibition or Injunction which may be pronounced against the erection, alteration, or demolition of a building. These prohibited works, however, whatever they may be, must not have advanced to completion. The *Nuntiatio* is granted *juris nostri conservandi causa;* that is to say, if in consequence of works commenced the substance of our land, or some co-existing attendant Right is menaced. As, for instance, when a third party erects a building on our ground, or demolishes one that already exists. It is also admissible *damni depellendi causa,* when the works threaten injury to neighbouring land, and Bail for eventual damage has

* These Interdicts presume that the party was entitled to bury at the given place, or to erect a tomb there.

not been given. Again, it takes place *publici juris tuendi causa*, when upon lands dedicated to public use unlawful works have been commenced. In the latter case, every citizen of full age may lay an Information; in the two first cases, every one having an interest in the same may take proceedings,* it matters not whether he be Owner, *Superficiarius*, Mortgagor, *Emphyteuta*, or *bonæ fidei* Possessor. Notice of Prohibition *(Nuntiatio)* must not only be given before the works have been completed, but it must be given in the presence of the *Dominus*, or of his Wife, or his Servants. The *Nuntiatio* operates in favour of the party from whom it has emanated, or in whose name it has been made. It is no exception to this rule, that a Right acquired by a party in consequence of the violation of the Prohibition has passed to his Heir. It operates *in rem*, that is to say, the claim of the Plaintiff to be reinstated in his former condition, may be demanded from any one. But the cost of reinstatement is only borne by the party who has continued the work after having been made aware of the objection raised thereto by the Plaintiff. Otherwise, if a party has not knowingly and wilfully disobeyed the notice, the judgment can only be for what is termed "*Patientia;*" that is, for Removal, which must be made at the expense of the Plaintiff. The effect of Prohibition or *Nuntiatio* is terminated: *a*. By remission made by a competent Judge, upon the application of the *Nuntiator*. This application is complied with when the *Nuntiator* refuses to take the Oath of Calumny, that is, if he refuses to take oath that he has a good ground of Action. Irre-

Who may lay the Information.

Patientia.

How the *Nuntiatio* is terminated.

* Namely, Servitudes, but only *Servitutes praediorum urbanorum.*

spective of this, the party may demand that a petitorial Suit shall be commenced, and that the *Nuntiator* shall accept to be the Plaintiff. Should he, however, fail to prove a *Jus prohibendi*, the Injunction is dissolved. The Action instituted by the *Nuntiator* is the *Actio confessoria* or *negatoria*. *b*. When the *Cautio de demoliendo* has been given; that is to say, when the party receiving Notice promises that in the event of his losing the Action, he will reinstate everything at his own cost. *c*. By the death of the *Nuntiator*, or Prohibitor, or by the loss of his Right to the land on account of which he has proceeded for an Injunction.

The *Interdictum quod vi.*

d. Proceedings for an Injunction. When any one undertakes to make an alteration with a piece of land by an *Opus novum*, any of the parties interested in the land may prohibit his doing so: and if, notwithstanding the Prohibition, the works be continued, the *Interdictum quod vi* becomes available. This has for its object the restoration of the *status quo*. *Vis*, in this case, operates as *clandestinitas;* hence the *Interdictum quod clam* is given. An *Opus* is *clam factum*, if it be made at the time that the Prohibition of a third party is anticipated. Prohibition may take place wherever there is an *Operis novi nuntiatio*. It must, however, be borne in mind that the conception of the term *Opus* in this case is far more comprehensive, and is by no means limited merely to buildings. The Right of Prohibition, or Injunction, is possessed by all parties interested, even, indeed, by the Usufructuary against the Owner. The effect of Prohibition ceases neither by the Death of the Owner, nor by the Alienation of the Thing prohibited. In every case of Prohibition,

The *Interdictum quod clam.*

The party prohibited is Plaintiff.

the party prohibited, not the Prohibitor, becomes Plaintiff. A Prohibition, or Injunction, must be made known, for the Prohibition operates only *in personam*. When it is once known, the *Interdictum de demoliendo* lies, not only against the wrong-doer, but also against innocent third parties in Possession; the latter, however, are exempt from costs of Restitution. Upon the whole, Prohibition appears to be more advantageous than *Nuntiatio*. It is, however, necessary to observe, that Prohibition contains a possessory element, and that to succeed, it is either necessary to be the Possessor, or at all events that the party prohibited be not such. When this is not the case, the party prohibited proceeds with the *Interdictum uti possidetis*, the Prohibition is dissolved, and the question of the *Jus prohibendi* is not dealt with at all. Thus, in the case under consideration, it is better to resort to the *Nuntiatio*, which does not involve the necessity of being in Possession. The effect of the Prohibition expires within a year.

Cautio damni infecti.

e. To guard against imminent danger, a Security is sometimes given, named *Cautio damni infecti*. It is employed as a precautionary Remedy against a Person who, for some lawful reasons carries on works upon our ground; as, for instance, the repairs of a Canal. In which case the Claim for Security is enforced by means of an *Exceptio* or Plea. The *Cautio* may also occur in another instance. When any party as Owner, Emphyteuta, etc., fears that damage may occur, owing to the defective condition of a neighbouring plot of land, arising it may be from some *vitium aedium*, or *vitium loci*, or *vitium operis*, to the plot of land which he possesses, either as Proprietor, Mortgagor, Usufructuary, or *Superficiarius;* in all of these instances he has the Right to demand that Security be given by his neighbour against the impending damage. He must show that he is the Owner, or that he stands in some other legal relation entitling him to set up this Claim, and he then takes the Oath of Calumny. After this his neighbour is called upon to give Security. In an *Opus* which has but just been commenced, the party who has undertaken it must find Security. The injury, however, for which Security is required to be given, must be immediate, or, as it is termed, *Damnum infectum.* Only after damage has been sustained, and an Action upon the Security has been brought, must the Right of demanding Security be proved. In the case of *Damnum praeteritum,* only the Right of retaining those portions of the building materials that may have fallen upon the endangered land is given. There are, however, some exceptions to this rule, as when there is no fault chargeable to the Owner of the adjacent land for his neglect in omitting to demand Security; it may then be demanded at a later period. For example, if Security were demanded, but the necessary measures to be taken were omitted in consequence of the neglect of a Magistrate.

Why Security is given.

The object of this Security is to found a Claim for compensatory Damages where such did not previously exist. Security cannot be claimed in this subsidiary way when other Remedies are already given. Hence the Hirer cannot make such a Claim upon the Letter, nor one Joint-Owner upon another. Further, a party who is himself the cause of the danger to his land is not in a position to claim Security, when, for example, he has himself erected the endangered building, having a knowledge of the danger. Nor, again, can he claim Security who has lost the land threatening danger to another party, because he had failed to find the required Security. The Security that must be given may be by a mere promise when the party liable is the Owner, or *bonæ fidei* Possessor; otherwise, actual Bail must be found. The Security need only be given for a certain time, but when the *causa* is continuous, the Security must be renewed. The Liability to find Security may be discharged by Dereliction. Failing this, or when refusal is made to provide Security, the party threatened with the damage, the Plaintiff, may claim the *Possessio naturalis* of the Property. Should this coercive Remedy, the so-called *Missio ex primo decreto*, fail, then the *Missio ex secundo decreto* follows, which gives the Ownership of the Property to the party threatened, provided Security be not found within a period of six weeks. The Right of Mortgage and of Usufruct becomes likewise extinguished, for the Mortgage Creditor and Usufructuary might have freed themselves, if they had been so minded, by providing Security. When Security has actually been given and damage ensues, resulting *in vitio aedium loci operisve*, not, however, by a natural event, but by the Delict of a third Person, an Action for compensatory Damages arises upon the Security given. This Action goes *in* and *ad heredes*. Thus, for example, damage must be made good which results from the removal of Tenants.

The *Missio ex primo* and *ex secundo decreto.*

Actio aquae pluviae arcendae.

f. For the removal of a contrivance by which the course of rain water has been changed so as to threaten danger to a piece of Rural land* *(Praedia rustica)* the *Actio aquae*

* This may be by levelling down or building up; but it must invariably be done by the hand of man.

pluviae arcendae is given. When the alteration is an accidental result, this Action will not lie. It is, however, also available in case of indirect damage; for example, the endangering of an Easement. Its purport is merely to secure the restitution of the *status quo*. The Defendant must bear the costs when he has caused the injury; otherwise they fall upon the Plaintiff. The Defendant is the Owner of the *Opus*, and likewise the Usufructuary. The Plaintiff is the Owner of the endangered Property, the *Emphyteuta*, or the Usufructuary.

Obligations arising from acts involving Public Danger.

VIII. Obligations arising out of Acts causing common Public Danger. Of this kind three require to be mentioned, namely, the *Effusum et Dejectum*, the *Positum et Suspensum*, and the keeping of dangerous animals. The Law ordains that he who keeps wild animals near a public thoroughfare, so that persons who pass by do or may sustain a damage, is liable, if human beings have perished, to be sued for the sum of two hundred *Aurei;* if only wounded by the animals, an arbitrary penalty must be paid. In the case of damage to Property the twofold value may be claimed. An *Actio popularis* for ten *Solidi* is given against any one who suspends, or places anything over a public thoroughfare, calculated to produce danger *(Positum vel suspensum habet)*. He who has sustained damage to his person or his Property by the throwing or pouring of anything from a house or room into a public place, may sue the Owner of the House, or of the Room, by the *Actio de effusis et dejectis* for compensatory Damages. The inmate has his redress against the wrong-doer.

SECTION LIII.—*Remaining miscellaneous cases of Obligations.*

Von Vangerow, ss. 707—710.
Arndts, ss. 340—348.
Puchta, ss. 316—318.
Glück XI., 167, 412; XXII., 108, 163 et seq.
Dig. ad exhibendum (10, 4).
Cod. " (3, 42).
Dig. de edendo (2, 13).
Cod. " (2, 1).
Dig. de testibus (22, 5).
Cod. " (4, 20).
Dig. de religiosis et sumtibus funerum, etc. (11, 7.)

Unjustifiable gain.

1. LIABILITY to refund unjustifiable Gain. He who obtains pecuniary benefit from the means of another without lawful reason renders himself liable to a Claim for Restitution. In this case the Transfer of the Property is always presumed. It is, however, only in this instance that the *Condictio*, of which mention will be made in this paragraph, is permissible. As far as a man's own Property is concerned, the *Condictio* is only allowed in case of *Furtum* or Theft. The absence of a lawful reason may be either present, or past; or it may lie in the illegal or immoral character of the Acquisition. If, on account of a *Causa futura honesta*, something has been handed over to be held in Ownership,* and the object contemplated has not been attained in consequence of *Casus* or *Culpa*, the *Condictio causa data causa non secuta* lies, for whatever the recipient has obtained, that is, for what he still

* But not on the ground of any relationship of indebtedness; for here the *solvendi causa* is not given *ob causam futuram*, but *ob causam praeteritam*.

possesses, including both Fruits and Accessions. The application of the *Condictio* to innominate Contracts (*Contracta innominata*) has fallen into disuse at the present time. But it still occurs occasionally, as in a *Donatio sub modo*, in a *Dos praenumerata*, in the *Conditionis implendae causa*, and in other instances. When a Debt has been paid under excusable error, the Payer and his Heirs have the *Condictio indebiti*, to the extent that the recipient has been benefited. When, however, the recipient takes in bad faith, the *Condictio indebiti* is inapplicable, and the *Condictio furtiva* lies. But an *Indebitum* exists when, in the case of a non-existing or an undetermined or satisfied Obligation, Payment has been made, even if it has been made by means of another Thing than the Thing due,* or to another Person than the lawful Creditor. The Plaintiff must prove the *Indebitum* and his error. This rule, however, does not apply to *Impuberes*, Minors, or Women. When the Defendant denies the receipt, the order of the Court burdens the Plaintiff with the proof of Payment, whilst the Defendant is burdened with the proof of indebtedness. The *Condictio* is employed to obtain the Restitution of that which is still in the Possession of the Defendant at the time of the *Litis contestatio*. What exists in kind must be returned; for that which no longer exists, a Surrogate, or something as a substitute for the Thing, may be demanded; and if the party sued has nothing, he is discharged. The rule that the party sued must make return in *quantum locupletior factus est*, is applicable to Fungibles. If he nevertheless

Payments made in Error.

* For example, it is believed that one is indebted in *Species*, whilst it was only in *Genera*, *etc.*

proves that he has not been benefited, he is discharged.

The *Condictio ob turpem causam.*

When a party has received something, *ob rem futuram*, which involves only for him as the recipient a *turpitudo*, the *Condictio ob turpem causam* lies. It may be that the Thing has been given to deter him from committing an act already forbidden, or to induce him to perform that which he is already bound by an Obligation to perform. When the *turpitudo* on the part of the Donor and on that of the Donee concur, the maxim applies, "*Possessor potior haberi debet.*" The *Condictio* is also excluded when the Donor only is chargeable with *turpitudo;* as, for example, in the case of a Gift to a strumpet.

The *Condictio injusta causa*

When a Person has derived a pecuniary benefit by the performance of a forbidden act, for example, by a Promise extorted by violence, the *Condictio injusta causa* lies. When a Person takes or receives Goods, which *ab initio* he had no Right to retain; or the Right to which has subsequently become extinct; in such a case, unless some other Action lies, the *Condictio sine causa* is given to him for the Restitution of the Thing, with the Fruits and Accessions. For example, when, as the result of a forbidden transaction, something has been paid; when something has been given for a legally impossible object, as for instance, Things as marriage Gifts, where the Marriage was not permissible; when Payment has been made by a Person who has no power of Alienation; when a Gift has been revoked on account of ingratitude; when a Marriage does not take place, in regard to the bridal Gifts; when Compensation is made for a Thing which, however, is subsequently recovered, etc. But the

The *Condictio sine causa.*

Condictio not only lies in those cases where a party has given his Property; but generally where *non ex justa causa* something has passed from the Estate of one Person to the Estate of another, and the other has thereby been inequitably enriched. Such, for example, is the case if my Property is held by a *Bonæ fidei possessor*, and he alienates. The *Condictio*, however, is only available when the Property has suffered a transition, as for instance by consumption; or, in other words, when it is impossible that it can be sued for by the *Vindicatio*.

The *Actio ad exhibendum*.

2. Liability to produce Moveable Property. He who possesses a Moveable Thing, in the inspection of which another Person has a pecuniary interest, on account of a Real or Personal Claim, is bound to exhibit or produce the Thing if required. Between these two Persons there is said to exist a legal Obligation. This Obligation is rendered valid by the *Actio ad exhibendum*. The Plaintiff must prove his amount of interest, that is, he must show upon what he founds his Claim for inspection. For this purpose a summary proceeding is provided. After production, the Plaintiff prosecutes his Claim according as it is either a Personal Right or a Real Right, by a Personal Action, or by an Action *in rem*, as the case may be. Thus the *Actio ad exhibendum* aids as preparatory to another Action. Either the exhibition is asked for in order to establish a certainty as to the identity and quality of a particular Thing; or for the purpose of the severance of the Thing from that with which it is united; or that something may be known in order that the Right of Election may be exercised. Separation can only take place when it is physically

Object of this *Actio*.

possible. It is of juridical importance, because without separation the Vindication would be impossible. The Action is not preparatory when the Defendant does not dispute the Right of the Plaintiff, nor claim any Right himself, nor when the Defendant *dolo desiit possidere*, and is condemned in the amount of the Plaintiff's interest. The reason is obvious: the Plaintiff has obtained his object. When, on account of defective pecuniary interest, the *Actio ad exhibendum* cannot take effect, other Remedies are given in order to afford relief; the *Interdicta de liberis exhibendis; de uxore exhibenda; de tabulis exhibendis.* The Liability to give up documents resembles the foregoing; this, however, is treated of in the Law of Evidence.

Remedies when the *Actio ad exhibendum* fails.

Interdictum de glande legenda.

3. Liability to allow the Removal of Things. To this belong: *a.* The Liability of an Owner of a piece of land to permit another to gather day by day the Fruits that have fallen into his ground, *Interdictum de glande legenda; b.* The Liability of the Owner of a piece of land to allow Property that has become buried in his ground to be removed, *Interdictum de thesauro. c.* The Liability of the Owner of a piece of land to allow his neighbour to lop off the branches of trees overhanging his neighbour's land, unless the Owner himself lops them off, *Interdictum de arboribus caedendis.*

Interdictum de thesauro.

Interdictum de arboribus caedendis.

Alimony.

4. Liability for Alimony. Parents and Grandparents must support their recognised helpless Children and Grandchildren; whilst Children must, in their turn, provide for their helpless Parents and Grandparents to the extent of their ability. Likewise, the Father of an illegitimate Child is liable for its maintenance.

Sepulture.

5. Liability for Sepulture. The following Persons

are liable: *a.* The Heir; *b.* The *Pater familias*, and the Husband and Wife; *c.* Those who take the *Dos* concurrently with the Heir. He who attends to a funeral without being compelled to do so has the *Actio funeraria* for Compensation against the party upon whom the law has imposed the duty.

SECTION LIV.—*Of the Securing of an Obligation by Guaranty or Bail.*

Von Vangerow, ss. 577—581.
Arndts, ss. 349—368.
Puchta, ss. 402—410.
Glück, XIII., 398; XIV., 433; XV., 1.
Instit. de fidejussoribus (3, 20).
Dig. de fidejussoribus et mandatoribus (46, 1).
Cod. " " " " (8, 41).
Gai. Comm. III., s. 115 et seq.
Dig. de pecunia constituta (13, 5).
Cod. de constituta pecunia (4, 18).
Dig. mandati vel contra (17, 1).
Cod. mandati (4, 35).
Dig. ad SC. Vellejanum (16, 1).
Cod. " " " (4, 29).

GENERALLY speaking, the Promise to answer for the Debt of another is expressed by the term "*Intercessio.*" By this is understood the undertaking of another's Obligation by means of a Legal Transaction with the Creditor. The Cash Payment of the Debt of another, however, does not constitute an *Intercessio.* Nor is it an *Intercessio* when any one makes himself responsible for the risk of any undertaking. Again, there is no *Intercessio* when any one makes *Aditio*, or Entrance upon an Inheritance. *Intercessio* is divisible into *Intercessio.*

Intercessio is privative or cumulative.

privative and *cumulative*. It is privative when the party interceding takes the place of the Debtor. This occurs in the case of the *Expromissio*, of which mention has been already made; and in what is denominated as Intervention, that is, the undertaking of another Debt, which would have been contracted without any intervention of a third party *(Tacita intercessio)*. This is, indeed, the only instance of *Intercessio* without a preexisting Obligation.

Intervention.

Cumulative *Intercessio*.

Intercessio is cumulative when the party interceding promises: *a*. To be answerable as principal Debtor *(in solidum)*; or *b*. To be answerable with the Debtor *(in subsidium)*. Collateral Liabilities incurred together with the Debtor are found in the creation of a Mortgage, in the case of the *Mandatum qualificatum*, and in Guaranty or Bail *(Fidejussio)*.

Guaranty or Bail.

Guaranty or Bail, is the Promise to become responsible for the Debt of another, in the event of the Debtor failing to pay his Debt at the proper time. In Modern Law, a mere *Pactum* suffices to constitute a Bail; according to the Roman Law in Justinian's time, a Stipulation also was required. As the Stipulation is now unfortunately, as Von Vangerow thinks, in disuse, there is no difference between the *Fidejussio* and the *Constitutum debiti alieni*. The party guaranteeing the Guarantor, is termed the Second Guarantor; and the party guaranteeing the Guarantor against loss by default of the Debtor, the Collateral Guarantor; the general term for both is *Fidejussor succedaneus*. Guaranty is allowable in all Obligations, both civil and natural. But the Guarantor cannot bind himself to another object,* than that which affects the principal Obligation; nor to a greater amount; nor can he place himself under more onerous Conditions; but he may place himself under less onerous ones. † Any collateral Security given in violation of these principles is void; except, indeed, in the case of the guaranteeing of a greater amount, when the Surety shall be responsible for the amount of the Debt.

Effect of a Guaranty

A Guaranty operates as follows: That the Guarantor shall be answerable in the same manner as the Debtor, unless it has been by Contract otherwise agreed. Whether he is liable for any Accessions, or answerable for conventional penalties, must depend upon the circumstances of each particular case. On the other hand, it is certain that the Guarantor is no longer liable when the Creditor by his own fault fails to obtain the satisfaction of his Debt. For example, if he lose it through negligence. To this category also belongs the inconsiderate prolongation of the time of performance.

The same Pleas may be used both by Debtor and Surety.

The Pleas which the Debtor may use against the Creditor are also available to the Surety; unless he has renounced them, or employed the *Intercessio* for the very object of securing the Creditor against them: or the Pleas must be purely personal, as in the *Exceptio competentiæ* and the *Pactum de non petendo*. The Guarantor has also Pleas peculiar to himself; namely, he has: *a*. The *Beneficium excussionis sive*

* If the principal Obligation is *simplex*, and the accessory one *alternative;* the Guaranty is void. It is, however, otherwise in the opposite case.

† More rigorous, for example, than the principal Obligation would be the accessory Obligation, should in the first instance the Debtor, in the second the Creditor, have the election. Most frequently it can only be subsequently ascertained whether a *causa durior* exists or not.

ordinis; that is, he may demand that the Creditor shall in the first instance proceed against the principal Debtor.* This *Beneficium* may be renounced beforehand, or it may be tacitly renounced by the declaration that a party makes himself the principal Debtor; for example, in answer to the Plea of the *In integrum restitutio* of the Minor. The Guarantor has: *b.* The *Beneficium divisionis (ex rescripto divi Hadriani);* that is to say, the Co-surety may claim division of the Claim.† He has also: *c.* The *Beneficium cedendarum actionum,* by which, before Payment, he may demand from the Creditor the Assignment of his Right. The Surety who has made Payment has three legal Remedies for the Recovery from the principal Debtor. If he have made *Intercessio* in consequence of a Mandate, he may institute the *Actio mandati contraria.* When he has interceded without a Mandate and has not availed himself of the *Beneficium cedendarum actionum,* he may, nevertheless, always institute the *Actio negotiorum gestorum contraria.* As against his Co-sureties, the Guarantor has only a Right of Recovery when he himself takes the Assignment of the Creditor's Claim.

The Rights of the Guarantor.

As against Co-Sureties.

Women protected by the *S.C. Velleja-num.*

The rule that all who have the Capacity to alienate may become Sureties, has an exception in the case of Women. This, however, only applies in actual Intercession. The *Senatus-Consultum Vellejanum* has made the Intercession of Women invalid to this extent, that the Woman who has made Intercession

* By virtue of this *Beneficium,* every Debtor is converted into a *fidejussor indemnitatis*; that is to say, the Guarantor of that which the Creditor cannot obtain from the Debtor.

† The Guarantors may also renounce this, but the Sureties of a Guardian are never allowed to do so.

on being sued for Payment may not only plead the *Senatus-Consultum Vellejanum*, but may recover by means of the *Condictio indebiti* what she has paid in Error. The Heirs also, and those who at her request have interceded, may raise the same Plea. When the *Exceptio* is taken advantage of, what, it may be asked, remains to the Creditor? In the case of *privative* Intercession, his original Right of Action against the Debtor revives; in the case of the *Tacita interventio* the Right of Action is given to him, which he would have had without the Intervention of the Woman. But some exceptional cases exist in which a Woman may intervene in spite of the *Senatus-Consultum*. Such cases are:

Right of the Creditor after the *SenatusConsultum* has been pleaded.

1. When the Intercession was made *animo donandi*.

2. When the Woman has been induced to make it by Loan.

3. When the Woman acts deceitfully.

4. When the Creditor is under an excusable Error in respect of the Intercession.

5. When the Creditor is a Minor, and the Debtor insolvent.

6. When, after the expiration of two years, the Woman again intervenes for the same Debt.

7. When the Intercession is made in respect of a *Dos*.

8. When the Mother or Grandmother, upon entering upon the Guardianship of a Child or Grandchild, has renounced the *Beneficium Senatus-Consulti*.

9. When the Woman undertakes the Suit of the Person who has the Right of Recovery against her.

10. When the Woman intercedes as a trader.

But even in these instances the Intercession is void, unless done by some public Instrument; that is, the Woman has always the *Exceptio Senatus-Consulti Vellejani* allowed her. In the Code, Justinian says: "Ne autem mulieres perperam sese pro aliis interponant, sancimus, non aliter eas in tali contractu posse pro aliis se obligare, *nisi instrumento publice confecto et a tribus testibus subsignato* accipiant homines a muliere pro aliis confessionem etc. Sin extra autem eandem observationem mulieres susceperint intercedentes, pro nihilo habeatur hujusmodi scriptura vel sine scriptis obligatio, tanquam nec confecta, nec penitus scripta, etc."*

But to this rule there are exceptions:

1. When a Loan has been made.

2. Where Intercession has been made *animo donandi*. That is when the interceding Woman intends, from the very commencement of the transaction, by becoming responsible for the Debt of another to give expression to an act of pure liberality.

3. When a Woman has interceded as a trader.

The *Intercessio* of a Wife for her Husband is invalid.

The ordinance, that every Intercession of a Wife for her Husband shall be void, emanated also from Justinian. To this Rule there are only two exceptions:

1. In cases of Renunciation on Oath.

2. Whenever the Creditor proves *quia pecuniae in propriam ipsius mulieris utilitatem expensae sunt*.

The last exception rests upon a Novel of Justinian, now cited as the *Authentica si qua mulier*.† If, for example, a man has obtained a Loan for the

* l. 23, s. 2, Cod. ad *S. C. Vellejanum* (4, 29).

† Nov. 134, c. 8.

repair of a house, and a Woman becomes security for the Loan, her Intercession, notwithstanding the *Senatus-Consultum*, is valid; if it can be shown that the money borrowed has been spent upon her house, or applied to cancel her Debt. A further modification of the strict rule has been introduced by the Canon Law. If a Woman choose to bind herself, even for her Husband, by Oath, it is deemed a transaction of so solemn a nature as entirely to overrule the more ancient Law in regard to her Intercession. In conclusion, when a question arises as to the Intercession of a Woman, the first enquiry to be made is, Has the Woman interceded for her Husband? If so, the general rule of Law is that her intercession is void *ab initio, nihil actum est.* If it be not for her Husband, the question is, Is there a public document made before three Witnesses? By the Prussian Code, however, the older and Roman Law is considerably modified. Any Person now, without regard to sex, who has the free disposition of Property, may become liable for the Obligation of another.*

* Confer. Preuss., Landrecht 1, 14, s. 221-226.

INDEX.

THE END.

GLASGOW: HAY NISBET, STEAM-POWER PRINTER, TRONGATE.

the translators have adopted of placing the Latin text and the translation side by side, renders the task of testing the fidelity of the latter exceedingly easy. The notes are at once explanations, illustrations, and additions, and, in their way, form a body of law which would not be disgraced by being placed by the side of such works as those of Sandars and Demangeat. The type is beautiful, and the book is in every respect one of the most valuable contributions from an English source to our legal literature which the last half-century has witnessed."—*Edinburgh Evening Courant.*

"In the year 1821, the first complete edition of the work was published in Germany. The value of the book thus discovered, which was in fact the basis upon which Justinian's work was founded, has always been recognised. It has been considered the best introduction to the study of the Civil Law; yet it has up to the present time remained comparatively inaccessible. It has never before appeared with an English translation. . . . . . The translation is carefully executed, and the annotations show extensive knowledge of the Roman Law."—*Athenæum.*

"The appearance of an English edition of Gaius, with a translation and notes, will be welcomed by all who are interested in the study of Roman Law. The original and translation are printed in parallel columns, and each section is followed with notes when explanation is deemed necessary."—*Solicitors' Journal.*

"The want of an edition of the Commentaries of Gaius for English students has now been supplied by Dr. Tomkins and Mr. Lemon in a manner which leaves nothing to be desired. The translation of the Latin text is excellent, and the notes, upon which the value of the work mainly depends, are full of the most ample learning upon the matter of the text. They contain numerous illustrations drawn from the laws of England, Germany, and France, as well as frequent quotations from various writers on the Roman Law. These illustrations and quotations we consider particularly valuable to the student, as they enable him to acquire a complete knowledge of the point in discussion at the smallest expense of time and labour. The introduction contains an account of all that is known of Gaius himself, as well as a graphic description of the discovery of his works in Verona. If Dr. Tomkins edits all the works he has promised to produce with the same care that he has bestowed on the parts already published of the "Institutes of Roman Law" and the "Commentaries of Gaius," those books will undoubtedly be the highest authorities on the subject."—*The Irish Law Times, May,* 1869.

Royal Octavo, 12*s. Cloth,*

THE INSTITUTES OF THE ROMAN LAW.

CONTAINING AN

ACCOUNT OF THE SOURCES OF THE ROMAN LAW AND ITS EXTERNAL HISTORY TO THE DECLINE OF THE EASTERN AND WESTERN EMPIRES.

BY

FREDERICK TOMKINS, Esq., M.A., D.C.L.,

OF LINCOLN'S INN, BARRISTER-AT-LAW.

"This work promises to be an important and valuable contribution to the study of the Roman Law."—*Law Magazine.*

"Of all the works on the Roman Law we believe this will be the best suited to law students. Mr. Tomkins gives us a simple English history of Roman Law, arranged most lucidly with marginal notes, and printed in a form calculated for easy reading and retention in the memory. We welcome the book of Mr. Tomkins. It is calculated to promote the study of Roman Law; and both at the Universities and in the Inns of Court, it is a work which may be safely and beneficially employed as a text-book."—*Law Times.*

"This work is pronounced by its author to be strictly elementary. But in regard to the labour bestowed, the research exercised, and the materials brought together, it seems to deserve a more ambitious title than that of an elementary treatise. The chapter on legal instruction, detailing the systems of legal education pursued in the various epochs of Rome, reflects great credit on the author, and so far as we know is purely original, in the sense that no preceding English writer has collated the matter therein contained."—*Law Journal.*

"Mr. Tomkins has chosen his subject wisely in at least one respect—there can be no doubt that a good introductory treatise on the Roman Law is sorely needed at present. The present part is only an instalment. But the present part is unquestionably both valuable in itself and of good promise for the future. We know of no other book in which anything like the same amount of information can be acquired with the same ease. We shall look with great interest for the publication of the remainder of this treatise. If the second part is as well executed as the first, and bears a due proportion to it, we think the work bids fair to become the standard text-book for English students.—*Solicitors' Journal.*

"This volume contains a sound account of the sources and history of the Roman Law. In the author's advocacy of the study of the Civil Law as a preparation for the construction of a scientific code, we heartily concur."—*Athenæum.*

"This is a learned, able, and successful performance. Dr. Tomkins enters minutely into the whole history of the Roman Law, beginning with an inquiry into the law-making powers of the different constituent bodies under the Republic. The different sources of the Roman Law are investigated, and we have a fuller and better account than in any other treatise with which we are acquainted of the different schools of the Roman jurists, of the character of the legal instruction conferred upon the students, and a minute review of the more distinguished jurists of the pre-Justinian era. The second division of the work treats of the legislation of Justinian, descriptively and historically; and the third of the fate of the Roman Law after the fall of the empire. It will doubtless be a recommendation to this work in England to know that the author studied at the feet of Mittermaier and Von Vangerow of Heidelberg. We can heartily recommend the volume as containing more exhaustive and erudite inquiry into the history of the Roman Law than any other work by an English author."—*Morning Star.*

This Work has been selected by the Council of Legal Education as one of the Books on the Civil Law in which Students for the Bar presenting themselves for Examination in Honours will be examined.

BUTTERWORTHS, 7, FLEET STREET, LONDON.